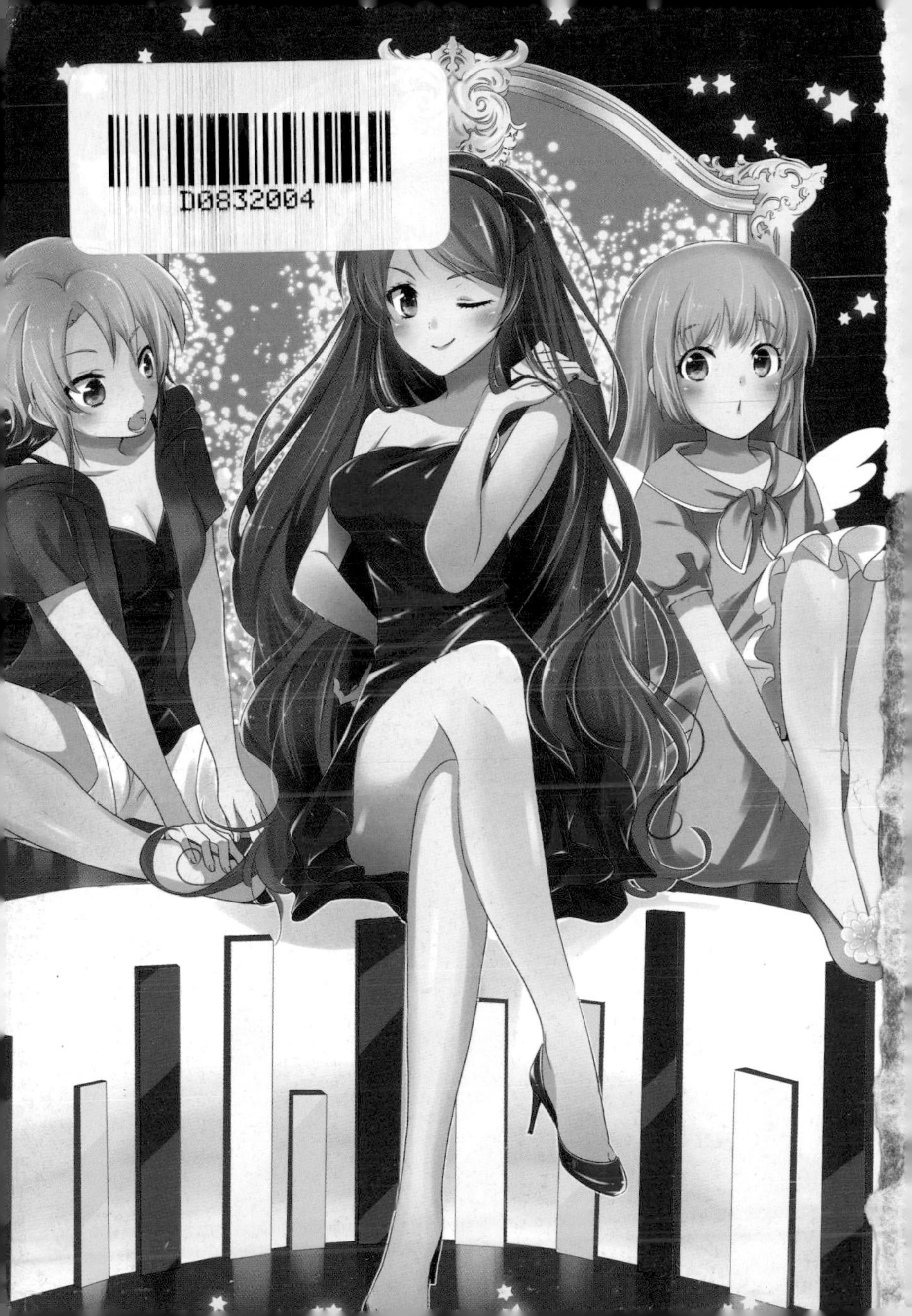

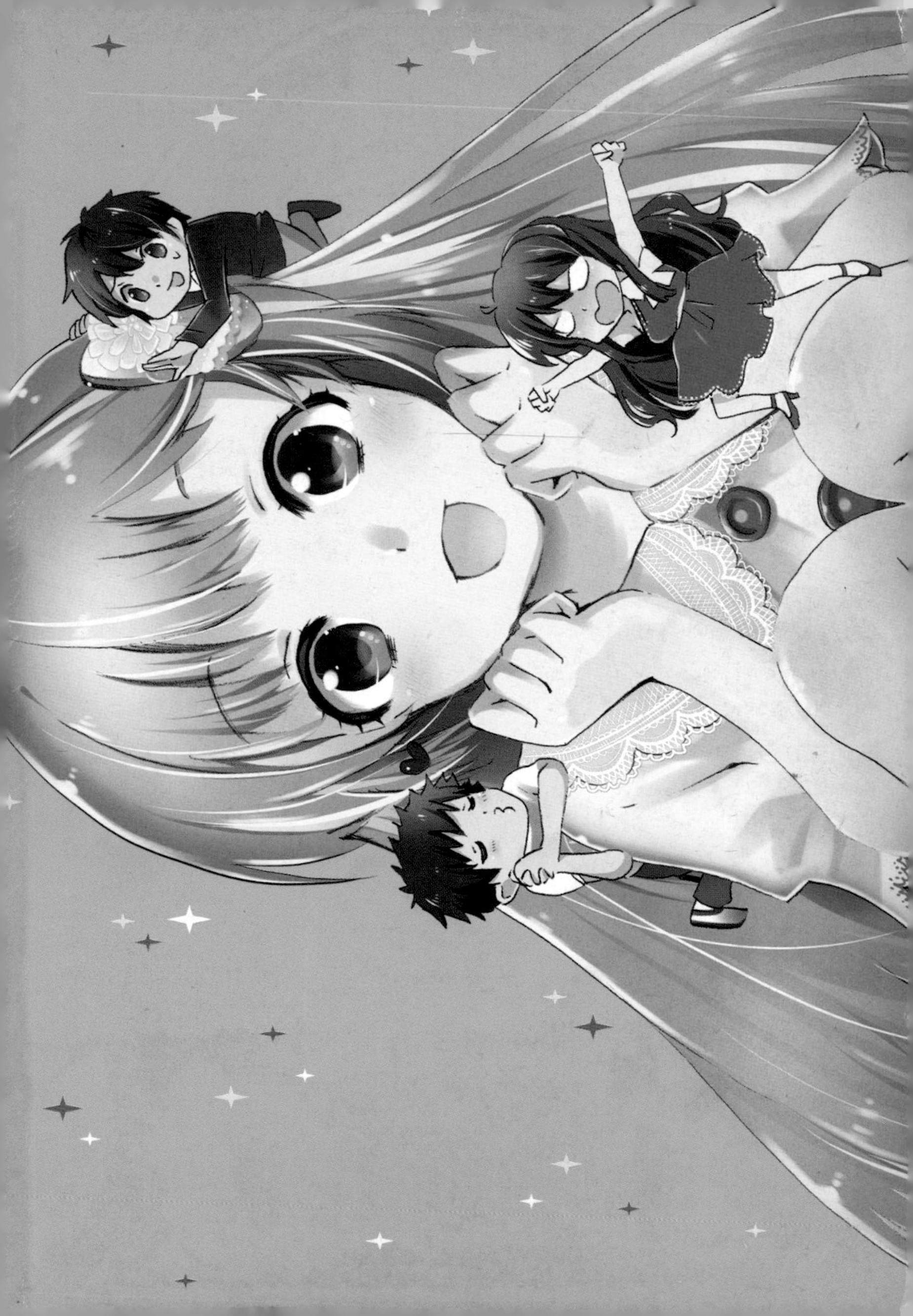

CHAPTER 7: Matador vs. Mori-girl

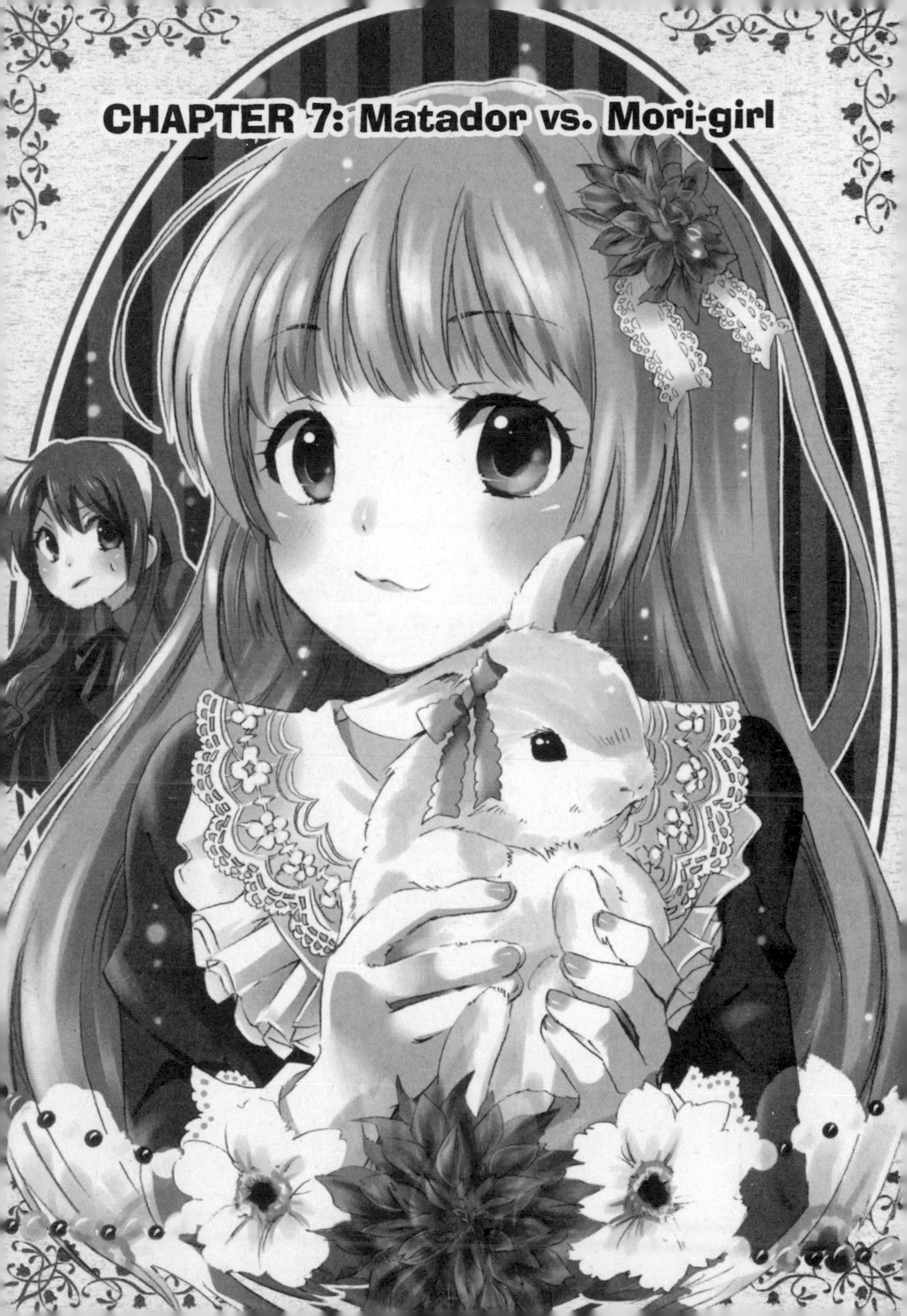

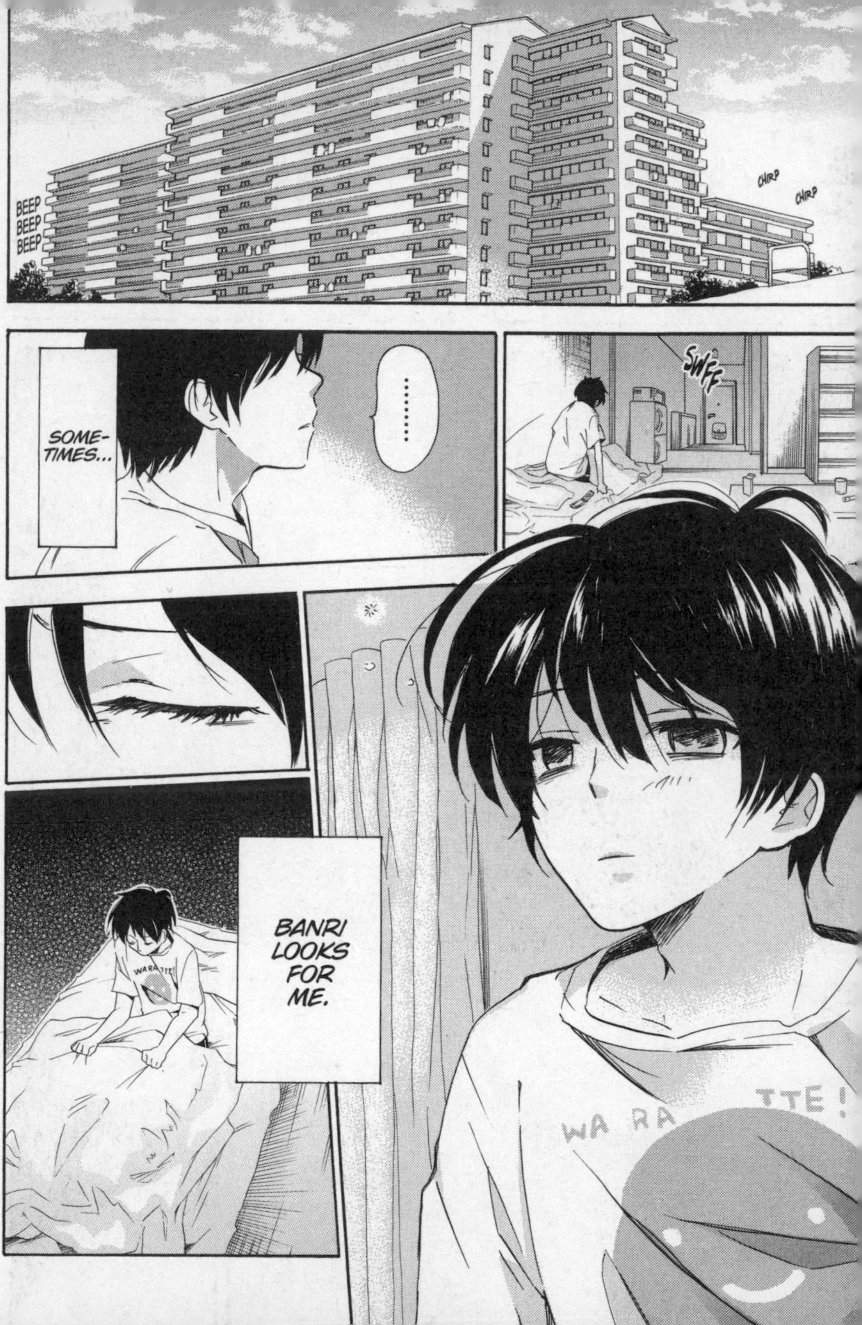
CHIRP
CHIRP
BEEP
BEEP
BEEP
SWFF
......
SOME-TIMES...
BANRI LOOKS FOR ME.
WA RA TTE!

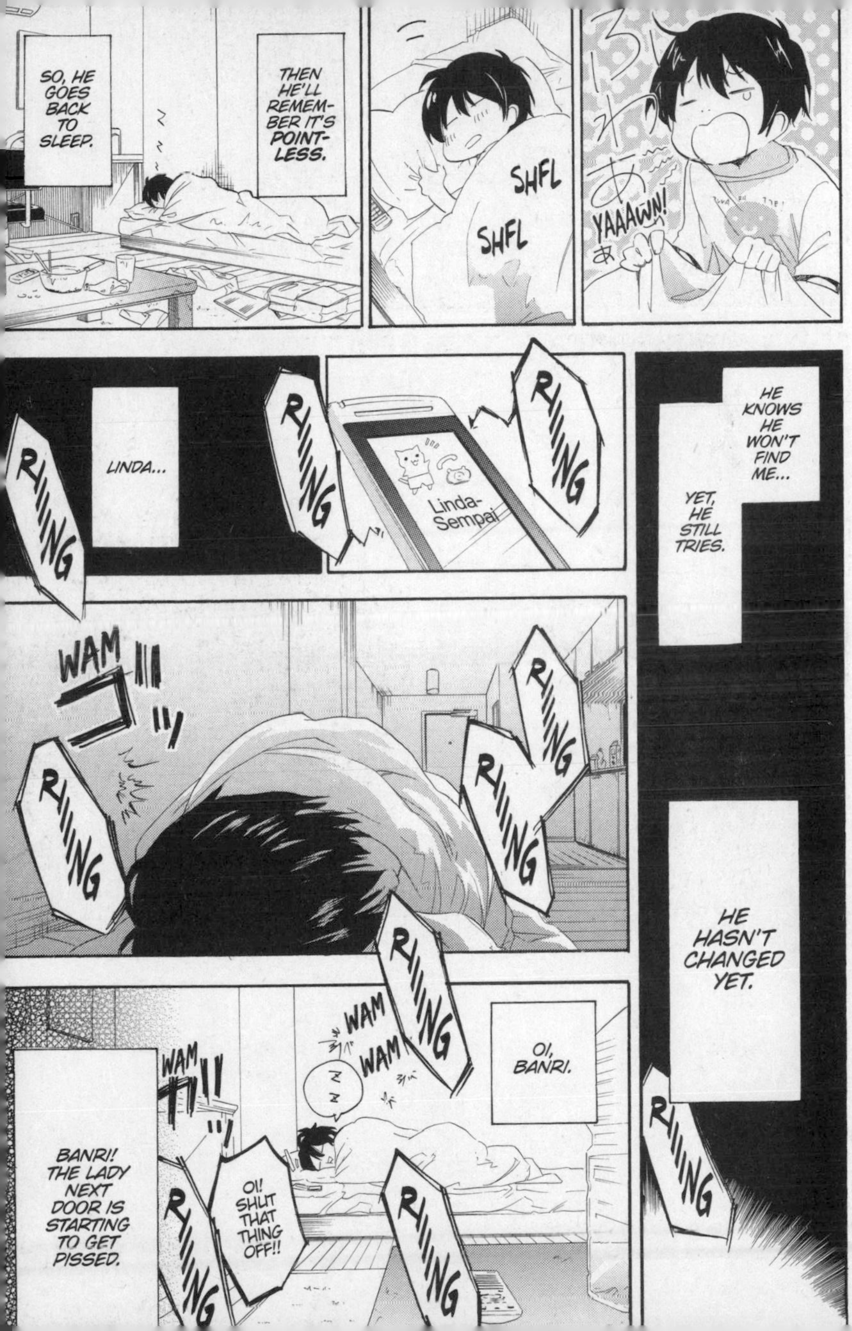
YAAAWN!
SHFL
SHFL
THEN HE'LL REMEMBER IT'S POINTLESS.
SO, HE GOES BACK TO SLEEP.
HE KNOWS HE WON'T FIND ME...
YET, HE STILL TRIES.
HE HASN'T CHANGED YET.
RIIING
RIIING
Linda-Sempai
RIIING
LINDA...
RIIING
RIIING
RIIING
WAM
RIIING
RIIING
OI, BANRI.
WAM
WAM
WAM
OI! SHUT THAT THING OFF!!
BANRI! THE LADY NEXT DOOR IS STARTING TO GET PISSED.
RIIING
RIIING

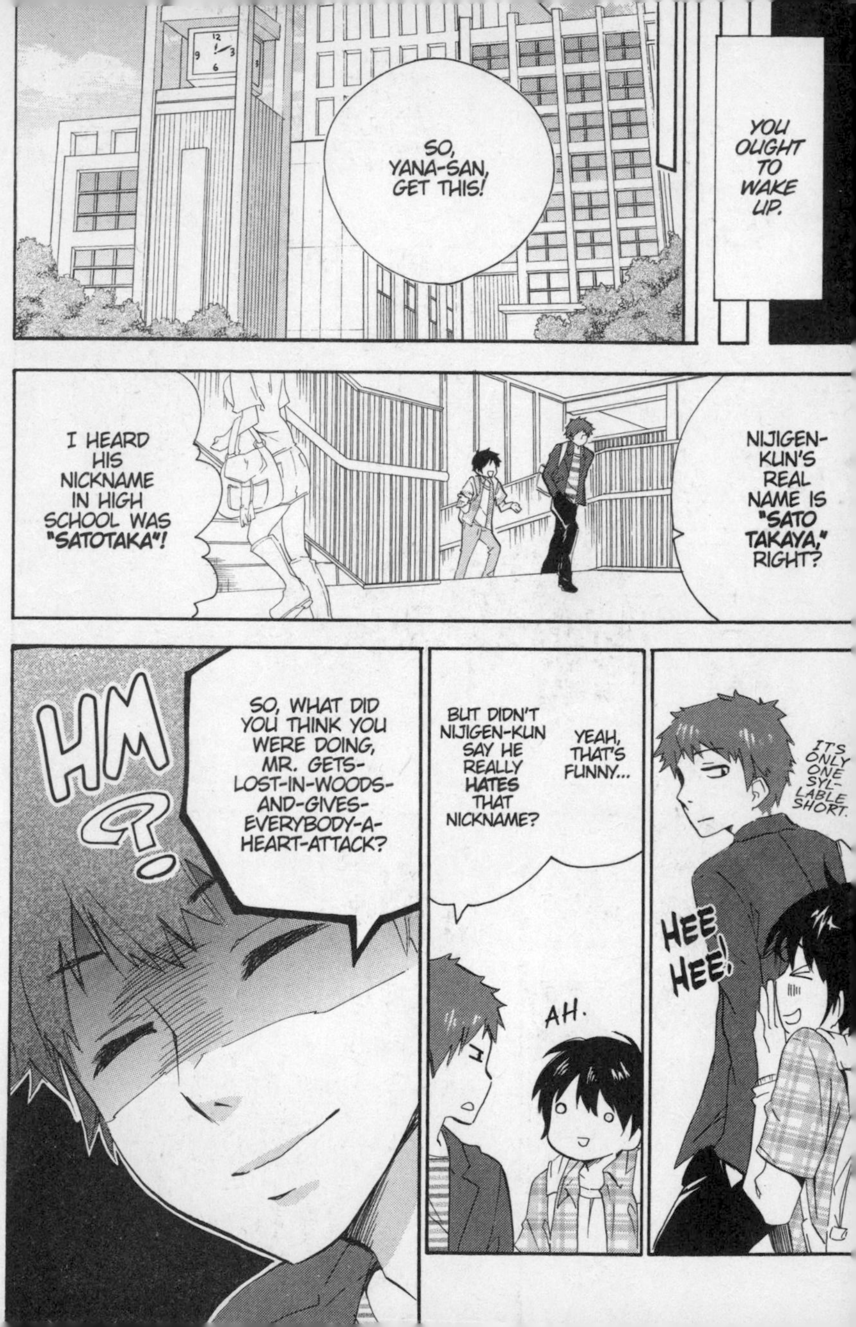
YOU OUGHT TO WAKE UP.
SO, YANA-SAN, GET THIS!
NIJIGEN-KUN'S REAL NAME IS "SATO TAKAYA," RIGHT?
I HEARD HIS NICKNAME IN HIGH SCHOOL WAS "SATOTAKA"!
IT'S ONLY ONE SYL-LABLE SHORT.
HEE HEE!
YEAH, THAT'S FUNNY...
BUT DIDN'T NIJIGEN-KUN SAY HE REALLY HATES THAT NICKNAME?
AH.
HM?
SO, WHAT DID YOU THINK YOU WERE DOING, MR. GETS-LOST-IN-WOODS-AND-GIVES-EVERYBODY-A-HEART-ATTACK?

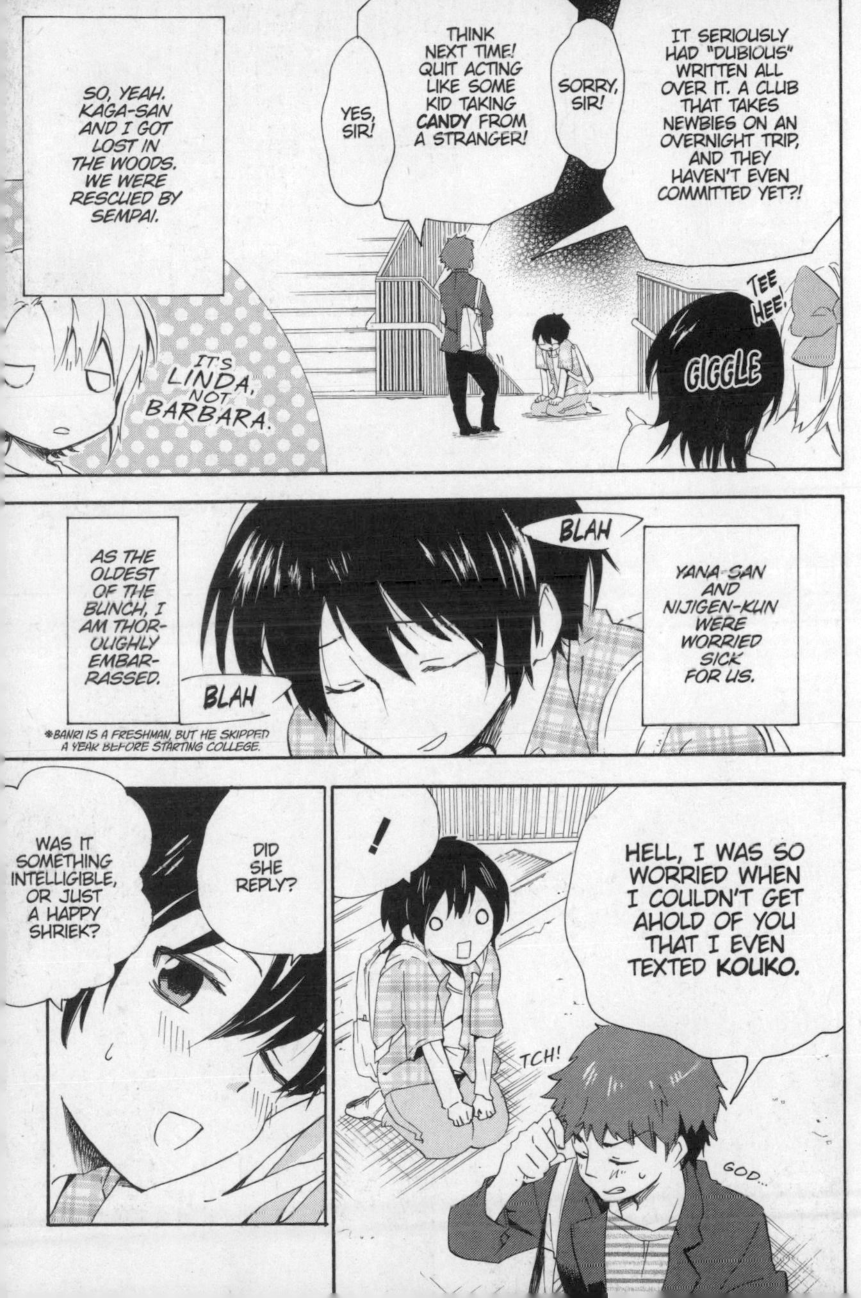
IT SERIOUSLY HAD "DUBIOUS" WRITTEN ALL OVER IT. A CLUB THAT TAKES NEWBIES ON AN OVERNIGHT TRIP, AND THEY HAVEN'T EVEN COMMITTED YET?!
SORRY, SIR!
THINK NEXT TIME! QUIT ACTING LIKE SOME KID TAKING CANDY FROM A STRANGER!
YES, SIR!
SO, YEAH. KAGA-SAN AND I GOT LOST IN THE WOODS. WE WERE RESCUED BY SEMPAI.
TEE HEE!
GIGGLE
IT'S LINDA, NOT BARBARA.
YANA-SAN AND NIJIGEN-KUN WERE WORRIED SICK FOR US.
BLAH
AS THE OLDEST OF THE BUNCH, I AM THOR-OUGHLY EMBAR-RASSED.
BLAH
*BANRI IS A FRESHMAN, BUT HE SKIPPED A YEAR BEFORE STARTING COLLEGE.
HELL, I WAS SO WORRIED WHEN I COULDN'T GET AHOLD OF YOU THAT I EVEN TEXTED KOUKO.
!
TCH!
GOD...
DID SHE REPLY?
WAS IT SOMETHING INTELLIGIBLE, OR JUST A HAPPY SHRIEK?

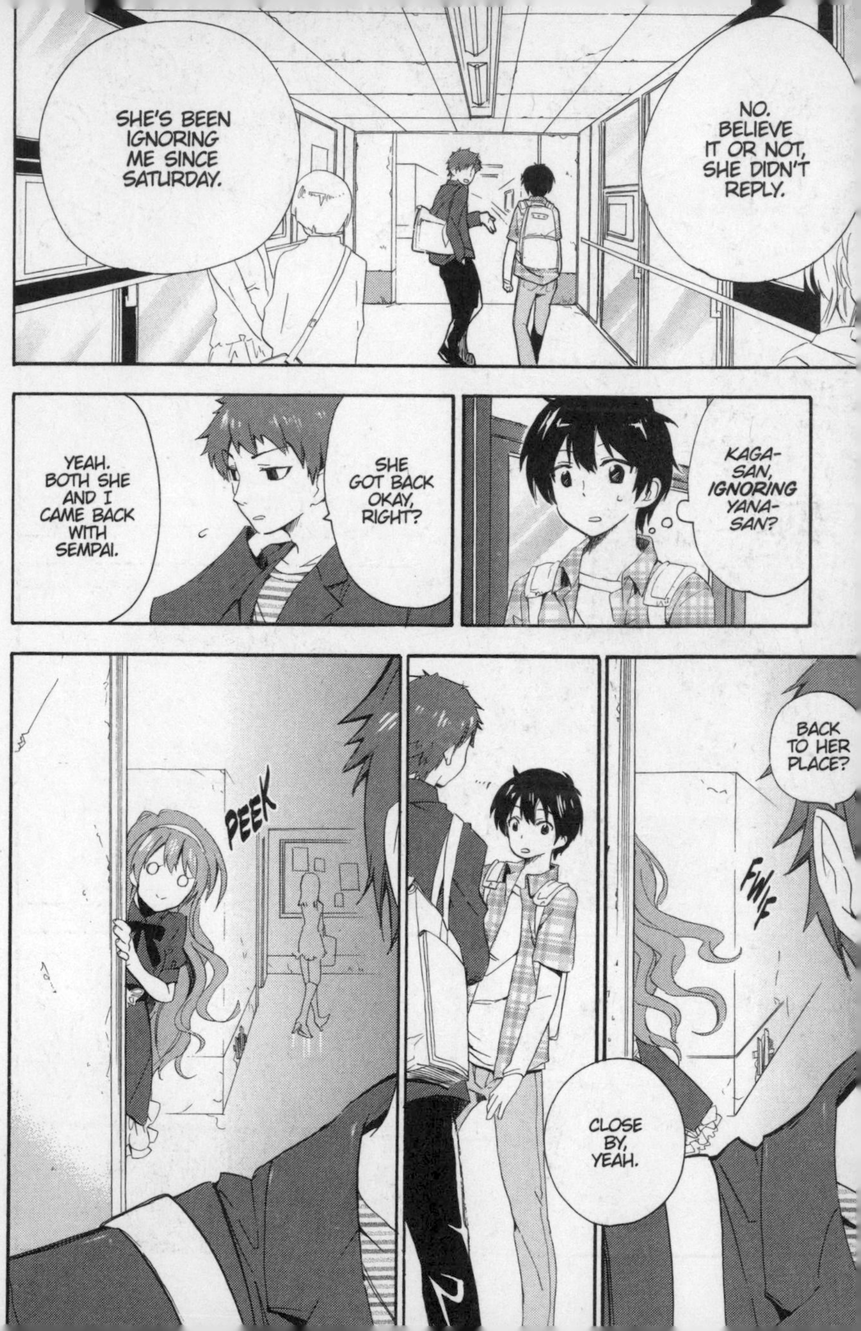
NO. BELIEVE IT OR NOT, SHE DIDN'T REPLY.
SHE'S BEEN IGNORING ME SINCE SATURDAY.
KAGA-SAN, IGNORING YANA-SAN?
SHE GOT BACK OKAY, RIGHT?
YEAH. BOTH SHE AND I CAME BACK WITH SEMPAI.
BACK TO HER PLACE?
FWIF
CLOSE BY, YEAH.
PEEK

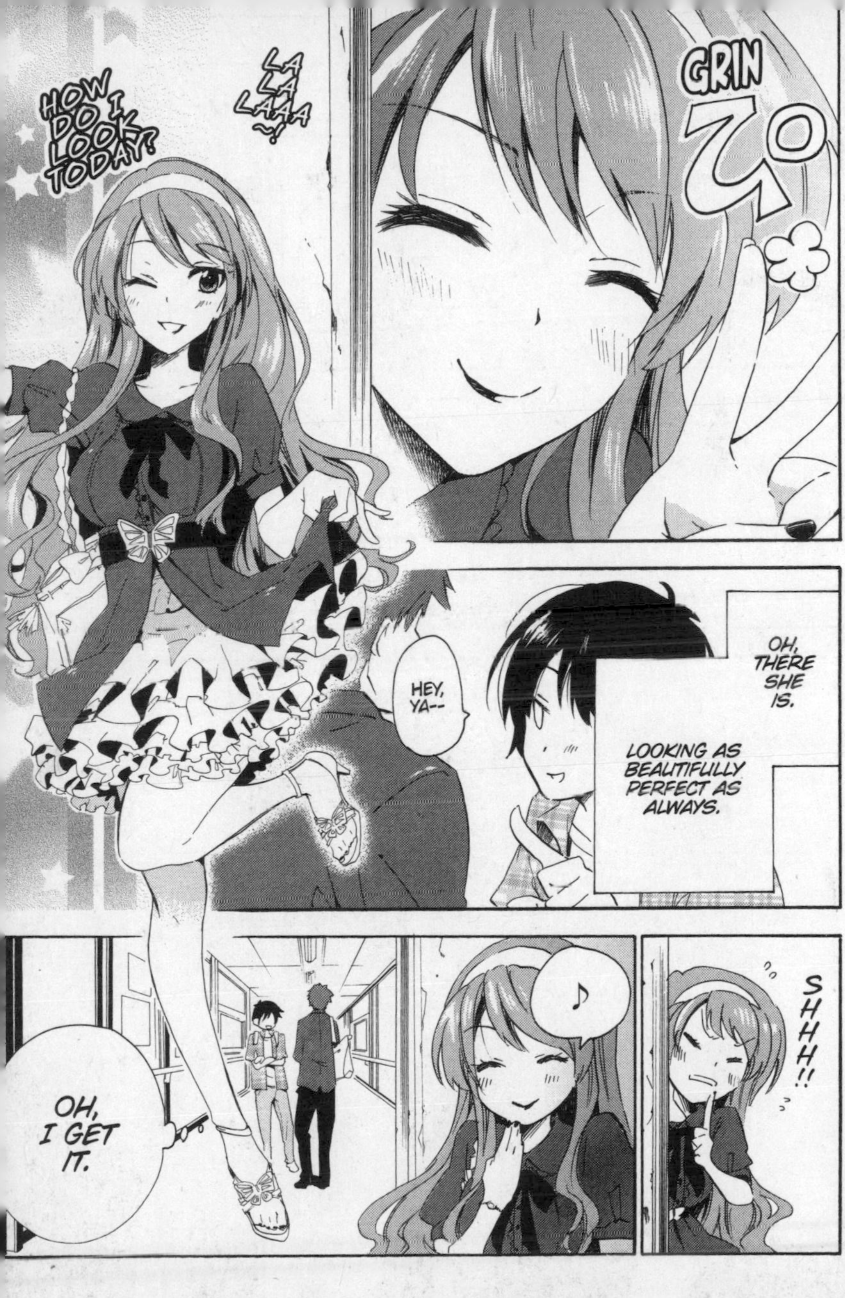
GRIN
OH, THERE SHE IS.
LOOKING AS BEAUTIFULLY PERFECT AS ALWAYS.
HEY, YA--
LA LA LAAA ~!
HOW DO I LOOK TODAY?
SHHH!!
♪
OH, I GET IT.

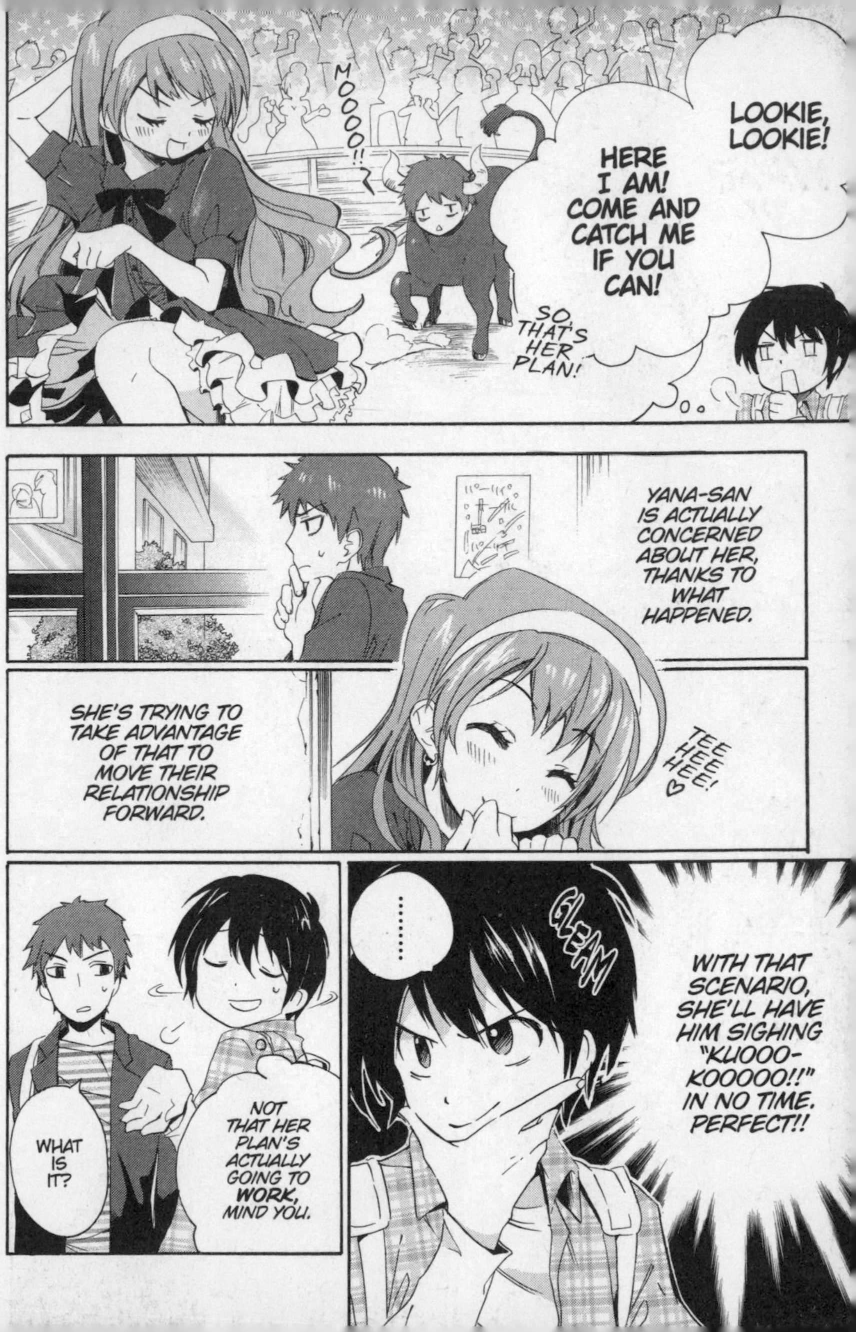
LOOKIE, LOOKIE!
HERE I AM! COME AND CATCH ME IF YOU CAN!
MOOOOO!!
SO, THAT'S HER PLAN!
YANA-SAN IS ACTUALLY CONCERNED ABOUT HER, THANKS TO WHAT HAPPENED.
TEE HEE HEE!
SHE'S TRYING TO TAKE ADVANTAGE OF THAT TO MOVE THEIR RELATIONSHIP FORWARD.
WITH THAT SCENARIO, SHE'LL HAVE HIM SIGHING "KUOOO-KOOOOO!!" IN NO TIME. PERFECT!!
GLEAM
......
NOT THAT HER PLAN'S ACTUALLY GOING TO WORK, MIND YOU.
WHAT IS IT?

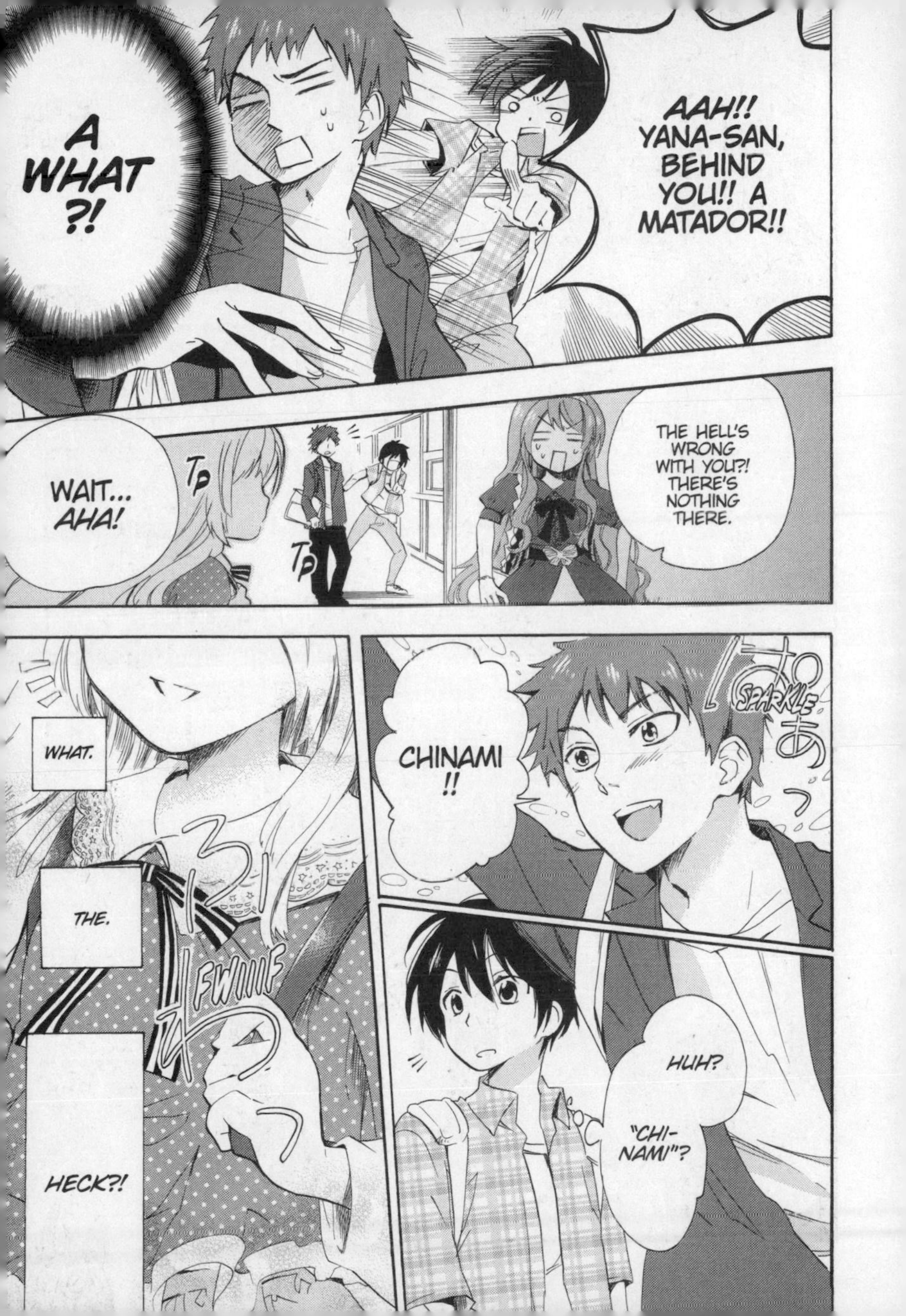
AAH!! YANA-SAN, BEHIND YOU!! A MATADOR!!
A WHAT?!
THE HELL'S WRONG WITH YOU?! THERE'S NOTHING THERE.
TP
TP
WAIT... AHA!
SPARKLE
CHINAMI!!
HUH?
"CHI-NAMI"?
WHAT.
THE.
HECK?!

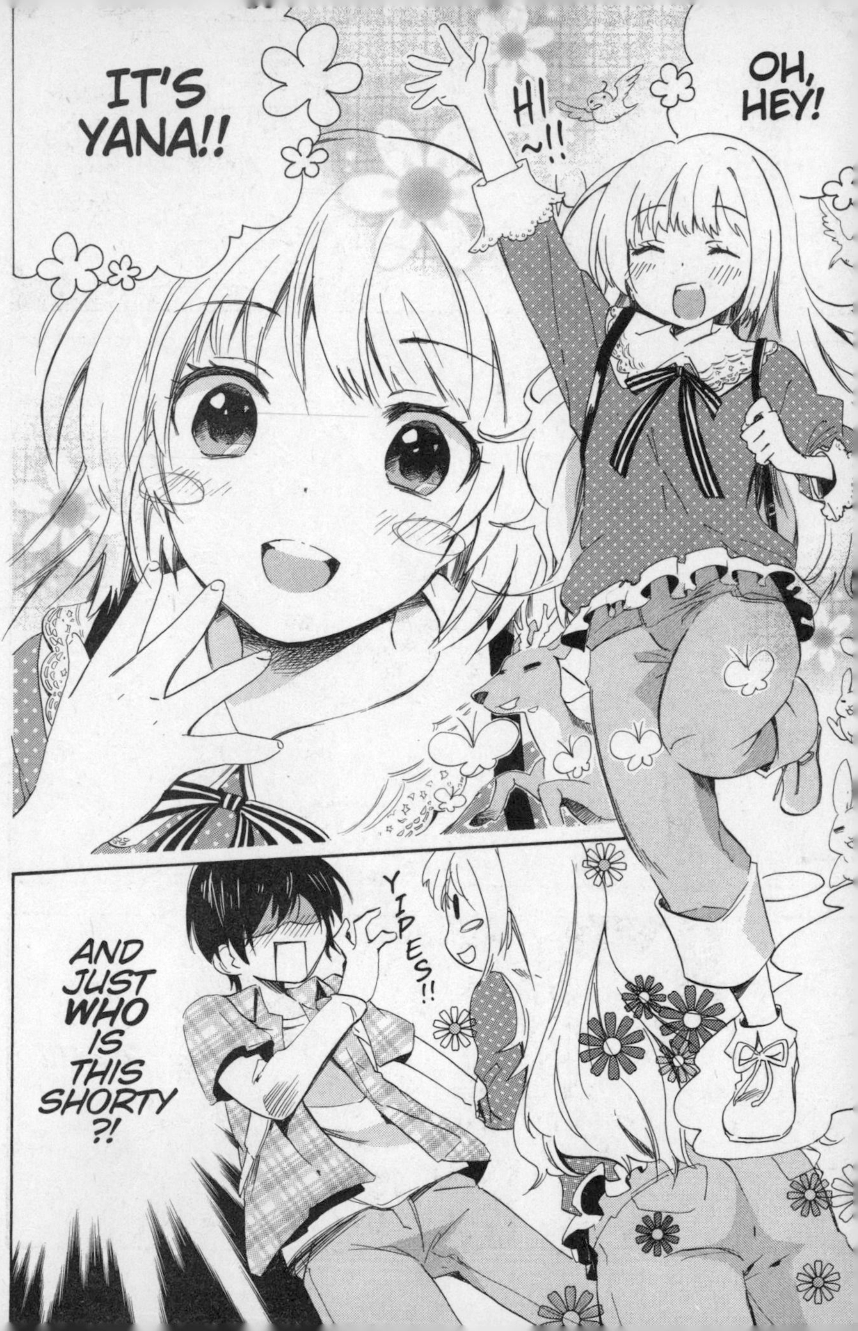
OH, HEY!
HI~!!
IT'S YANA!!
YIPES!!
AND JUST WHO IS THIS SHORTY?!

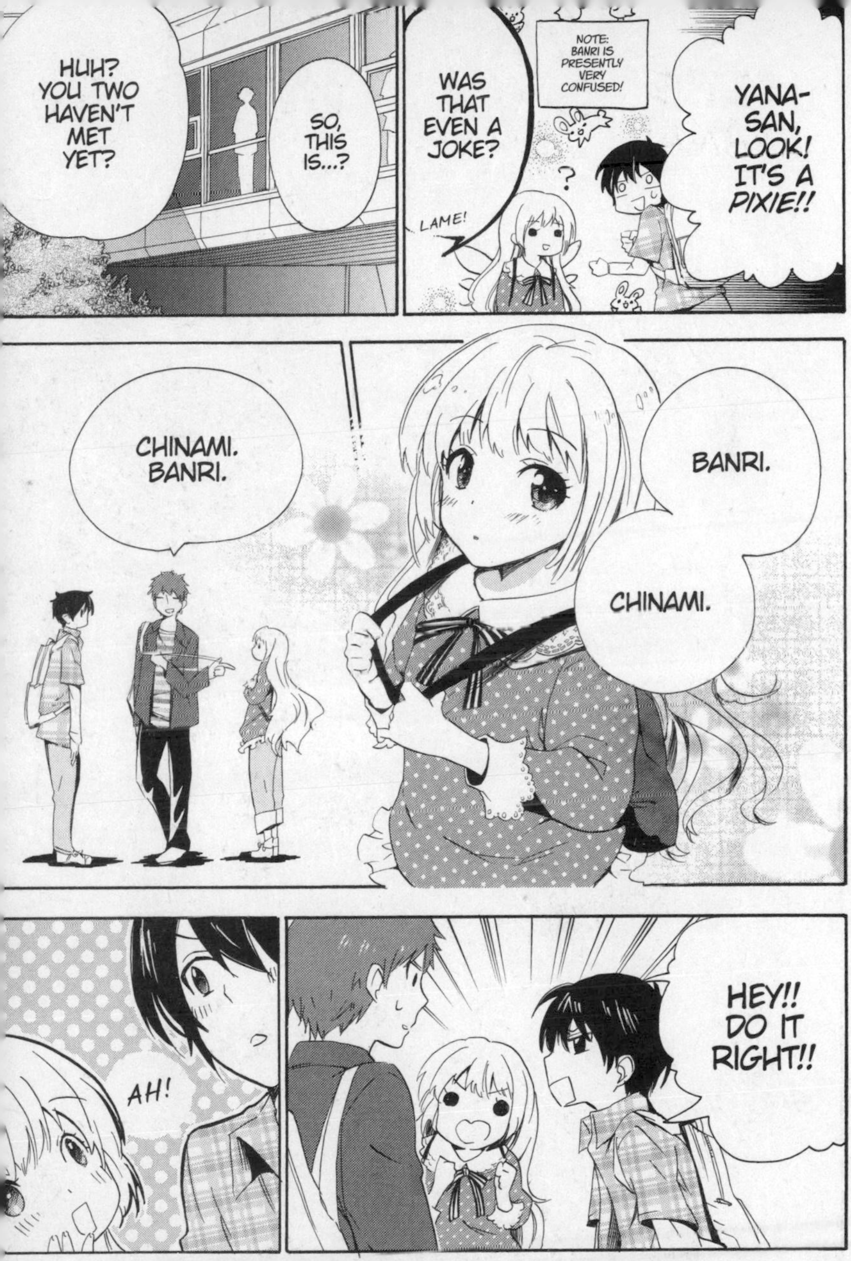
YANA-SAN, LOOK! IT'S A PIXIE!!
NOTE: BANRI IS PRESENTLY VERY CONFUSED!
WAS THAT EVEN A JOKE?
LAME!
SO, THIS IS...?
HUH? YOU TWO HAVEN'T MET YET?
BANRI.
CHINAMI.
CHINAMI. BANRI.
HEY!! DO IT RIGHT!!
AH!

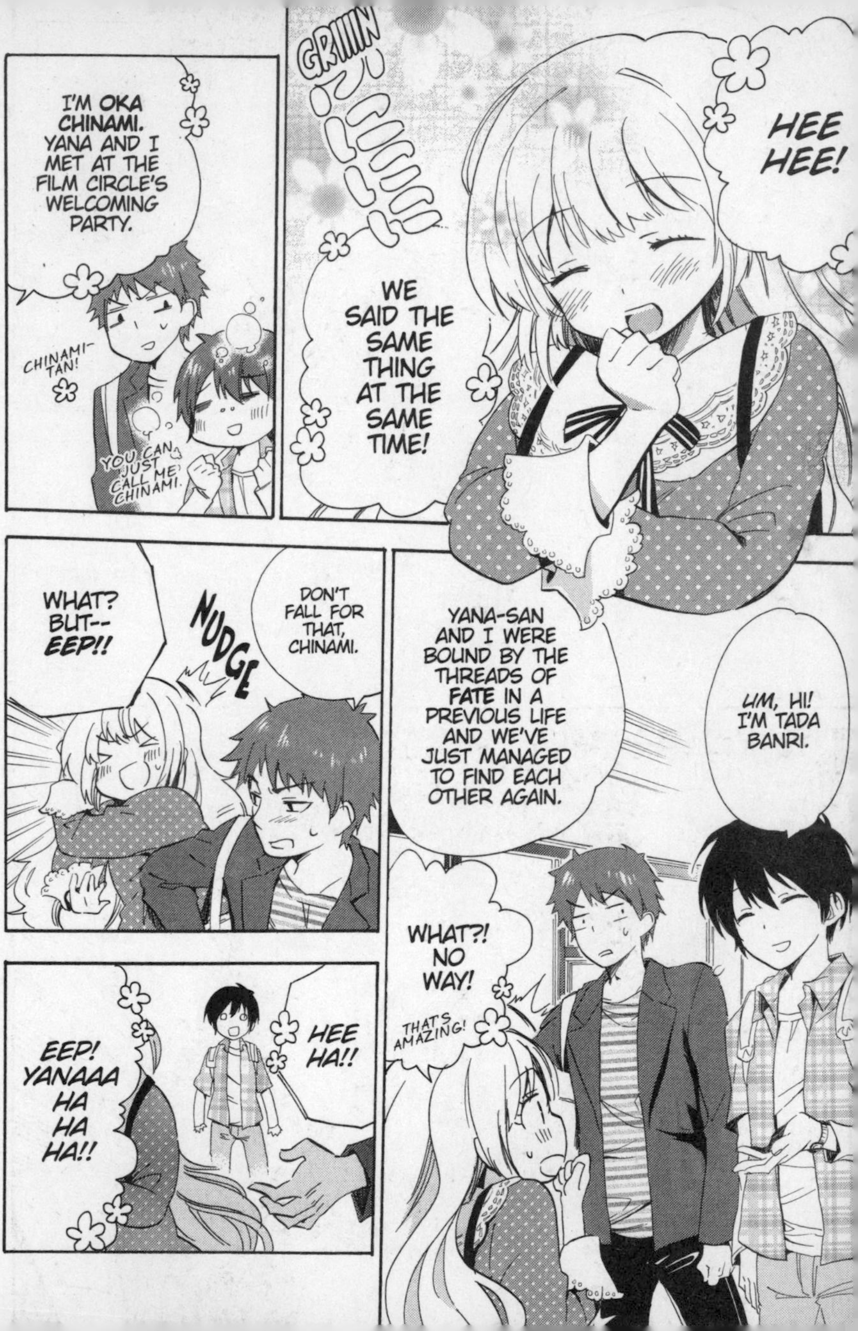
GRIIIIN
HEE HEE!
WE SAID THE SAME THING AT THE SAME TIME!
I'M OKA CHINAMI. YANA AND I MET AT THE FILM CIRCLE'S WELCOMING PARTY.
CHINAMI-TAN!
YOU CAN JUST CALL ME CHINAMI.
UM, HI! I'M TADA BANRI.
YANA-SAN AND I WERE BOUND BY THE THREADS OF FATE IN A PREVIOUS LIFE AND WE'VE JUST MANAGED TO FIND EACH OTHER AGAIN.
WHAT?! NO WAY!
THAT'S AMAZING!
DON'T FALL FOR THAT, CHINAMI.
NUDGE
WHAT? BUT-- EEP!!
HEE HA!!
EEP! YANAAA HA HA HA HA!!

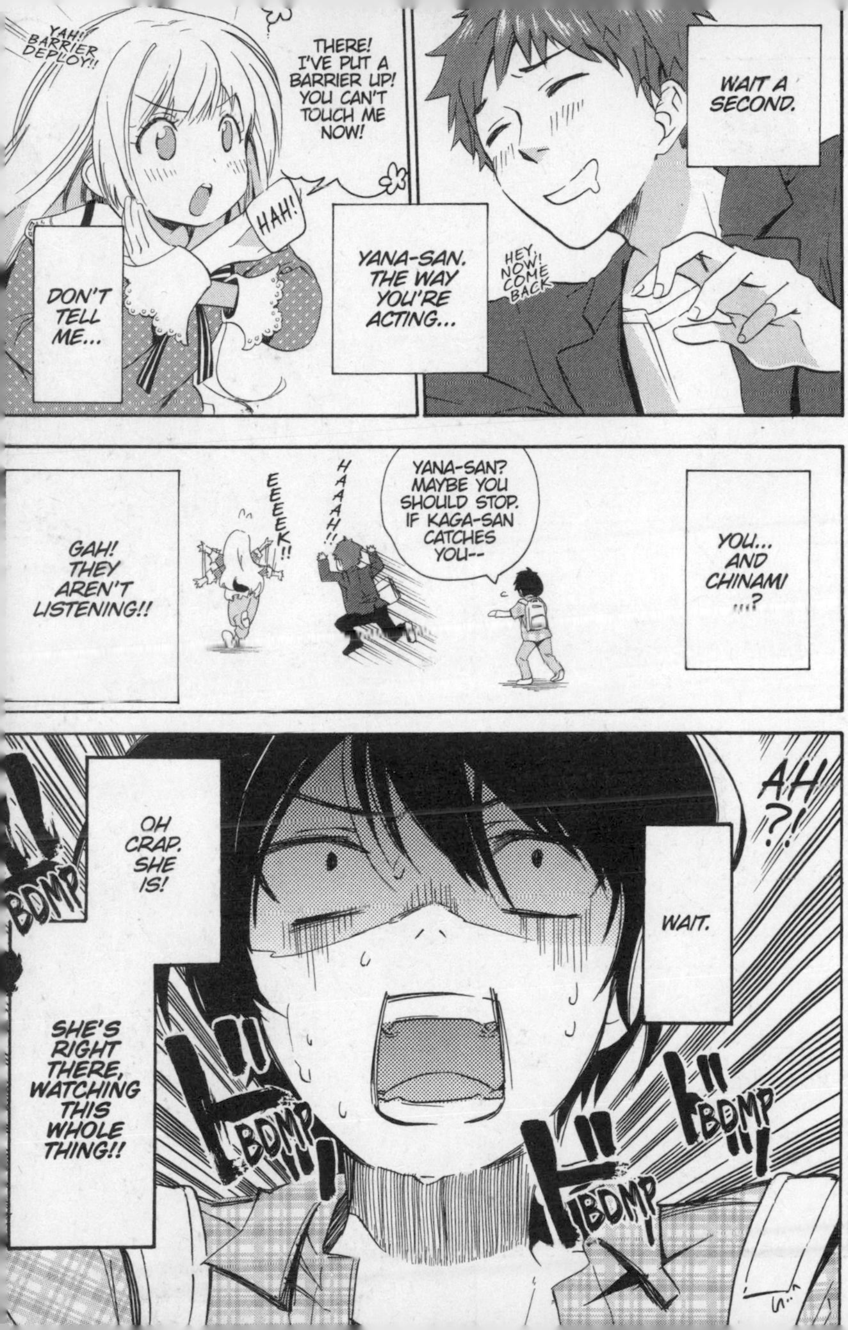
WAIT A SECOND.
YANA-SAN. THE WAY YOU'RE ACTING...
HEY, NOW! COME BACK
YAH!! BARRIER DEPLOY!!
THERE! I'VE PUT A BARRIER UP! YOU CAN'T TOUCH ME NOW!
HAH!
DON'T TELL ME...
YOU... AND CHINAMI ...?
YANA-SAN? MAYBE YOU SHOULD STOP. IF KAGA-SAN CATCHES YOU--
HAAAAH!!
EEEEK!!
GAH! THEY AREN'T LISTENING!!
AH ?!
WAIT.
OH CRAP. SHE IS!
SHE'S RIGHT THERE, WATCHING THIS WHOLE THING!!
BDMP
BDMP
BDMP
BDMP

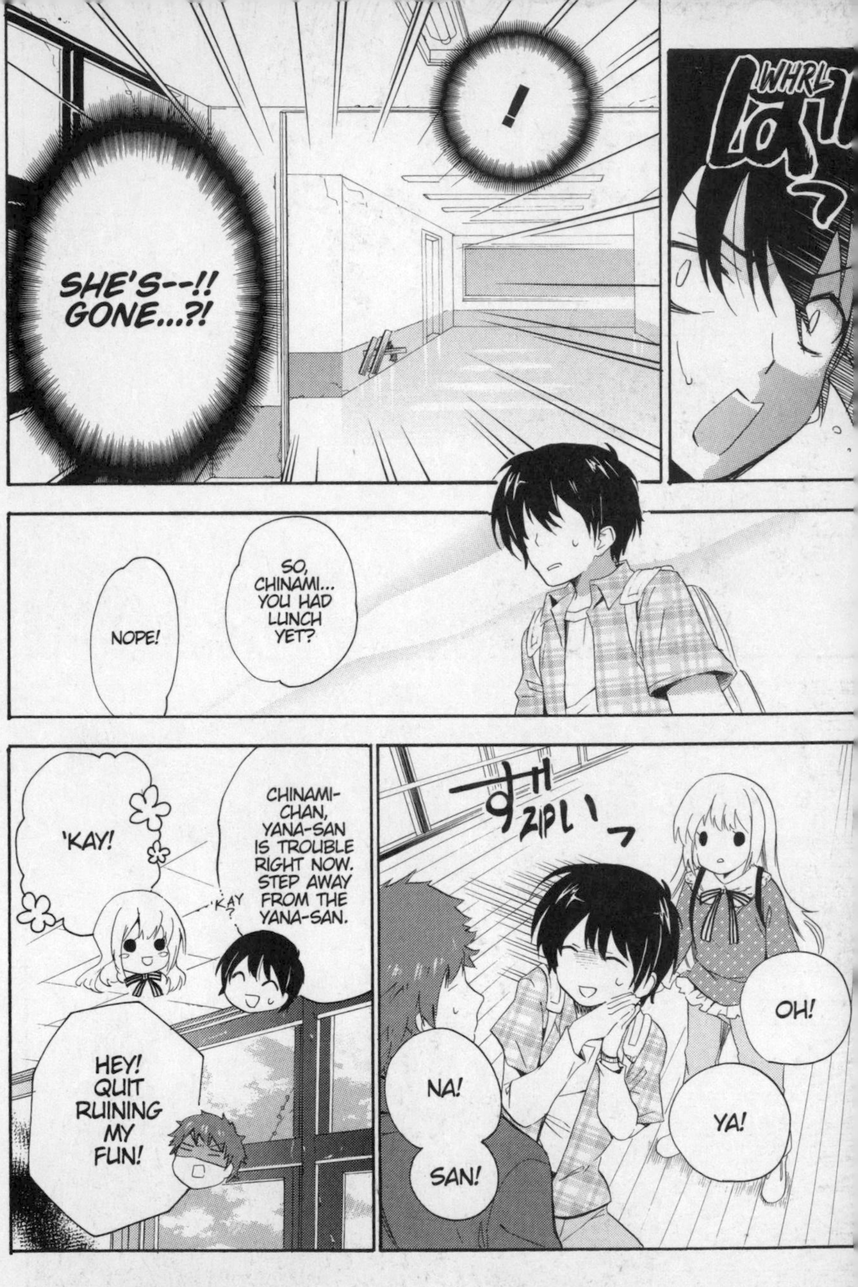
WHRL
!
SHE'S--!! GONE...?!
SO, CHINAMI... YOU HAD LUNCH YET?
NOPE!
ZIP
OH!
YA!
NA!
SAN!
CHINAMI-CHAN, YANA-SAN IS TROUBLE RIGHT NOW. STEP AWAY FROM THE YANA-SAN.
'KAY!
'KAY?
HEY! QUIT RUINING MY FUN!

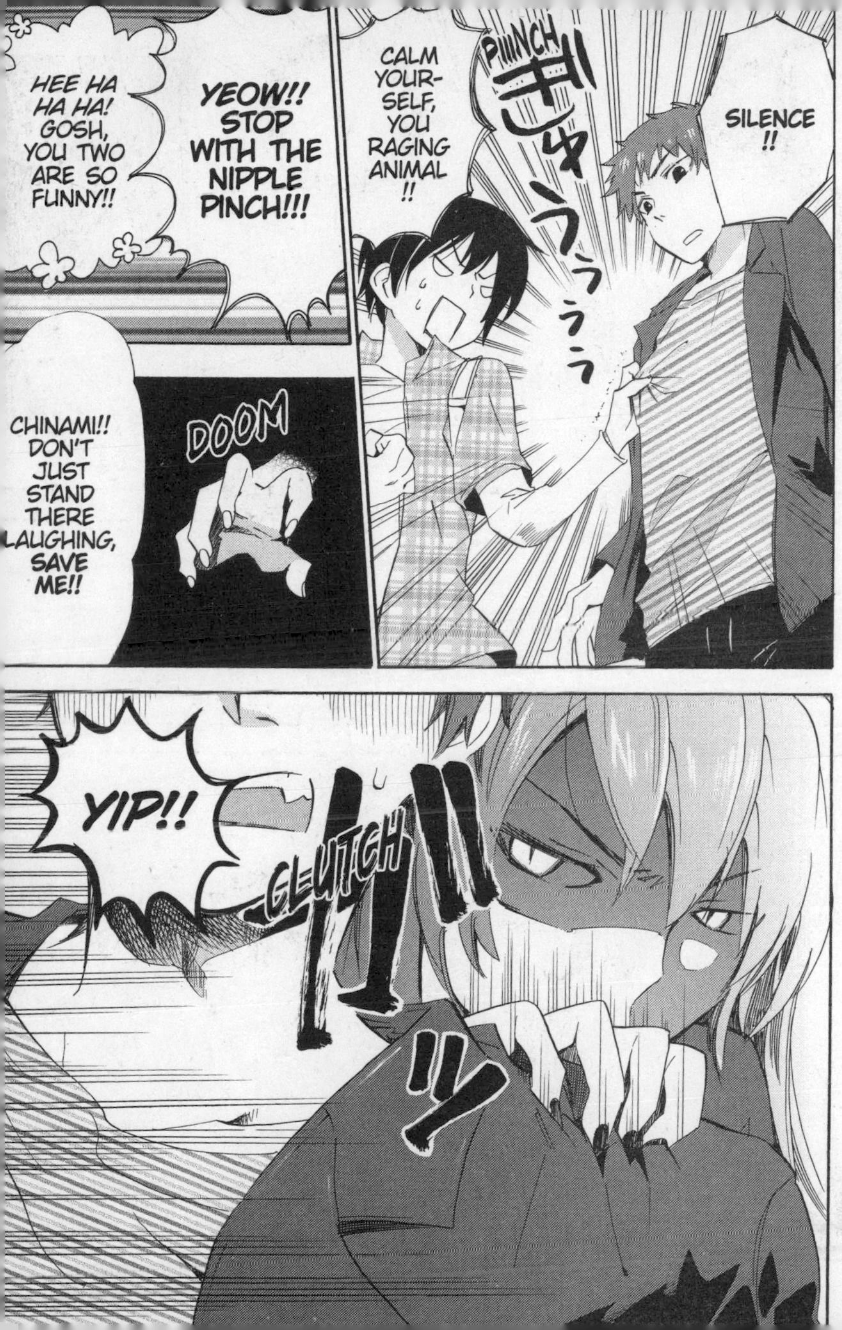
SILENCE!!
PIIINCH
CALM YOURSELF, YOU RAGING ANIMAL!!
YEOW!! STOP WITH THE NIPPLE PINCH!!!
HEE HA HA HA! GOSH, YOU TWO ARE SO FUNNY!!
CHINAMI!! DON'T JUST STAND THERE LAUGHING, SAVE ME!!
DOOM
CLUTCH
YIP!!

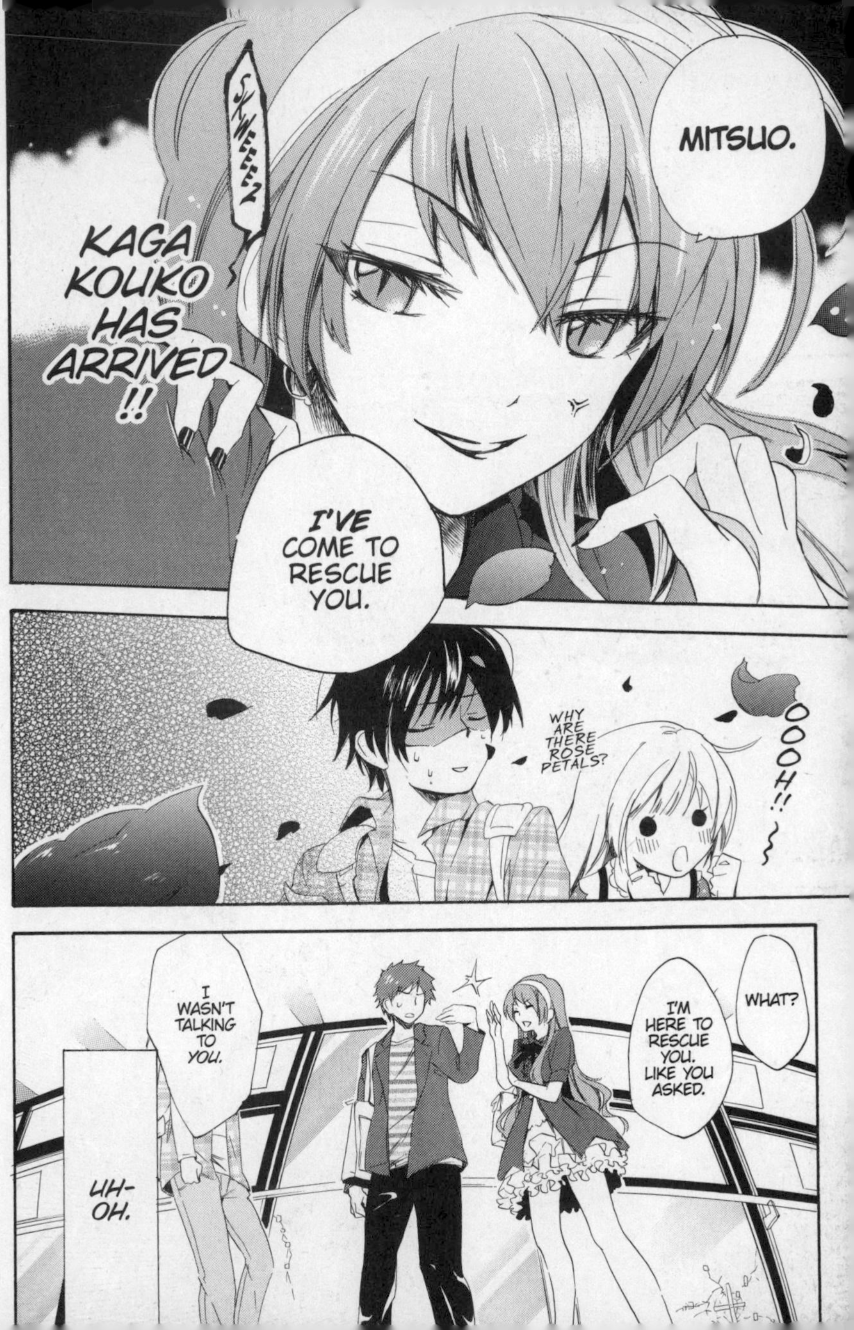
MITSUO.
SKWEEEZ
KAGA KOUKO HAS ARRIVED!!
I'VE COME TO RESCUE YOU.
OOOOH!!
WHY ARE THERE ROSE PETALS?
WHAT?
I'M HERE TO RESCUE YOU. LIKE YOU ASKED.
I WASN'T TALKING TO YOU.
UH-OH.

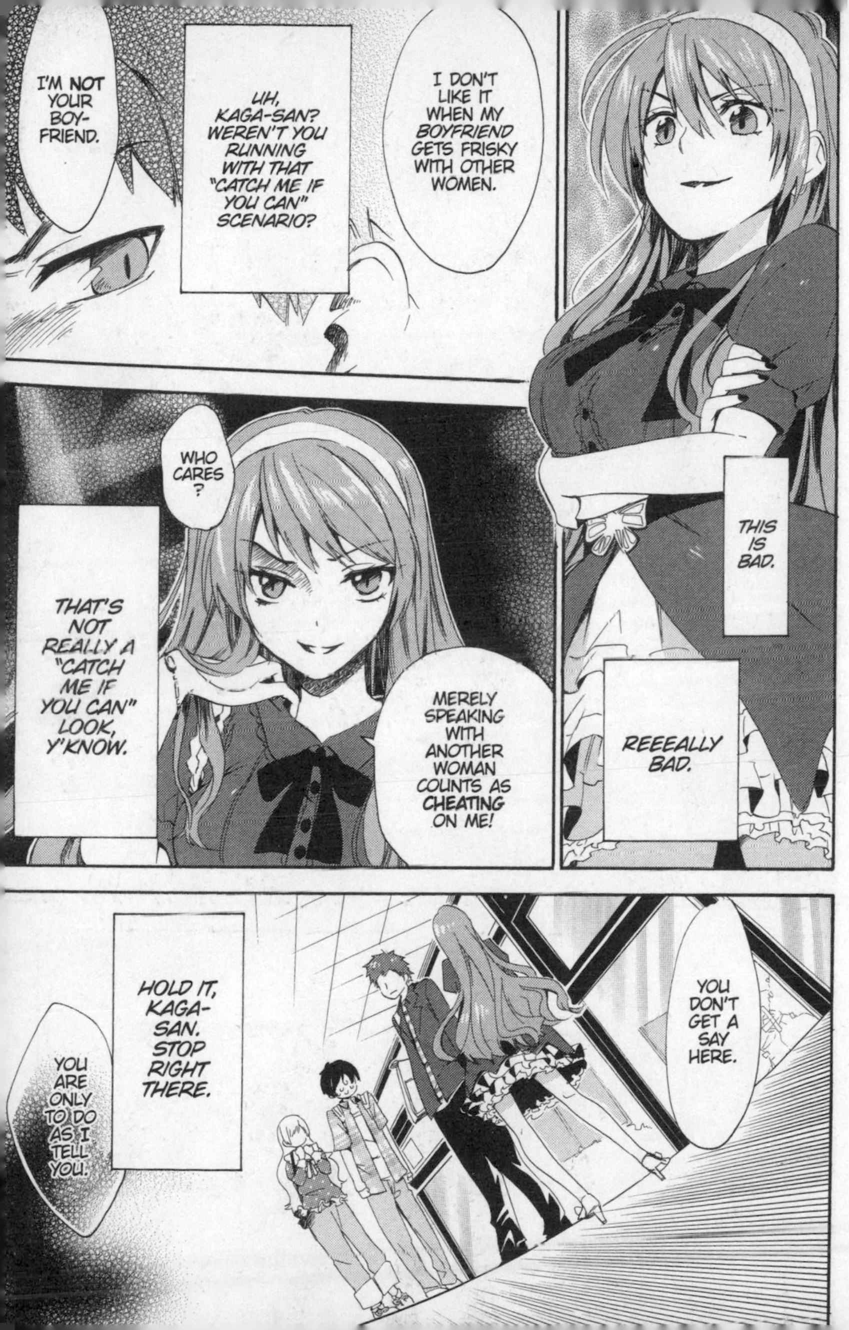
THIS IS BAD.
REEEALLY BAD.
I DON'T LIKE IT WHEN MY BOYFRIEND GETS FRISKY WITH OTHER WOMEN.
UH, KAGA-SAN? WEREN'T YOU RUNNING WITH THAT "CATCH ME IF YOU CAN" SCENARIO?
I'M NOT YOUR BOY-FRIEND.
MERELY SPEAKING WITH ANOTHER WOMAN COUNTS AS CHEATING ON ME!
WHO CARES?
THAT'S NOT REALLY A "CATCH ME IF YOU CAN" LOOK, Y'KNOW.
YOU DON'T GET A SAY HERE.
HOLD IT, KAGA-SAN. STOP RIGHT THERE.
YOU ARE ONLY TO DO AS I TELL YOU.

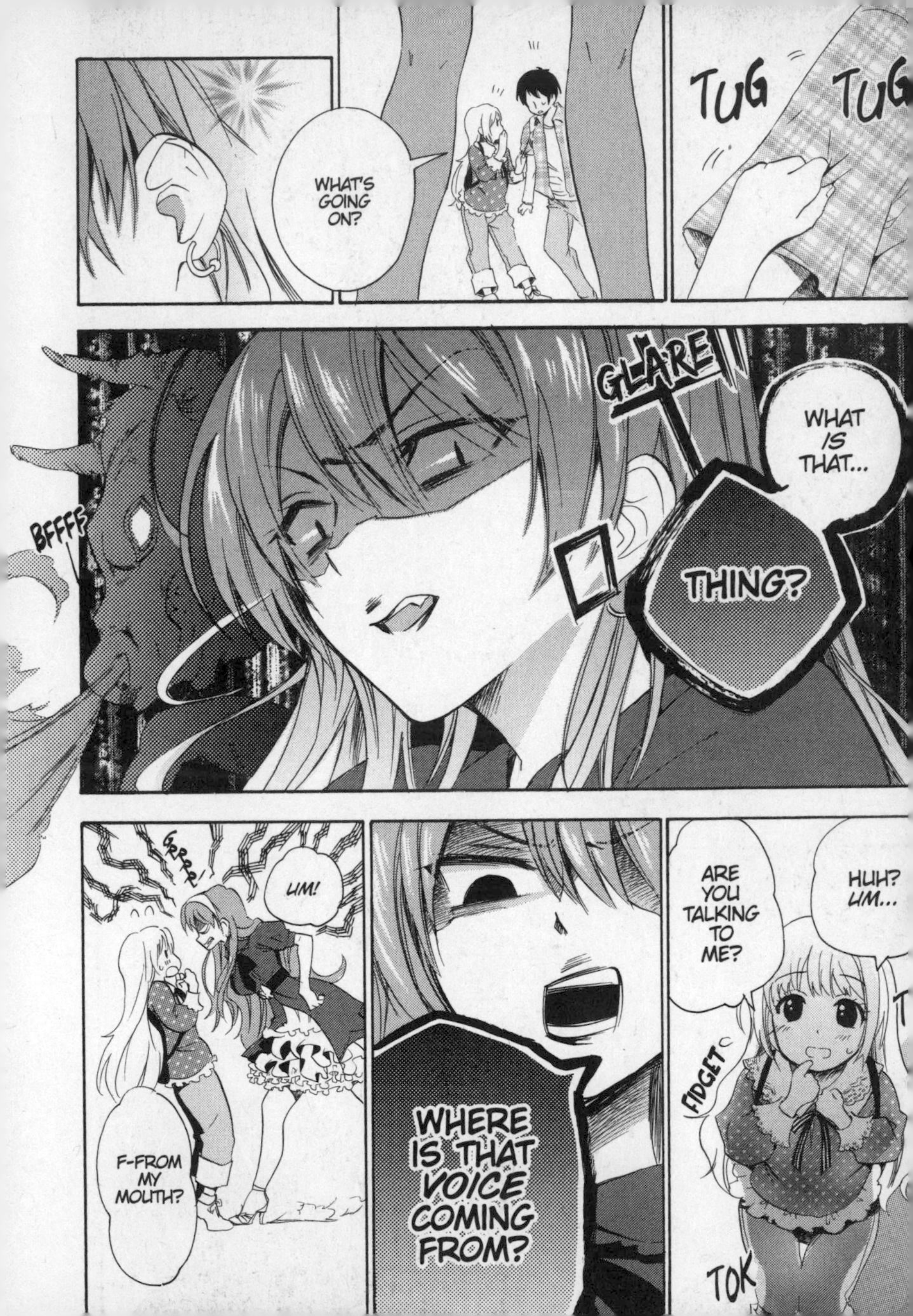
TUG TUG
WHAT'S GOING ON?
WHAT IS THAT...
THING?
GLARE
BFFFF
HUH? UM...
ARE YOU TALKING TO ME?
FIDGET
TOK
WHERE IS THAT VOICE COMING FROM?
UM!
GRRR!
F-FROM MY MOUTH?

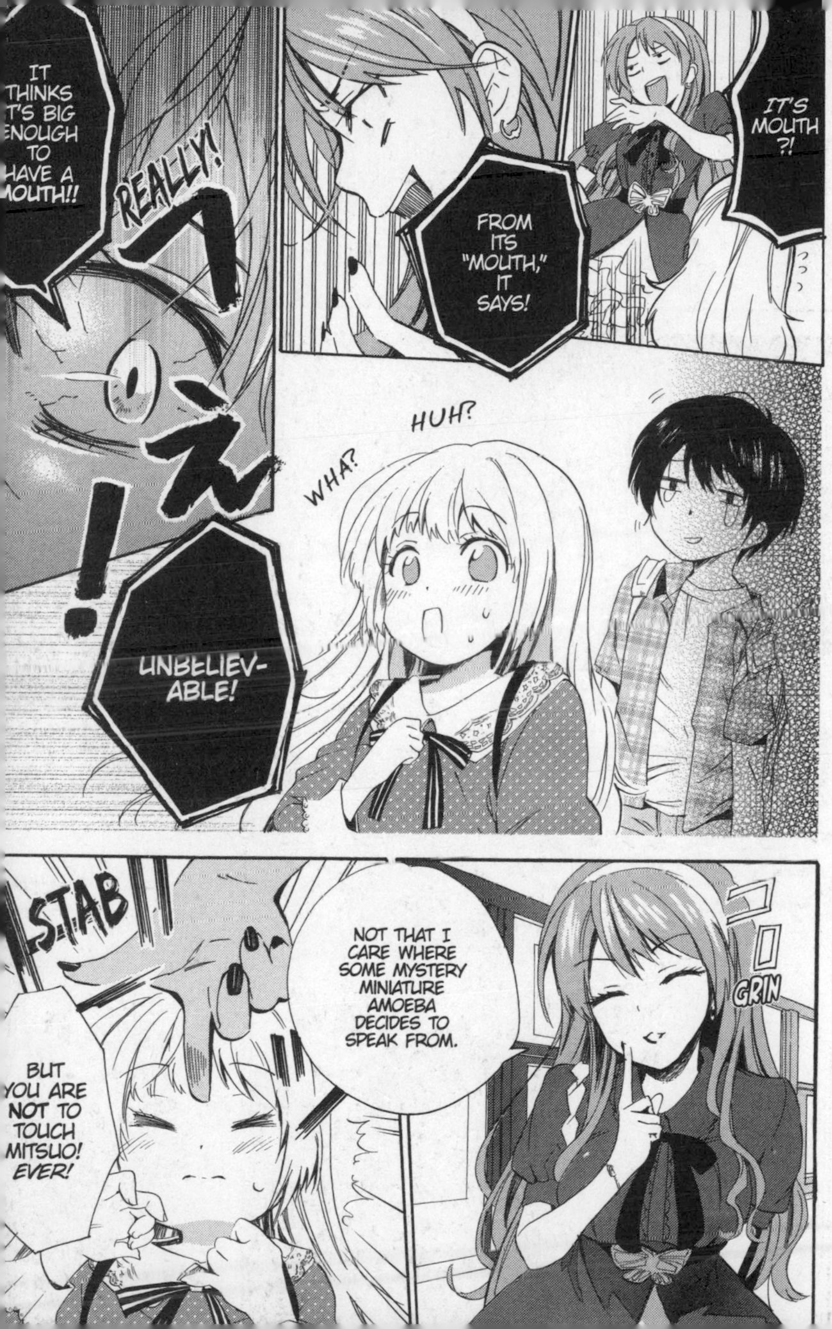

IT'S MOUTH?!
FROM ITS "MOUTH," IT SAYS!
HUH?
WHA?
REALLY!
IT THINKS IT'S BIG ENOUGH TO HAVE A MOUTH!!
UNBELIEV-ABLE!
GRIN
NOT THAT I CARE WHERE SOME MYSTERY MINIATURE AMOEBA DECIDES TO SPEAK FROM.
STAB
BUT YOU ARE NOT TO TOUCH MITSUO! EVER!

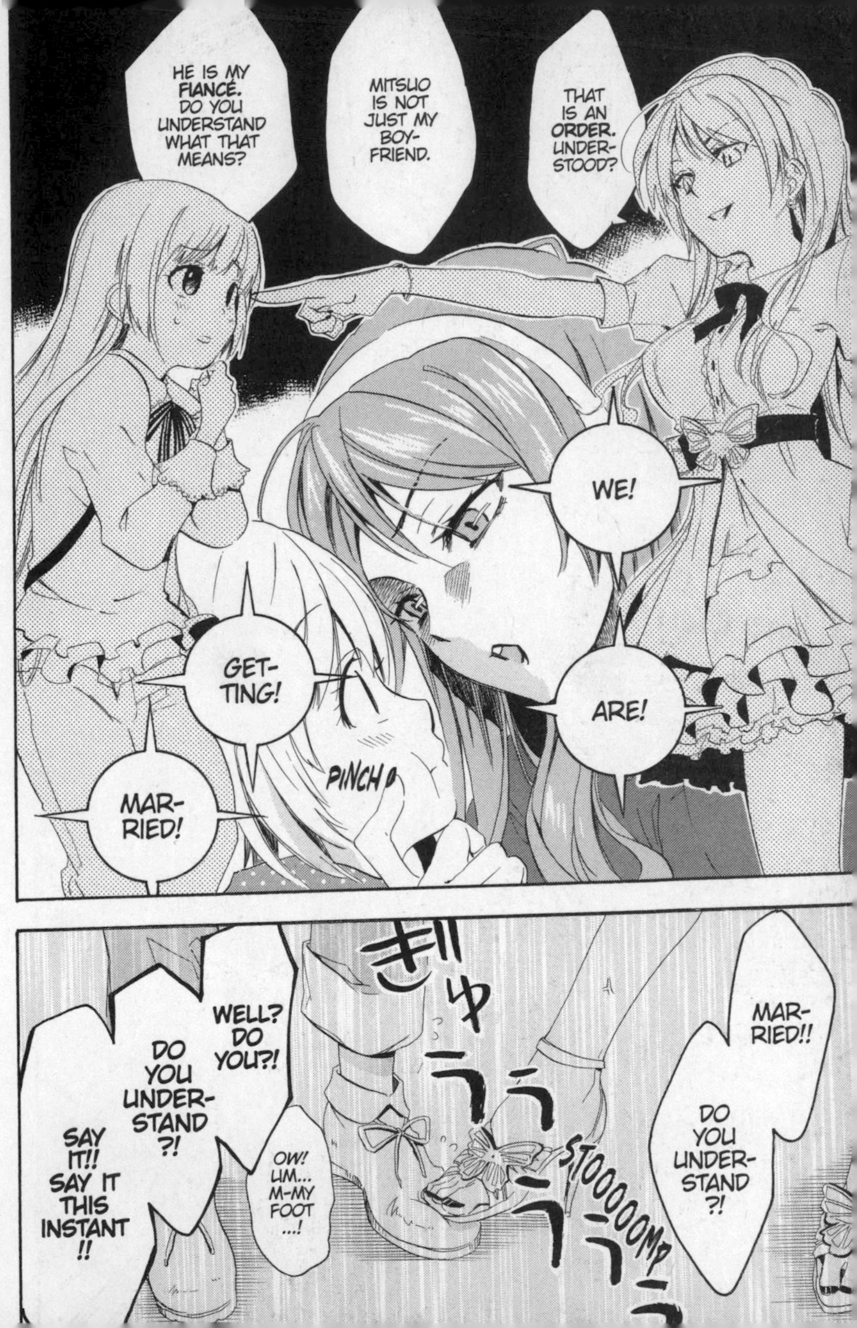
THAT IS AN ORDER. UNDERSTOOD?
MITSUO IS NOT JUST MY BOY-FRIEND.
HE IS MY FIANCÉ. DO YOU UNDERSTAND WHAT THAT MEANS?
WE!
ARE!
GET-TING!
MAR-RIED!
PINCH
MAR-RIED!!
DO YOU UNDER-STAND?!
STOOOOOMP
OW! UM... M-MY FOOT ...!
WELL? DO YOU?!
DO YOU UNDER-STAND?!
SAY IT!! SAY IT THIS INSTANT!!

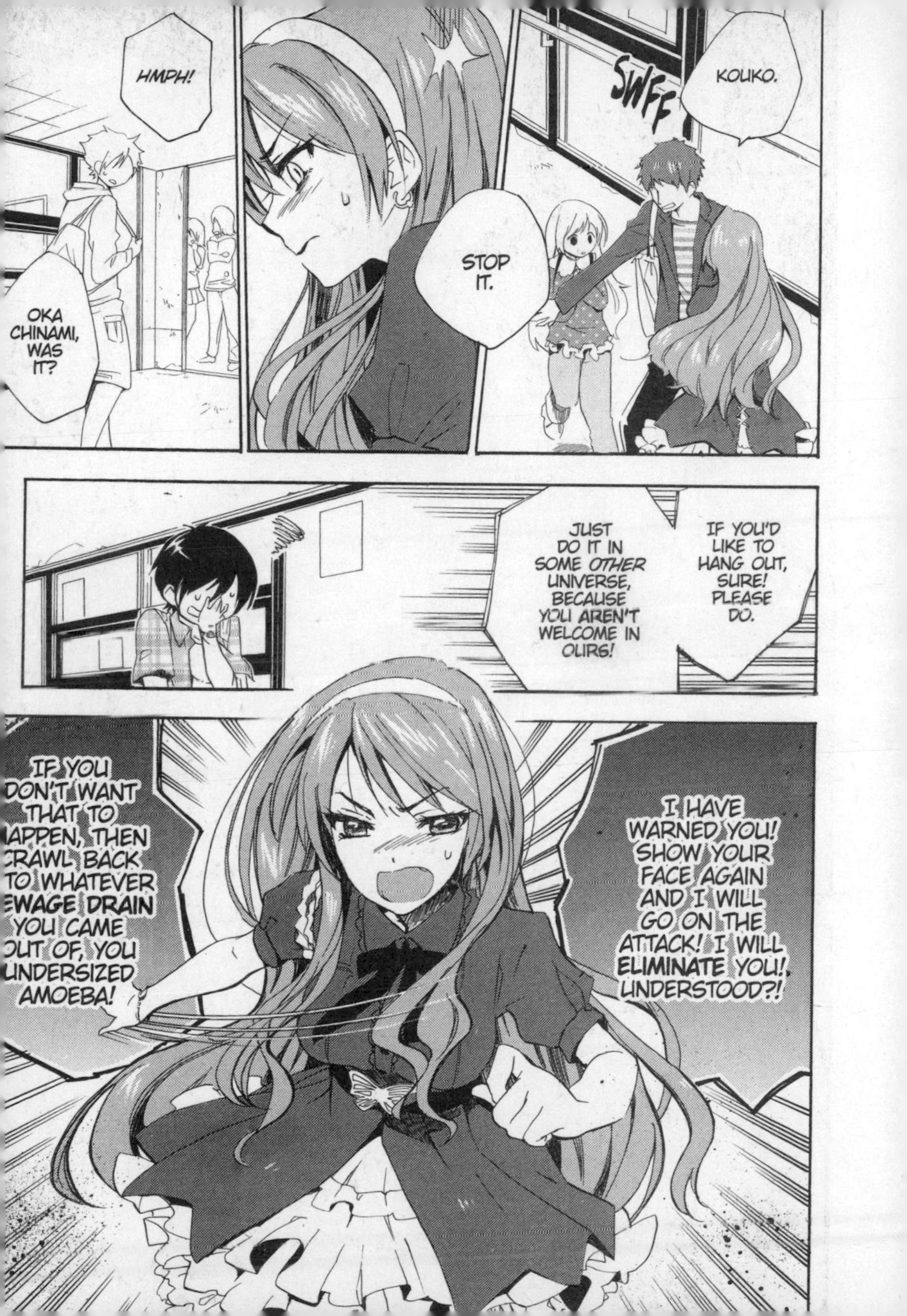
KOUKO.
SWFF
STOP IT.
HMPH!
OKA CHINAMI, WAS IT?
IF YOU'D LIKE TO HANG OUT, SURE! PLEASE DO.
JUST DO IT IN SOME *OTHER* UNIVERSE, BECAUSE YOU AREN'T WELCOME IN OURS!
I HAVE WARNED YOU! SHOW YOUR FACE AGAIN AND I WILL GO ON THE ATTACK! I WILL ELIMINATE YOU! UNDERSTOOD?!
IF YOU DON'T WANT THAT TO APPEN, THEN RAWL BACK TO WHATEVER EWAGE DRAIN YOU CAME UT OF, YOU UNDERSIZED AMOEBA!

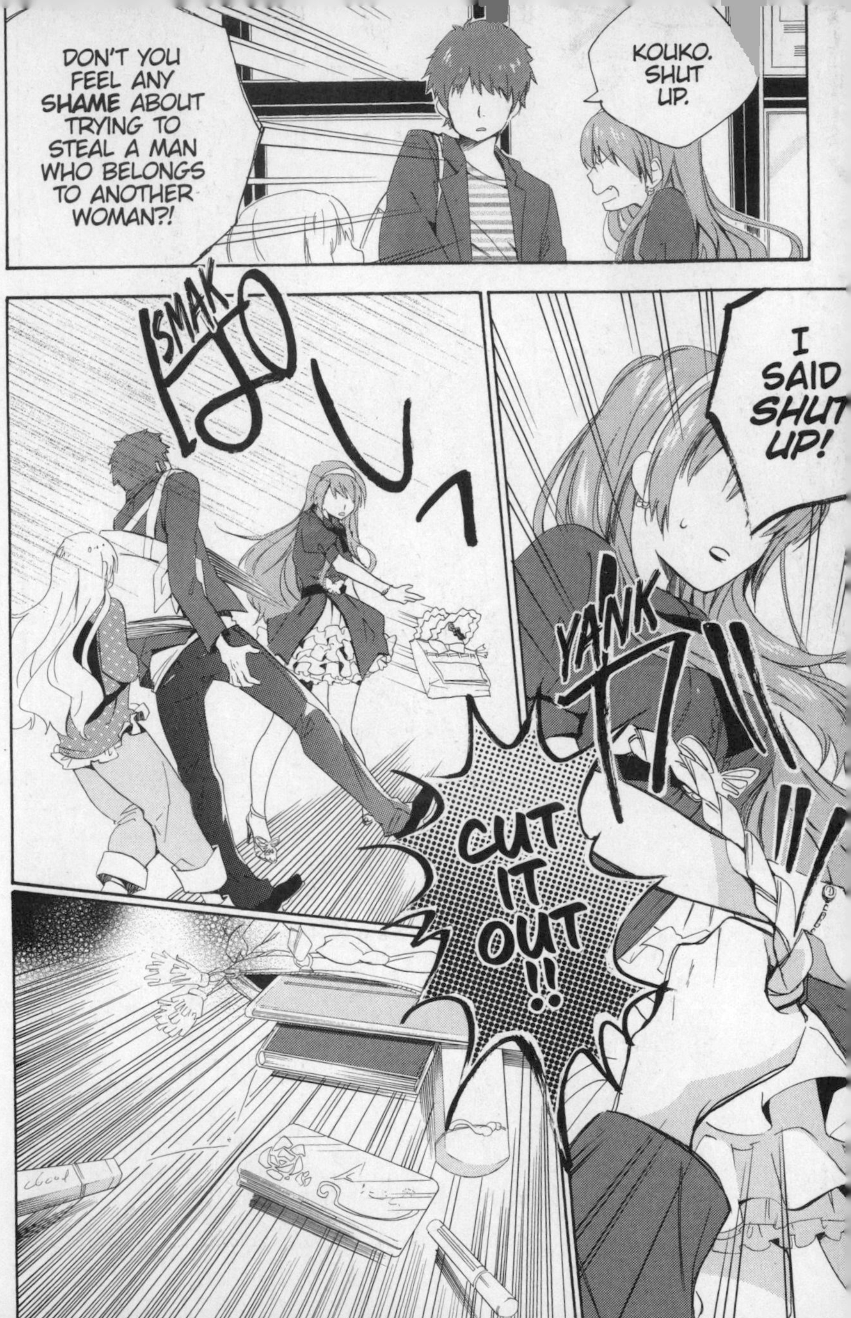
KOUKO. SHUT UP.
DON'T YOU FEEL ANY SHAME ABOUT TRYING TO STEAL A MAN WHO BELONGS TO ANOTHER WOMAN?!
I SAID SHUT UP!
YANK
CUT IT OUT!!
SMAK

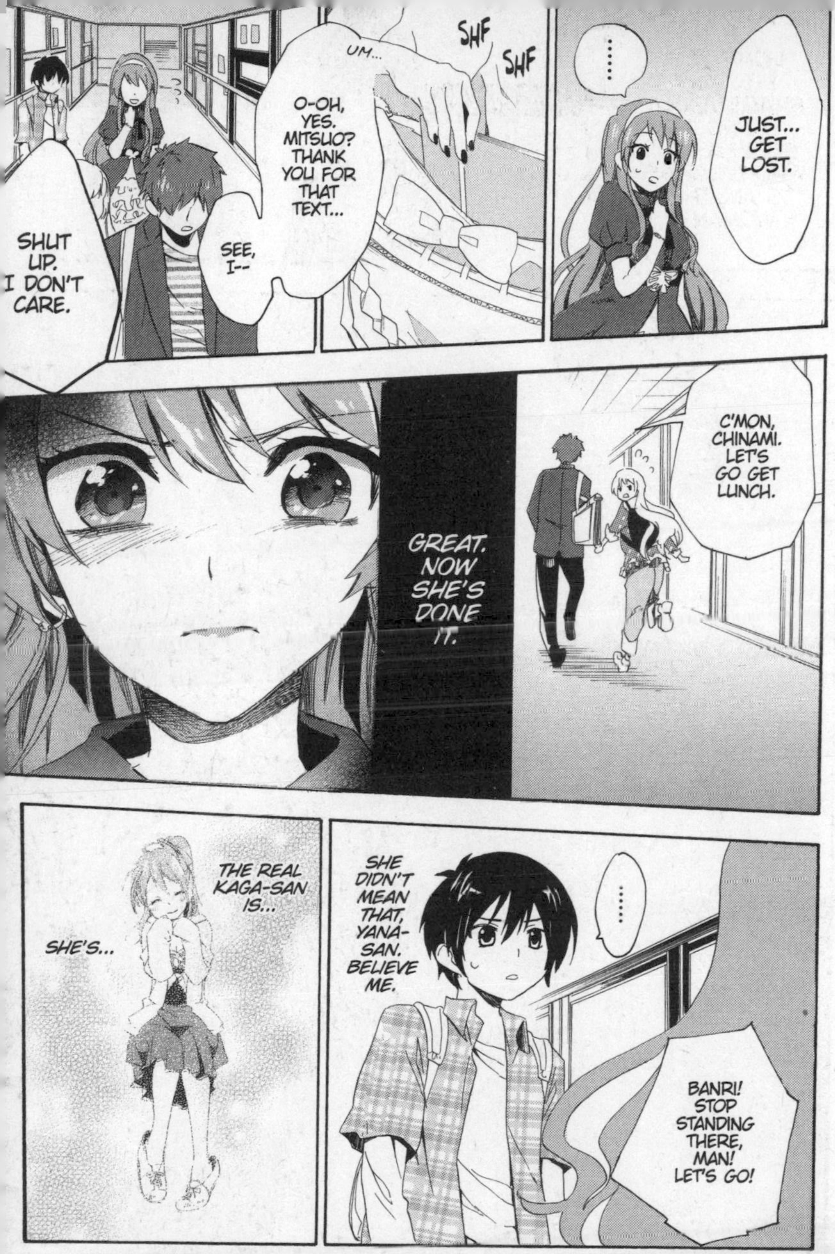
......
JUST... GET LOST.
SHF
SHF
UM...
O-OH, YES. MITSUO? THANK YOU FOR THAT TEXT...
SEE, I--
SHUT UP. I DON'T CARE.
C'MON, CHINAMI. LET'S GO GET LUNCH.
GREAT. NOW SHE'S DONE IT.
......
SHE DIDN'T MEAN THAT, YANA-SAN. BELIEVE ME.
BANRI! STOP STANDING THERE, MAN! LET'S GO!
THE REAL KAGA-SAN IS...
SHE'S...

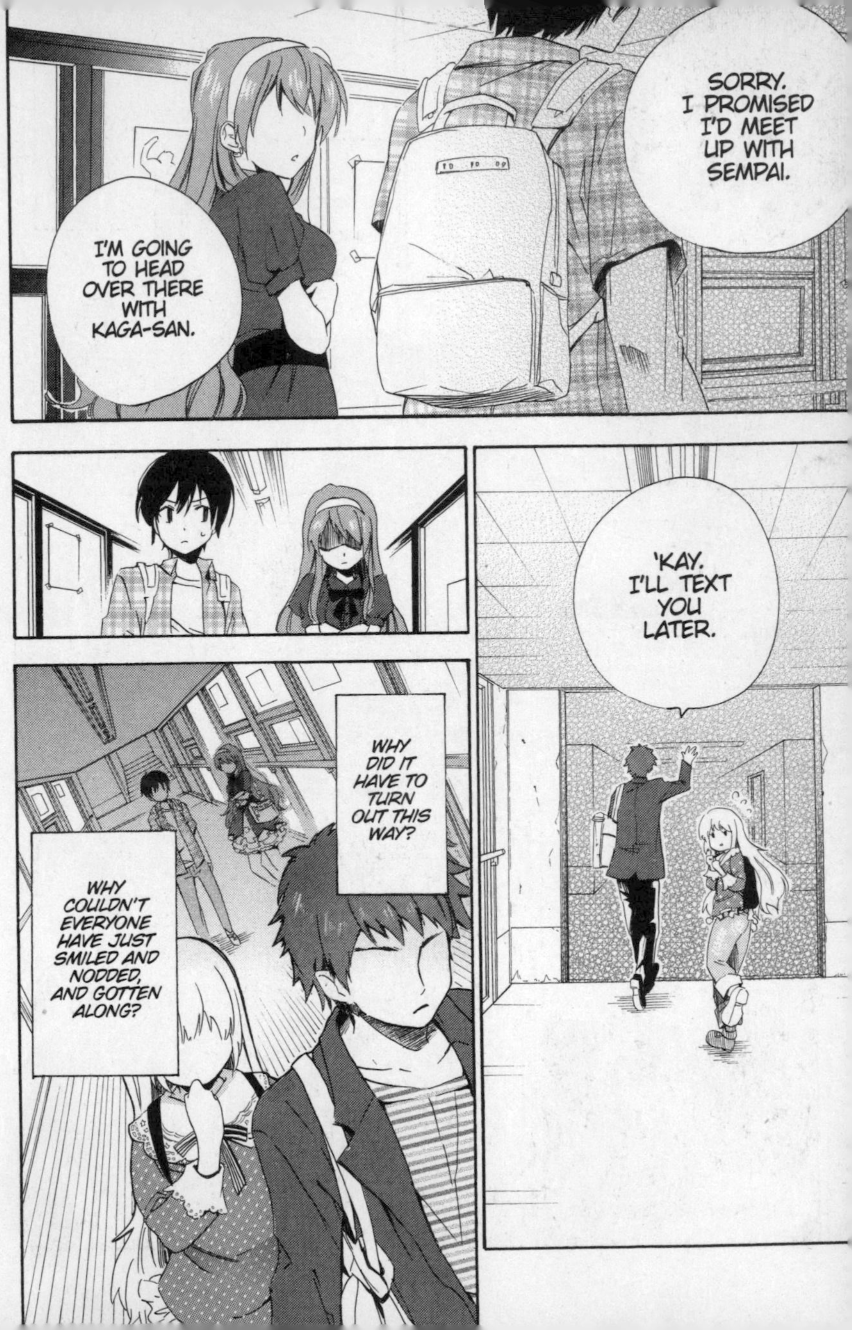
SORRY. I PROMISED I'D MEET UP WITH SEMPAI.
I'M GOING TO HEAD OVER THERE WITH KAGA-SAN.
'KAY. I'LL TEXT YOU LATER.
WHY DID IT HAVE TO TURN OUT THIS WAY?
WHY COULDN'T EVERYONE HAVE JUST SMILED AND NODDED, AND GOTTEN ALONG?

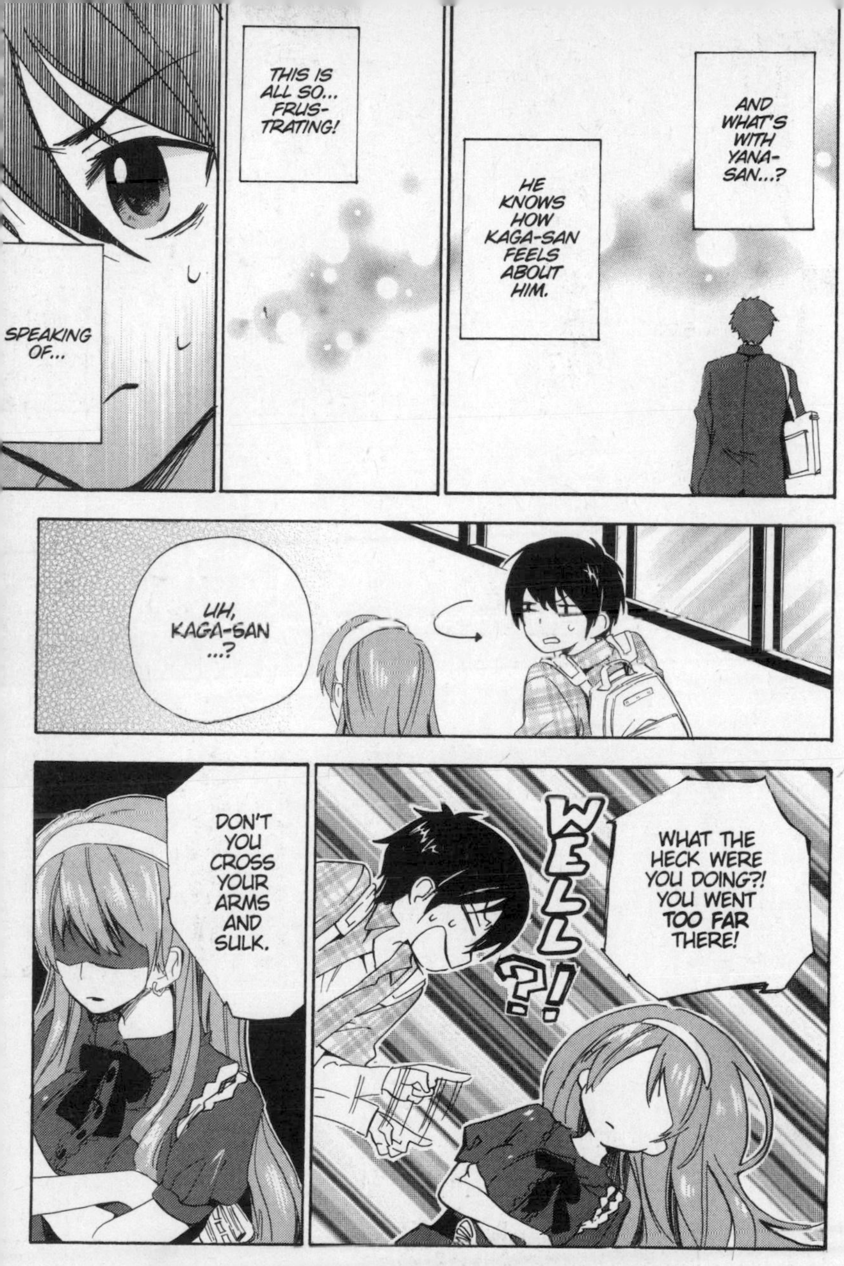
AND WHAT'S WITH YANA-SAN...?
HE KNOWS HOW KAGA-SAN FEELS ABOUT HIM.
THIS IS ALL SO... FRUS-TRATING!
SPEAKING OF...
UH, KAGA-SAN ...?
WHAT THE HECK WERE YOU DOING?! YOU WENT TOO FAR THERE!
WELL?!
DON'T YOU CROSS YOUR ARMS AND SULK.

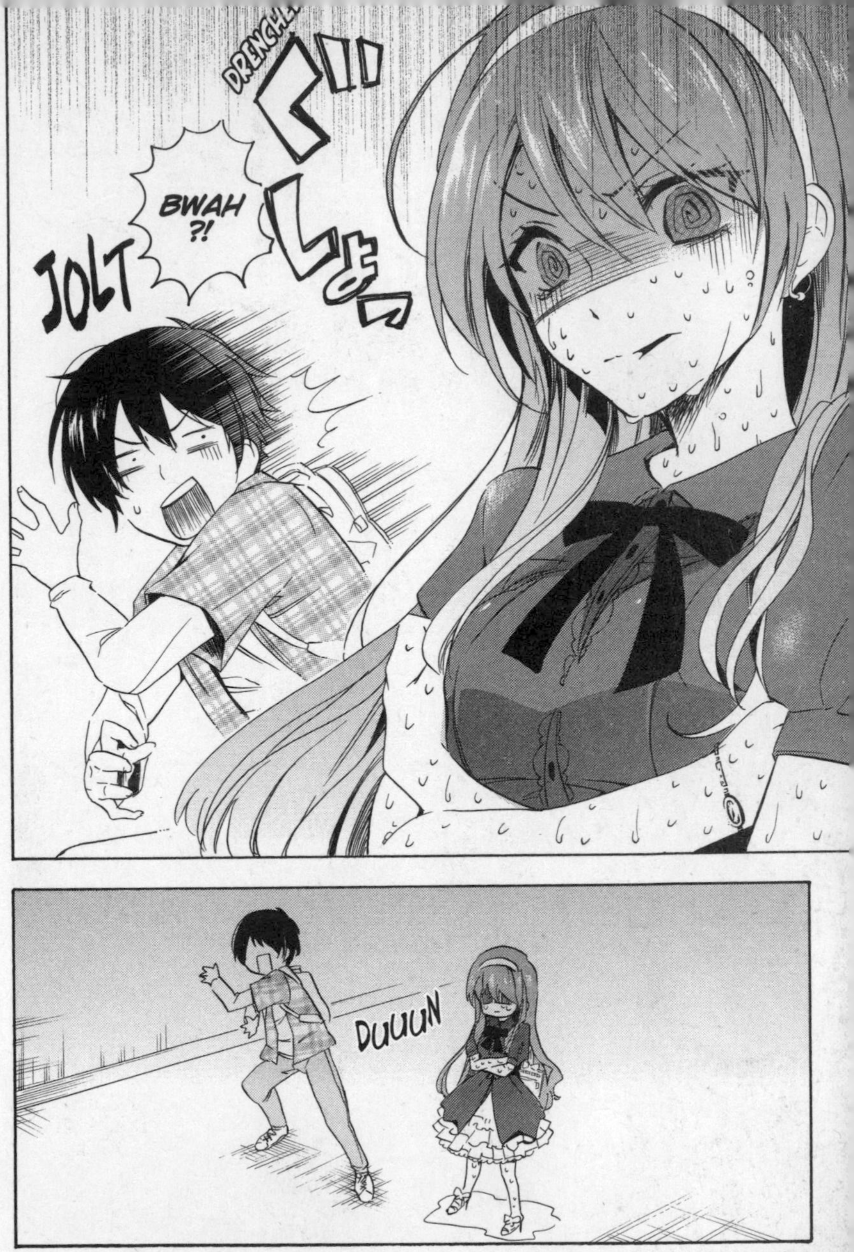
DRENCHE
ぐしょっ
BWAH ?!
JOLT
DUUUN

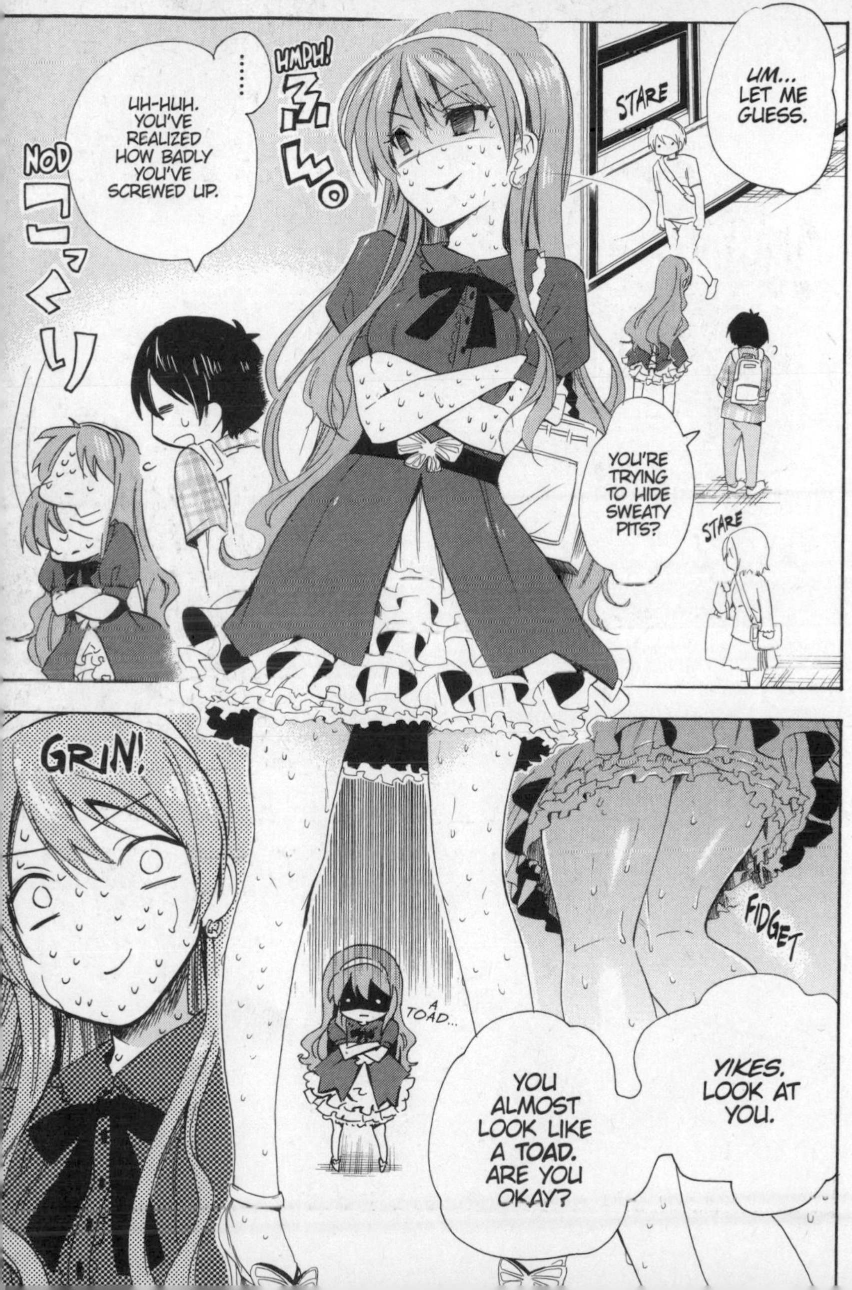
UM... LET ME GUESS.
STARE
YOU'RE TRYING TO HIDE SWEATY PITS?
STARE
HMPH!
......
UH-HUH. YOU'VE REALIZED HOW BADLY YOU'VE SCREWED UP.
NOD
FIDGET
YIKES. LOOK AT YOU.
YOU ALMOST LOOK LIKE A TOAD. ARE YOU OKAY?
A TOAD...
GRIN!

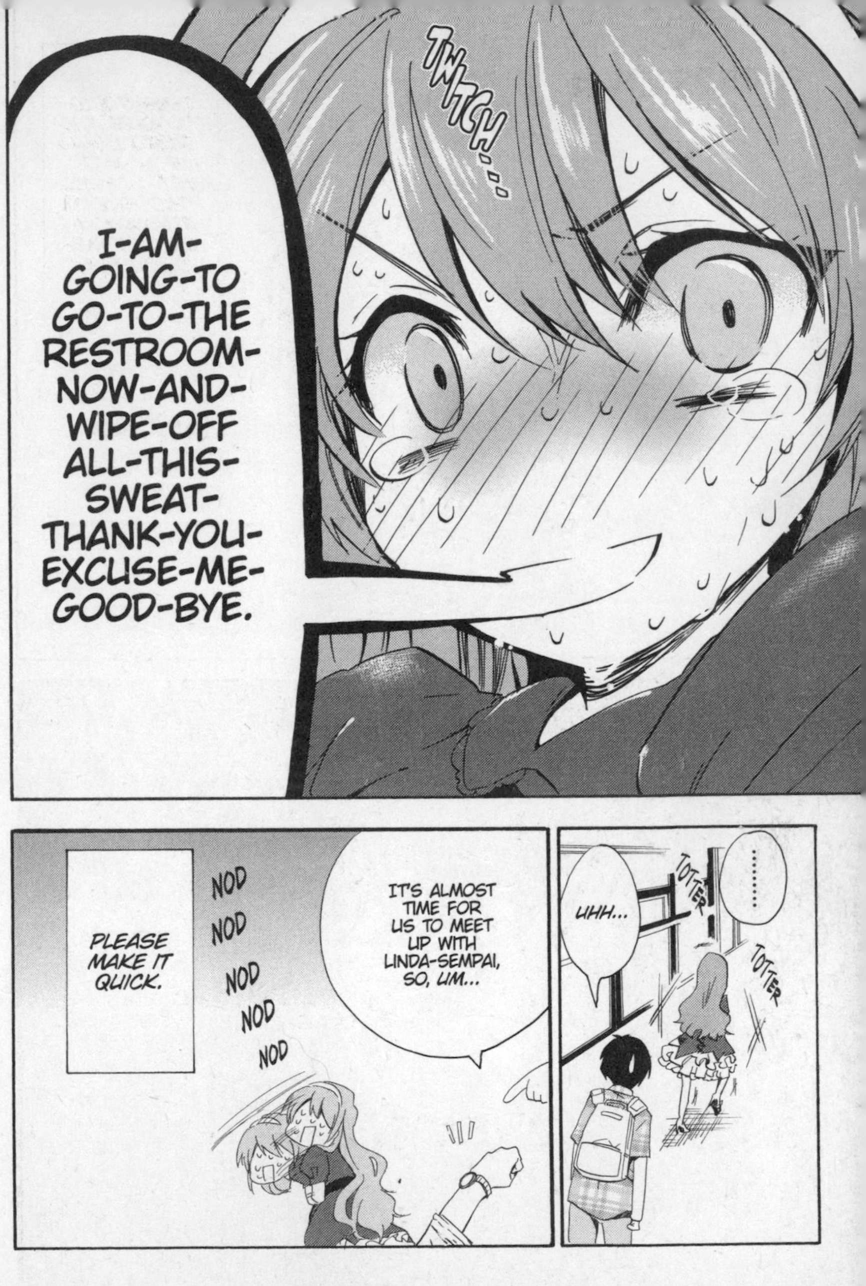
TWITCH...
I-AM-GOING-TO GO-TO-THE RESTROOM-NOW-AND-WIPE-OFF ALL-THIS-SWEAT-THANK-YOU-EXCUSE-ME-GOOD-BYE.
......
UHH...
TOTTER
TOTTER
IT'S ALMOST TIME FOR US TO MEET UP WITH LINDA-SEMPAI, SO, UM...
NOD
NOD
NOD
NOD
NOD
PLEASE MAKE IT QUICK.

CHAPTER 8

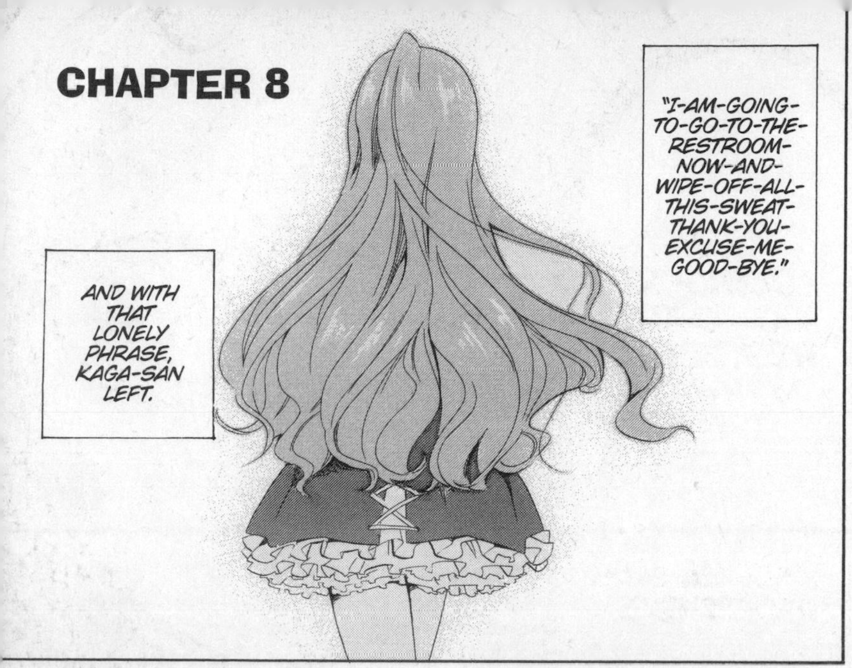
"I-AM-GOING-TO-GO-TO-THE-RESTROOM-NOW-AND-WIPE-OFF-ALL-THIS-SWEAT-THANK-YOU-EXCUSE-ME-GOOD-BYE."
AND WITH THAT LONELY PHRASE, KAGA-SAN LEFT.

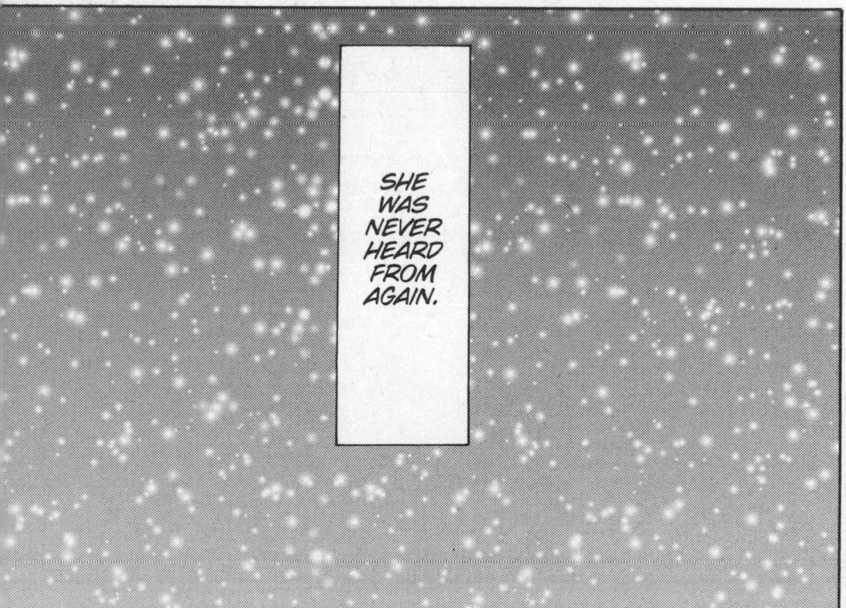
SHE WAS NEVER HEARD FROM AGAIN.

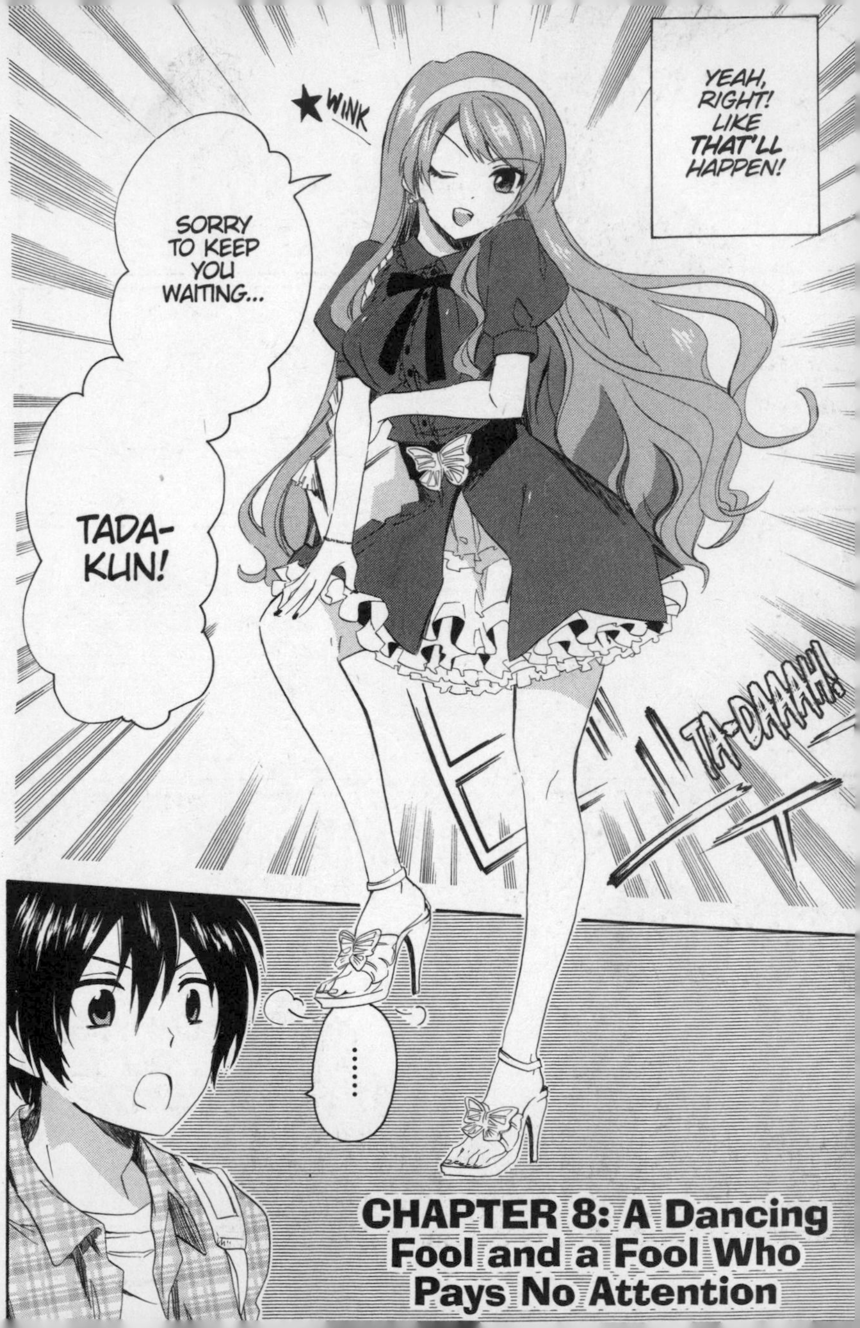
YEAH, RIGHT! LIKE THAT'LL HAPPEN!
WINK
SORRY TO KEEP YOU WAITING...
TADA-KUN!
TA-DAAAH!
......

CHAPTER 8: A Dancing Fool and a Fool Who Pays No Attention

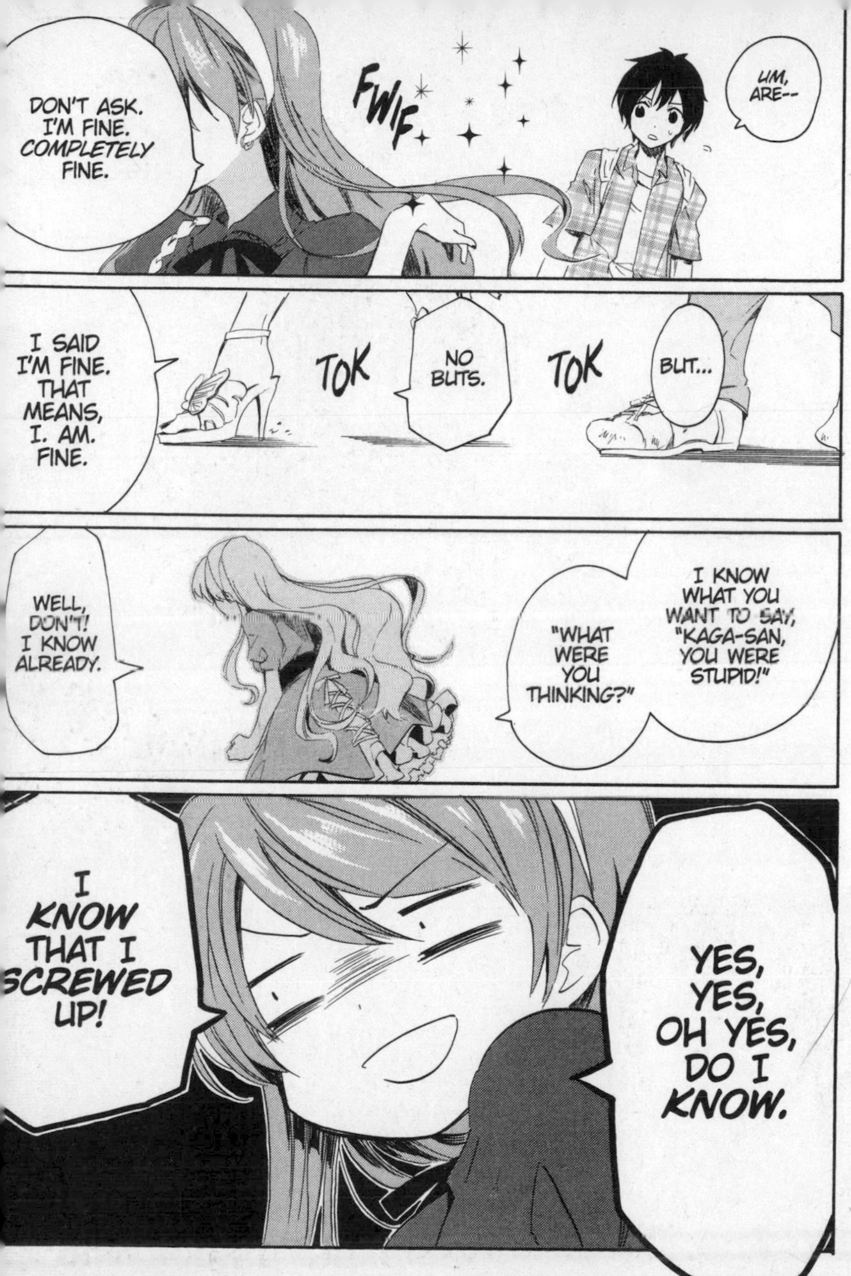
UM, ARE--
FWIF
DON'T ASK. I'M FINE. COMPLETELY FINE.
BUT...
TOK
NO BUTS.
TOK
I SAID I'M FINE. THAT MEANS, I. AM. FINE.
I KNOW WHAT YOU WANT TO SAY, "KAGA-SAN, YOU WERE STUPID!"
"WHAT WERE YOU THINKING?"
WELL, DON'T! I KNOW ALREADY.
YES, YES, OH YES, DO I KNOW.
I KNOW THAT I SCREWED UP!

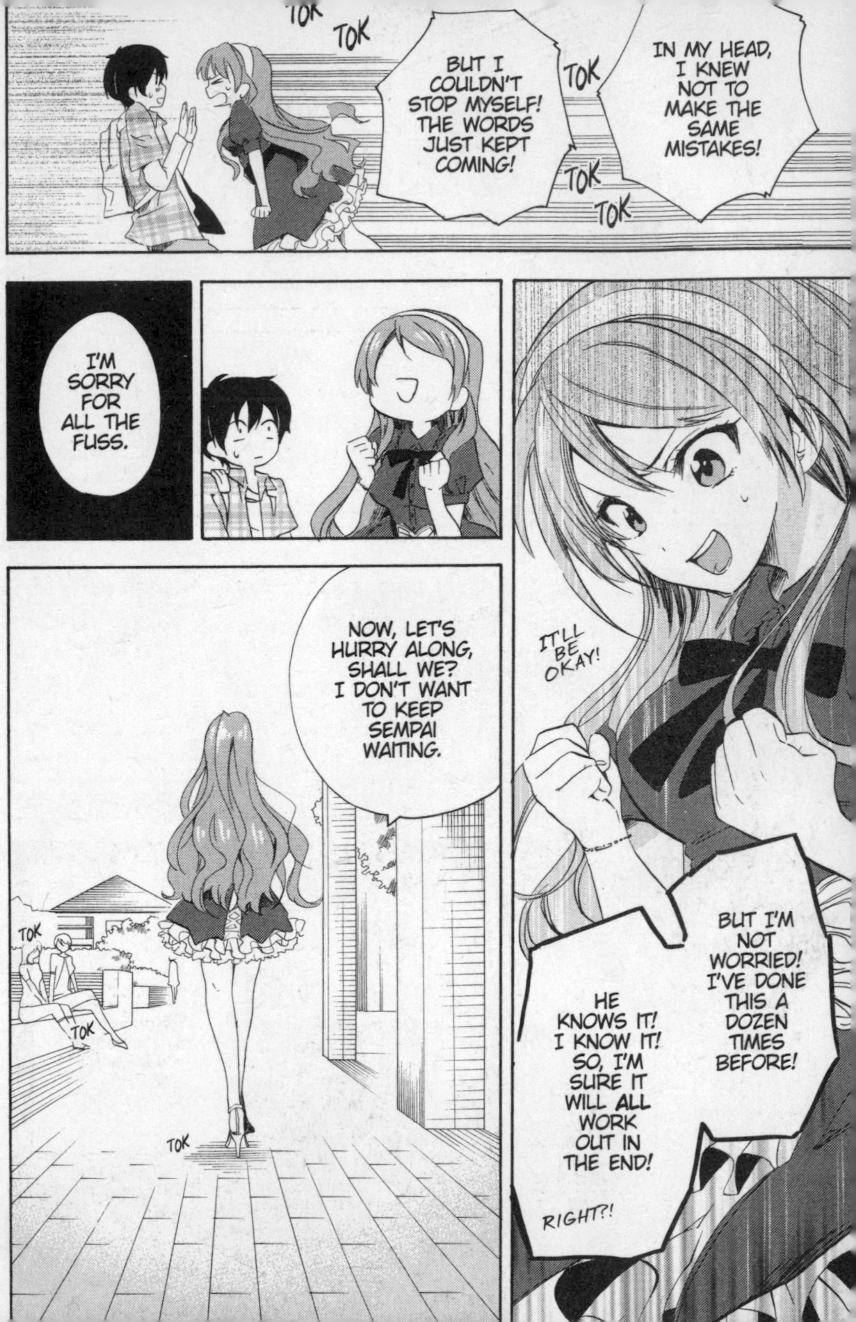
TOK
TOK
IN MY HEAD, I KNEW NOT TO MAKE THE SAME MISTAKES!
TOK
BUT I COULDN'T STOP MYSELF! THE WORDS JUST KEPT COMING!
TOK
TOK
IT'LL BE OKAY!
BUT I'M NOT WORRIED! I'VE DONE THIS A DOZEN TIMES BEFORE!
HE KNOWS IT! I KNOW IT! SO, I'M SURE IT WILL ALL WORK OUT IN THE END!
RIGHT?!
I'M SORRY FOR ALL THE FUSS.
NOW, LET'S HURRY ALONG, SHALL WE? I DON'T WANT TO KEEP SEMPAI WAITING.
TOK
TOK
TOK

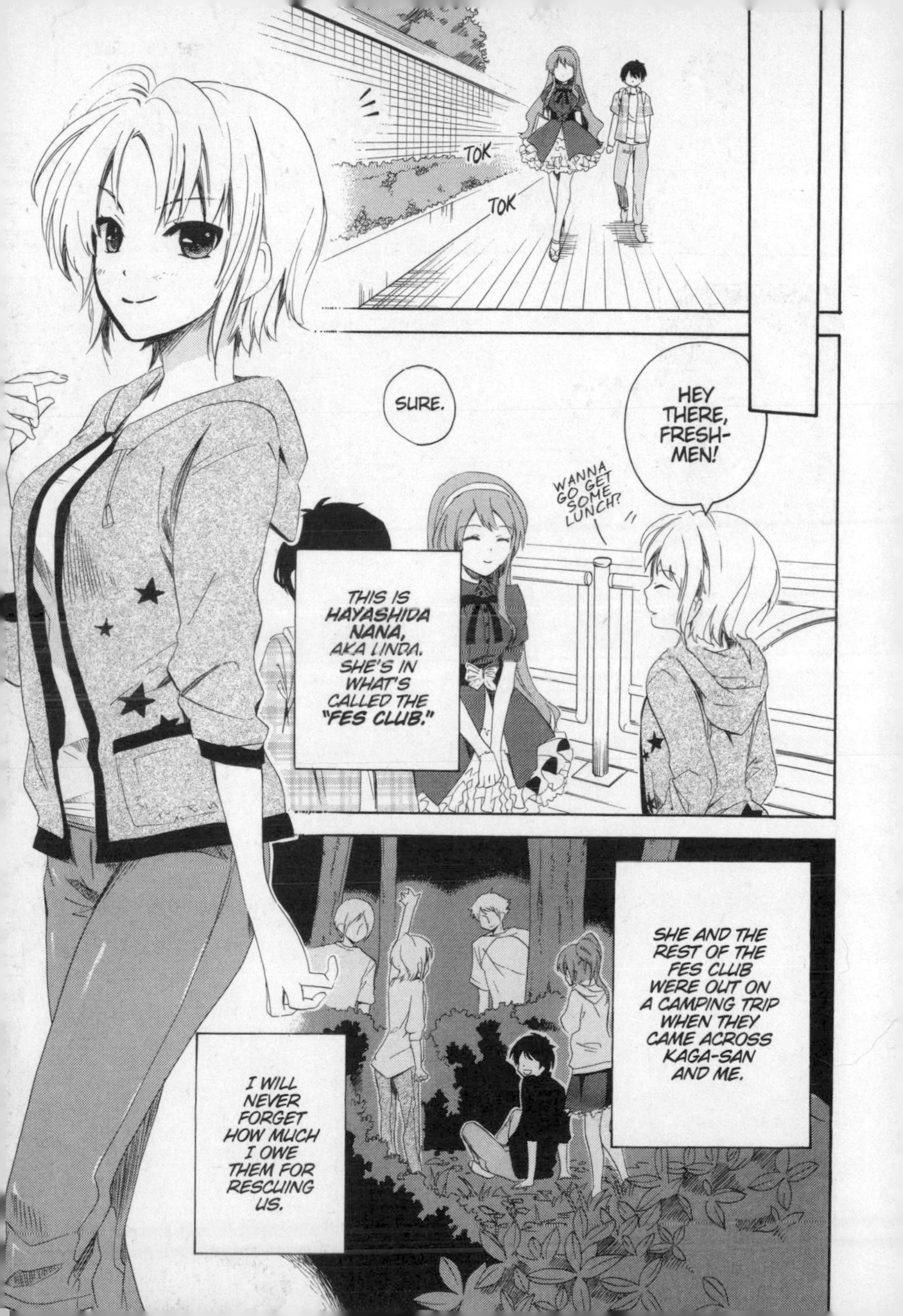
TOK
TOK
HEY THERE, FRESHMEN!
WANNA GO GET SOME LUNCH?
SURE.
THIS IS HAYASHIDA NANA, AKA LINDA. SHE'S IN WHAT'S CALLED THE "FES CLUB."
SHE AND THE REST OF THE FES CLUB WERE OUT ON A CAMPING TRIP WHEN THEY CAME ACROSS KAGA-SAN AND ME.
I WILL NEVER FORGET HOW MUCH I OWE THEM FOR RESCUING US.

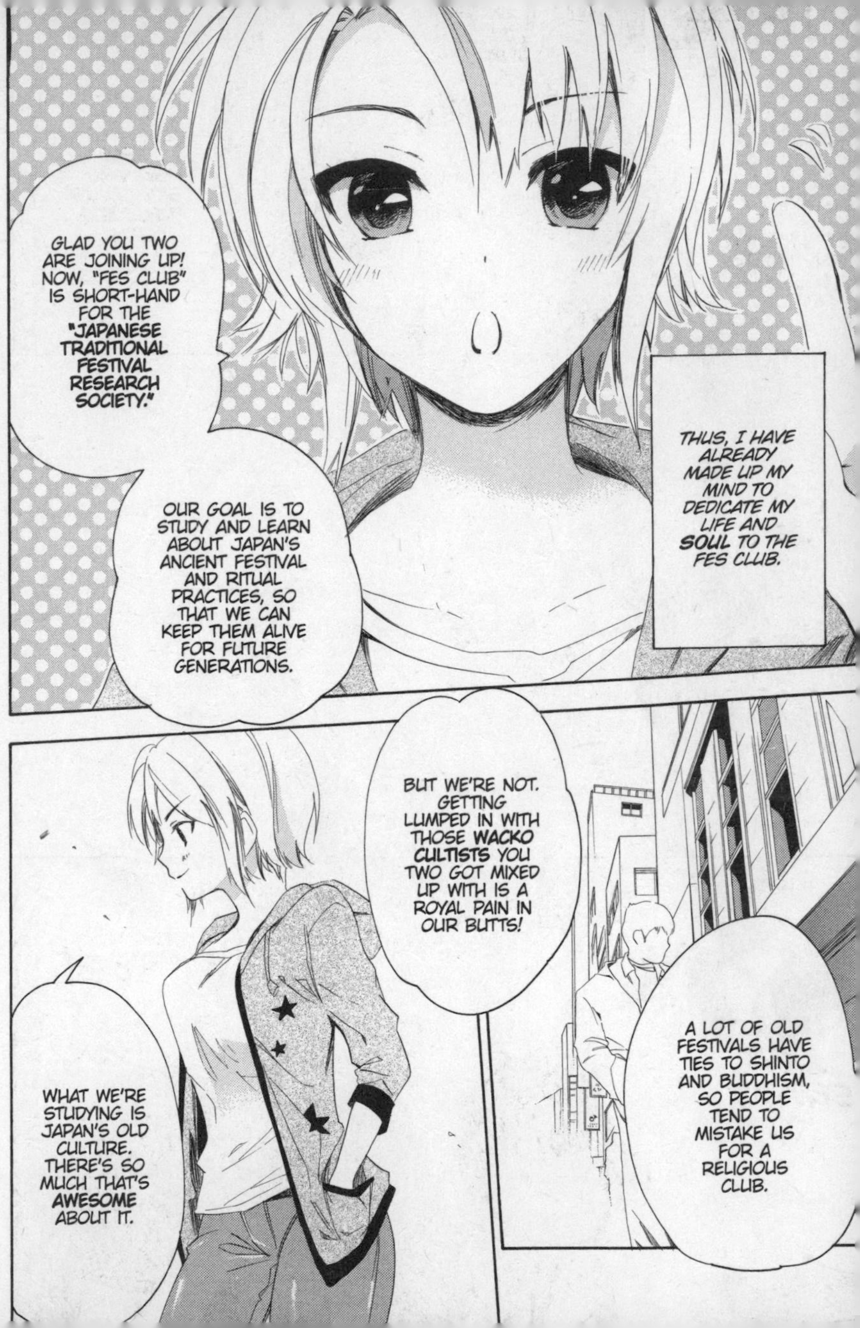
GLAD YOU TWO ARE JOINING UP! NOW, "FES CLUB" IS SHORT-HAND FOR THE "JAPANESE TRADITIONAL FESTIVAL RESEARCH SOCIETY."
OUR GOAL IS TO STUDY AND LEARN ABOUT JAPAN'S ANCIENT FESTIVAL AND RITUAL PRACTICES, SO THAT WE CAN KEEP THEM ALIVE FOR FUTURE GENERATIONS.
THUS, I HAVE ALREADY MADE UP MY MIND TO DEDICATE MY LIFE AND SOUL TO THE FES CLUB.
A LOT OF OLD FESTIVALS HAVE TIES TO SHINTO AND BUDDHISM, SO PEOPLE TEND TO MISTAKE US FOR A RELIGIOUS CLUB.
BUT WE'RE NOT. GETTING LUMPED IN WITH THOSE WACKO CULTISTS YOU TWO GOT MIXED UP WITH IS A ROYAL PAIN IN OUR BUTTS!
WHAT WE'RE STUDYING IS JAPAN'S OLD CULTURE. THERE'S SO MUCH THAT'S AWESOME ABOUT IT.

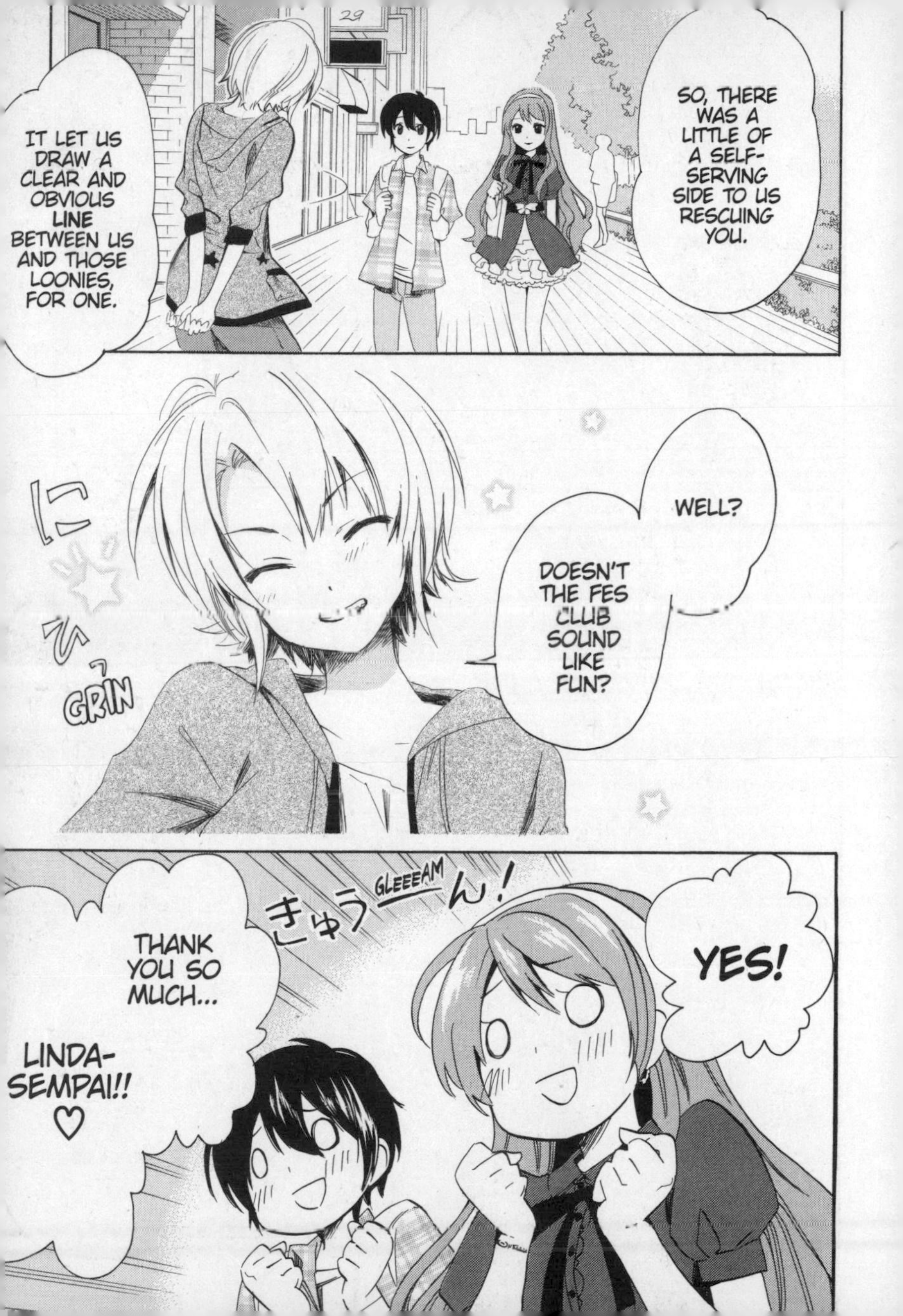
SO, THERE WAS A LITTLE OF A SELF-SERVING SIDE TO US RESCUING YOU.
IT LET US DRAW A CLEAR AND OBVIOUS LINE BETWEEN US AND THOSE LOONIES, FOR ONE.
WELL?
DOESN'T THE FES CLUB SOUND LIKE FUN?
にっ
GRIN
YES!
きゅうーん!
GLEEEAM
THANK YOU SO MUCH...
LINDA-SEMPAI!! ♡

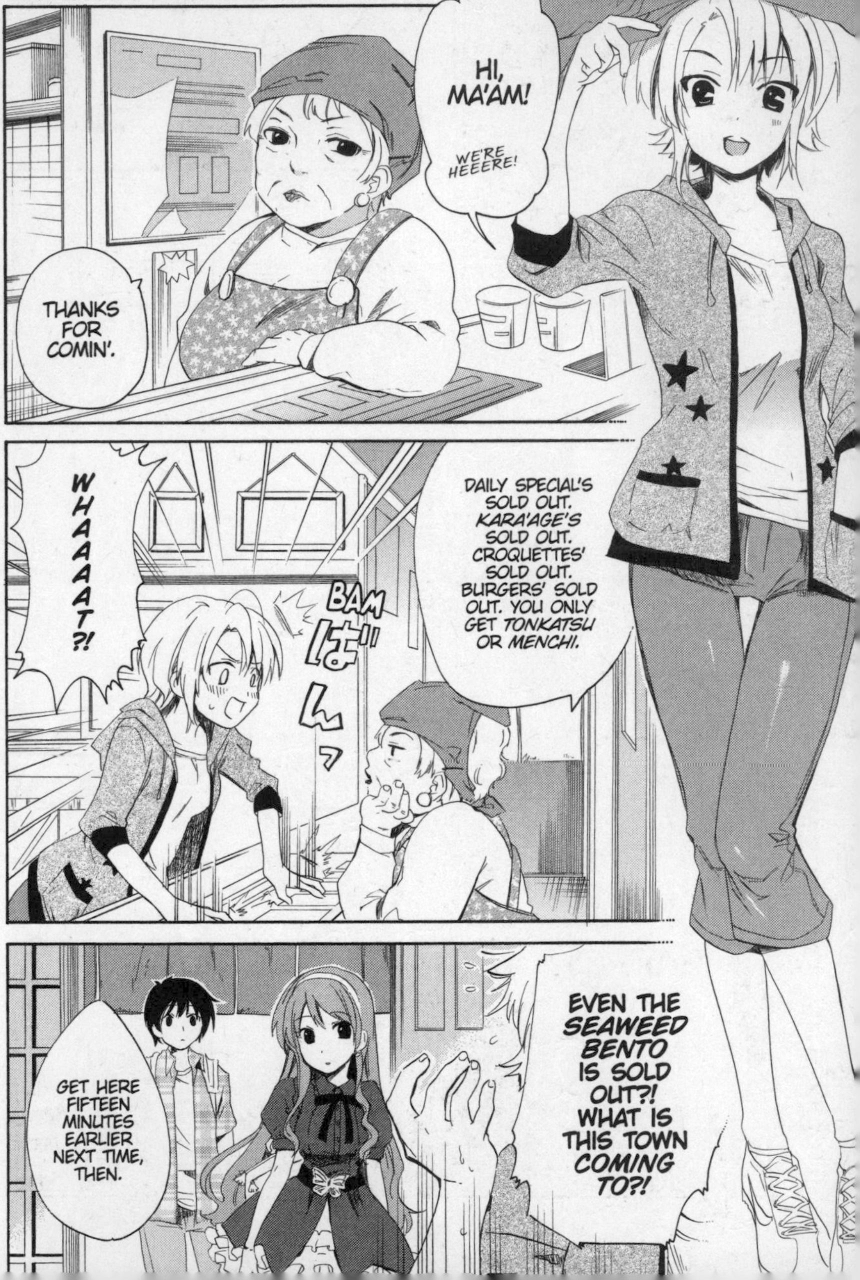
HI, MA'AM!
WE'RE HEEEERE!
THANKS FOR COMIN'.
DAILY SPECIAL'S SOLD OUT. KARA'AGE'S SOLD OUT. CROQUETTES' SOLD OUT. BURGERS' SOLD OUT. YOU ONLY GET TONKATSU OR MENCHI.
BAM
ばんっ
WHAAAAAT?!
EVEN THE SEAWEED BENTO IS SOLD OUT?! WHAT IS THIS TOWN COMING TO?!
GET HERE FIFTEEN MINUTES EARLIER NEXT TIME, THEN.

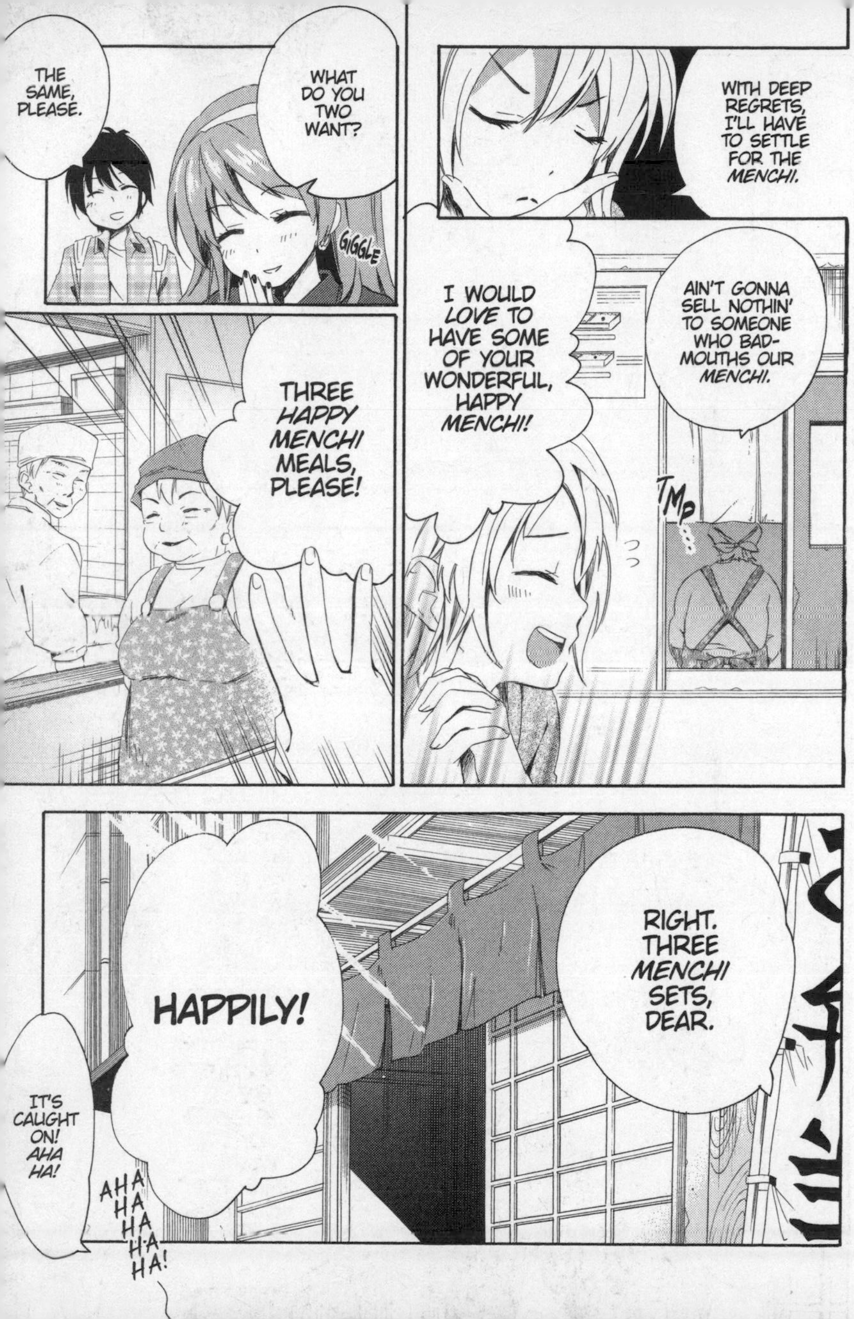
WITH DEEP REGRETS, I'LL HAVE TO SETTLE FOR THE *MENCHI*.
WHAT DO YOU TWO WANT?
GIGGLE
THE SAME, PLEASE.
AIN'T GONNA SELL NOTHIN' TO SOMEONE WHO BAD-MOUTHS OUR *MENCHI*.
TMP
I WOULD *LOVE* TO HAVE SOME OF YOUR WONDERFUL, HAPPY *MENCHI*!
THREE *HAPPY MENCHI* MEALS, PLEASE!
RIGHT. THREE *MENCHI* SETS, DEAR.
HAPPILY!
IT'S CAUGHT ON! *AHA HA!*
AHAHAHAHAHA!

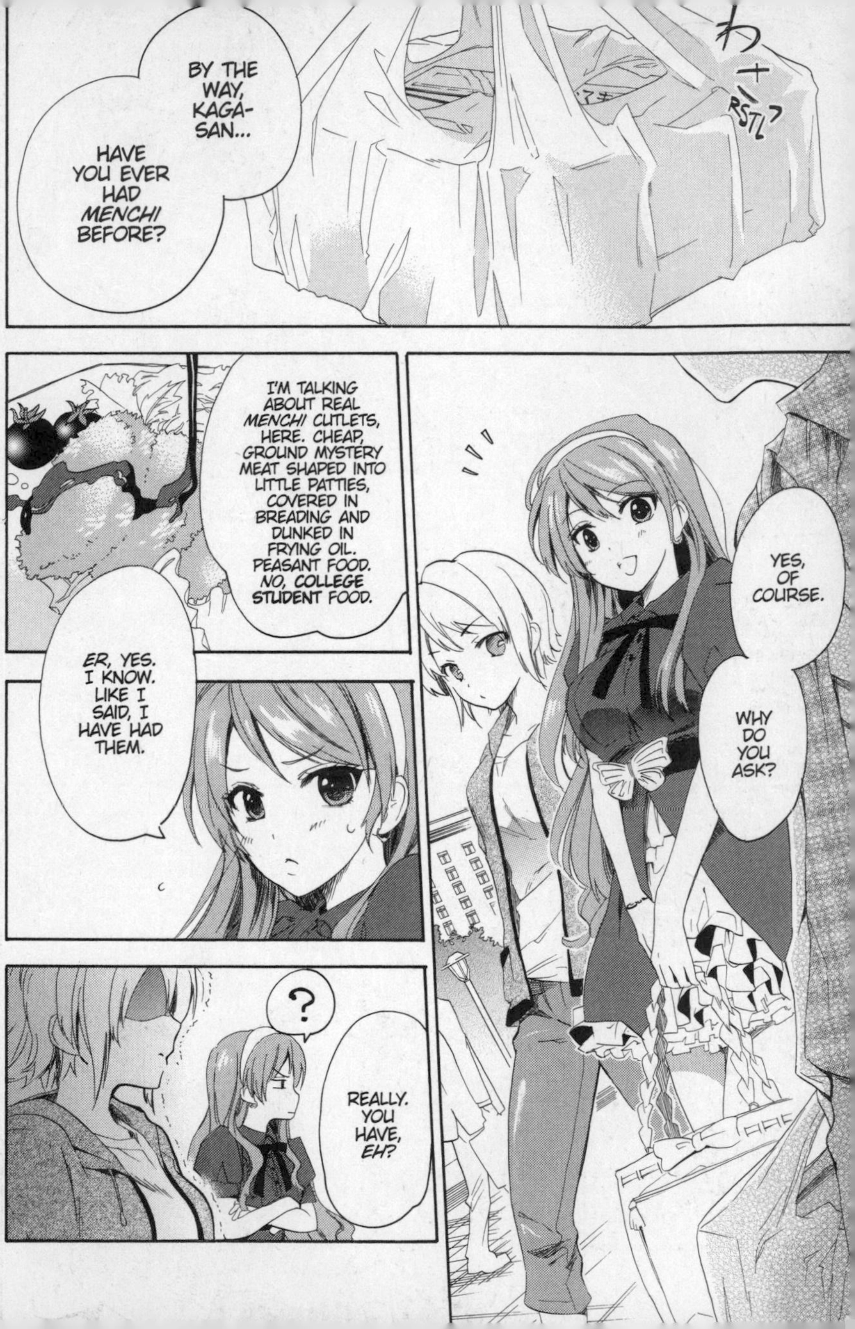
RSTL?
BY THE WAY, KAGA-SAN...
HAVE YOU EVER HAD MENCHI BEFORE?
YES, OF COURSE.
WHY DO YOU ASK?
I'M TALKING ABOUT REAL MENCHI CUTLETS, HERE. CHEAP, GROUND MYSTERY MEAT SHAPED INTO LITTLE PATTIES, COVERED IN BREADING AND DUNKED IN FRYING OIL. PEASANT FOOD. NO, COLLEGE STUDENT FOOD.
ER, YES. I KNOW. LIKE I SAID, I HAVE HAD THEM.
?
REALLY. YOU HAVE, EH?

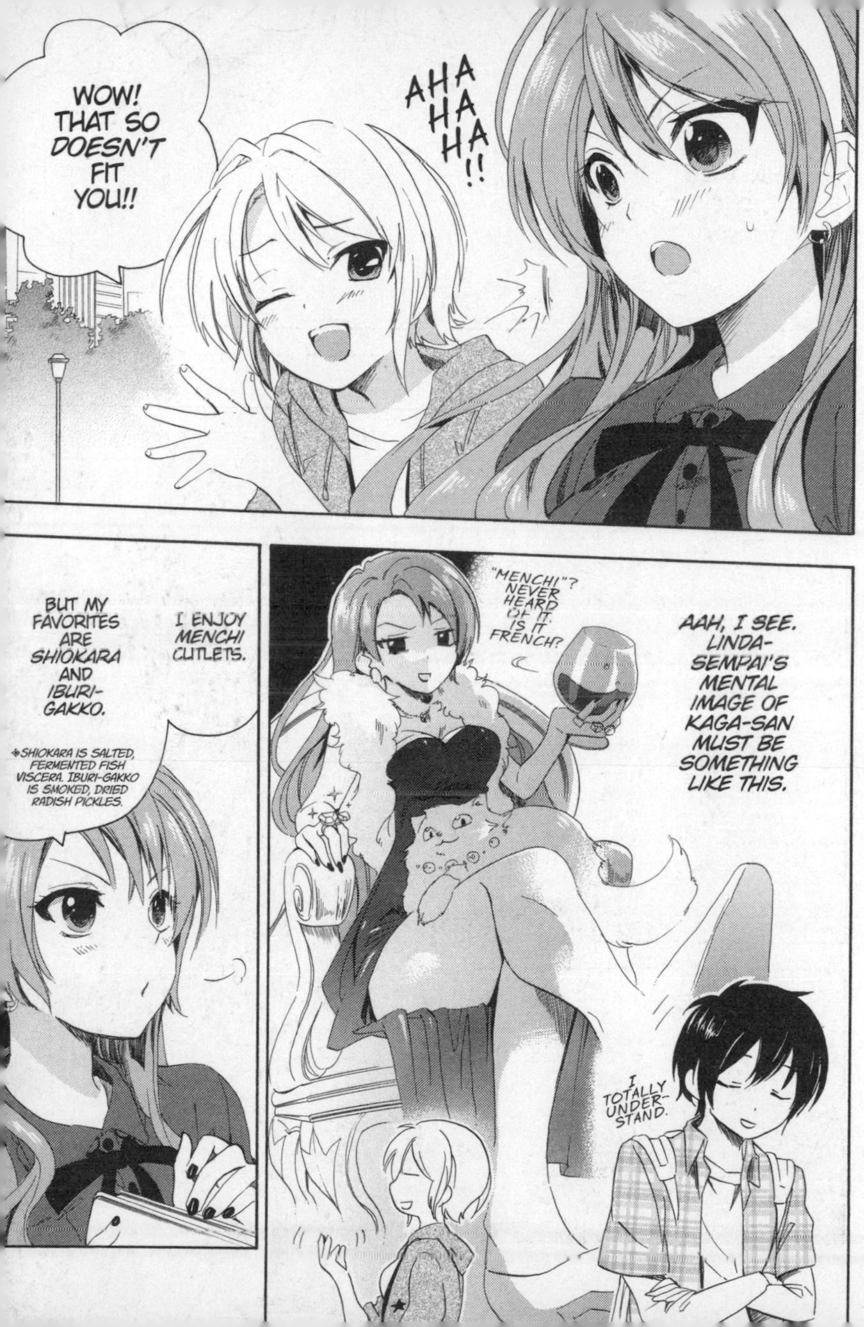
AHAHAHA!!
WOW! THAT SO DOESN'T FIT YOU!!
AAH, I SEE. LINDA-SEMPAI'S MENTAL IMAGE OF KAGA-SAN MUST BE SOMETHING LIKE THIS.
"MENCHI"? NEVER HEARD OF IT. IS IT FRENCH?
I TOTALLY UNDER-STAND.
I ENJOY MENCHI CUTLETS.
BUT MY FAVORITES ARE SHIOKARA AND IBURI-GAKKO.
*SHIOKARA IS SALTED, FERMENTED FISH VISCERA. IBURI-GAKKO IS SMOKED, DRIED RADISH PICKLES.

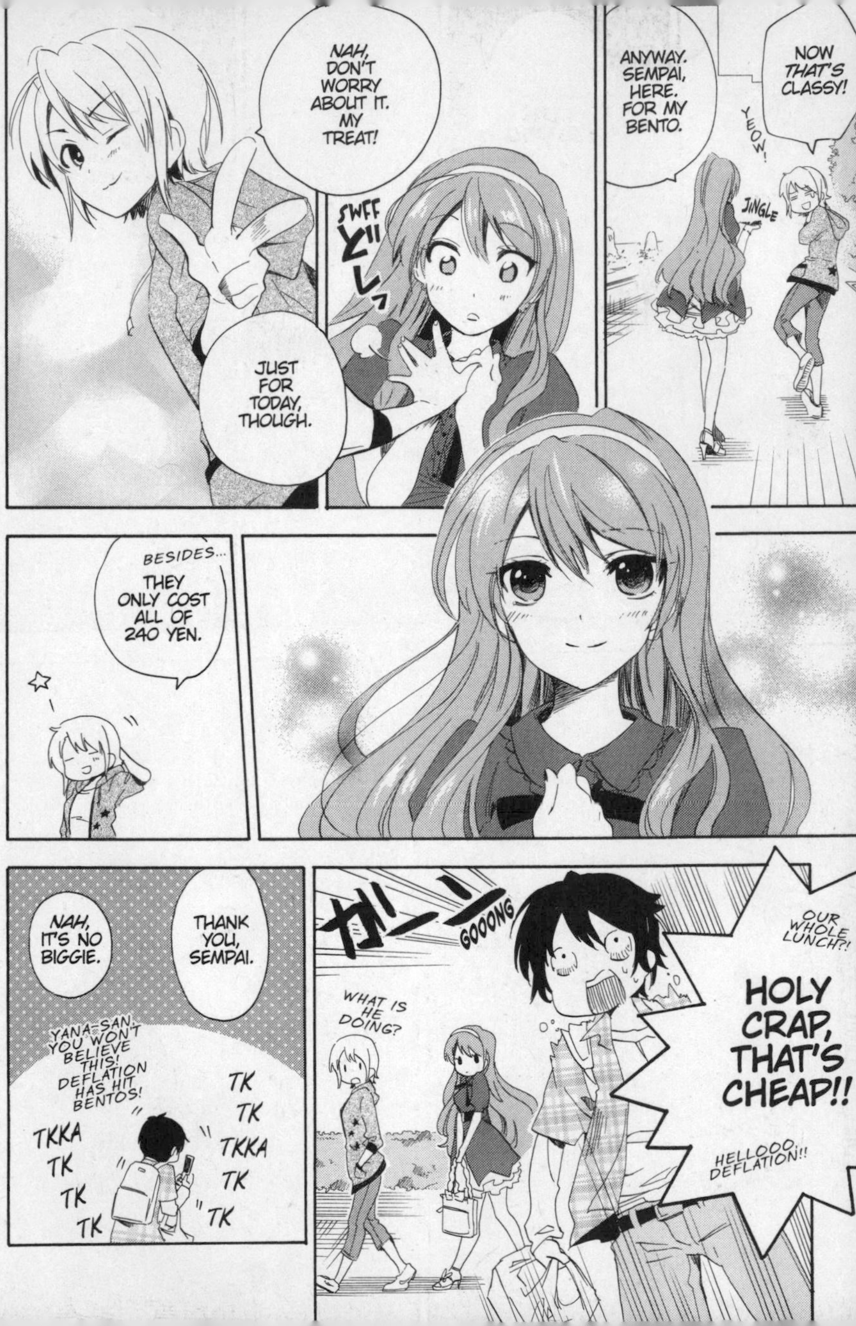
NOW THAT'S CLASSY!
YEOW!
ANYWAY. SEMPAI, HERE. FOR MY BENTO.
JINGLE
SWFF
NAH, DON'T WORRY ABOUT IT. MY TREAT!
JUST FOR TODAY, THOUGH.
BESIDES... THEY ONLY COST ALL OF 240 YEN.
OUR WHOLE LUNCH?!
GOOONG
HOLY CRAP, THAT'S CHEAP!!
WHAT IS HE DOING?
HELLOOO DEFLATION!!
THANK YOU, SEMPAI.
NAH, IT'S NO BIGGIE.
YANA-SAN, YOU WON'T BELIEVE THIS! DEFLATION HAS HIT BENTOS!
TK TK TKKA TK TK
TKKA TK TK TK

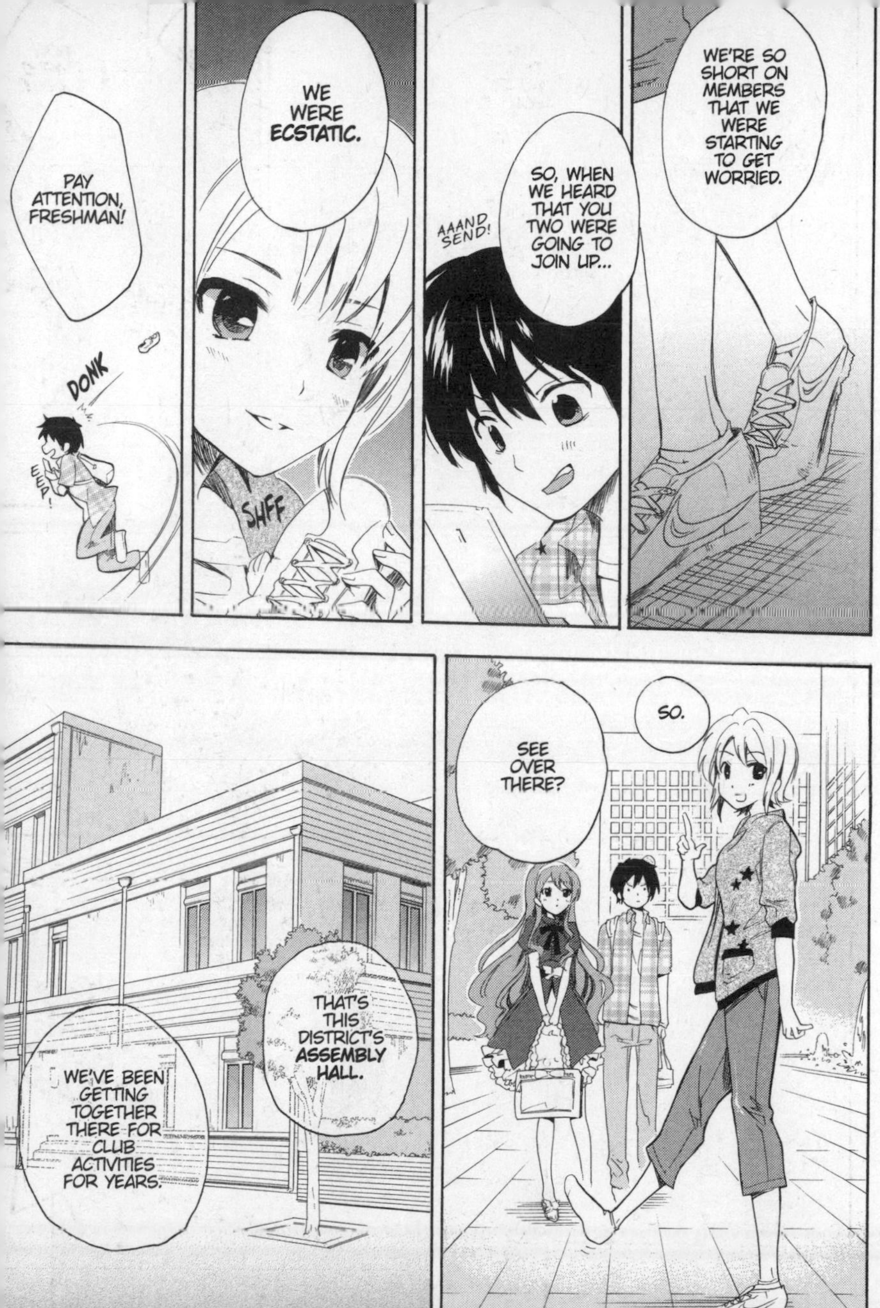
WE'RE SO SHORT ON MEMBERS THAT WE WERE STARTING TO GET WORRIED.
SO, WHEN WE HEARD THAT YOU TWO WERE GOING TO JOIN UP...
AAAND SEND!
WE WERE ECSTATIC.
SHFF
PAY ATTENTION, FRESHMAN!
DONK
EEP!
SO.
SEE OVER THERE?
THAT'S THIS DISTRICT'S ASSEMBLY HALL.
WE'VE BEEN GETTING TOGETHER THERE FOR CLUB ACTIVITIES FOR YEARS.

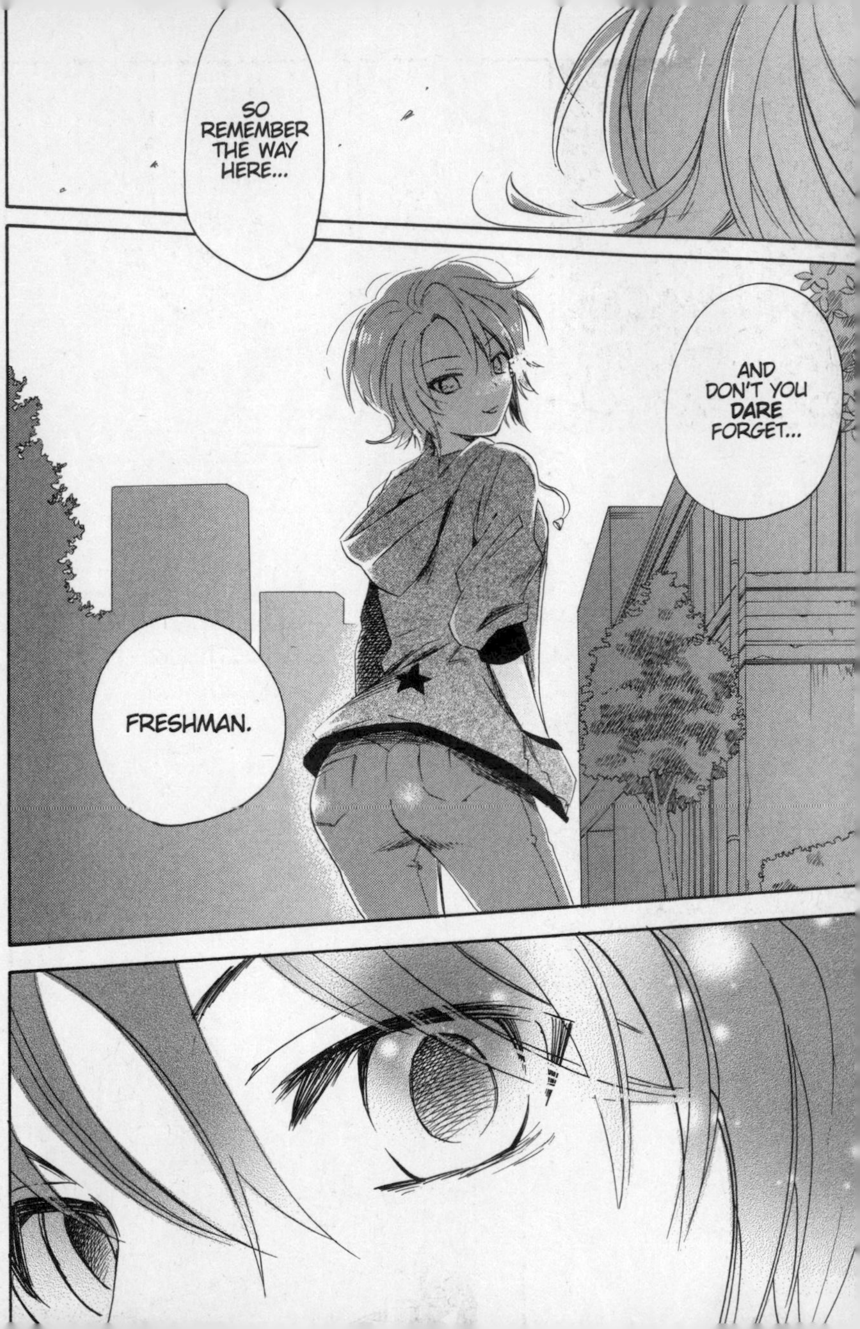
SO REMEMBER THE WAY HERE...
AND DON'T YOU DARE FORGET...
FRESHMAN.

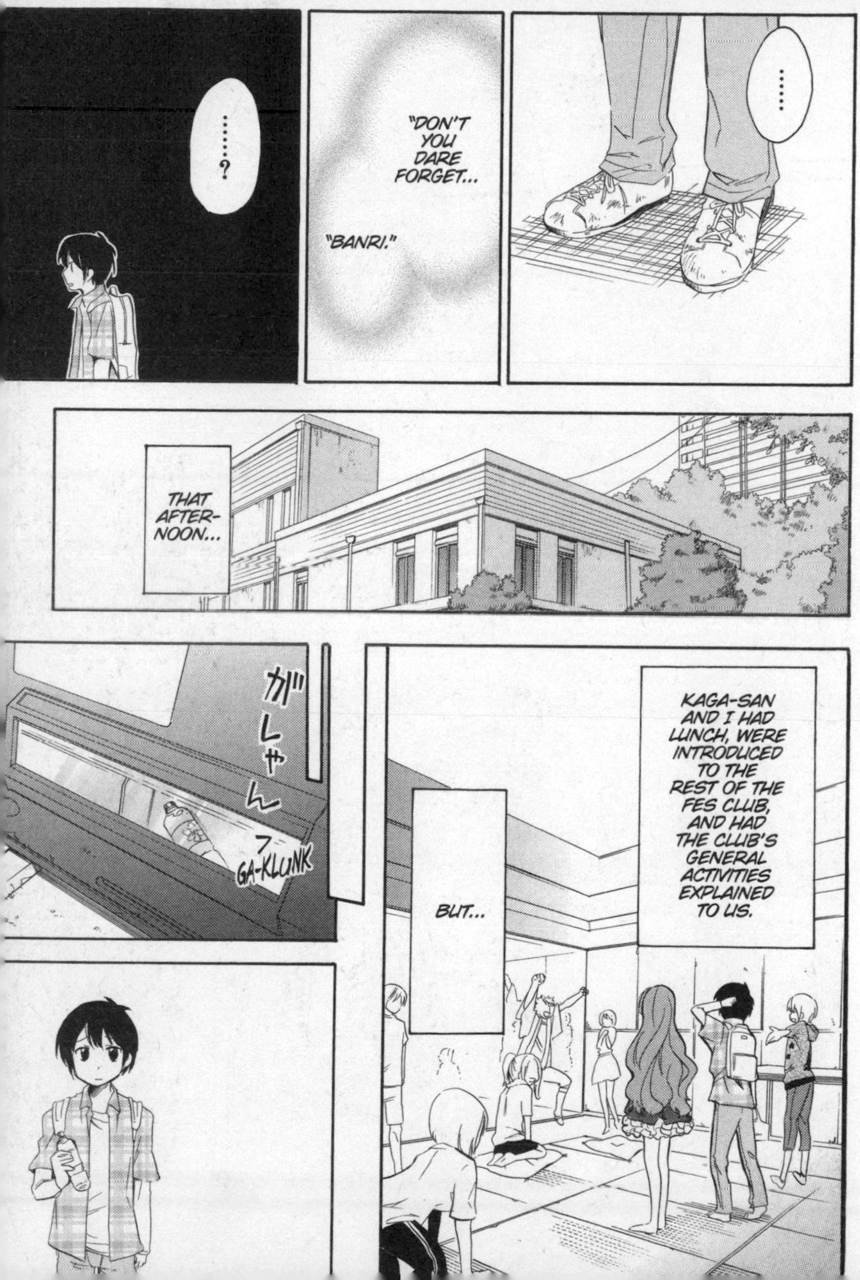
……
"DON'T YOU DARE FORGET...
"BANRI."
……?
THAT AFTERNOON...
KAGA-SAN AND I HAD LUNCH, WERE INTRODUCED TO THE REST OF THE FES CLUB, AND HAD THE CLUB'S GENERAL ACTIVITIES EXPLAINED TO US.
BUT...
がしゃん
GA-KLUNK

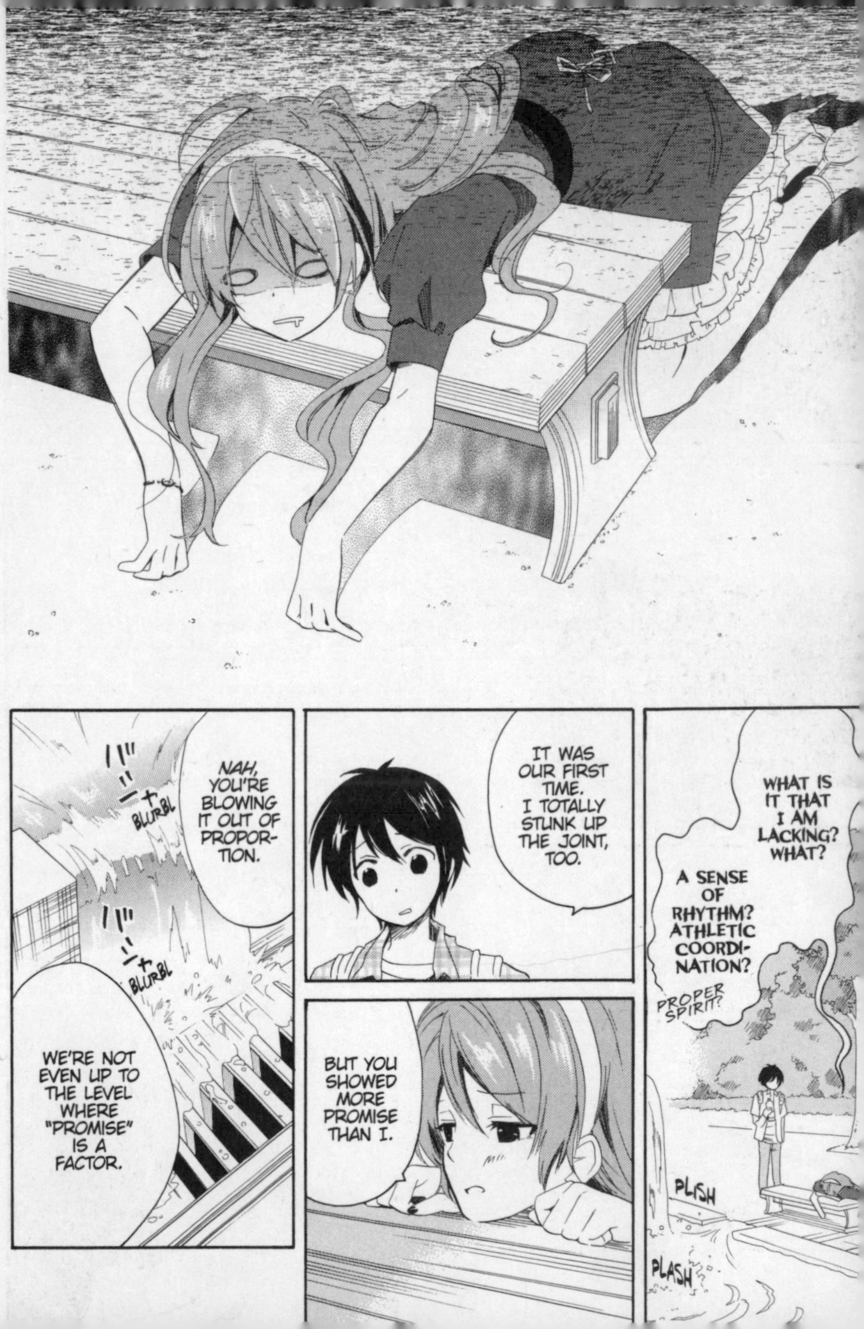
WHAT IS IT THAT I AM LACKING? WHAT?
A SENSE OF RHYTHM? ATHLETIC COORDI-NATION?
PROPER SPIRIT?
PLISH
PLASH
IT WAS OUR FIRST TIME. I TOTALLY STUNK UP THE JOINT, TOO.
BUT YOU SHOWED MORE PROMISE THAN I.
NAH, YOU'RE BLOWING IT OUT OF PROPOR-TION.
BLURBL
BLURBL
WE'RE NOT EVEN UP TO THE LEVEL WHERE "PROMISE" IS A FACTOR.

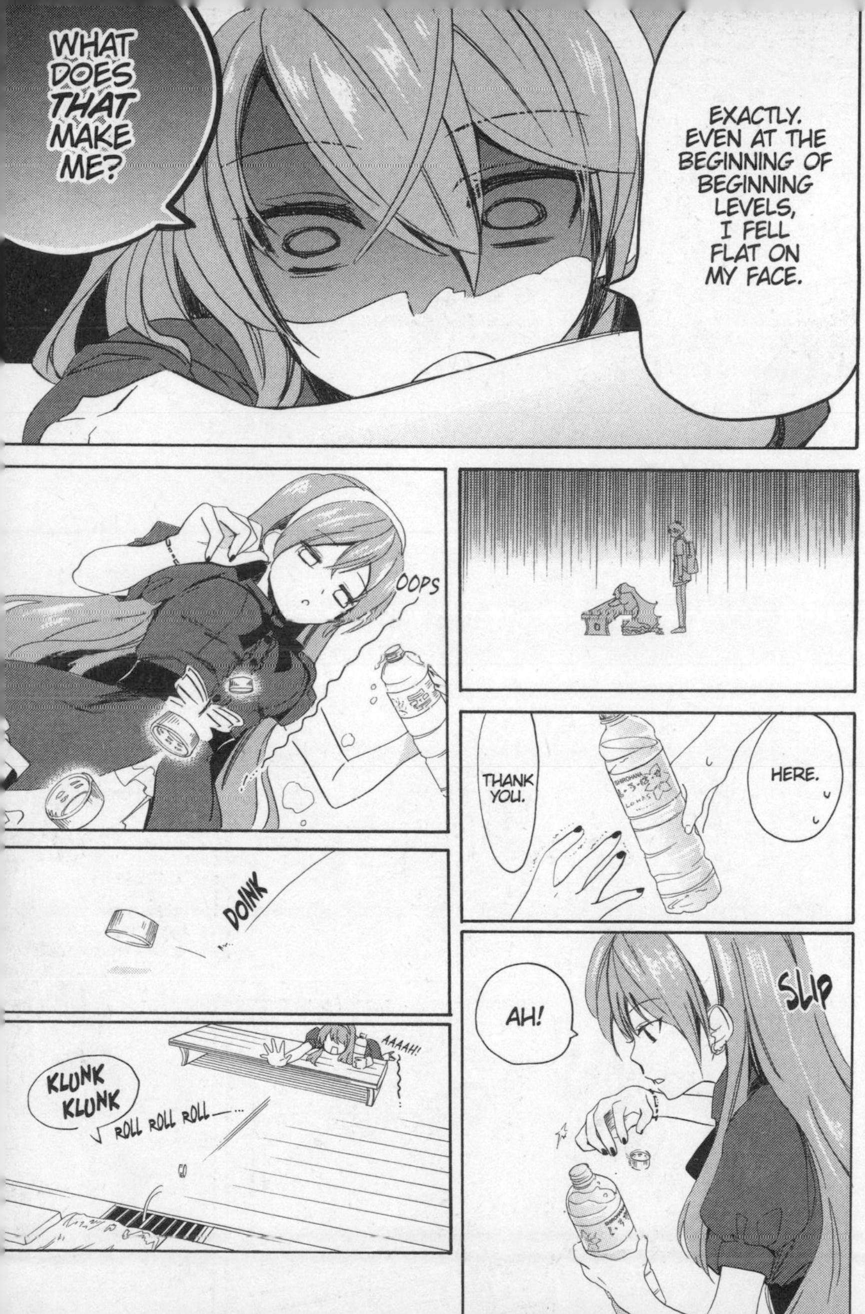
EXACTLY. EVEN AT THE BEGINNING OF BEGINNING LEVELS, I FELL FLAT ON MY FACE.
WHAT DOES THAT MAKE ME?
HERE.
THANK YOU.
SLIP
AH!
OOPS
DOINK
AAAAH!
KLUNK KLUNK
ROLL ROLL ROLL...

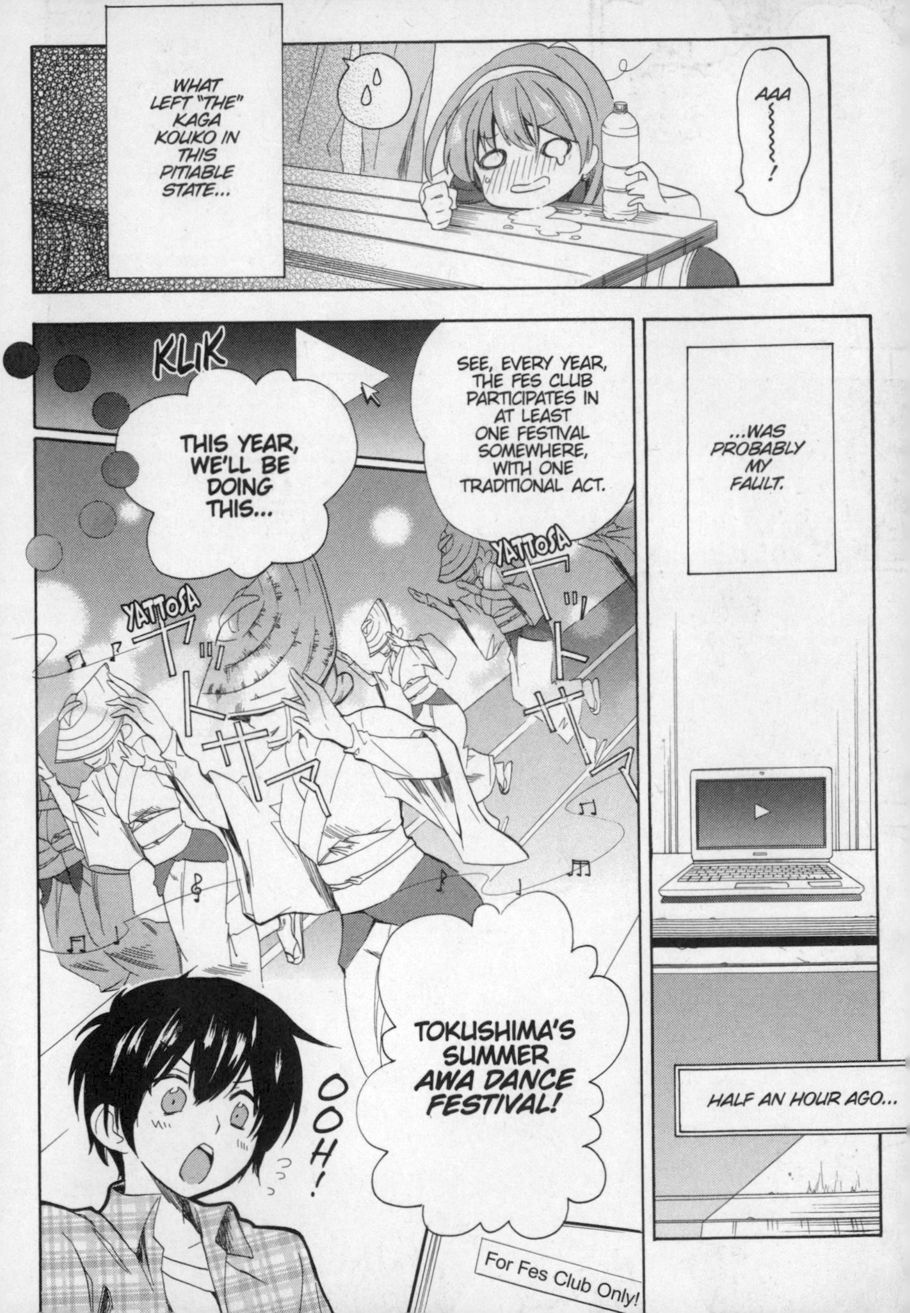
AAA~~~!
WHAT LEFT "THE" KAGA KOUKO IN THIS PITIABLE STATE...
...WAS PROBABLY MY FAULT.
HALF AN HOUR AGO...
KLIK
SEE, EVERY YEAR, THE FES CLUB PARTICIPATES IN AT LEAST ONE FESTIVAL SOMEWHERE, WITH ONE TRADITIONAL ACT.
THIS YEAR, WE'LL BE DOING THIS...
YATTOSA
YATTOSA
TOKUSHIMA'S SUMMER AWA DANCE FESTIVAL!
OOOH!
For Fes Club Only!

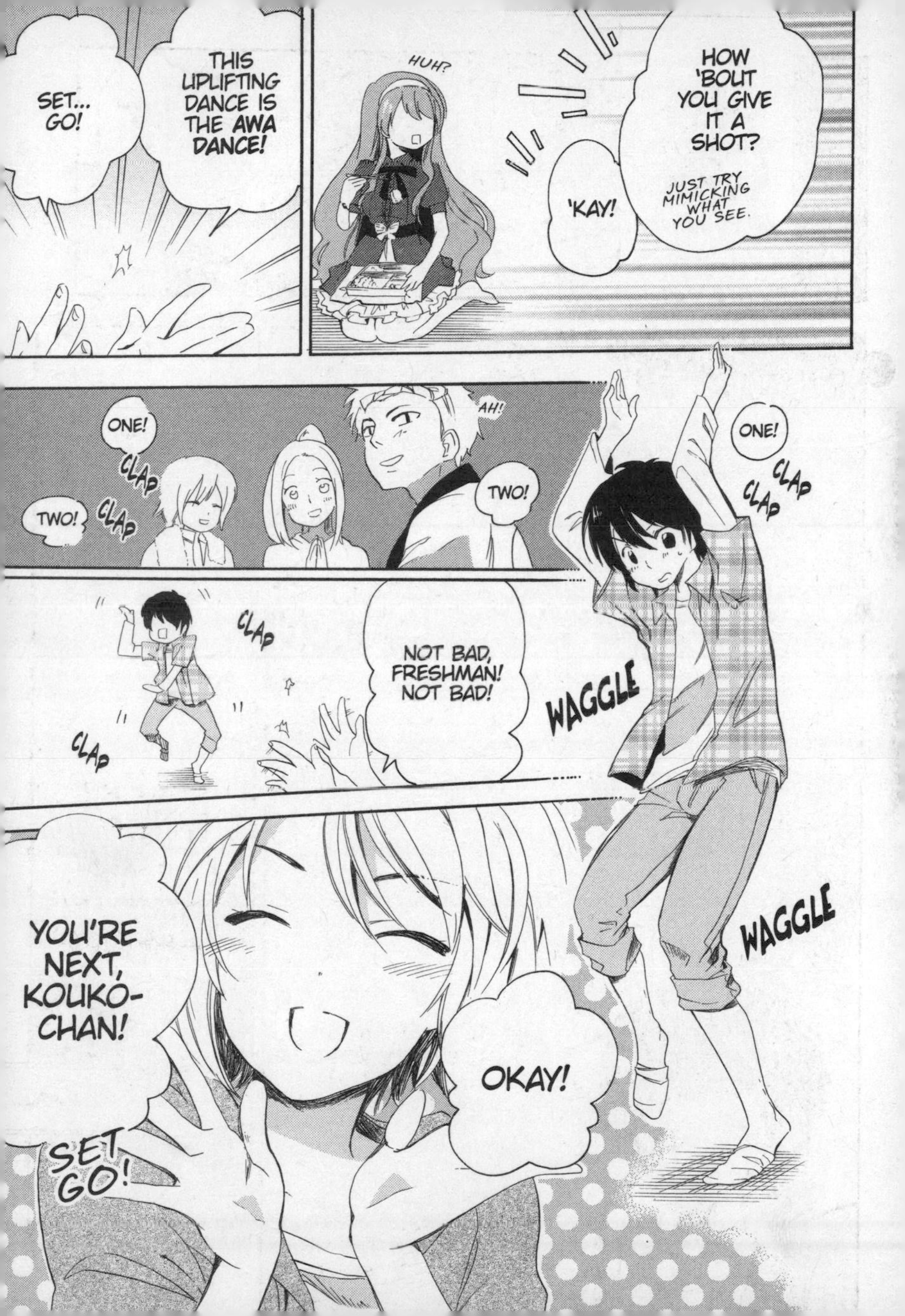
HOW 'BOUT YOU GIVE IT A SHOT?
JUST TRY MIMICKING WHAT YOU SEE.
'KAY!
HUH?
THIS UPLIFTING DANCE IS THE AWA DANCE!
SET... GO!
ONE!
CLAP
CLAP
WAGGLE
WAGGLE
AH!
TWO!
ONE!
CLAP
TWO!
CLAP
NOT BAD, FRESHMAN! NOT BAD!
CLAP
CLAP
OKAY!
YOU'RE NEXT, KOUKO-CHAN!
SET GO!

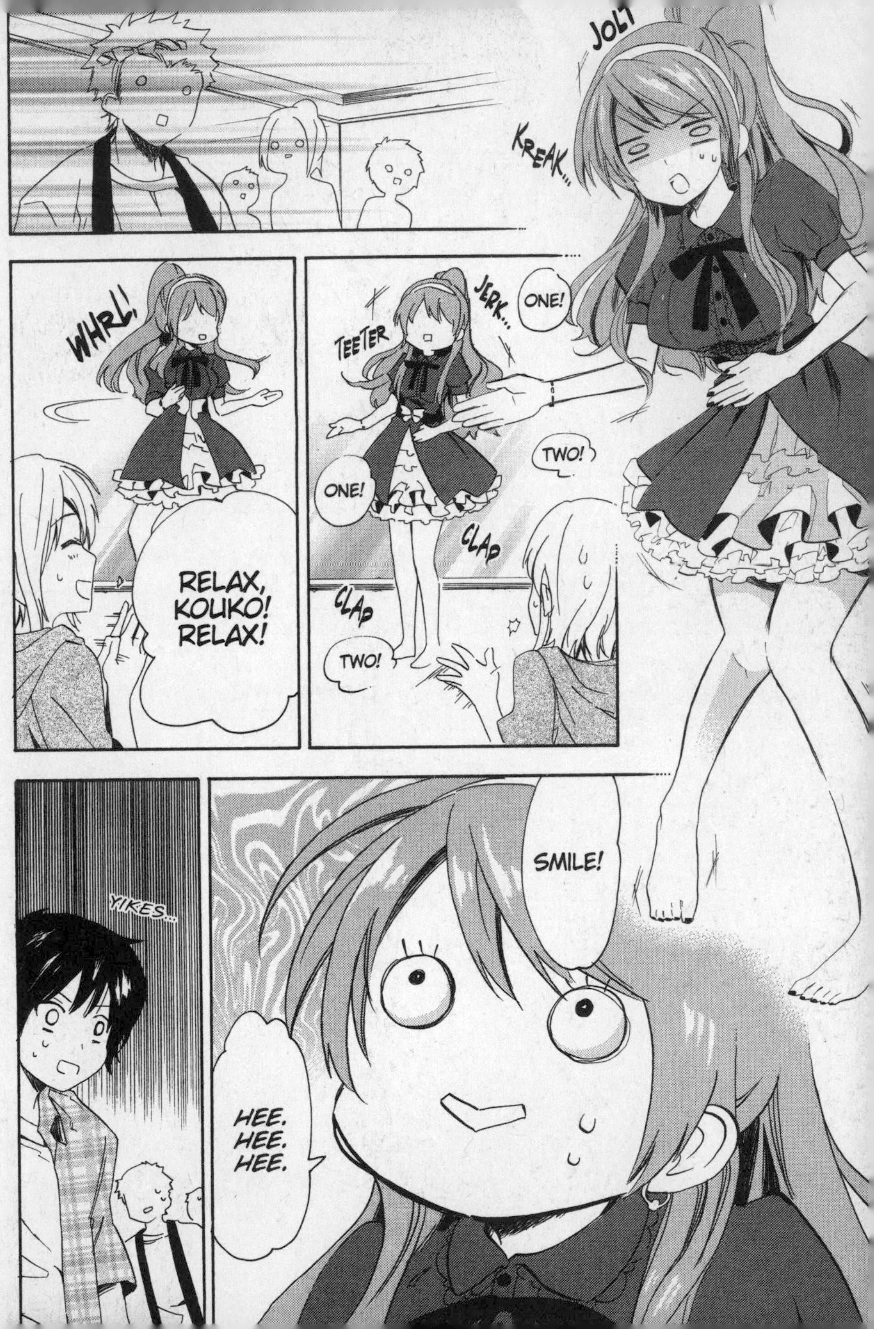
JOLT
KREAK...
JERK...
ONE!
TEETER
TWO!
ONE!
CLAP
CLAP
TWO!
WHRL!
RELAX, KOUKO! RELAX!
SMILE!
HEE. HEE. HEE.
YIKES...

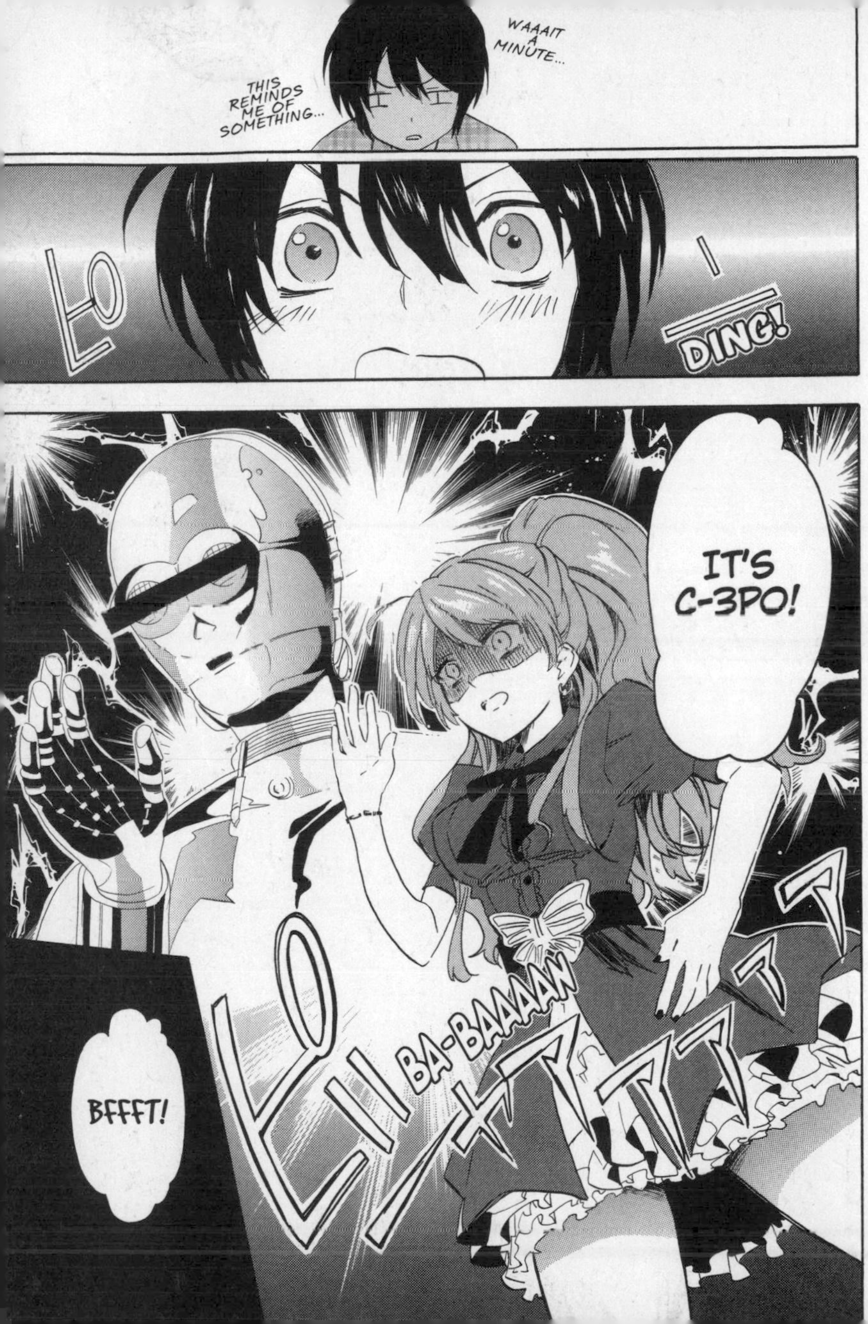
WAAAIT A MINUTE...
THIS REMINDS ME OF SOMETHING...
DING!
IT'S C-3PO!
BA-BAAAAN
BFFFT!

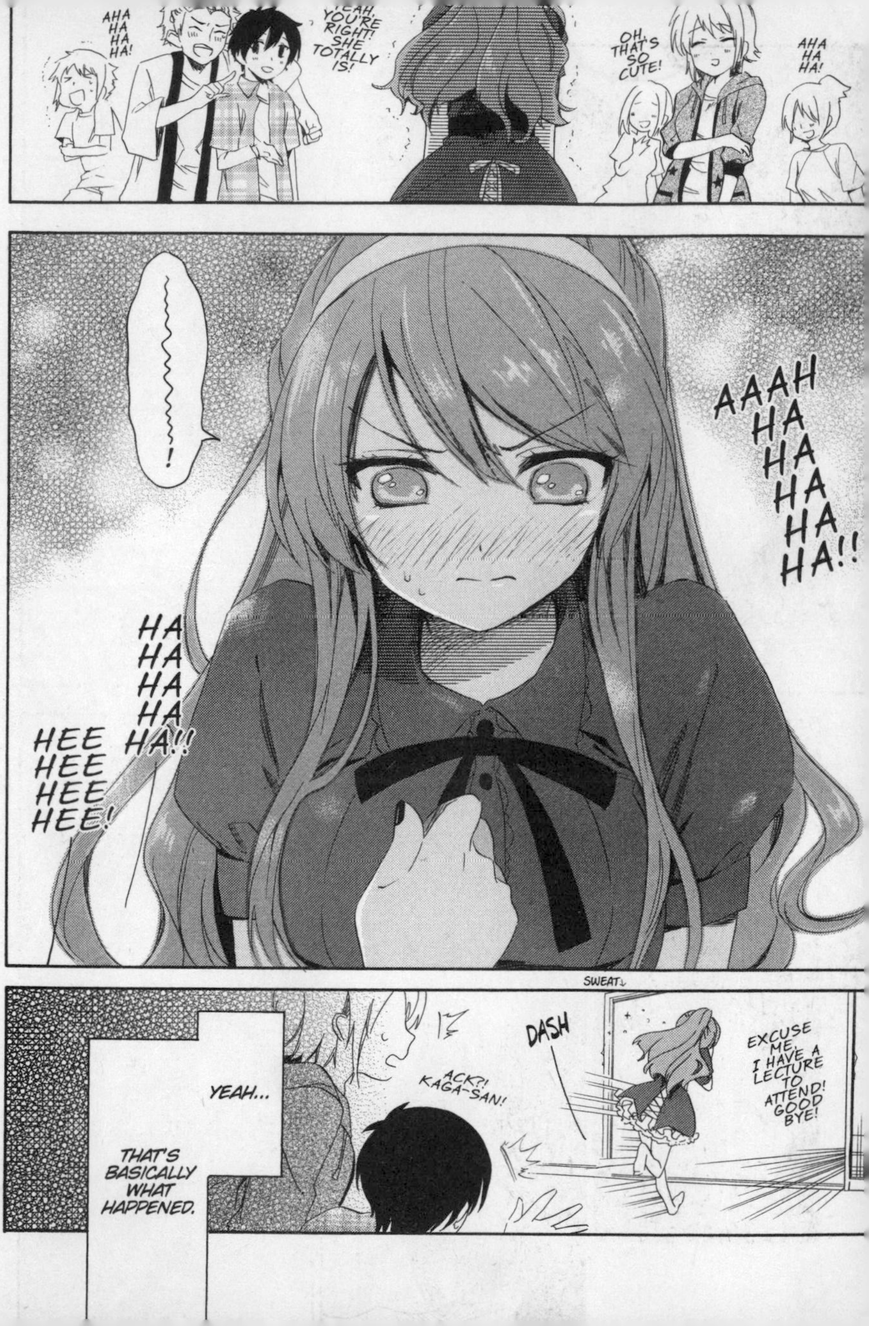
AHA HA HA!
OH, THAT'S SO CUTE!
YEAH, YOU'RE RIGHT! SHE TOTALLY IS!
AHA HA HA HA!
AAAH HA HA HA HA HA!!
~~~~!
HA HA HA HA HA HA!!
HEE HEE HEE HEE!
SWEAT
EXCUSE ME, I HAVE A LECTURE TO ATTEND! GOOD BYE!
DASH
ACK?! KAGA-SAN!
YEAH...
THAT'S BASICALLY WHAT HAPPENED.
~~~~

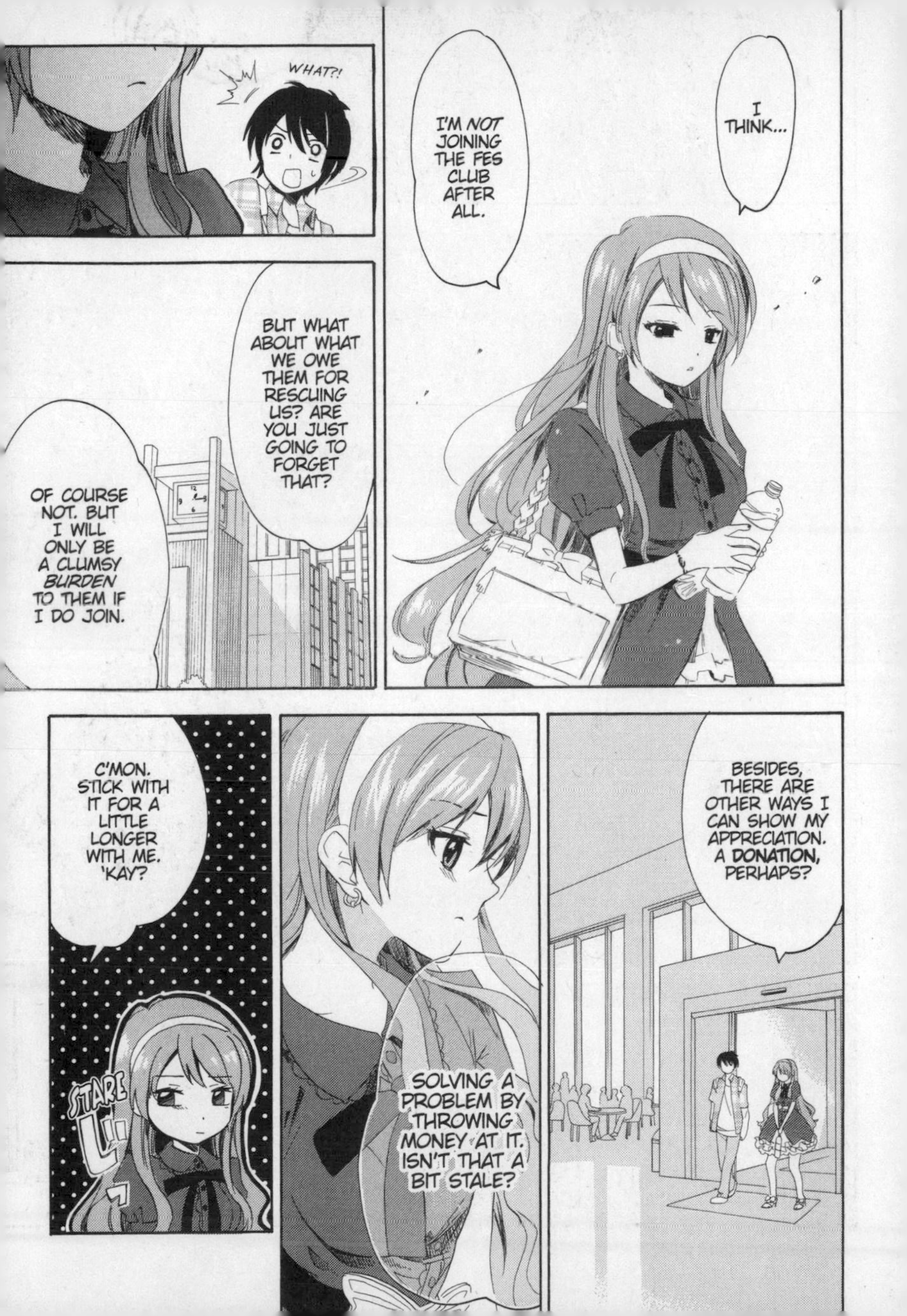
I THINK...
I'M NOT JOINING THE FES CLUB AFTER ALL.
WHAT?!
BUT WHAT ABOUT WHAT WE OWE THEM FOR RESCUING US? ARE YOU JUST GOING TO FORGET THAT?
OF COURSE NOT. BUT I WILL ONLY BE A CLUMSY BURDEN TO THEM IF I DO JOIN.
BESIDES, THERE ARE OTHER WAYS I CAN SHOW MY APPRECIATION. A DONATION, PERHAPS?
SOLVING A PROBLEM BY THROWING MONEY AT IT. ISN'T THAT A BIT STALE?
C'MON. STICK WITH IT FOR A LITTLE LONGER WITH ME. 'KAY?
STARE

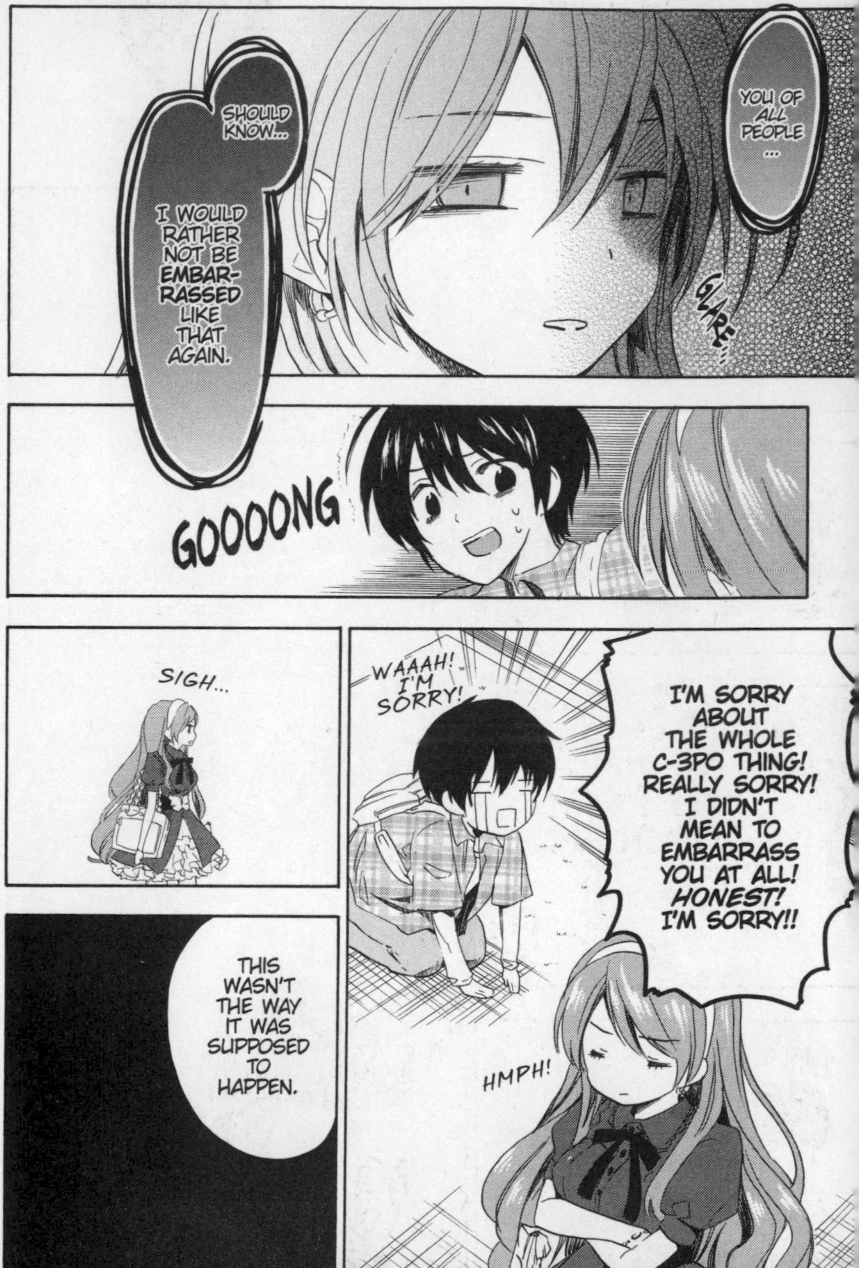
YOU OF ALL PEOPLE ...
SHOULD KNOW...
I WOULD RATHER NOT BE EMBARRASSED LIKE THAT AGAIN.
GLARE...
GOOOONG
I'M SORRY ABOUT THE WHOLE C-3PO THING! REALLY SORRY! I DIDN'T MEAN TO EMBARRASS YOU AT ALL! HONEST! I'M SORRY!!
WAAAH! I'M SORRY!
HMPH!
SIGH...
THIS WASN'T THE WAY IT WAS SUPPOSED TO HAPPEN.

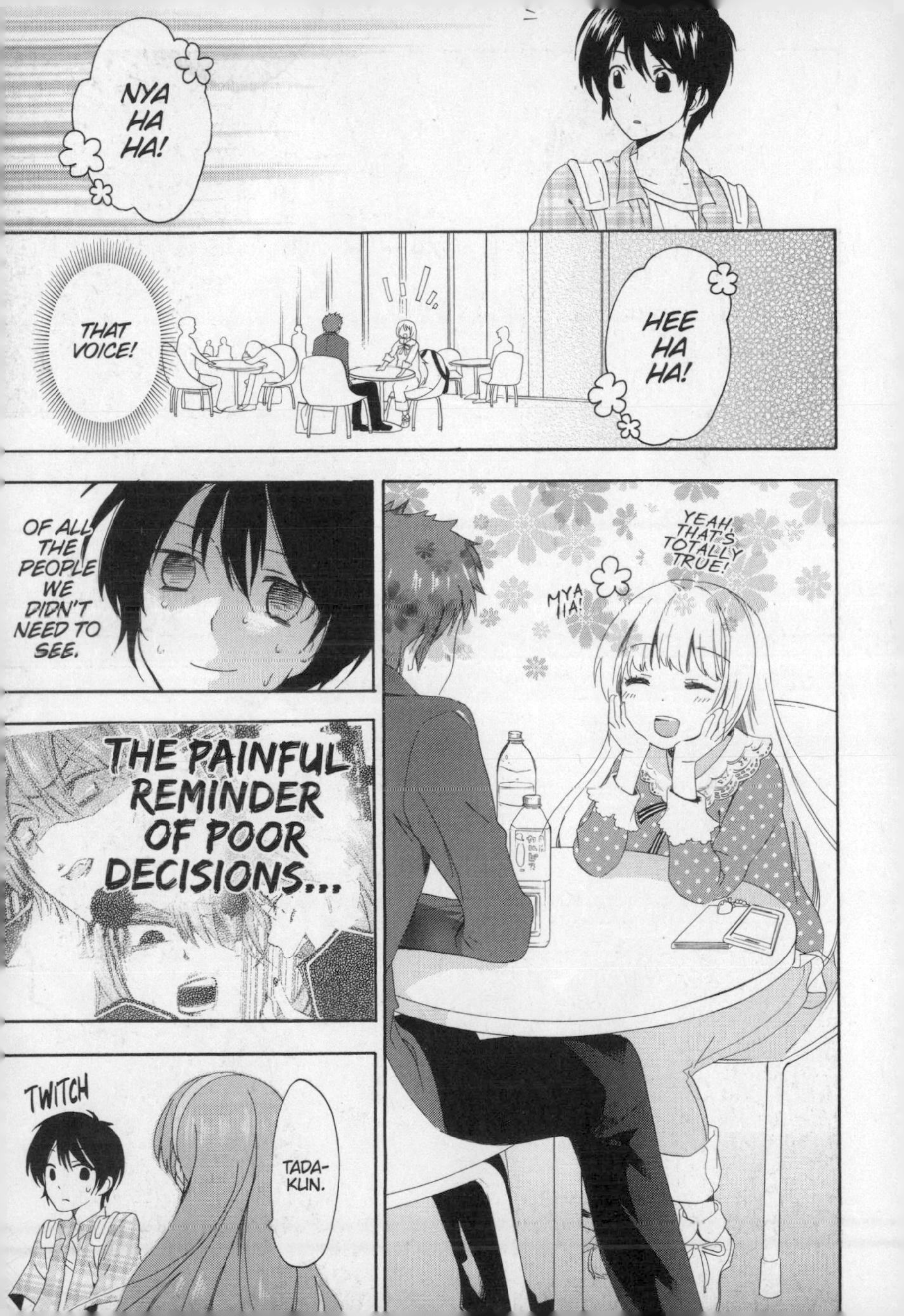
NYA HA HA!
HEE HA HA!
THAT VOICE!
YEAH, THAT'S TOTALLY TRUE!
MYA HA!
OF ALL THE PEOPLE WE DIDN'T NEED TO SEE.
THE PAINFUL REMINDER OF POOR DECISIONS...
TADA-KUN.
TWITCH

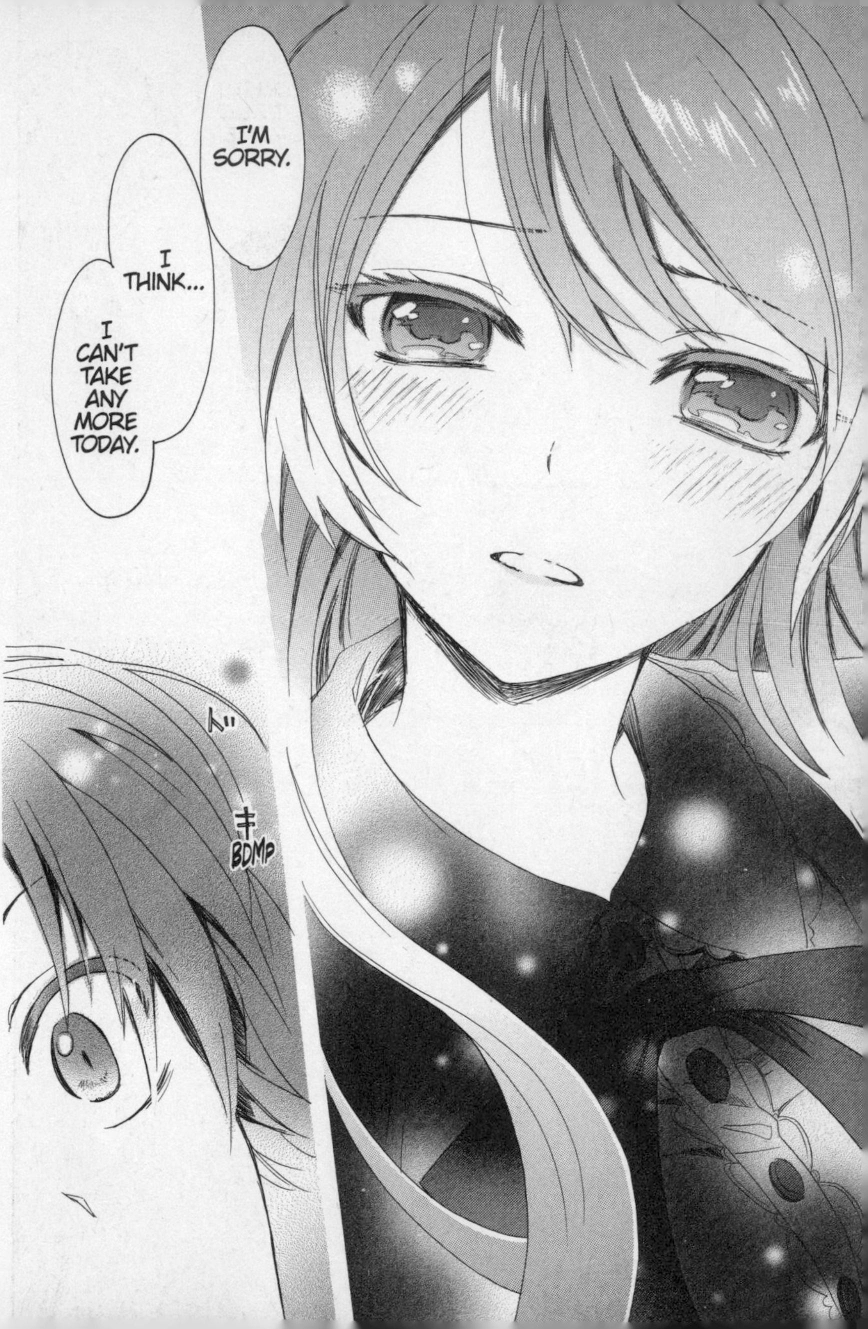
I'M SORRY.
I THINK...
I CAN'T TAKE ANY MORE TODAY.
ドッ
キ
BDMP

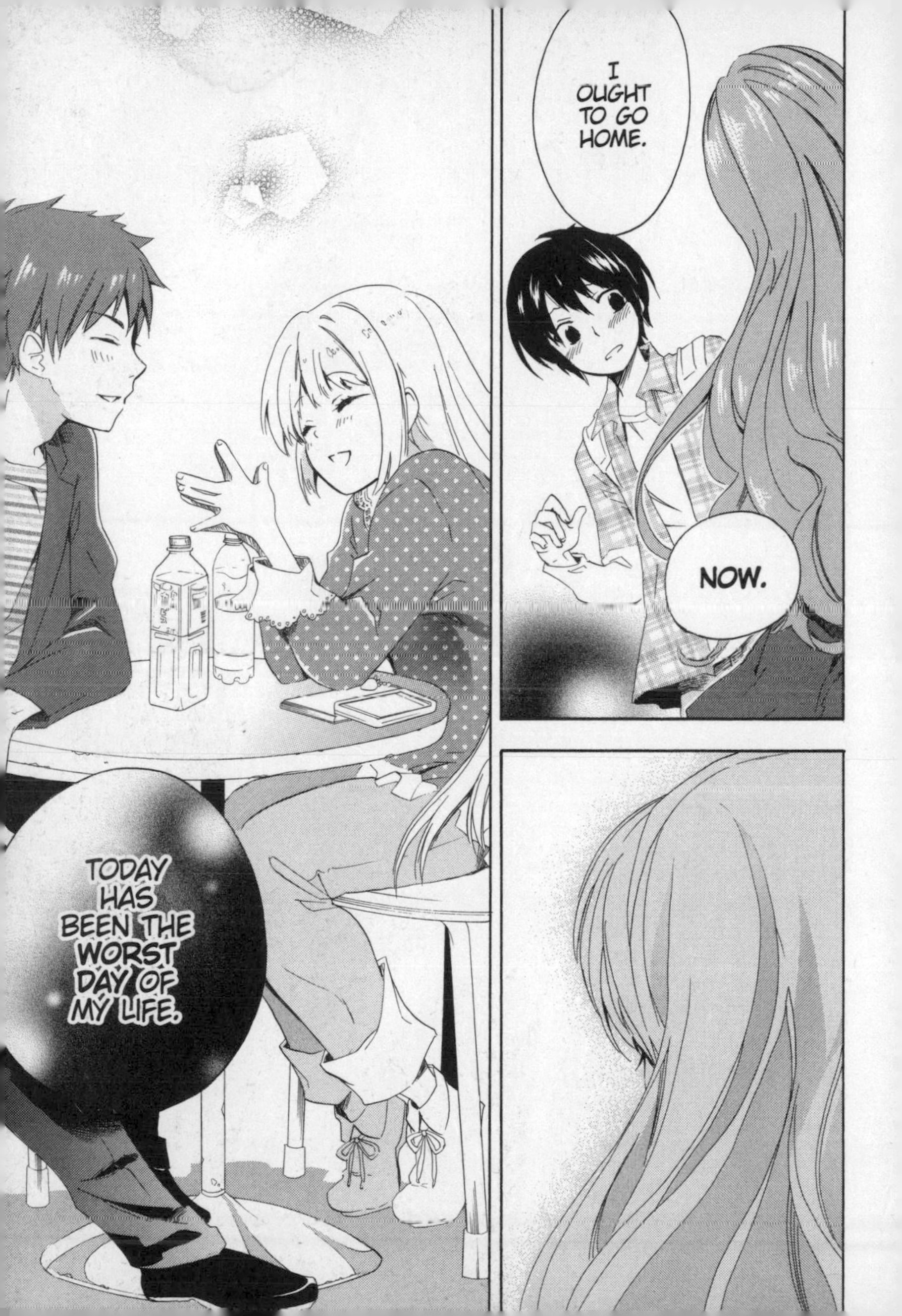
I OUGHT TO GO HOME.
NOW.
TODAY HAS BEEN THE WORST DAY OF MY LIFE.

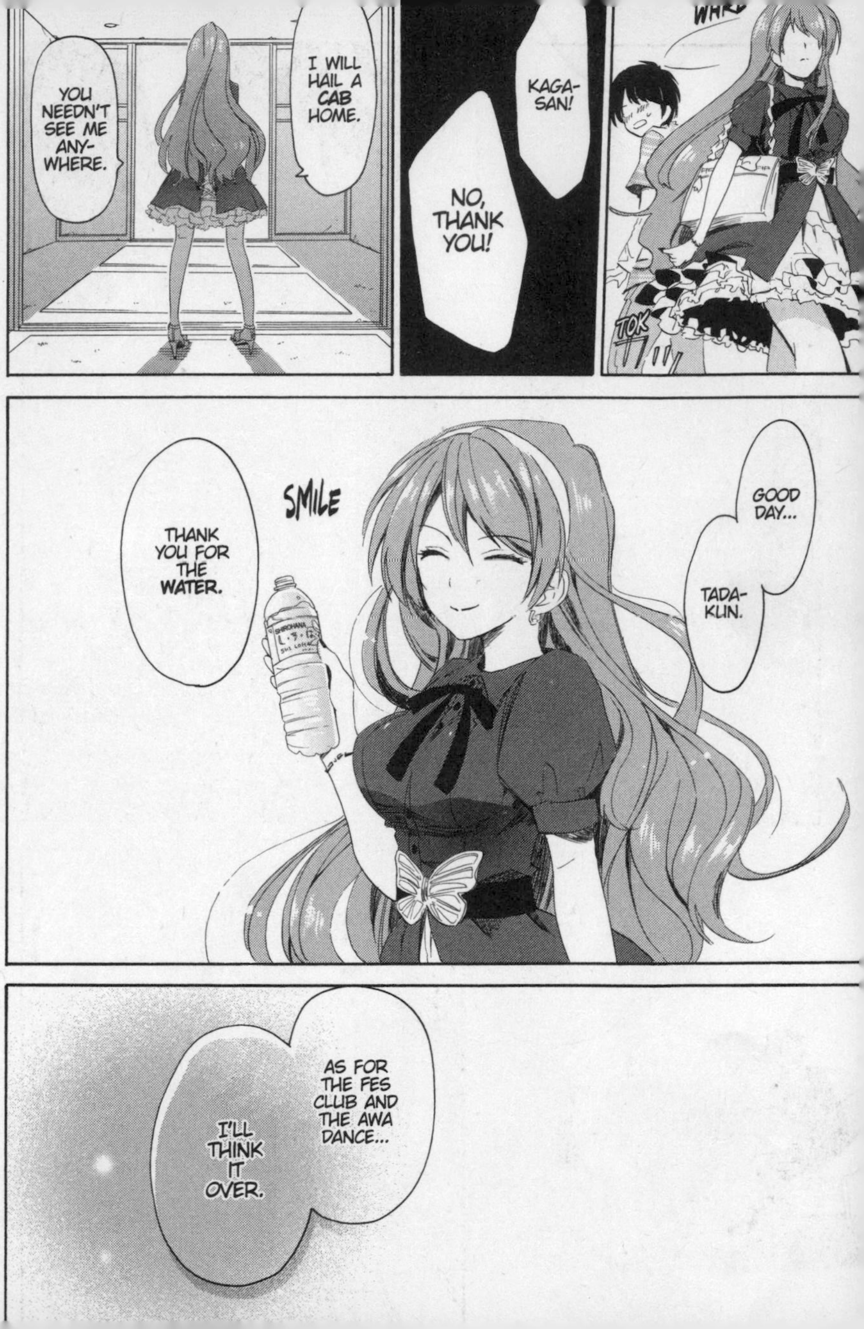
TOK
KAGA-SAN!
NO, THANK YOU!
I WILL HAIL A CAB HOME.
YOU NEEDN'T SEE ME ANYWHERE.
GOOD DAY...
TADA-KUN.
SMILE
THANK YOU FOR THE WATER.
AS FOR THE FES CLUB AND THE AWA DANCE...
I'LL THINK IT OVER.

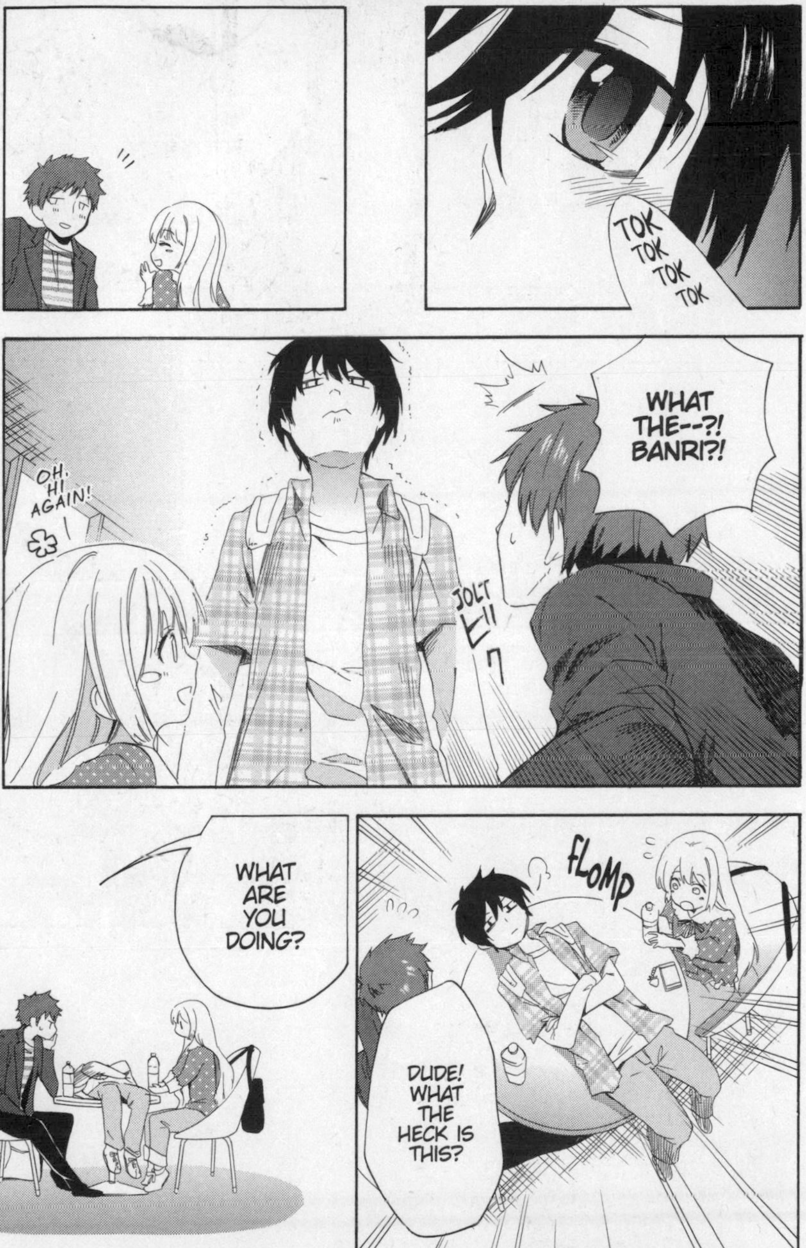
TOK TOK TOK TOK
WHAT THE--?! BANRI?!
JOLT
OH, HI AGAIN!
FLOMP
DUDE! WHAT THE HECK IS THIS?
WHAT ARE YOU DOING?

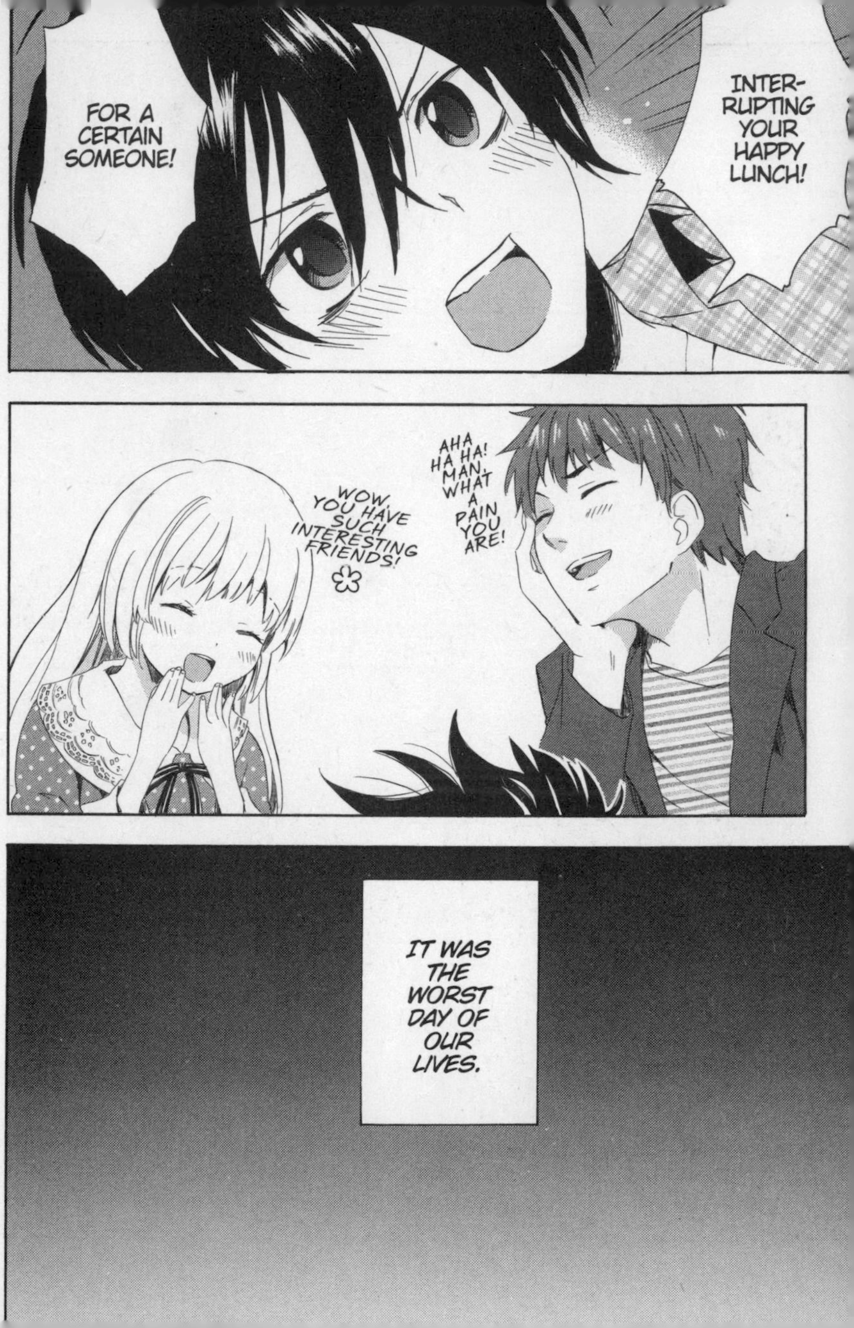
INTER-RUPTING YOUR HAPPY LUNCH!
FOR A CERTAIN SOMEONE!
AHA HA HA! MAN, WHAT A PAIN YOU ARE!
WOW, YOU HAVE SUCH INTERESTING FRIENDS!
IT WAS THE WORST DAY OF OUR LIVES.

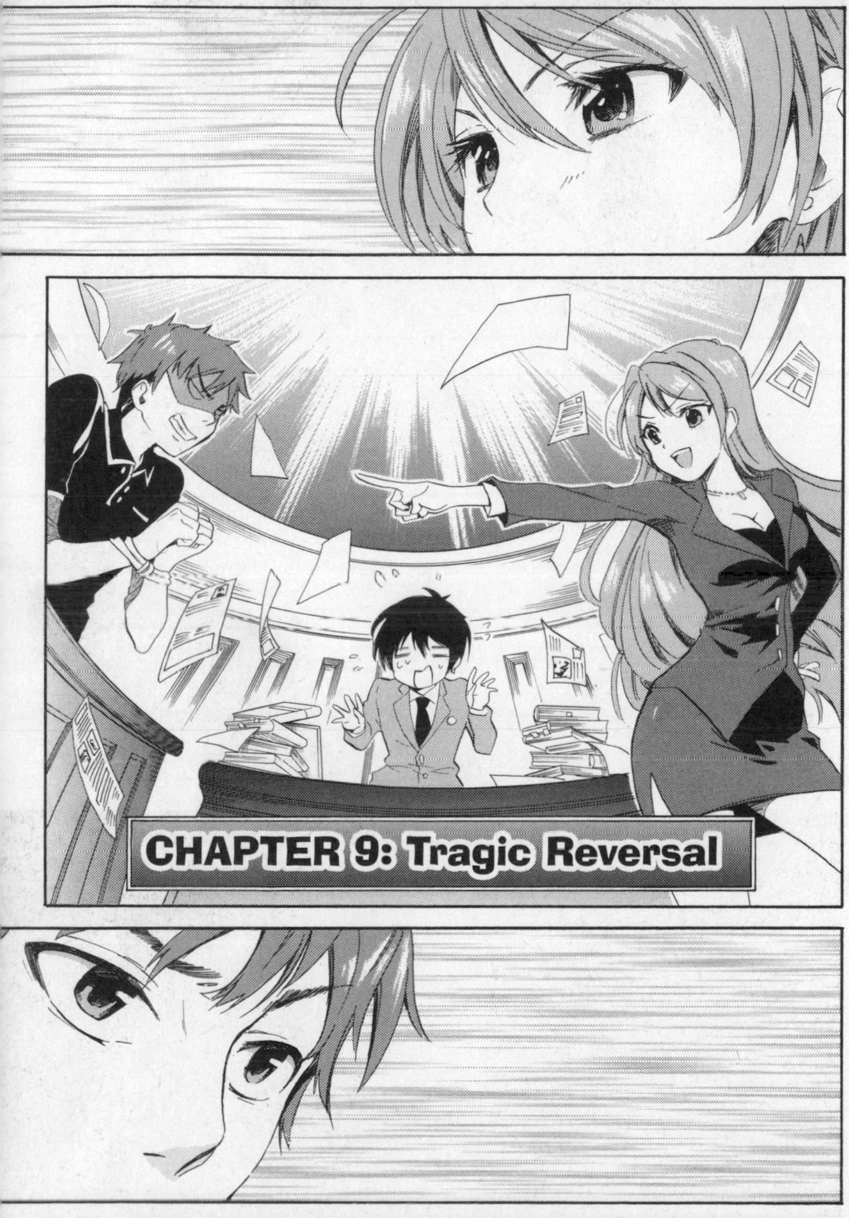
CHAPTER 9: Tragic Reversal

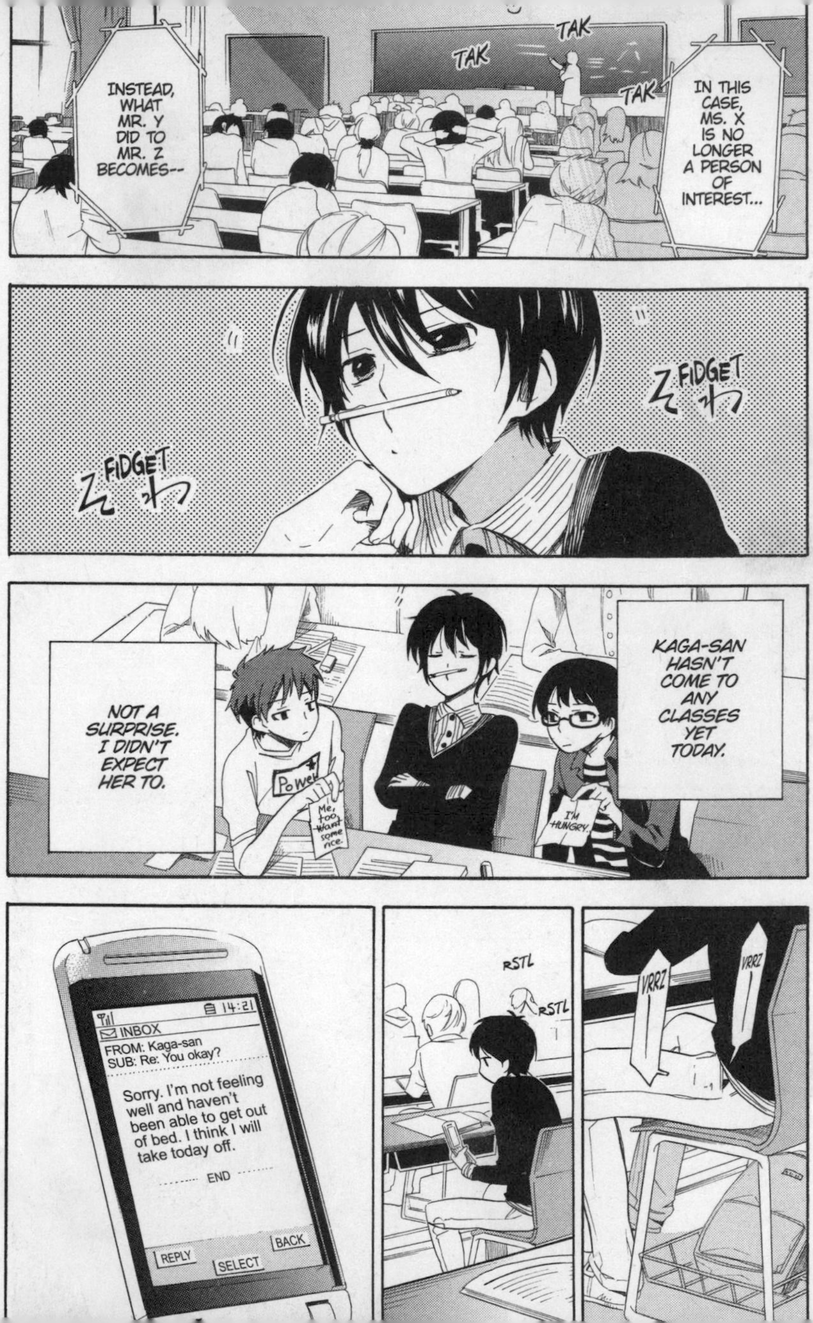
TAK
TAK
TAK
IN THIS CASE, MS. X IS NO LONGER A PERSON OF INTEREST...
INSTEAD, WHAT MR. Y DID TO MR. Z BECOMES--
FIDGET
FIDGET
KAGA-SAN HASN'T COME TO ANY CLASSES YET TODAY.
I'M HUNGRY.
Power
Me, too. Want some rice.
NOT A SURPRISE. I DIDN'T EXPECT HER TO.
VRRZ
VRRZ
RSTL
RSTL
14:21
INBOX
FROM: Kaga-san
SUB: Re: You okay?
Sorry. I'm not feeling well and haven't been able to get out of bed. I think I will take today off.
END
REPLY
SELECT
BACK

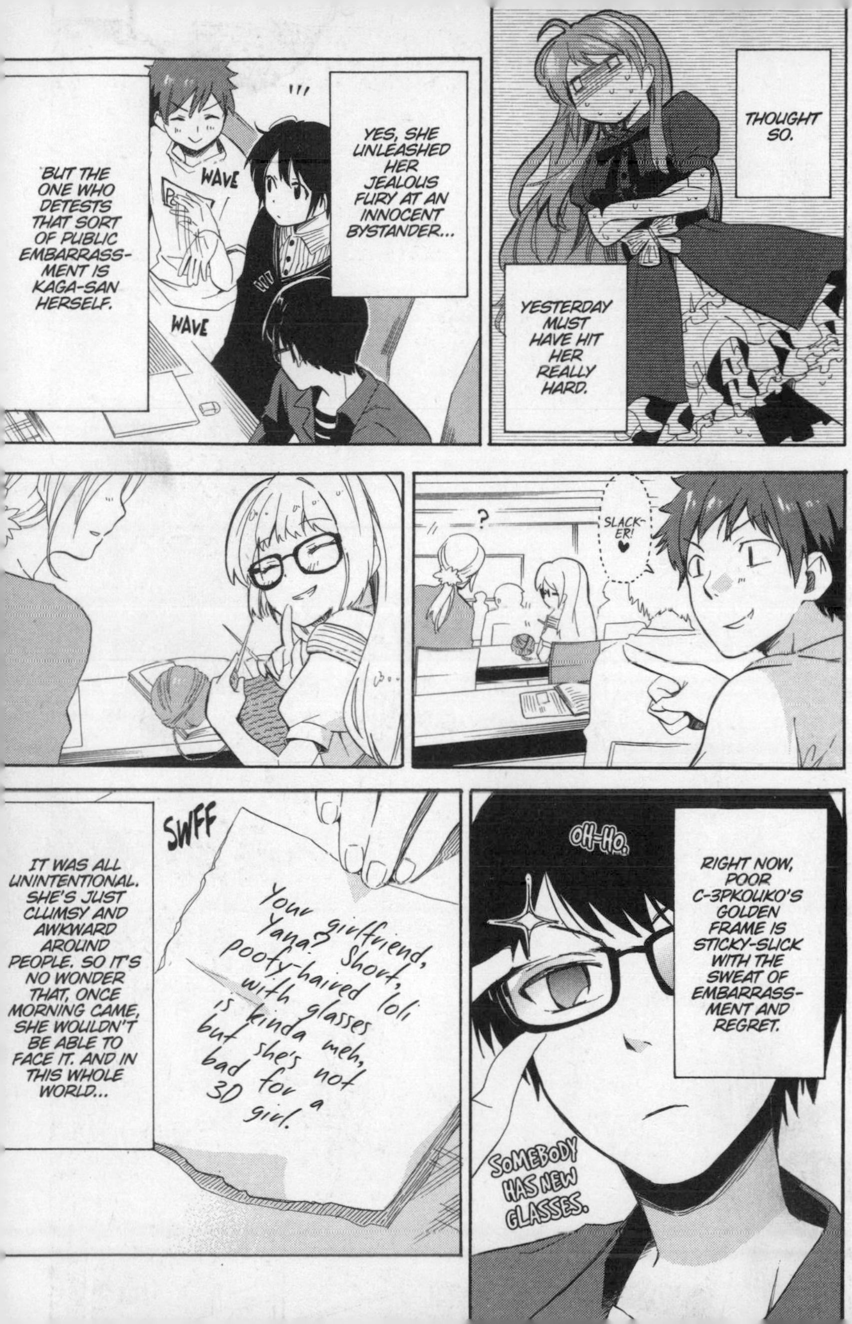
THOUGHT SO.
YESTERDAY MUST HAVE HIT HER REALLY HARD.
YES, SHE UNLEASHED HER JEALOUS FURY AT AN INNOCENT BYSTANDER...
WAVE
WAVE
BUT THE ONE WHO DETESTS THAT SORT OF PUBLIC EMBARRASS-MENT IS KAGA-SAN HERSELF.
SLACK-ER!
OH-HO.
RIGHT NOW, POOR C-3PKOUKO'S GOLDEN FRAME IS STICKY-SLICK WITH THE SWEAT OF EMBARRASS-MENT AND REGRET.
SOMEBODY HAS NEW GLASSES.
SWFF
Your girlfriend, Yana? Short, poofy-haired loli with glasses is kinda meh, but she's not bad for a 3D girl.
IT WAS ALL UNINTENTIONAL. SHE'S JUST CLUMSY AND AWKWARD AROUND PEOPLE. SO IT'S NO WONDER THAT, ONCE MORNING CAME, SHE WOULDN'T BE ABLE TO FACE IT. AND IN THIS WHOLE WORLD...

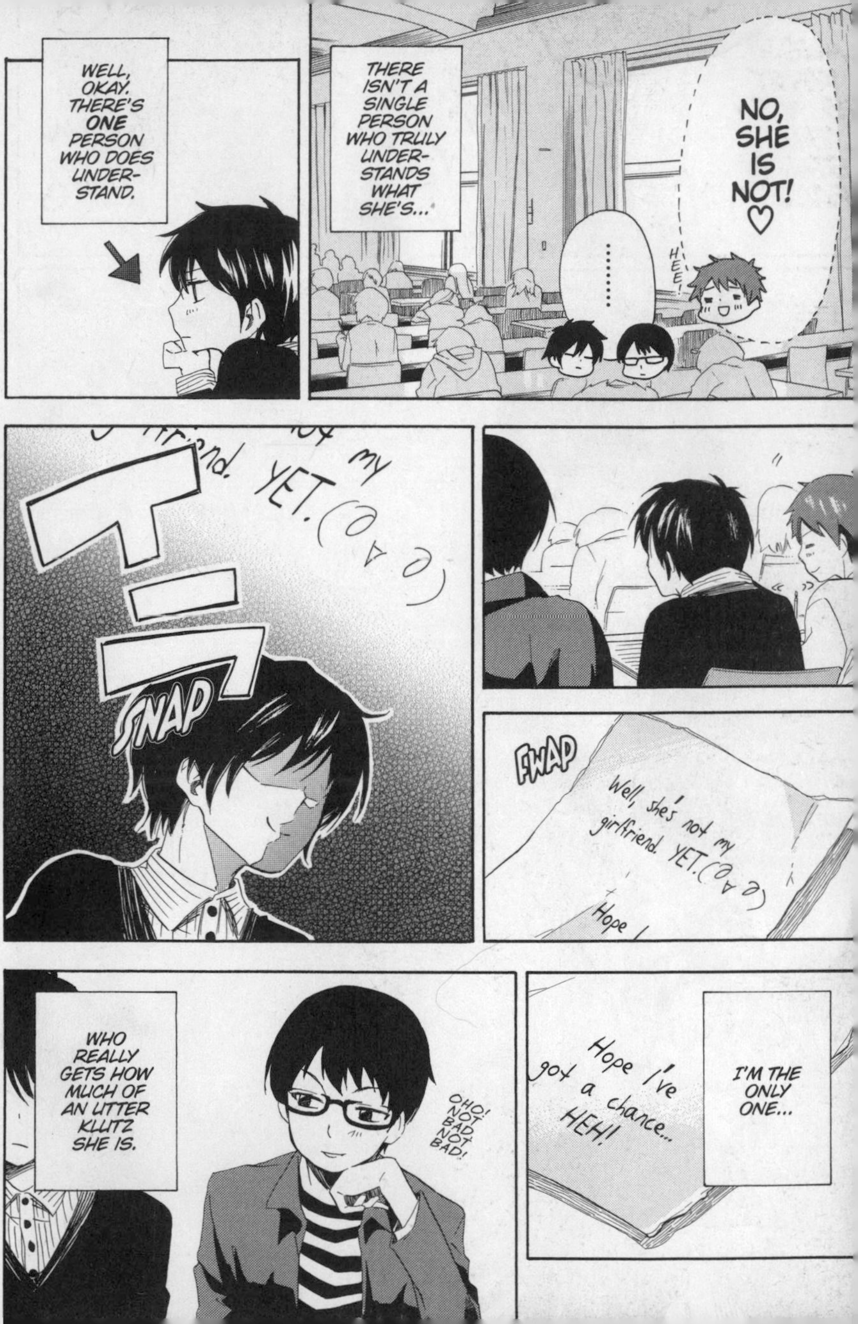
NO, SHE IS NOT! ♡
HEE!
THERE ISN'T A SINGLE PERSON WHO TRULY UNDER-STANDS WHAT SHE'S...
......
WELL, OKAY. THERE'S ONE PERSON WHO DOES UNDER-STAND.
FWAP
Well, she's not my girlfriend. YET.
Hope I
not my friend. YET.
SNAP
I'M THE ONLY ONE...
Hope I've got a chance... HEH!
WHO REALLY GETS HOW MUCH OF AN UTTER KLUTZ SHE IS.
OHO! NOT BAD NOT BAD!

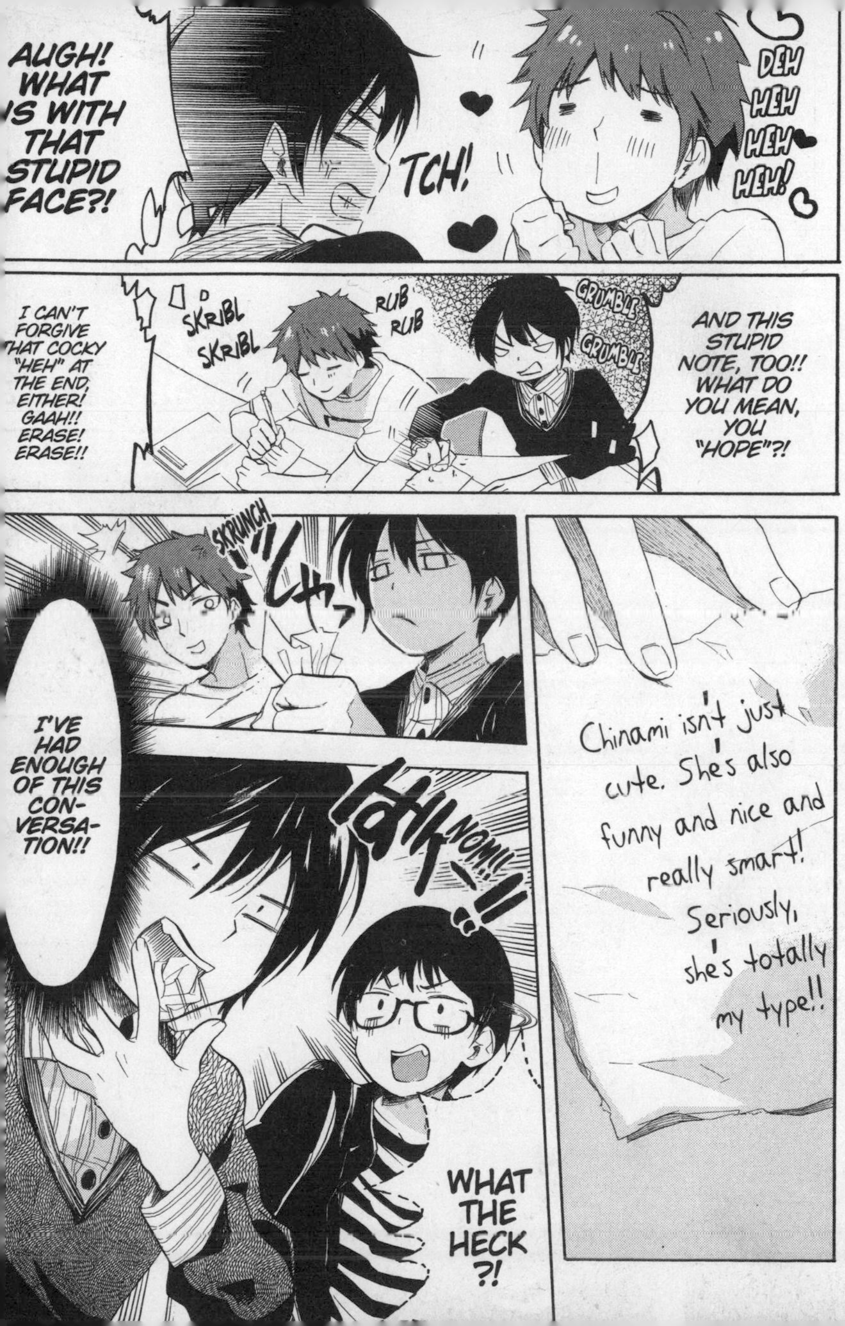
DEH HEH HEH HEH!
TCH!
AUGH! WHAT IS WITH THAT STUPID FACE?!
AND THIS STUPID NOTE, TOO!! WHAT DO YOU MEAN, YOU "HOPE"?!
GRUMBLE GRUMBLE
RUB RUB
SKRIBL SKRIBL
I CAN'T FORGIVE THAT COCKY "HEH" AT THE END, EITHER! GAAH!! ERASE! ERASE!!
Chinami isn't just cute. She's also funny and nice and really smart! Seriously, she's totally my type!!
SKRUNCH
NOM!!!
WHAT THE HECK?!
I'VE HAD ENOUGH OF THIS CONVERSATION!!

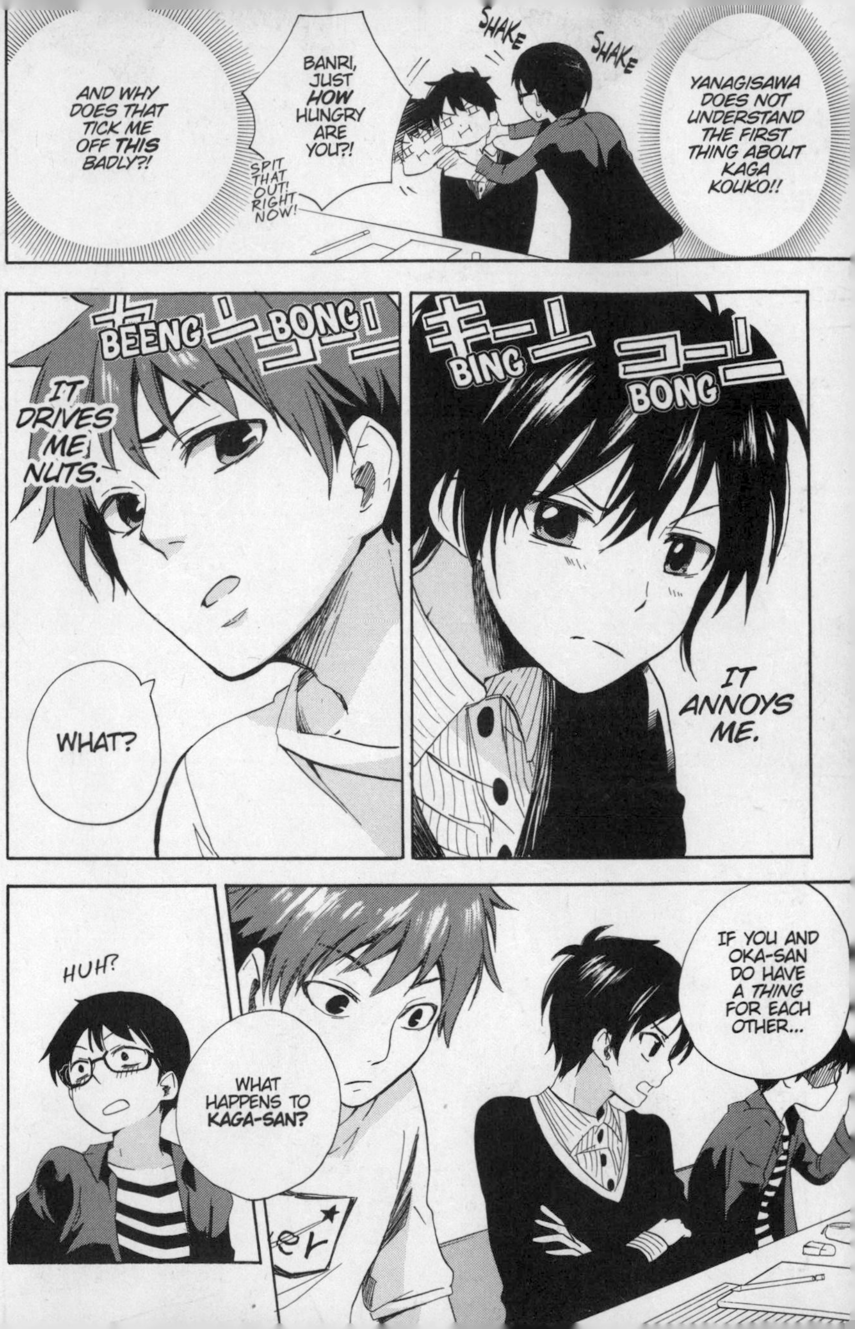
YANAGISAWA DOES NOT UNDERSTAND THE FIRST THING ABOUT KAGA KOUKO!!
SHAKE
SHAKE
BANRI, JUST HOW HUNGRY ARE YOU?!
SPIT THAT OUT! RIGHT NOW!
AND WHY DOES THAT TICK ME OFF THIS BADLY?!
BING
BONG
IT ANNOYS ME.
BEENG
BONG
IT DRIVES ME NUTS.
WHAT?
IF YOU AND OKA-SAN DO HAVE A THING FOR EACH OTHER...
WHAT HAPPENS TO KAGA-SAN?
HUH?

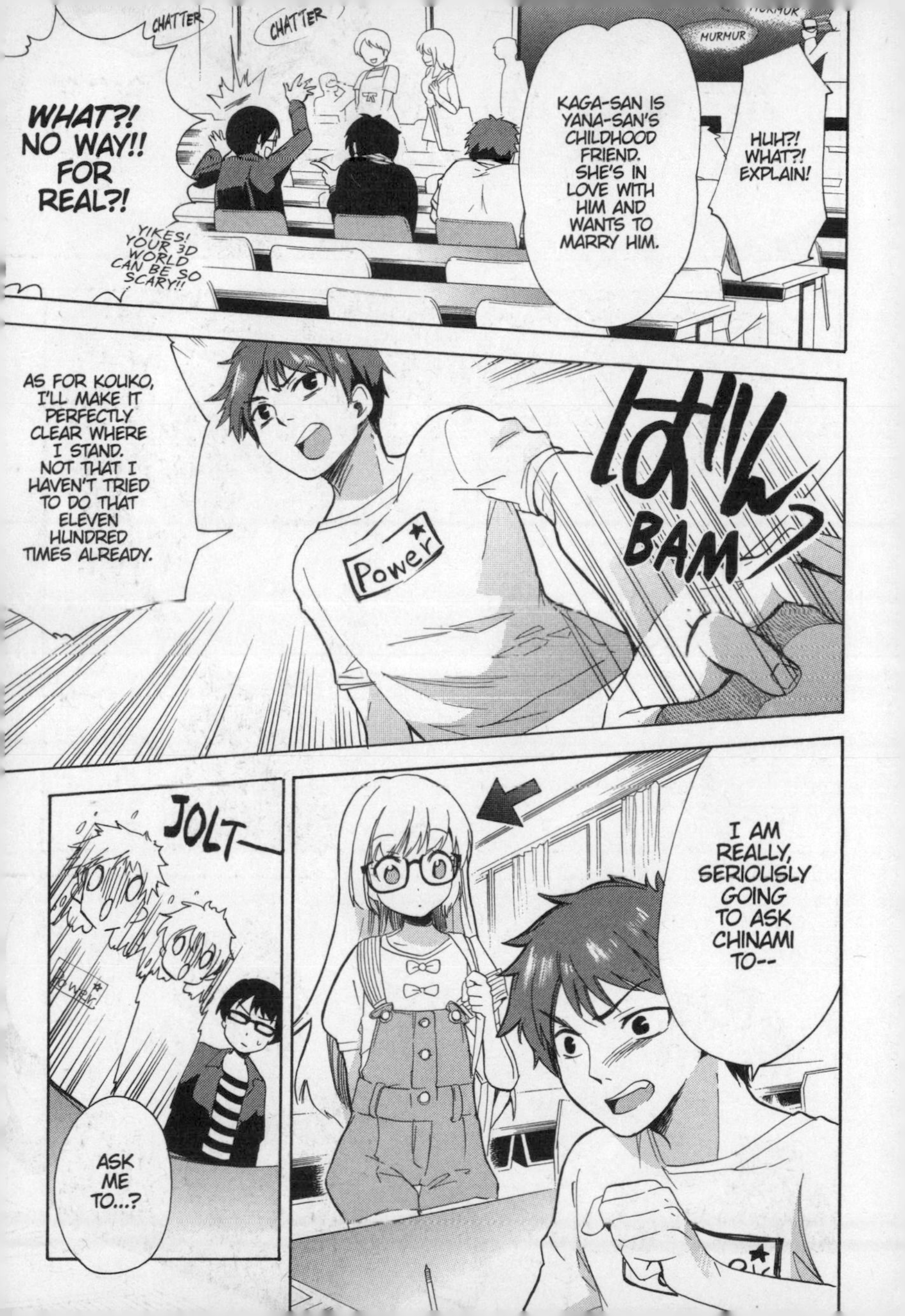
MURMUR
HUH?! WHAT?! EXPLAIN!
KAGA-SAN IS YANA-SAN'S CHILDHOOD FRIEND. SHE'S IN LOVE WITH HIM AND WANTS TO MARRY HIM.
CHATTER
CHATTER
WHAT?! NO WAY!! FOR REAL?!
YIKES! YOUR 3D WORLD CAN BE SO SCARY!!
はん
BAM
Power
AS FOR KOUKO, I'LL MAKE IT PERFECTLY CLEAR WHERE I STAND. NOT THAT I HAVEN'T TRIED TO DO THAT ELEVEN HUNDRED TIMES ALREADY.
I AM REALLY, SERIOUSLY GOING TO ASK CHINAMI TO--
JOLT—
ASK ME TO...?

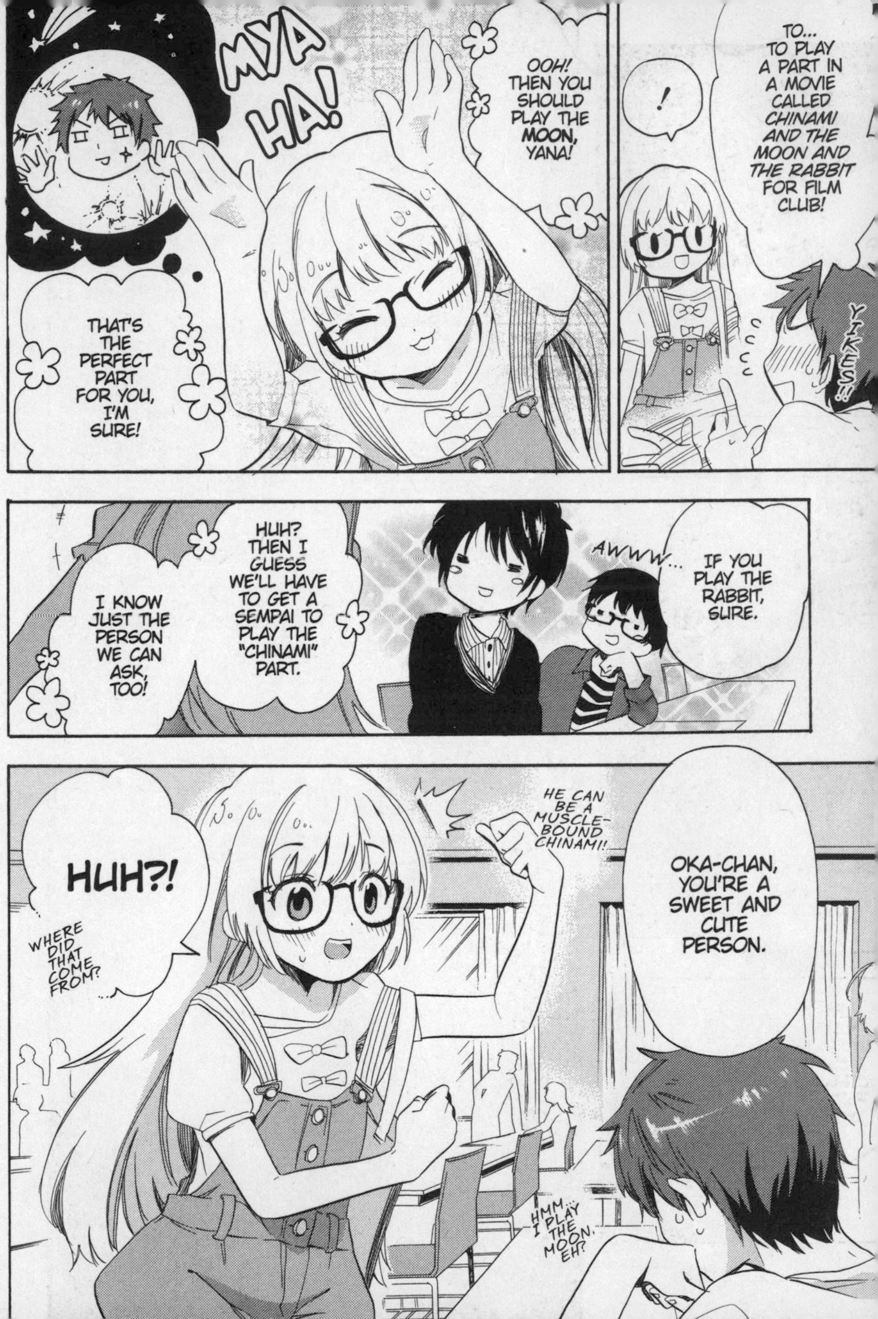
TO... TO PLAY A PART IN A MOVIE CALLED CHINAMI AND THE MOON AND THE RABBIT FOR FILM CLUB!
!
YIKES!!
OOH! THEN YOU SHOULD PLAY THE MOON, YANA!
MYA HA!
THAT'S THE PERFECT PART FOR YOU, I'M SURE!
IF YOU PLAY THE RABBIT, SURE.
AWWW...
HUH? THEN I GUESS WE'LL HAVE TO GET A SEMPAI TO PLAY THE "CHINAMI" PART.
I KNOW JUST THE PERSON WE CAN ASK, TOO!
OKA-CHAN, YOU'RE A SWEET AND CUTE PERSON.
HMM... I PLAY THE MOON, EH?
HE CAN BE A MUSCLE-BOUND CHINAMI!!
HUH?!
WHERE DID THAT COME FROM?

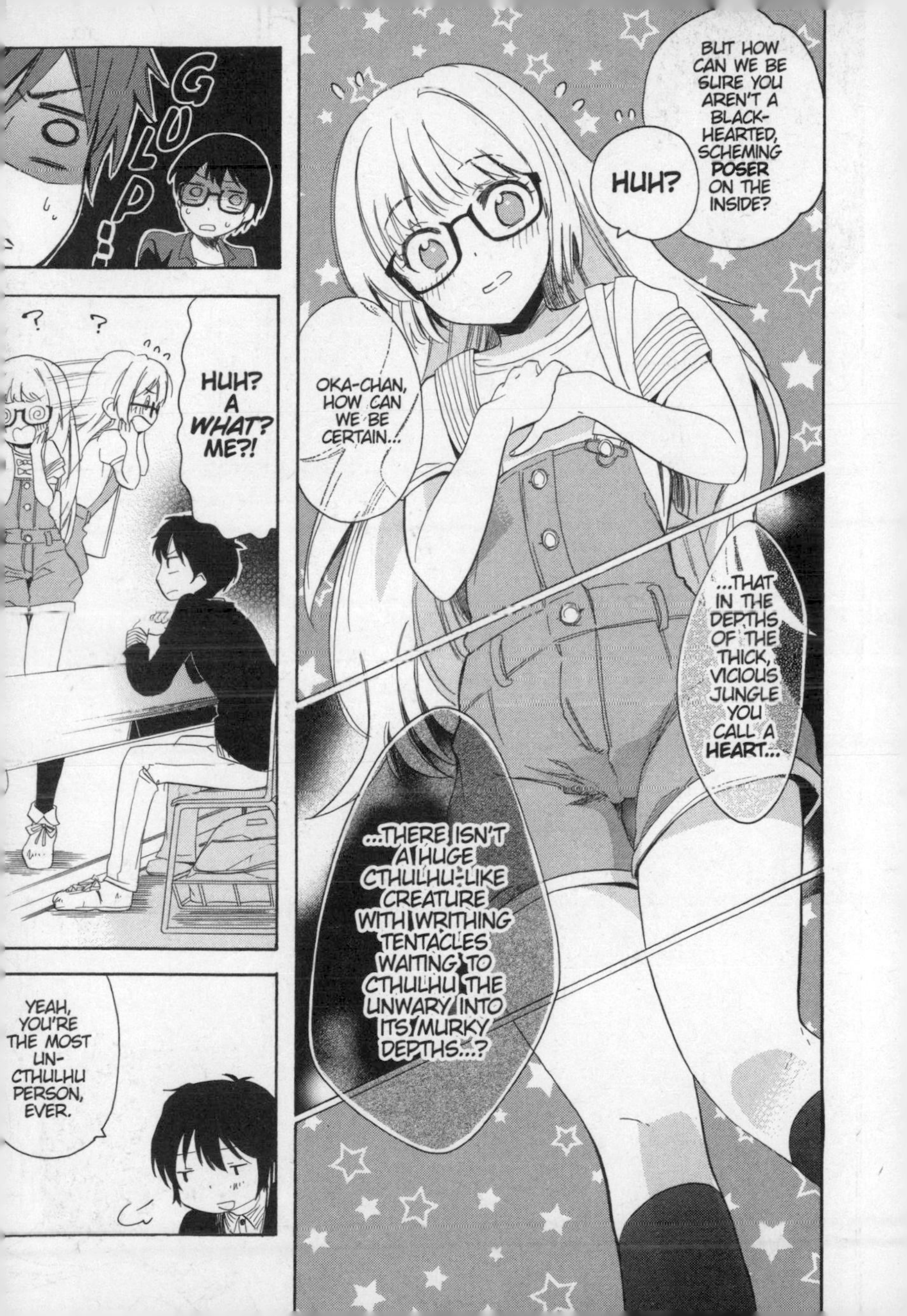
BUT HOW CAN WE BE SURE YOU AREN'T A BLACK-HEARTED, SCHEMING POSER ON THE INSIDE?
HUH?
OKA-CHAN, HOW CAN WE BE CERTAIN...
...THAT IN THE DEPTHS OF THE THICK, VICIOUS JUNGLE YOU CALL A HEART...
...THERE ISN'T A HUGE CTHULHU-LIKE CREATURE WITH WRITHING TENTACLES WAITING TO CTHULHU THE UNWARY INTO ITS MURKY DEPTHS...?
GULP
HUH? A WHAT? ME?!
YEAH, YOU'RE THE MOST UN-CTHULHU PERSON, EVER.

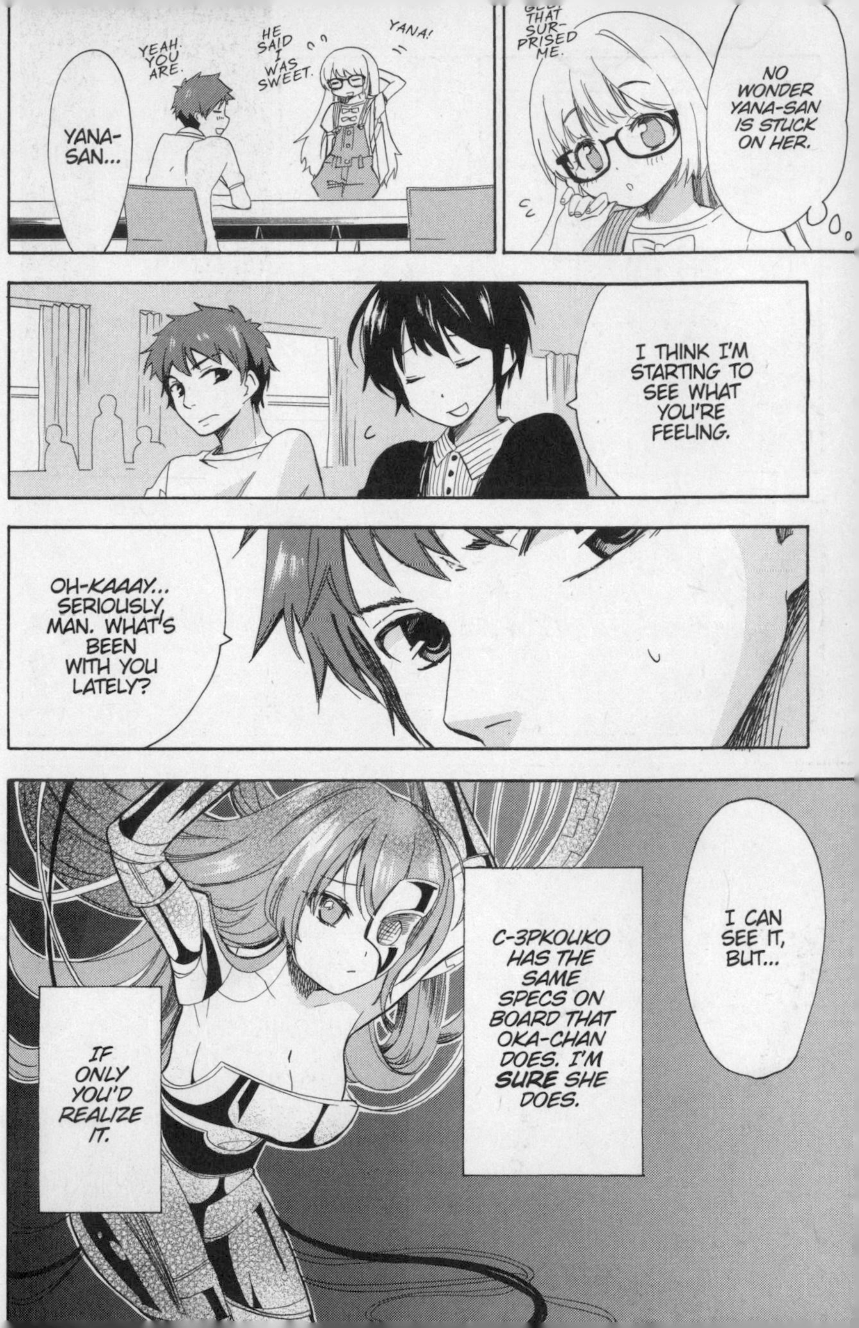

THAT SUR-PRISED ME.
NO WONDER YANA-SAN IS STUCK ON HER.
YANA!
HE SAID I WAS SWEET.
YEAH. YOU ARE.
YANA-SAN...
I THINK I'M STARTING TO SEE WHAT YOU'RE FEELING.
OH-KAAAY... SERIOUSLY, MAN. WHAT'S BEEN WITH YOU LATELY?
I CAN SEE IT, BUT...
C-3PKOUKO HAS THE SAME SPECS ON BOARD THAT OKA-CHAN DOES. I'M SURE SHE DOES.
IF ONLY YOU'D REALIZE IT.

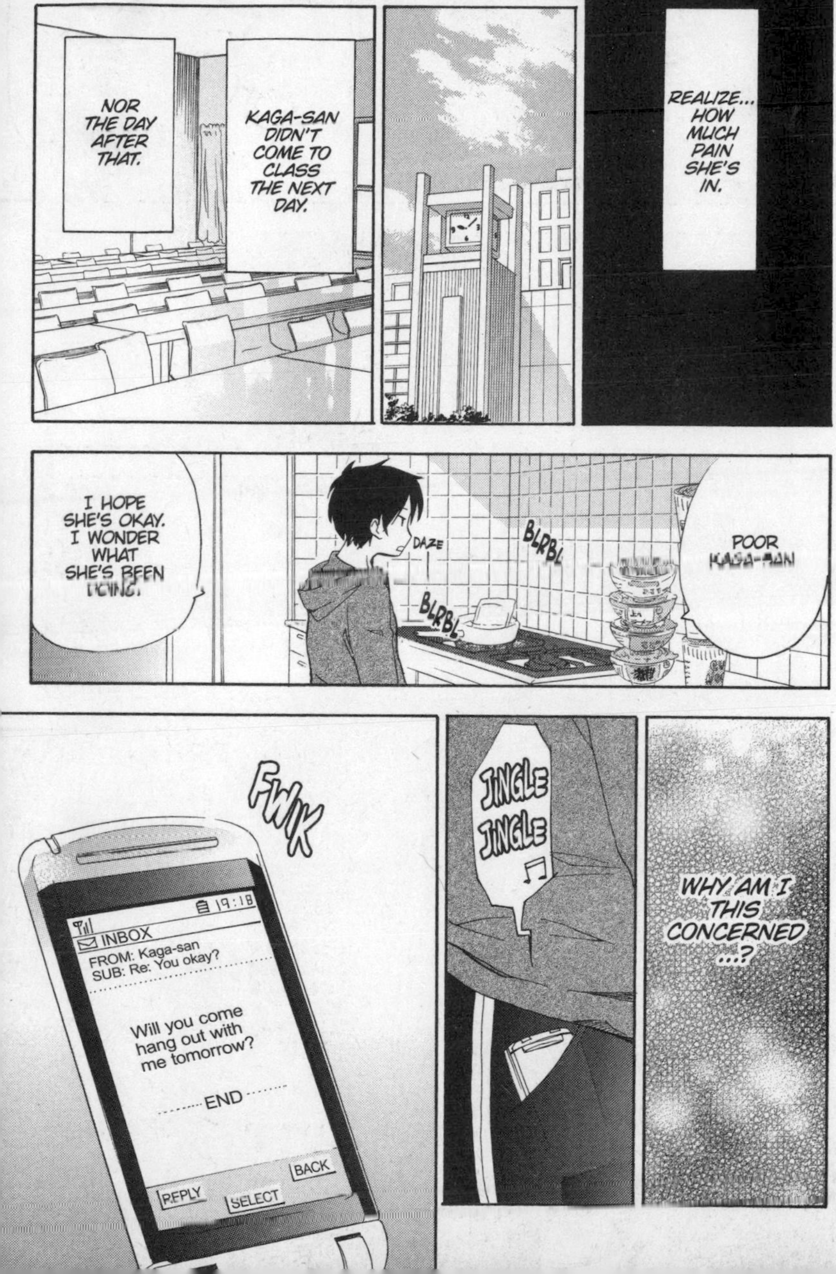
REALIZE... HOW MUCH PAIN SHE'S IN.
KAGA-SAN DIDN'T COME TO CLASS THE NEXT DAY.
NOR THE DAY AFTER THAT.
POOR KAGA-SAN
BLRBL
BLRBL
DAZE
I HOPE SHE'S OKAY. I WONDER WHAT SHE'S BEEN DOING.
WHY AM I THIS CONCERNED ...?
JINGLE JINGLE ♪
FWIK
19:18
INBOX
FROM: Kaga-san
SUB: Re: You okay?
Will you come hang out with me tomorrow?
END
BACK
REPLY
SELECT

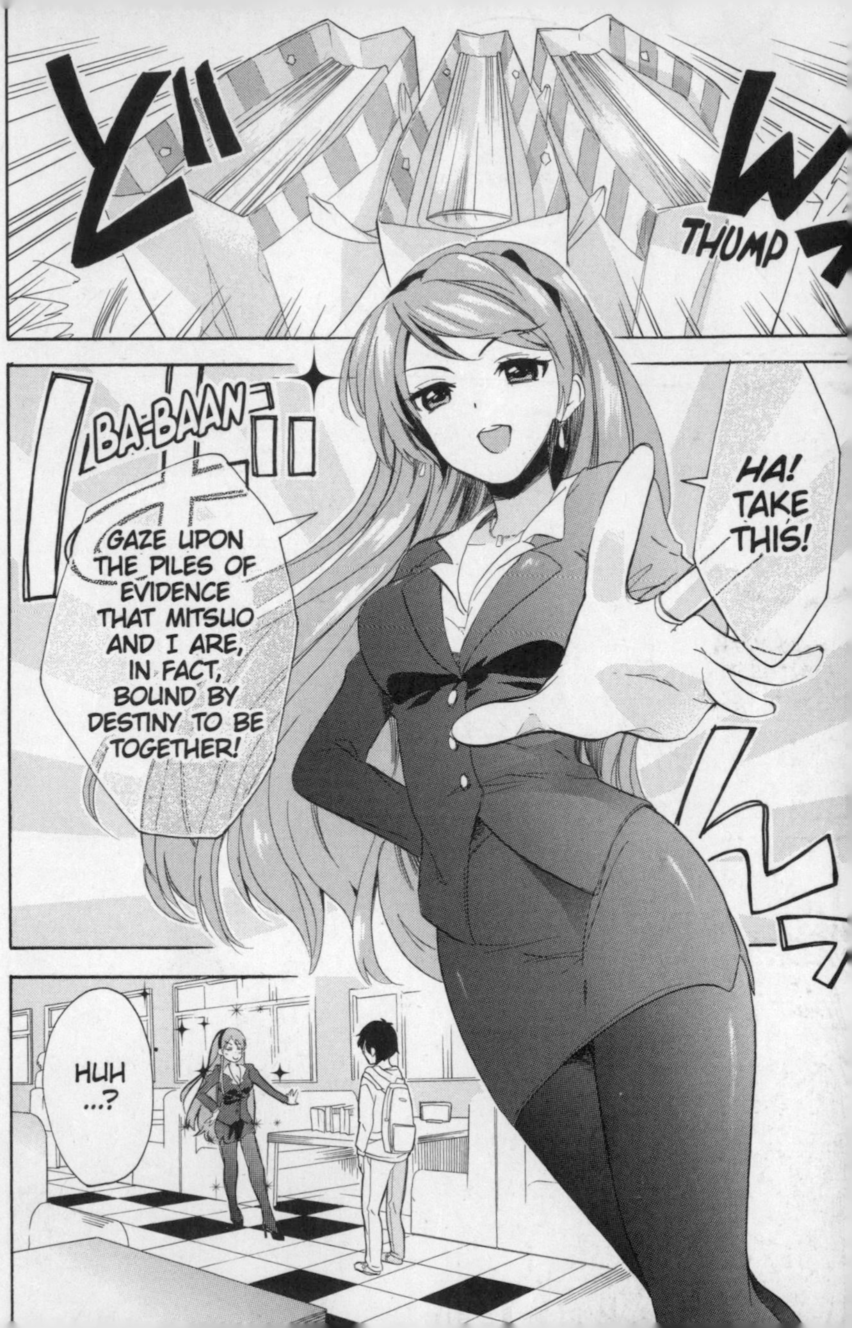
THUMP
HA! TAKE THIS!
BA-BAAN
GAZE UPON THE PILES OF EVIDENCE THAT MITSUO AND I ARE, IN FACT, BOUND BY DESTINY TO BE TOGETHER!
HUH ...?

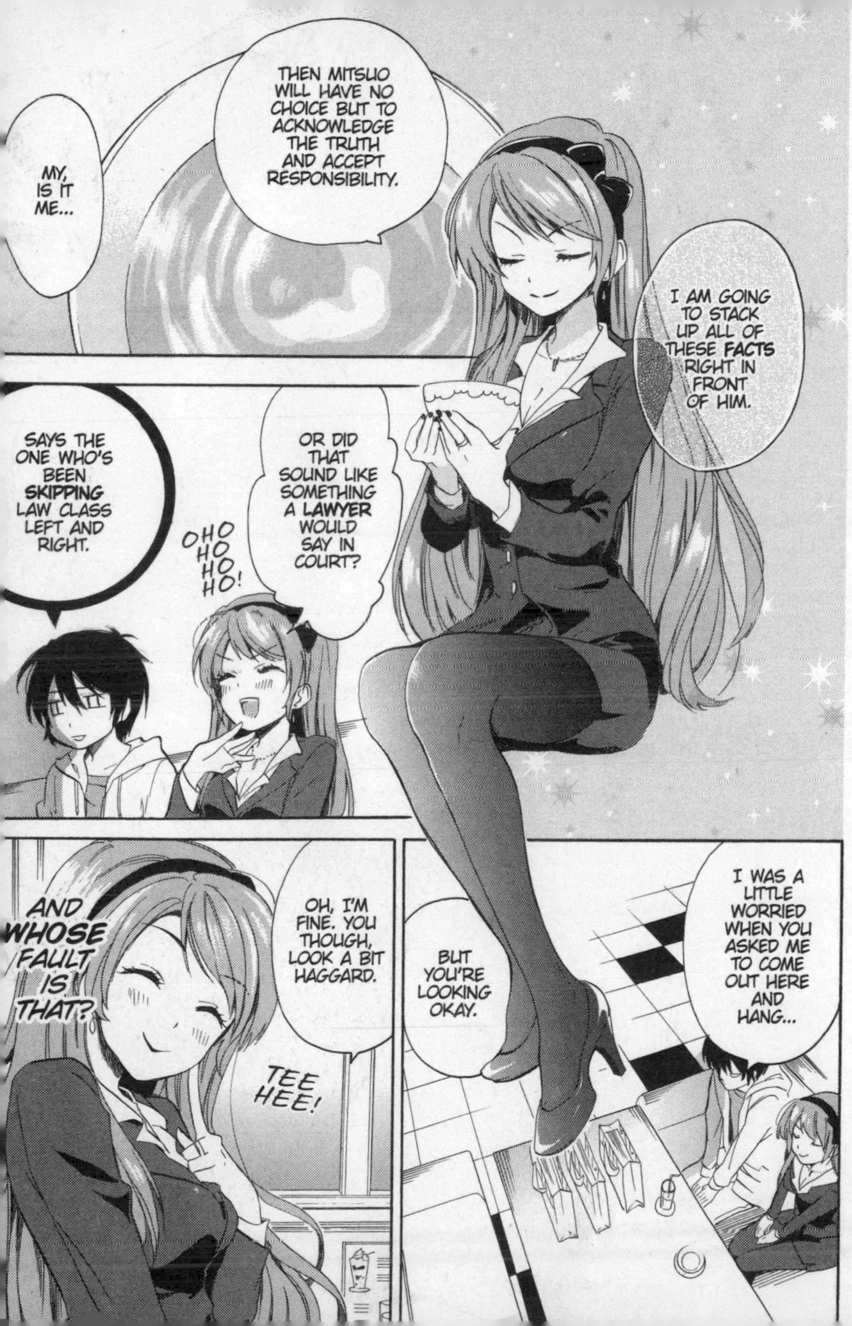
I AM GOING TO STACK UP ALL OF THESE FACTS RIGHT IN FRONT OF HIM.
THEN MITSUO WILL HAVE NO CHOICE BUT TO ACKNOWLEDGE THE TRUTH AND ACCEPT RESPONSIBILITY.
MY, IS IT ME...
OR DID THAT SOUND LIKE SOMETHING A LAWYER WOULD SAY IN COURT?
OHO HO HO HO!
SAYS THE ONE WHO'S BEEN SKIPPING LAW CLASS LEFT AND RIGHT.
I WAS A LITTLE WORRIED WHEN YOU ASKED ME TO COME OUT HERE AND HANG...
BUT YOU'RE LOOKING OKAY.
OH, I'M FINE. YOU THOUGH, LOOK A BIT HAGGARD.
TEE HEE!
AND WHOSE FAULT IS THAT?

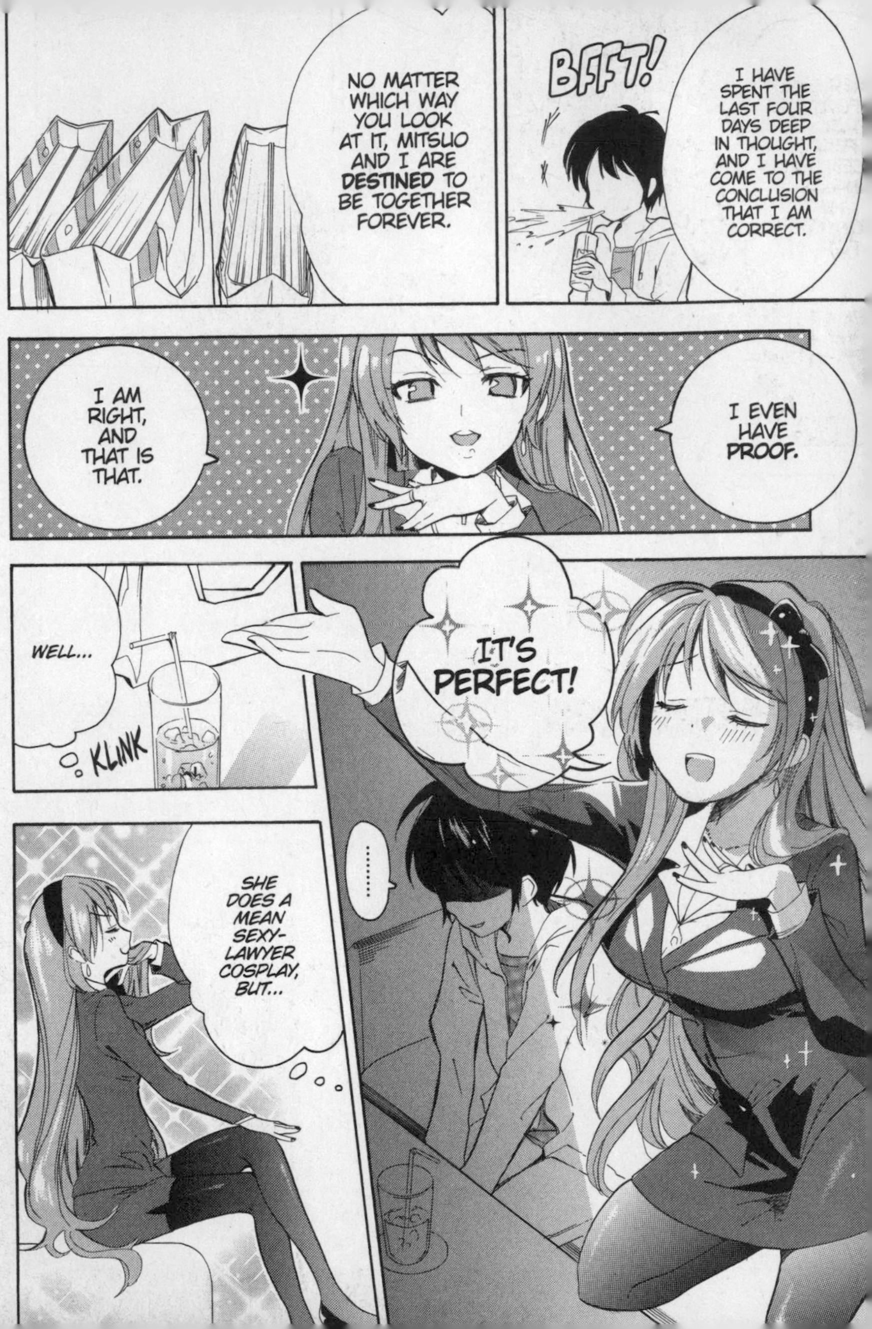
BFFT!
I HAVE SPENT THE LAST FOUR DAYS DEEP IN THOUGHT, AND I HAVE COME TO THE CONCLUSION THAT I AM CORRECT.
NO MATTER WHICH WAY YOU LOOK AT IT, MITSUO AND I ARE DESTINED TO BE TOGETHER FOREVER.
I EVEN HAVE PROOF.
I AM RIGHT, AND THAT IS THAT.
IT'S PERFECT!
......
WELL...
KLINK
SHE DOES A MEAN SEXY-LAWYER COSPLAY, BUT...

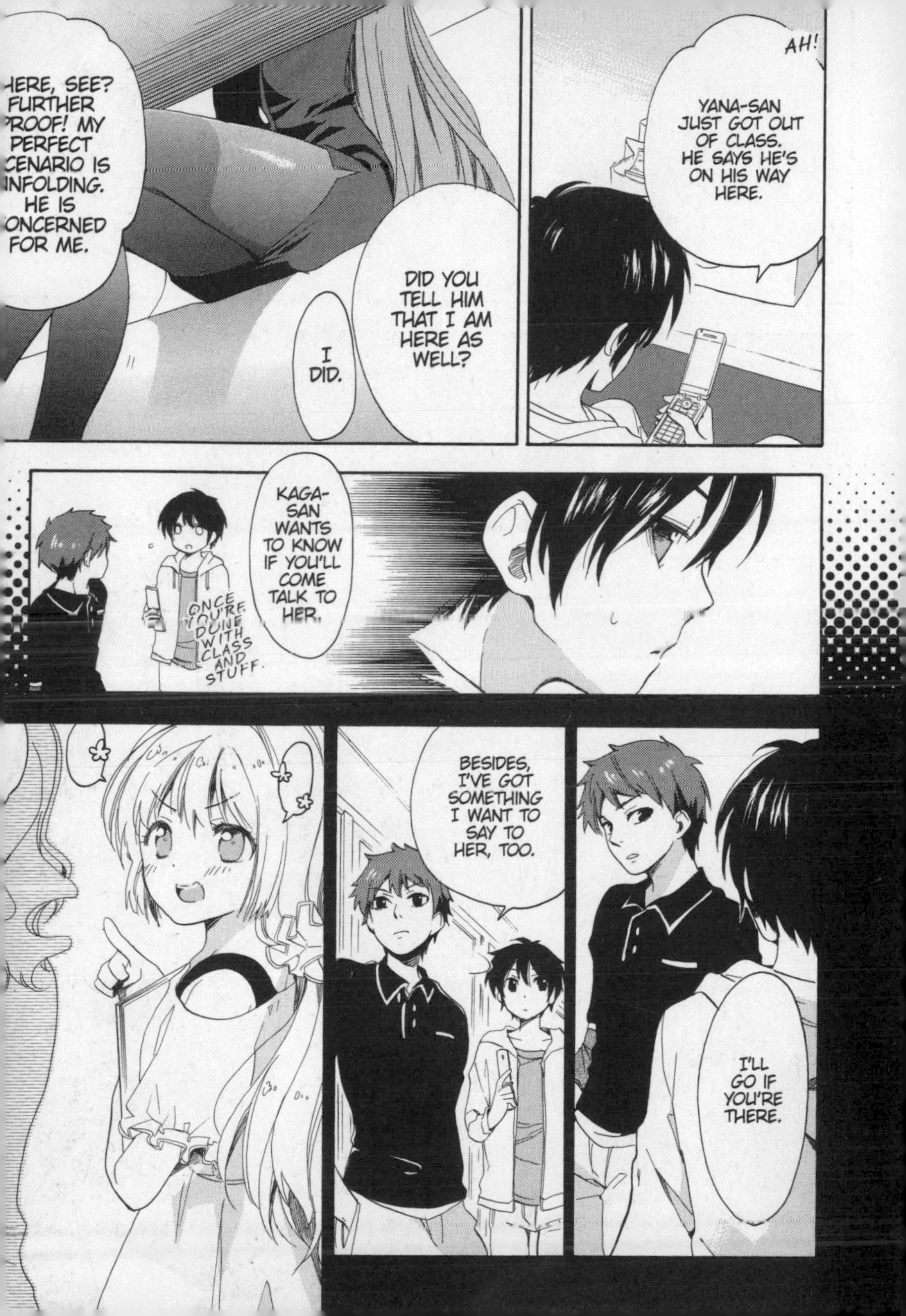
AH!
YANA-SAN JUST GOT OUT OF CLASS. HE SAYS HE'S ON HIS WAY HERE.
DID YOU TELL HIM THAT I AM HERE AS WELL?
I DID.
HERE, SEE? FURTHER PROOF! MY PERFECT CENARIO IS INFOLDING. HE IS ONCERNED FOR ME.
KAGA-SAN WANTS TO KNOW IF YOU'LL COME TALK TO HER.
ONCE YOU'RE DONE WITH CLASS AND STUFF.
I'LL GO IF YOU'RE THERE.
BESIDES, I'VE GOT SOMETHING I WANT TO SAY TO HER, TOO.

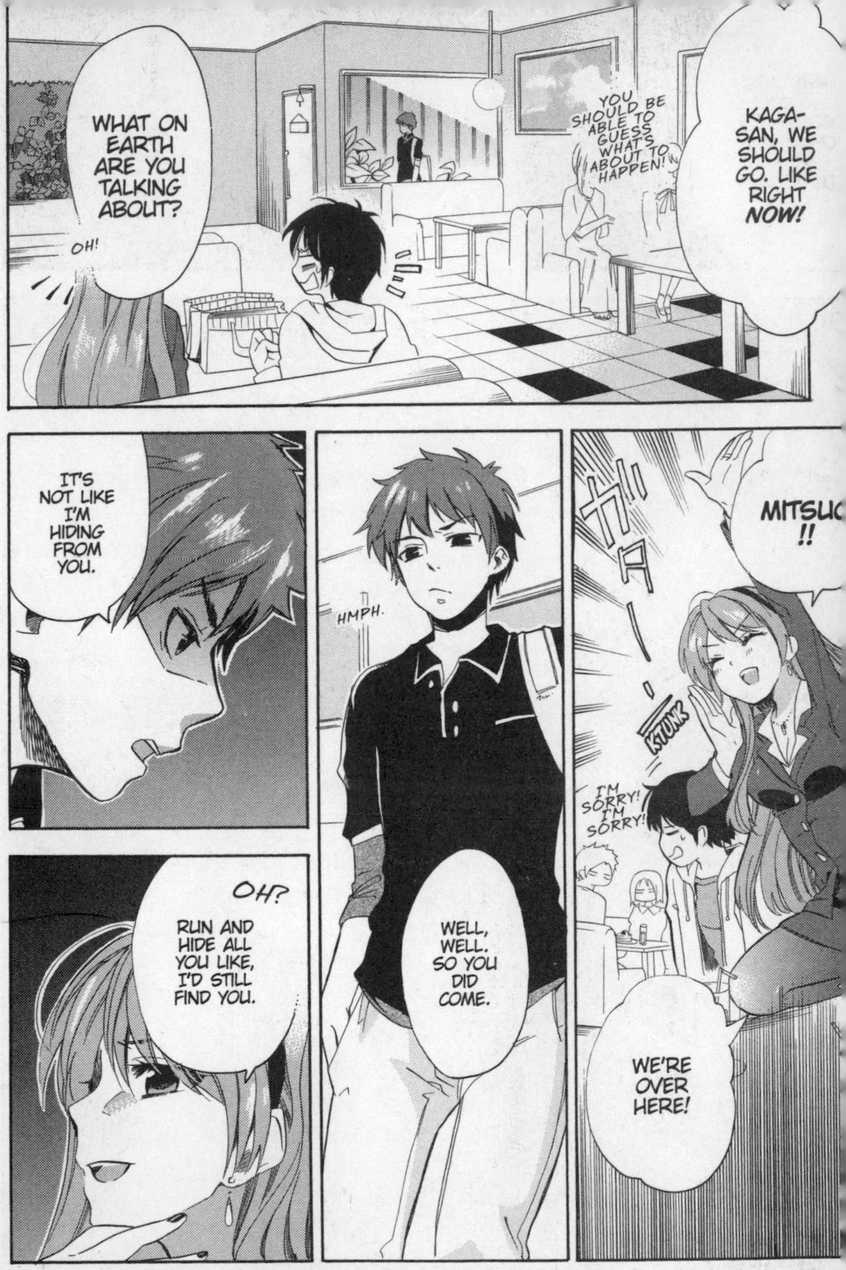
KAGA-SAN, WE SHOULD GO. LIKE RIGHT NOW!
YOU SHOULD BE ABLE TO GUESS WHAT'S ABOUT TO HAPPEN!
WHAT ON EARTH ARE YOU TALKING ABOUT?
OH!
MITSUO!!
KTUNK
I'M SORRY! I'M SORRY!
WE'RE OVER HERE!
HMPH.
WELL, WELL. SO YOU DID COME.
IT'S NOT LIKE I'M HIDING FROM YOU.
OH?
RUN AND HIDE ALL YOU LIKE, I'D STILL FIND YOU.

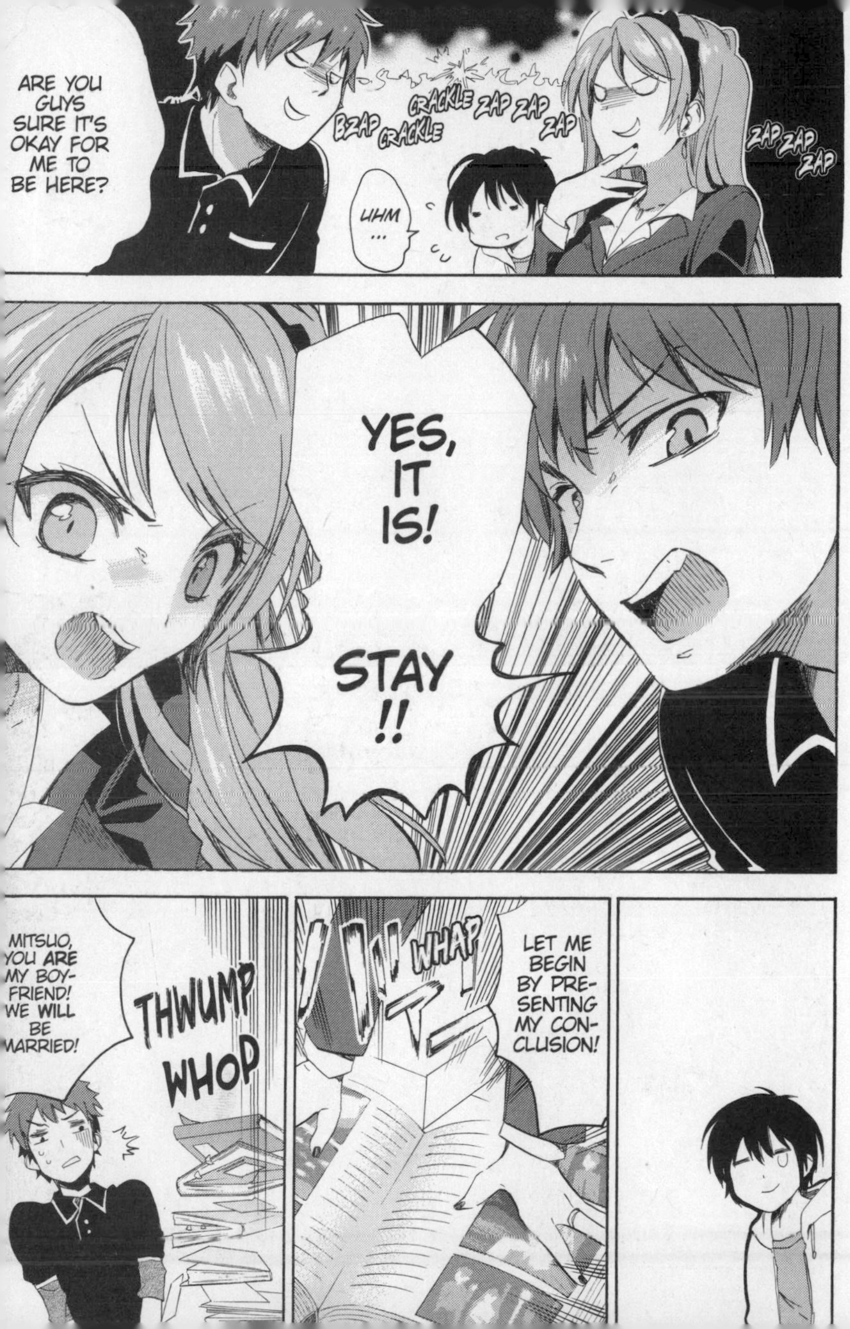
ZAP ZAP ZAP
CRACKLE ZAP ZAP ZAP
BZAP CRACKLE
ARE YOU GUYS SURE IT'S OKAY FOR ME TO BE HERE?
UHM ...
YES, IT IS!
STAY !!
LET ME BEGIN BY PRE-SENTING MY CON-CLUSION!
WHAP
MITSUO, YOU ARE MY BOY-FRIEND! WE WILL BE MARRIED!
THWUMP WHOP

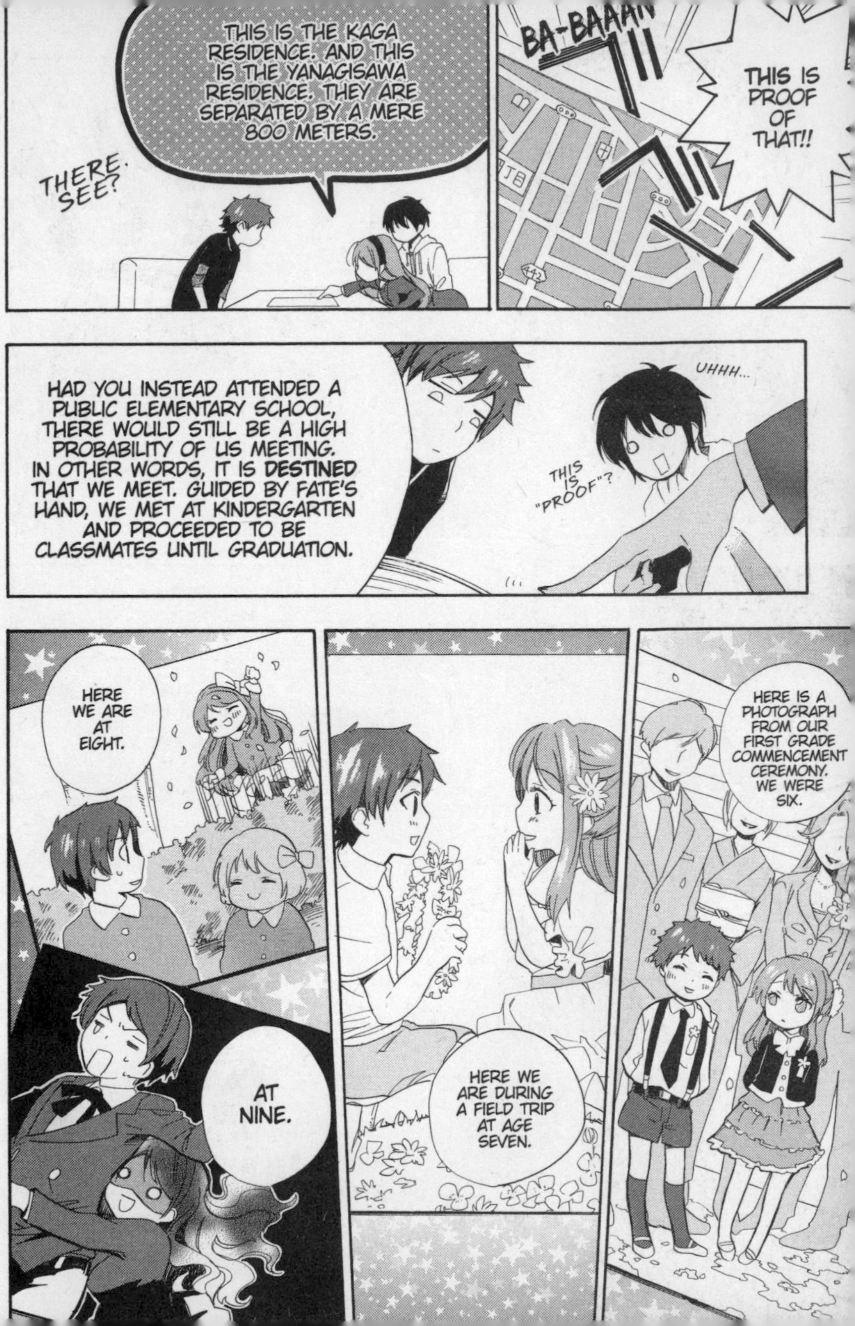
BA-BAAAN
THIS IS PROOF OF THAT!!
THIS IS THE KAGA RESIDENCE. AND THIS IS THE YANAGISAWA RESIDENCE. THEY ARE SEPARATED BY A MERE 800 METERS.
THERE. SEE?
UHHH...
THIS IS "PROOF"?
HAD YOU INSTEAD ATTENDED A PUBLIC ELEMENTARY SCHOOL, THERE WOULD STILL BE A HIGH PROBABILITY OF US MEETING. IN OTHER WORDS, IT IS DESTINED THAT WE MEET. GUIDED BY FATE'S HAND, WE MET AT KINDERGARTEN AND PROCEEDED TO BE CLASSMATES UNTIL GRADUATION.
HERE IS A PHOTOGRAPH FROM OUR FIRST GRADE COMMENCEMENT CEREMONY. WE WERE SIX.
HERE WE ARE DURING A FIELD TRIP AT AGE SEVEN.
HERE WE ARE AT EIGHT.
AT NINE.

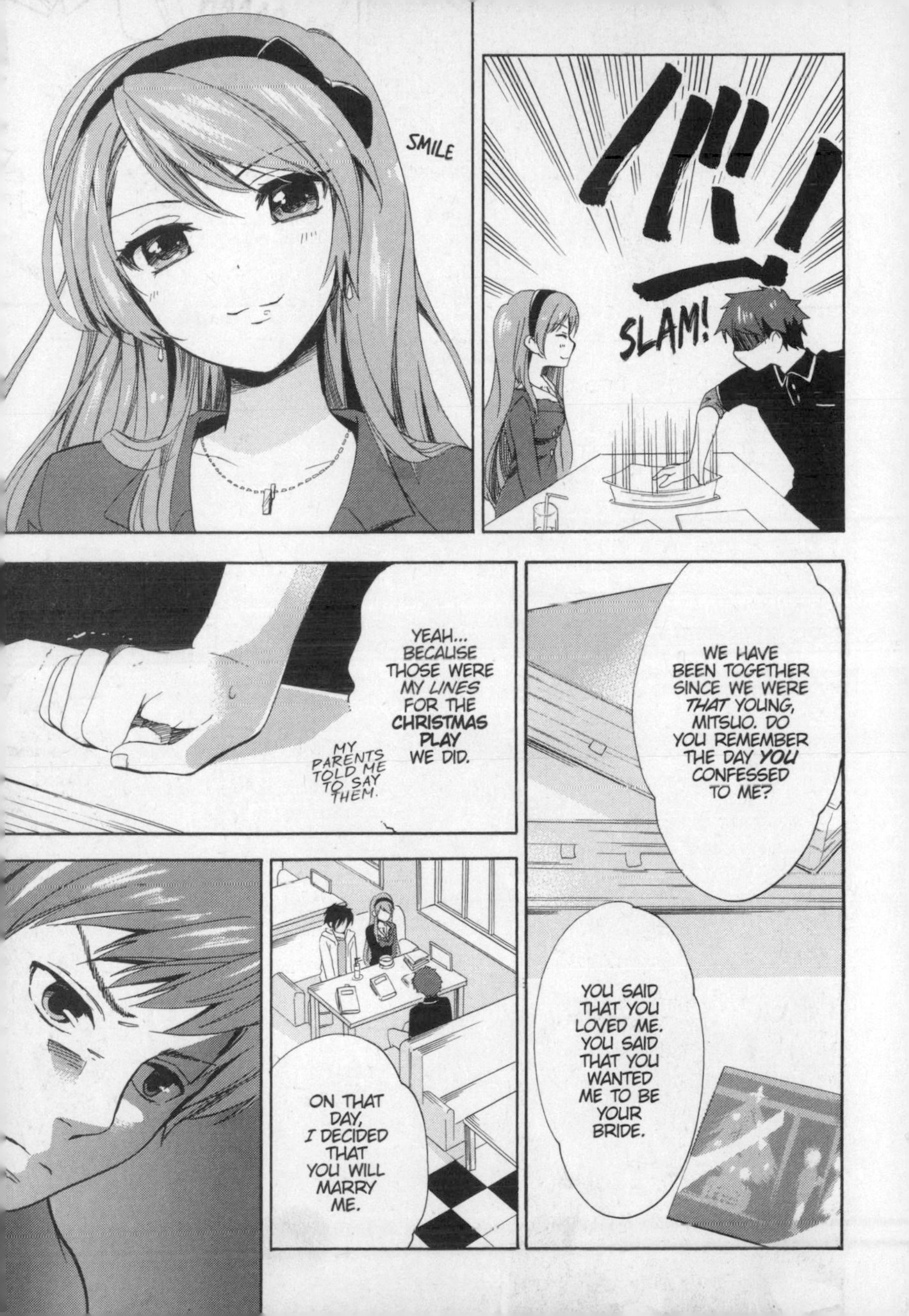
SLAM!
SMILE
WE HAVE BEEN TOGETHER SINCE WE WERE *THAT* YOUNG, MITSUO. DO YOU REMEMBER THE DAY ***YOU*** CONFESSED TO ME?
YEAH... BECAUSE THOSE WERE MY *LINES* FOR THE **CHRISTMAS PLAY** WE DID.
MY PARENTS TOLD ME TO SAY THEM.
YOU SAID THAT YOU LOVED ME. YOU SAID THAT YOU WANTED ME TO BE YOUR BRIDE.
ON THAT DAY, *I* DECIDED THAT YOU WILL MARRY ME.

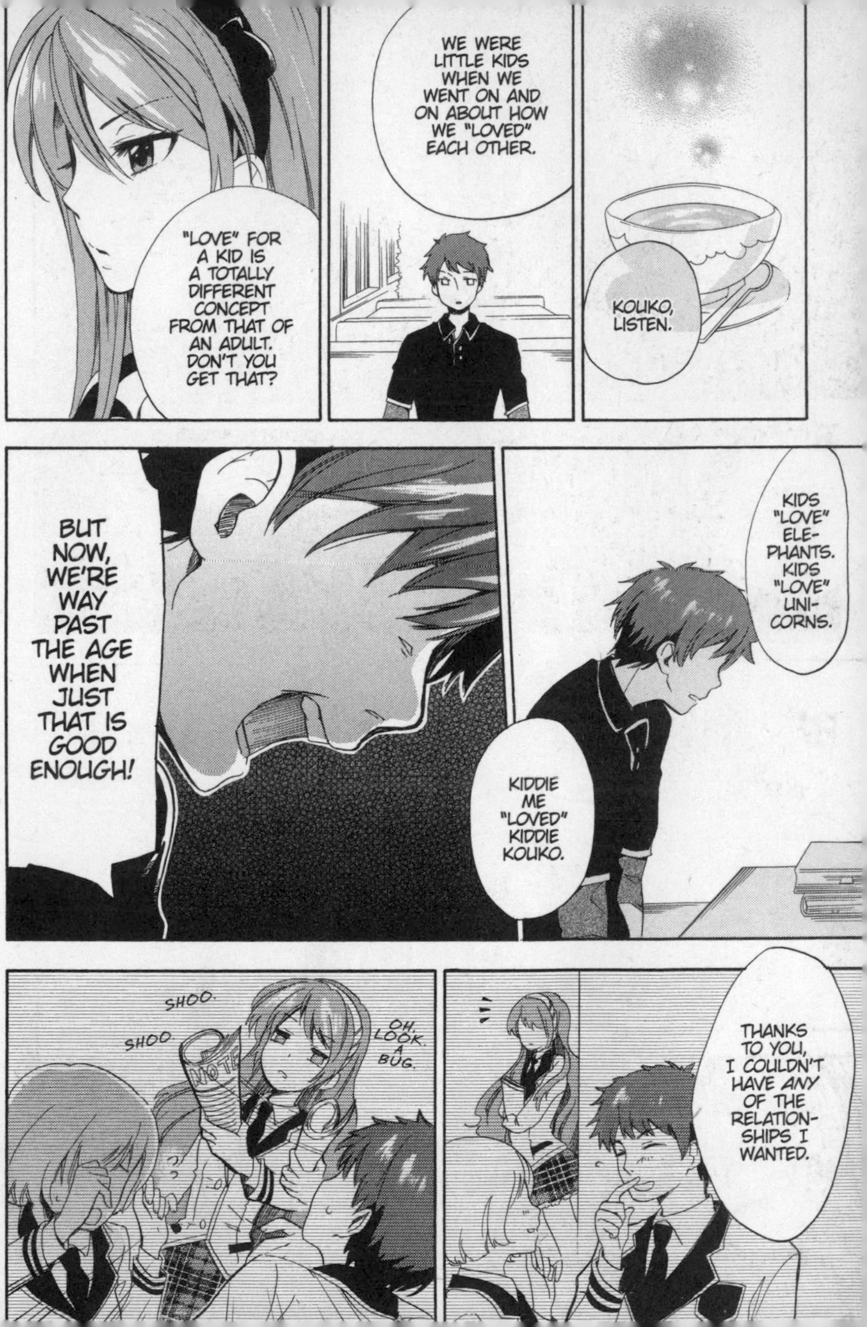
KOUKO, LISTEN.
WE WERE LITTLE KIDS WHEN WE WENT ON AND ON ABOUT HOW WE "LOVED" EACH OTHER.
"LOVE" FOR A KID IS A TOTALLY DIFFERENT CONCEPT FROM THAT OF AN ADULT. DON'T YOU GET THAT?
KIDS "LOVE" ELE-PHANTS. KIDS "LOVE" UNI-CORNS.
KIDDIE ME "LOVED" KIDDIE KOUKO.
BUT NOW, WE'RE WAY PAST THE AGE WHEN JUST THAT IS GOOD ENOUGH!
THANKS TO YOU, I COULDN'T HAVE *ANY* OF THE RELATION-SHIPS I WANTED.
SHOO.
SHOO.
OH, LOOK A BUG.

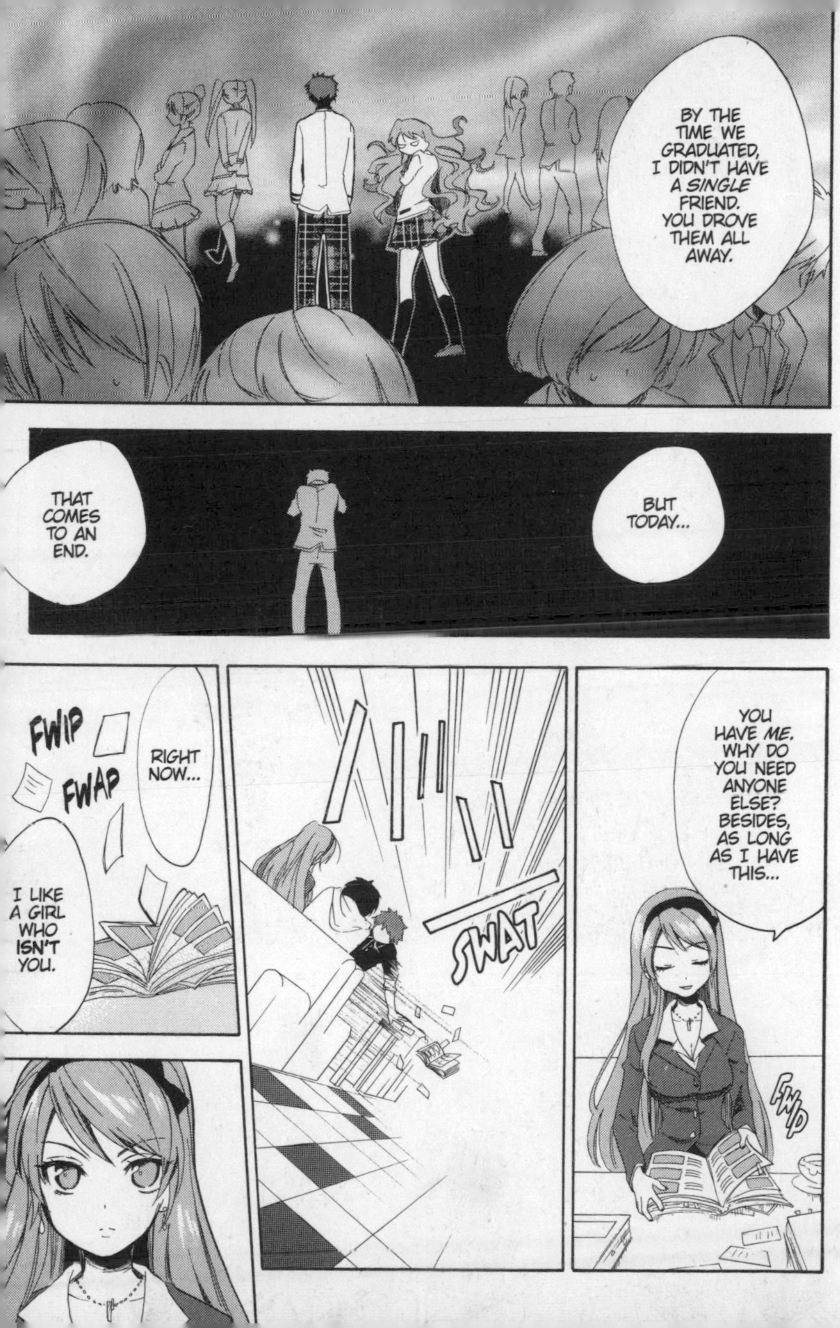
BY THE TIME WE GRADUATED, I DIDN'T HAVE A SINGLE FRIEND. YOU DROVE THEM ALL AWAY.
BUT TODAY...
THAT COMES TO AN END.
YOU HAVE ME. WHY DO YOU NEED ANYONE ELSE? BESIDES, AS LONG AS I HAVE THIS...
FWIP
SWAT
RIGHT NOW...
FWIP
FWAP
I LIKE A GIRL WHO ISN'T YOU.

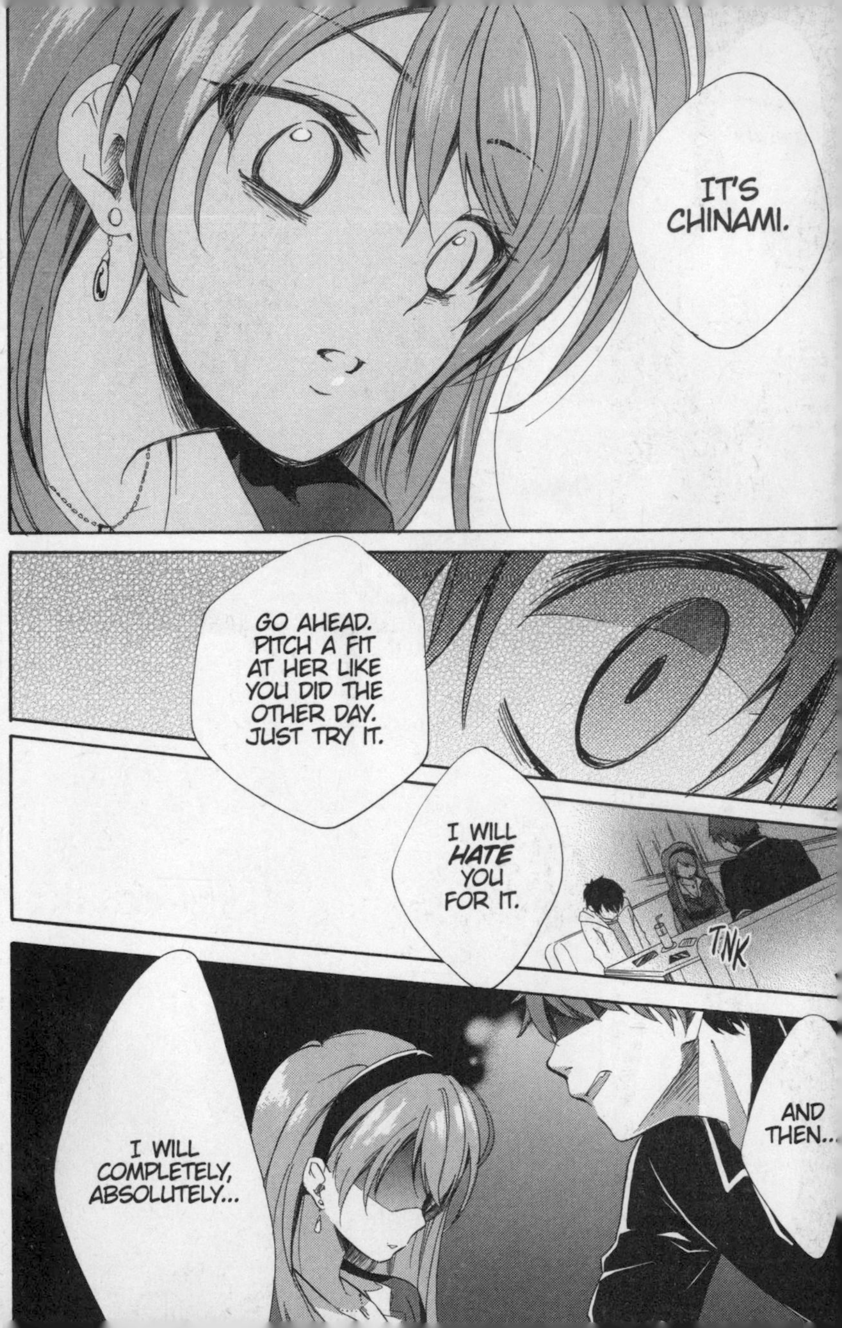
IT'S CHINAMI.
GO AHEAD. PITCH A FIT AT HER LIKE YOU DID THE OTHER DAY. JUST TRY IT.
I WILL HATE YOU FOR IT.
TINK
AND THEN...
I WILL COMPLETELY, ABSOLUTELY...

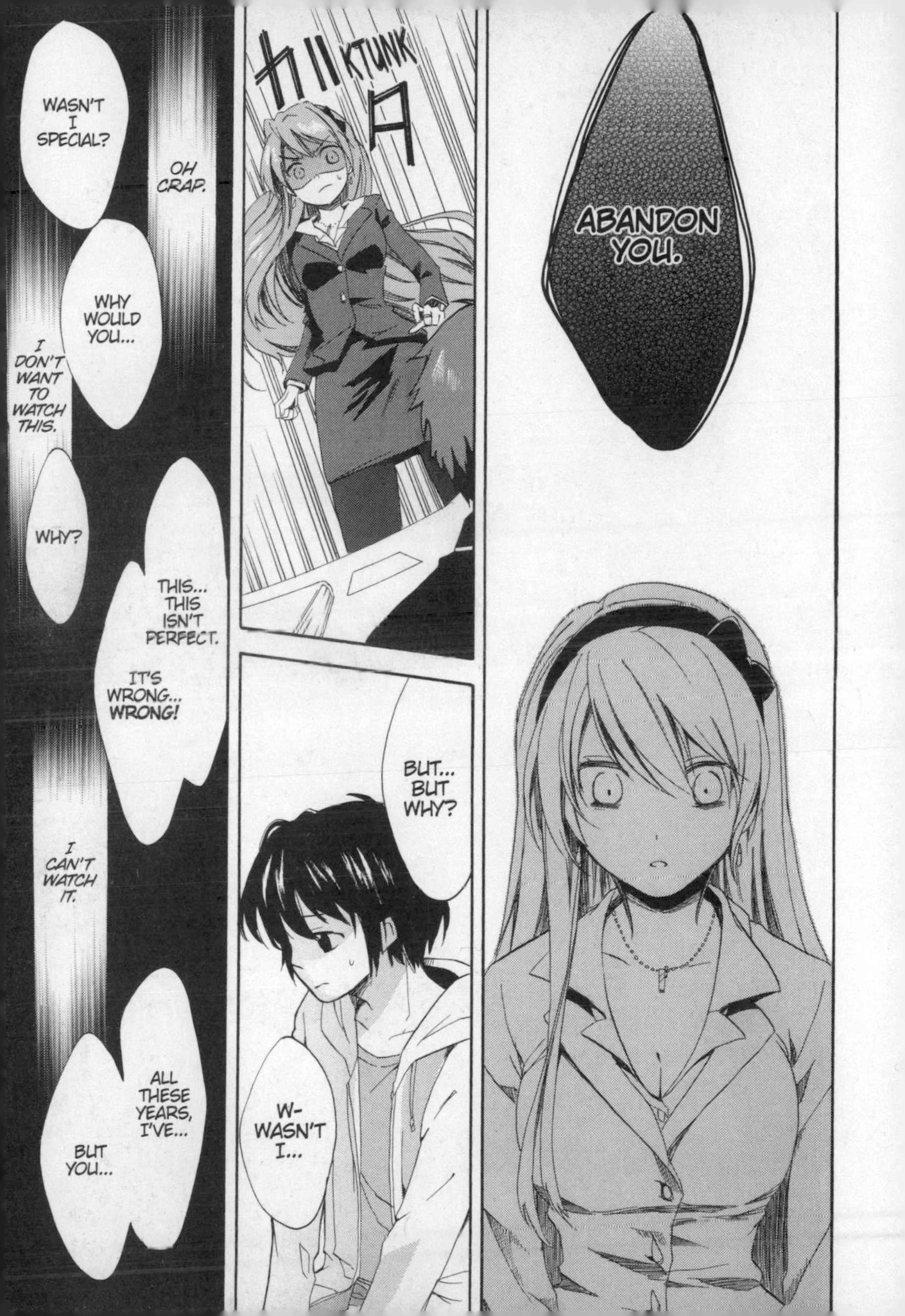
ABANDON YOU.
KTUNK
BUT... BUT WHY?
W-WASN'T I...
WASN'T I SPECIAL?
OH CRAP.
WHY WOULD YOU...
I DON'T WANT TO WATCH THIS.
WHY?
THIS... THIS ISN'T PERFECT.
IT'S WRONG... WRONG!
I CAN'T WATCH IT.
ALL THESE YEARS, I'VE...
BUT YOU...

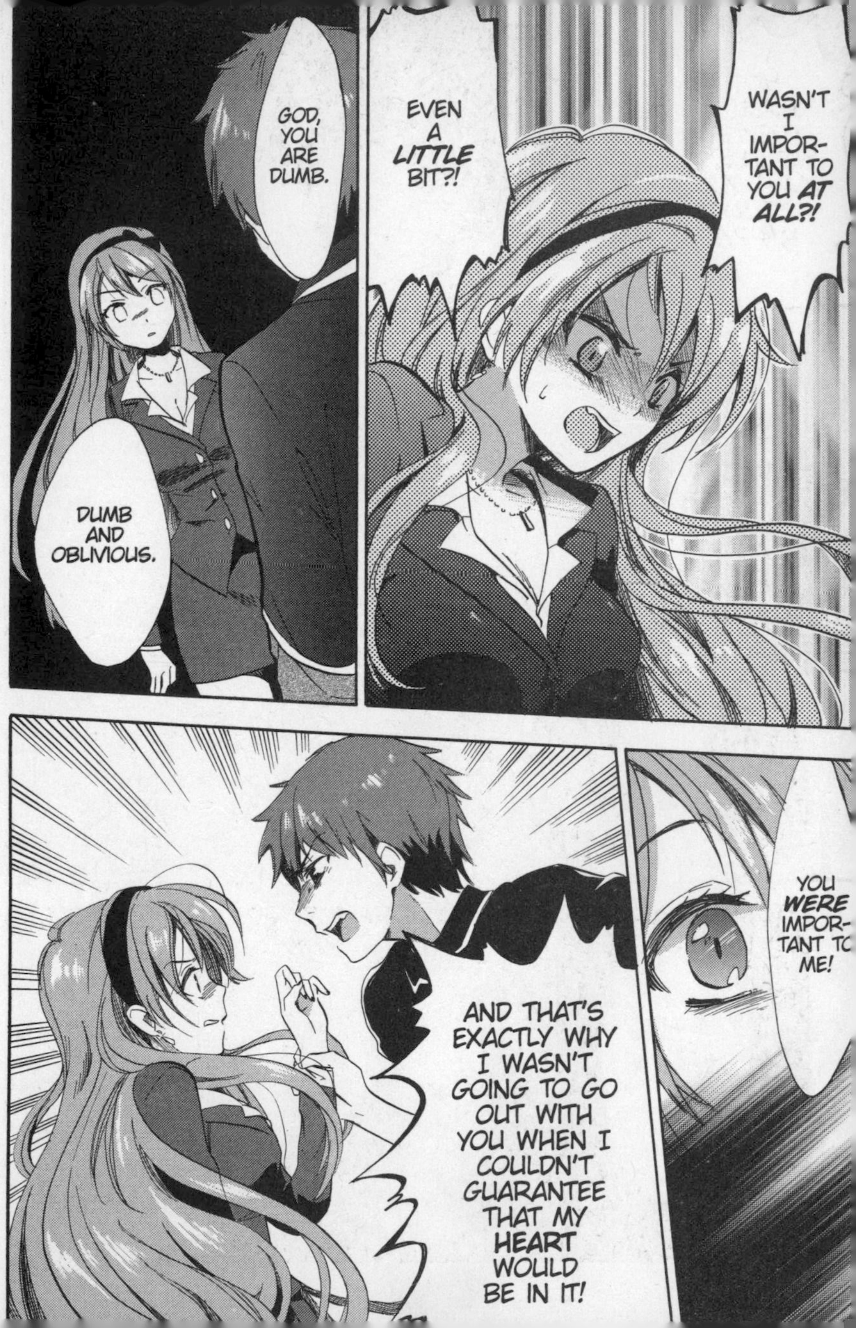
WASN'T I IMPORTANT TO YOU AT ALL?!
EVEN A LITTLE BIT?!
GOD, YOU ARE DUMB.
DUMB AND OBLIVIOUS.
YOU WERE IMPORTANT TO ME!
AND THAT'S EXACTLY WHY I WASN'T GOING TO GO OUT WITH YOU WHEN I COULDN'T GUARANTEE THAT MY HEART WOULD BE IN IT!

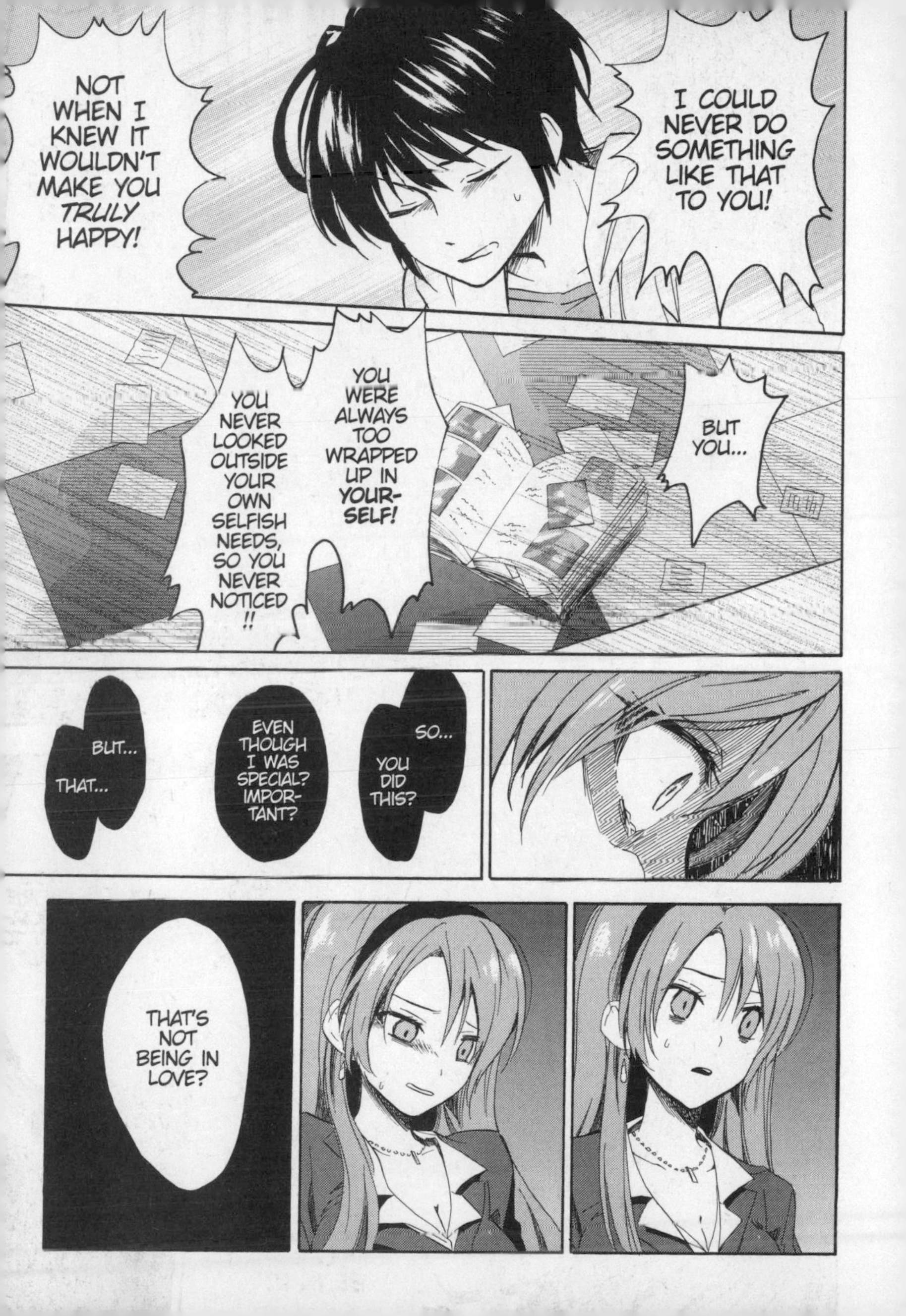
I COULD NEVER DO SOMETHING LIKE THAT TO YOU!
NOT WHEN I KNEW IT WOULDN'T MAKE YOU *TRULY* HAPPY!
BUT YOU...
YOU WERE ALWAYS TOO WRAPPED UP IN **YOURSELF**!
YOU NEVER LOOKED OUTSIDE YOUR OWN SELFISH NEEDS, SO YOU NEVER NOTICED!!
SO... YOU DID THIS?
EVEN THOUGH I WAS SPECIAL? IMPORTANT?
BUT... THAT...
THAT'S NOT BEING IN LOVE?

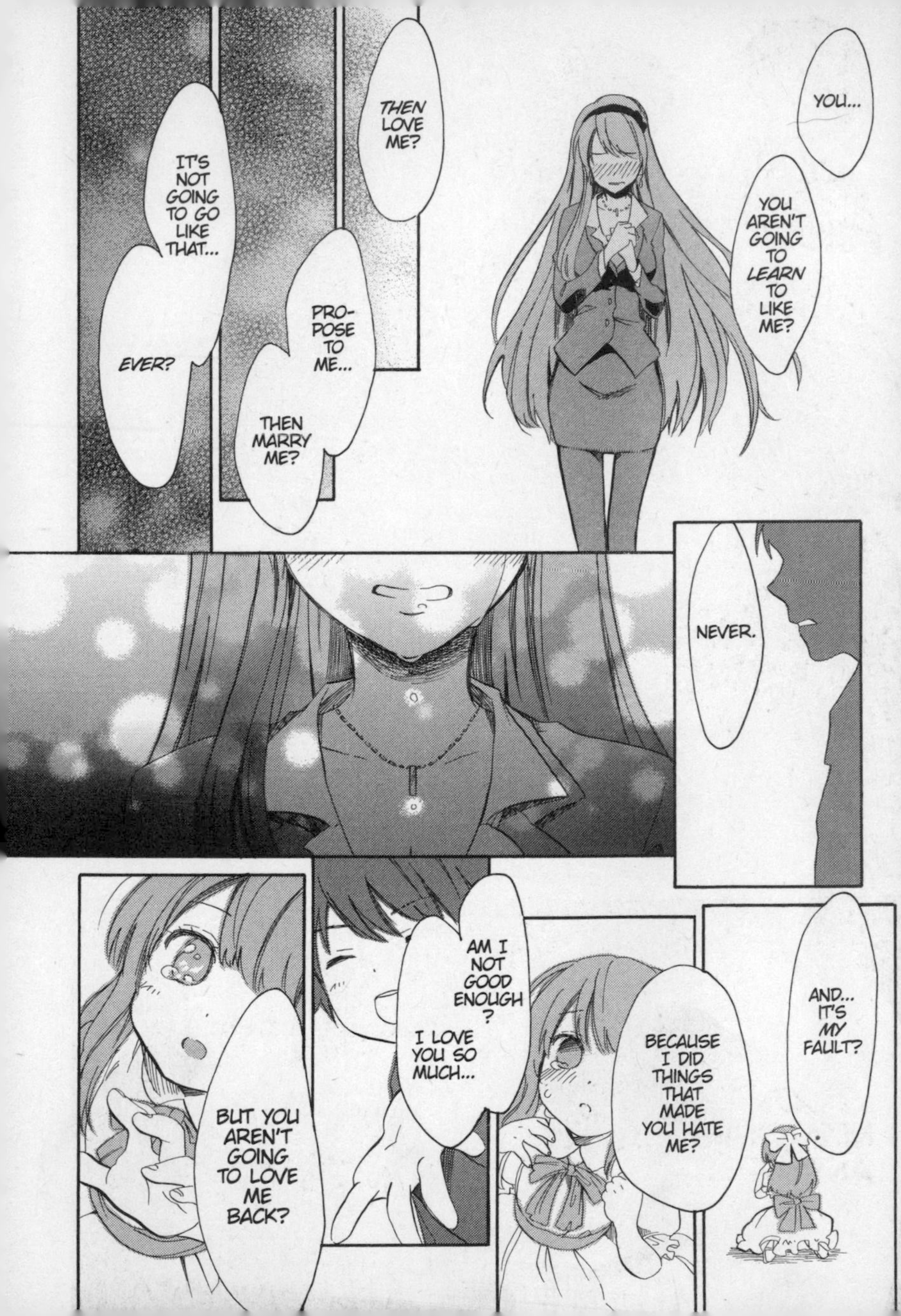
YOU...
YOU AREN'T GOING TO LEARN TO LIKE ME?
THEN LOVE ME?
PRO-POSE TO ME...
THEN MARRY ME?
IT'S NOT GOING TO GO LIKE THAT...
EVER?
NEVER.
AND... IT'S MY FAULT?
BECAUSE I DID THINGS THAT MADE YOU HATE ME?
AM I NOT GOOD ENOUGH?
I LOVE YOU SO MUCH...
BUT YOU AREN'T GOING TO LOVE ME BACK?

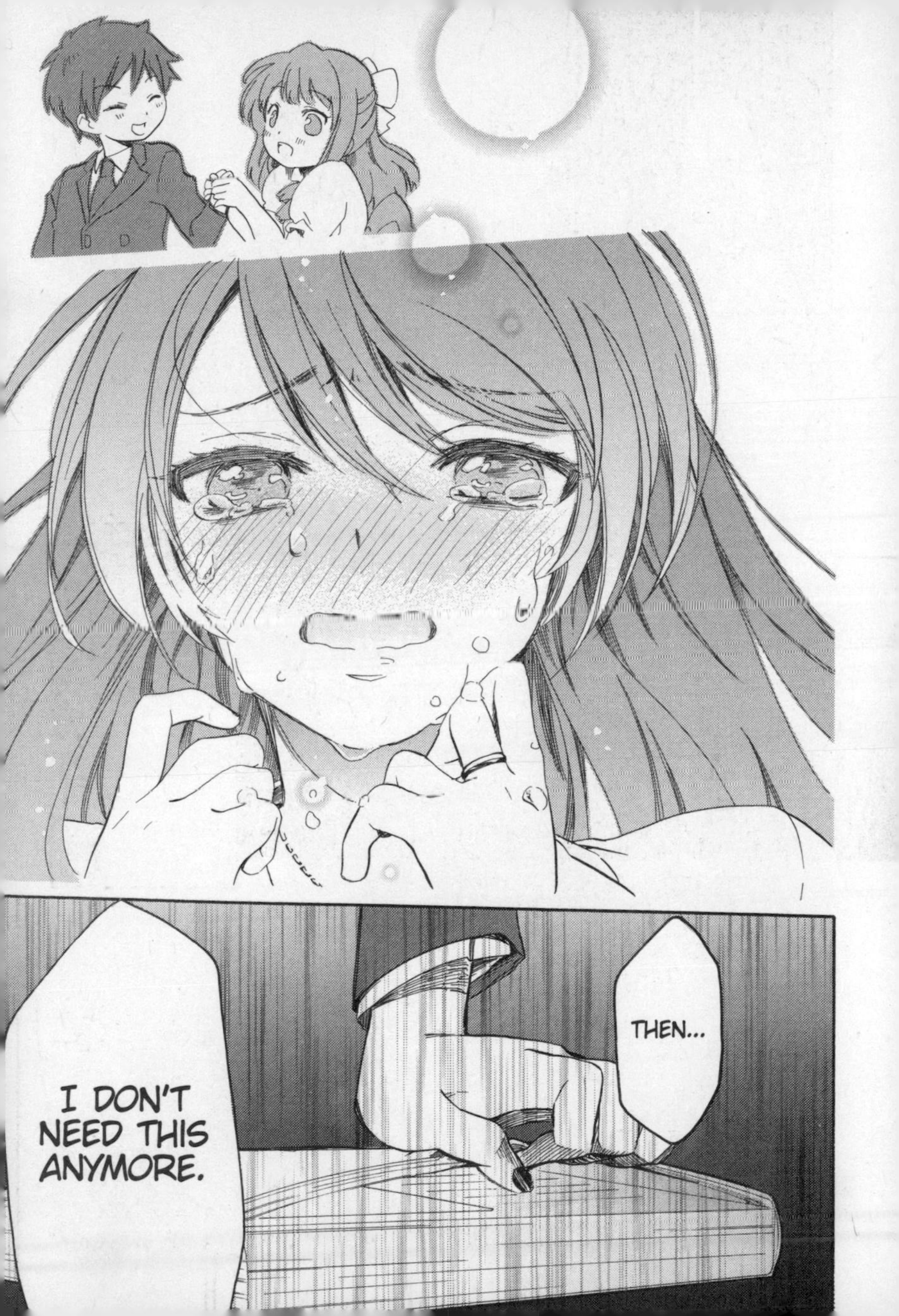
THEN...
I DON'T NEED THIS ANYMORE.

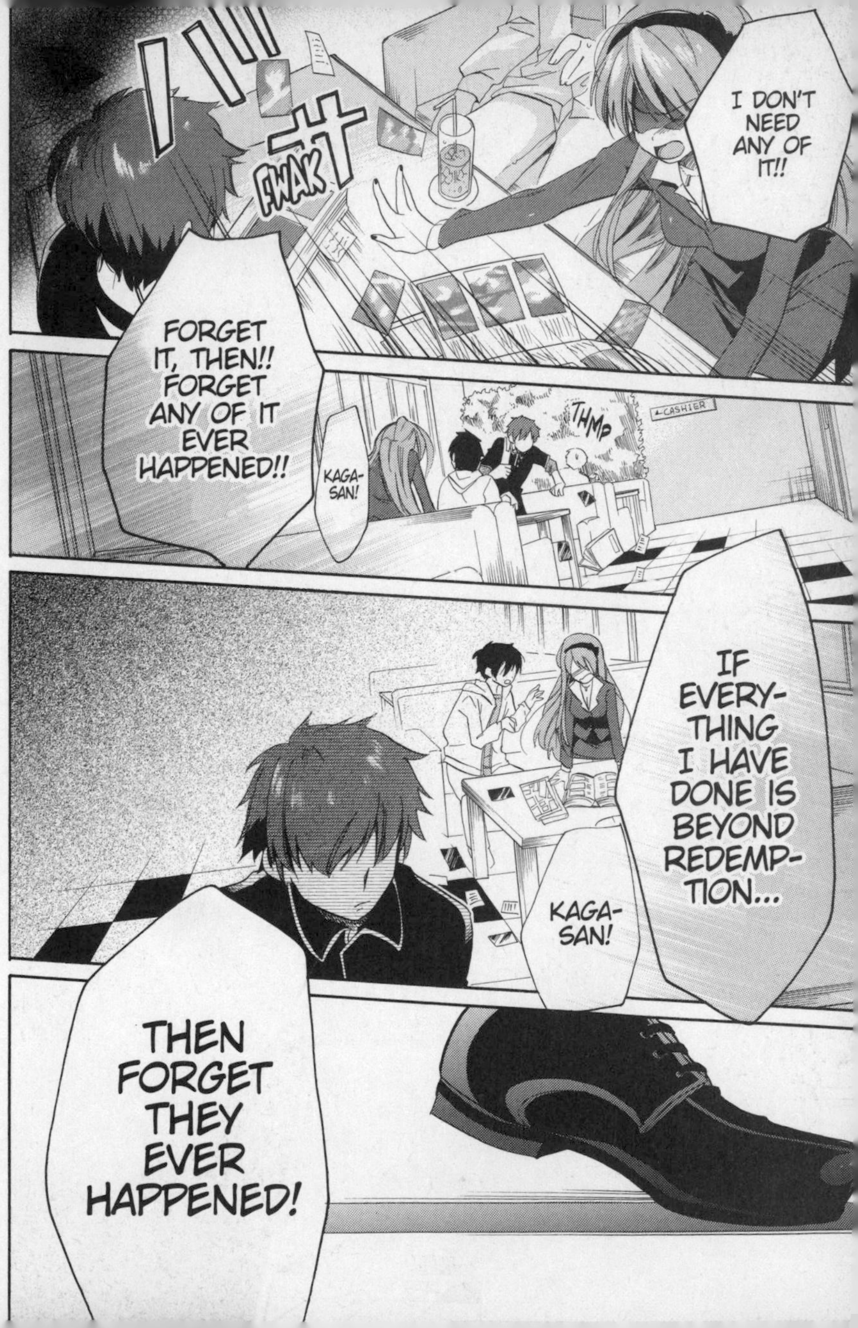
I DON'T NEED ANY OF IT!!
FWAK
FORGET IT, THEN!! FORGET ANY OF IT EVER HAPPENED!!
←CASHIER
THMP
KAGA-SAN!
IF EVERY-THING I HAVE DONE IS BEYOND REDEMP-TION...
KAGA-SAN!
THEN FORGET THEY EVER HAPPENED!

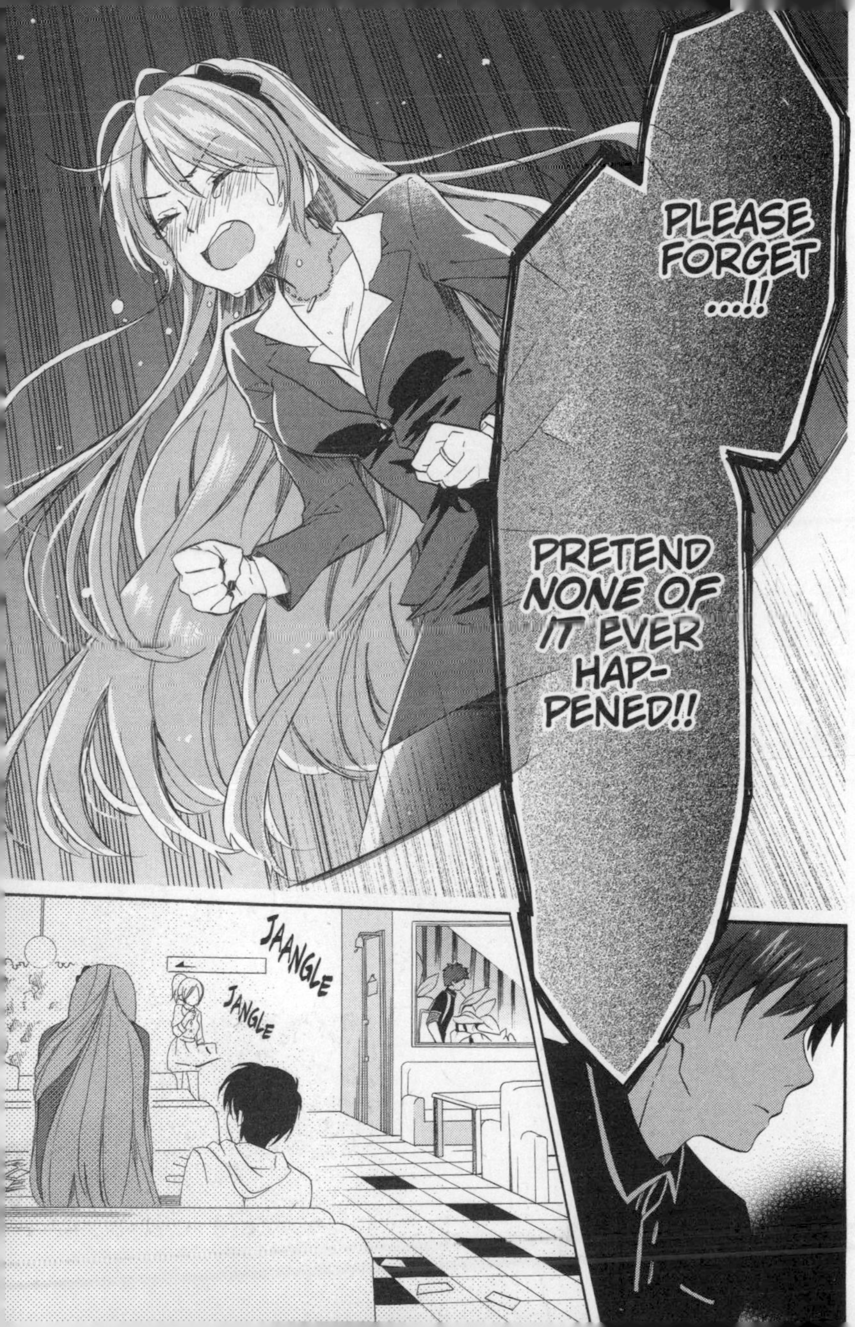
PLEASE FORGET ...!!
PRETEND NONE OF IT EVER HAP-PENED!!
JAANGLE
JANGLE

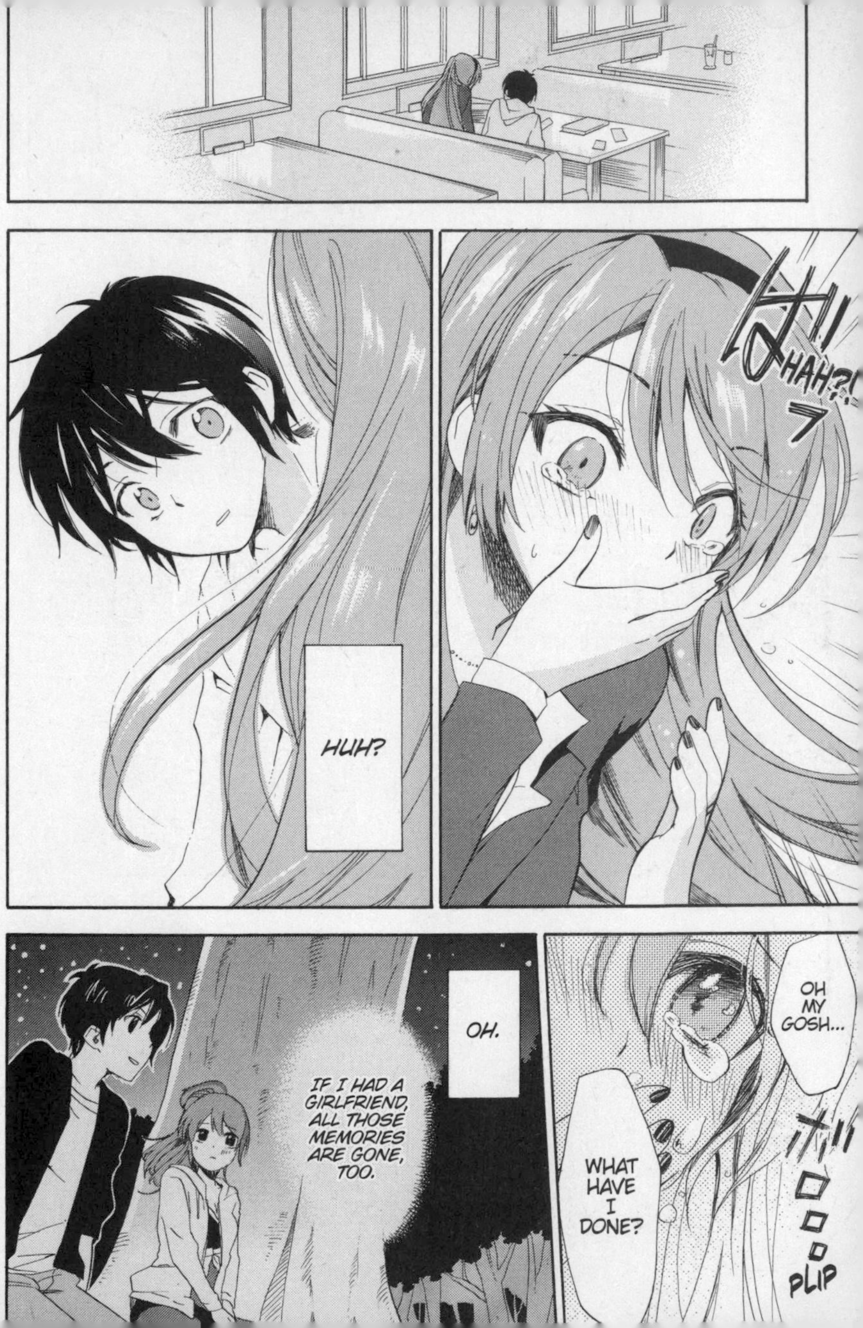
HAH?!
HUH?
OH MY GOSH...
WHAT HAVE I DONE?
PLIP
OH.
IF I HAD A GIRLFRIEND, ALL THOSE MEMORIES ARE GONE, TOO.

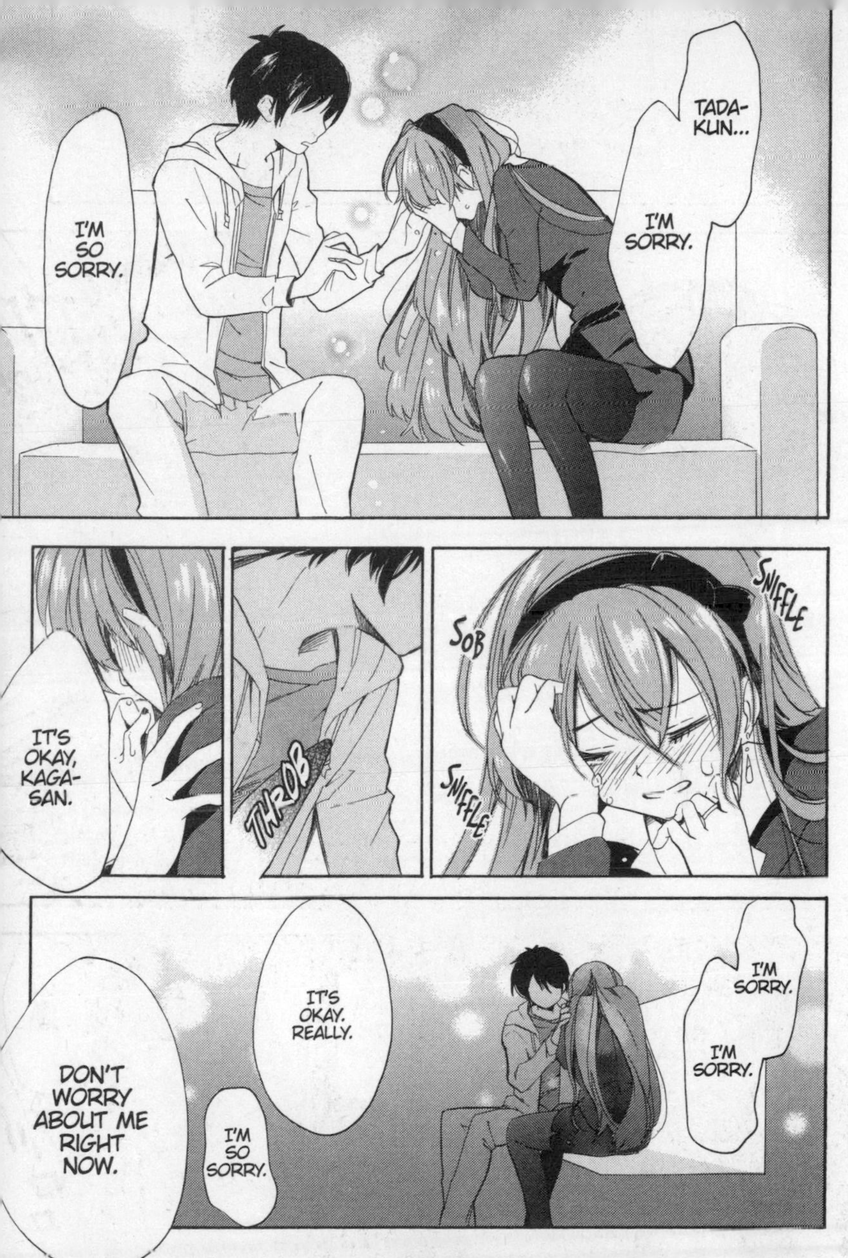
TADA-KUN... I'M SORRY.
I'M SO SORRY.
SNIFFLE
SOB
SNIFFLE
THROB
IT'S OKAY, KAGA-SAN.
I'M SORRY.
I'M SORRY.
IT'S OKAY. REALLY.
DON'T WORRY ABOUT ME RIGHT NOW.
I'M SO SORRY.

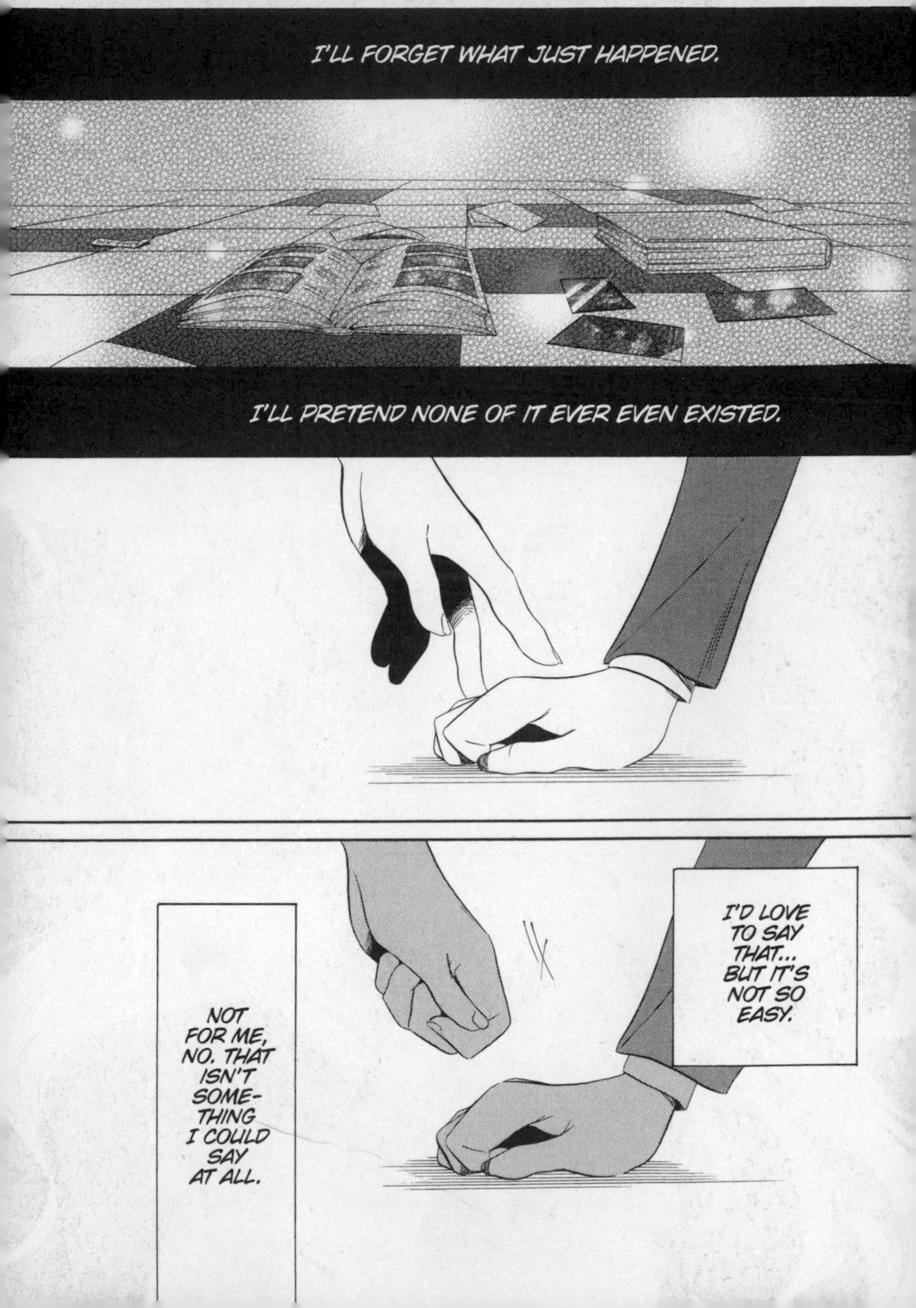
I'LL FORGET WHAT JUST HAPPENED.
I'LL PRETEND NONE OF IT EVER EVEN EXISTED.
I'D LOVE TO SAY THAT... BUT IT'S NOT SO EASY.
NOT FOR ME, NO. THAT ISN'T SOME-THING I COULD SAY AT ALL.

CHAPTER 10: Kill Me

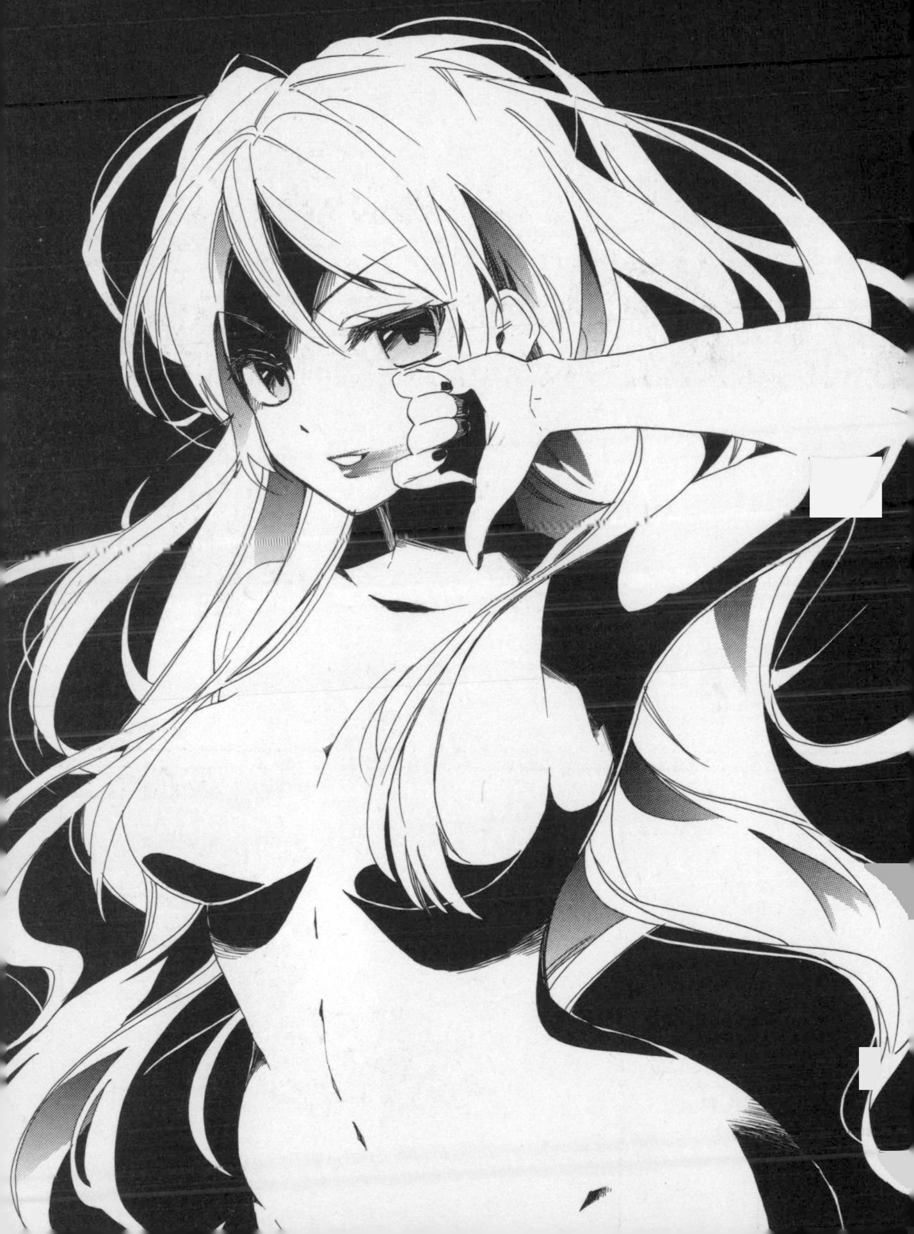

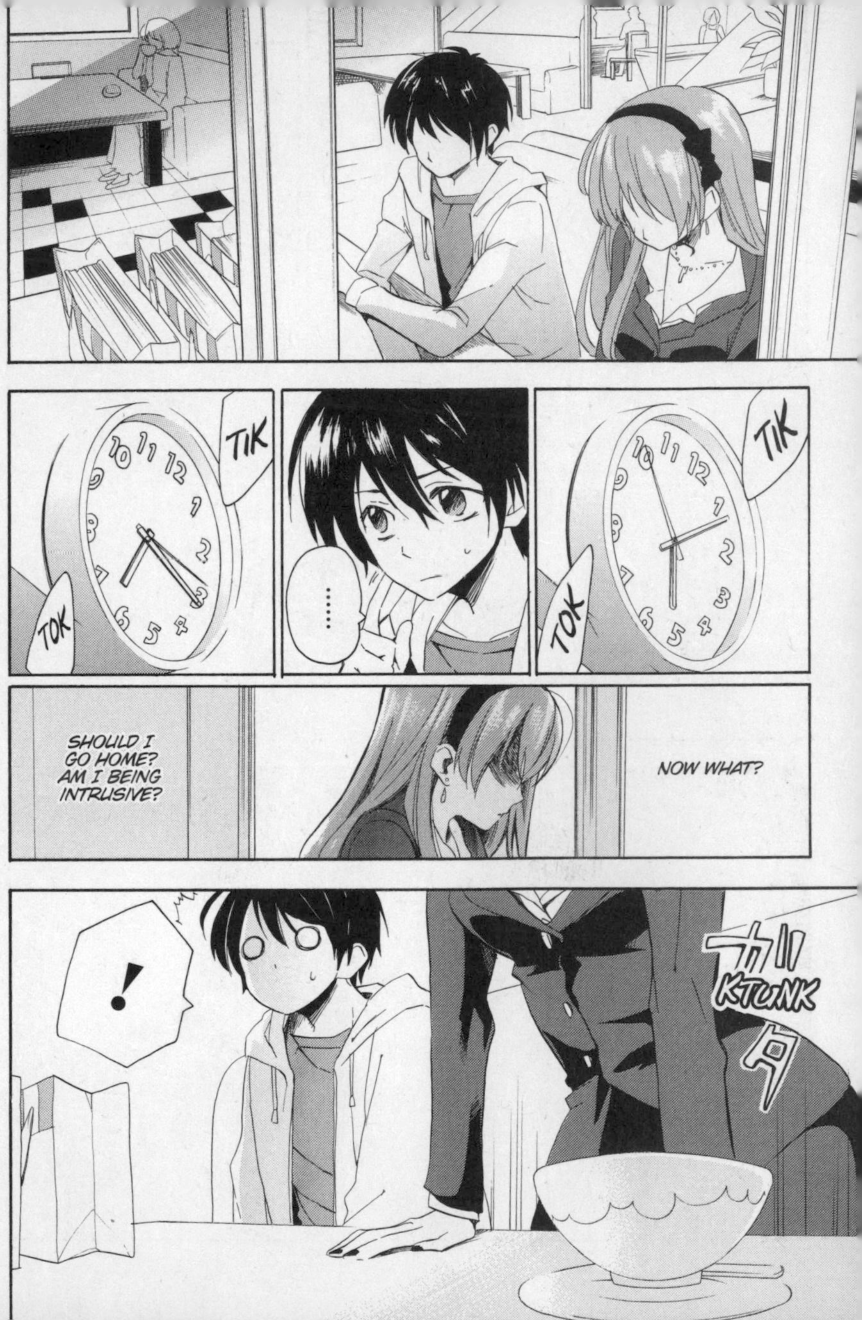
TIK
TOK
......
TIK
TOK
NOW WHAT?
SHOULD I GO HOME? AM I BEING INTRUSIVE?
KTUNK
!

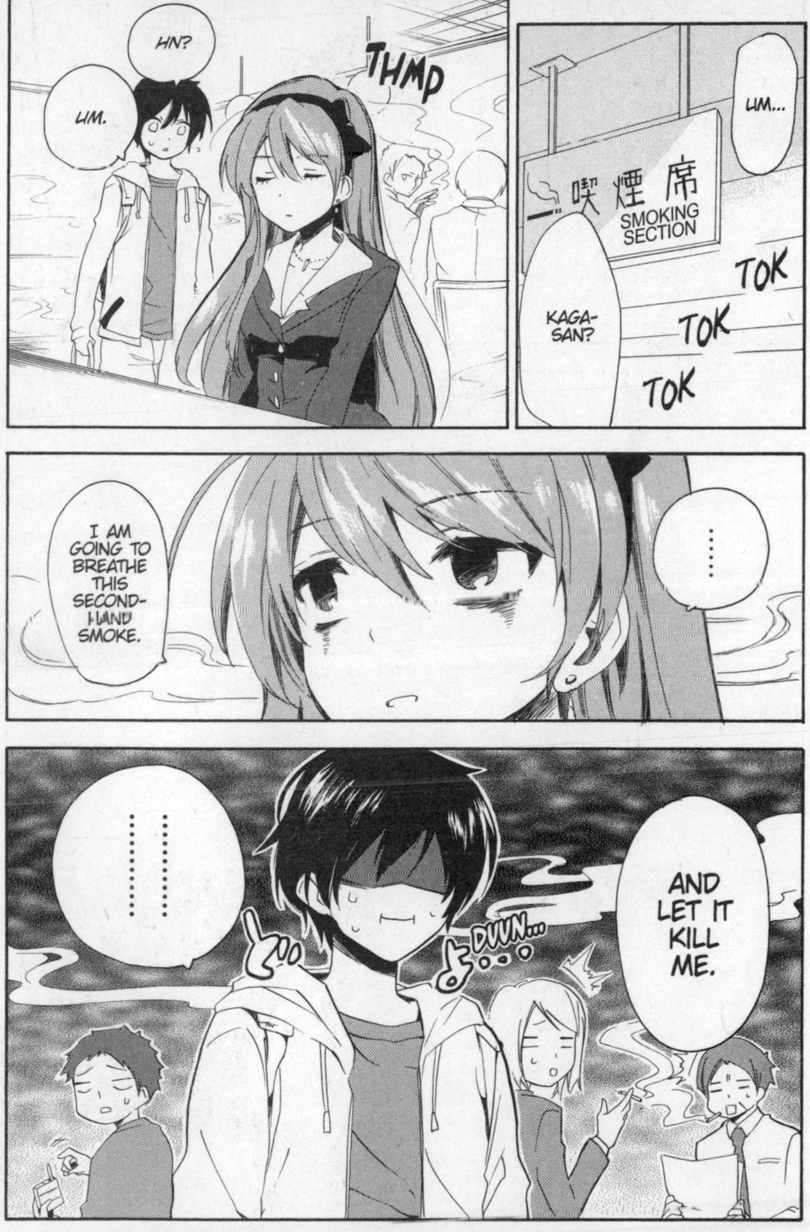
UM...
喫煙席
SMOKING SECTION
KAGA-SAN?
TOK
TOK
TOK
THMP
HN?
UM.
......
I AM GOING TO BREATHE THIS SECOND-HAND SMOKE.
AND LET IT KILL ME.
DUUN...
......

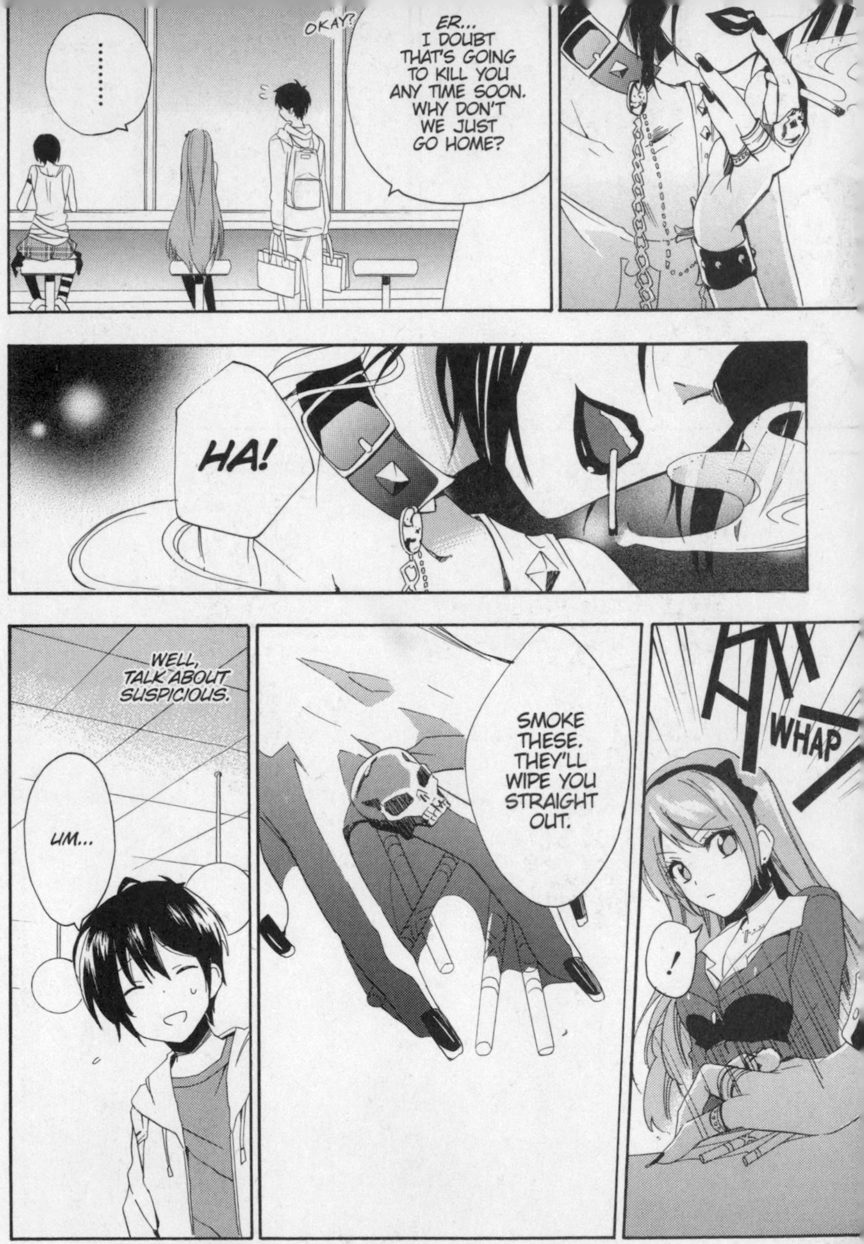
ER... I DOUBT THAT'S GOING TO KILL YOU ANY TIME SOON. WHY DON'T WE JUST GO HOME?
OKAY?
......
HA!
WHAP
!
SMOKE THESE. THEY'LL WIPE YOU STRAIGHT OUT.
WELL, TALK ABOUT SUSPICIOUS.
UM...

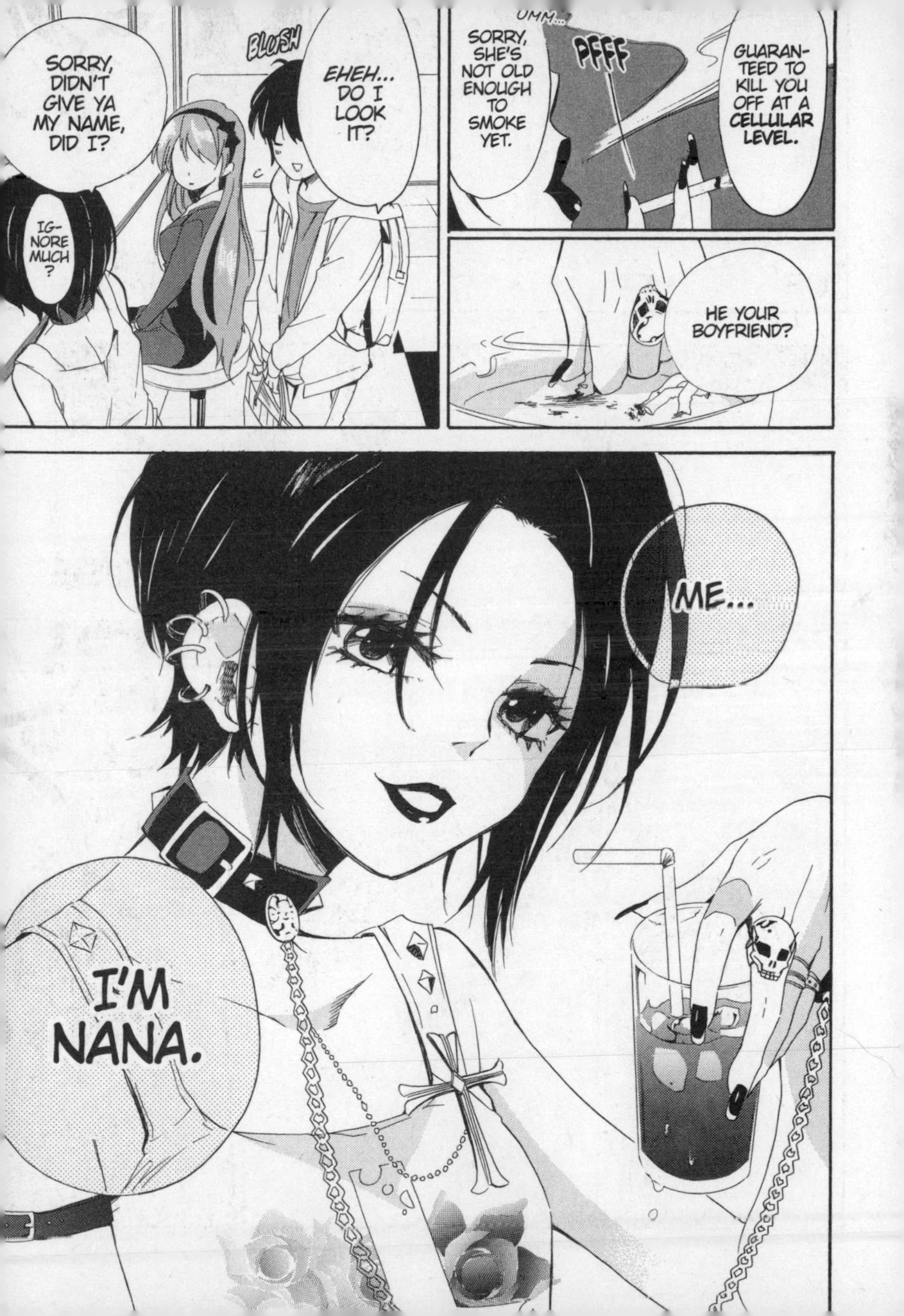
GUARAN-TEED TO KILL YOU OFF AT A CELLULAR LEVEL.
PFFF
UMM...?
SORRY, SHE'S NOT OLD ENOUGH TO SMOKE YET.
HE YOUR BOYFRIEND?
EHEH... DO I LOOK IT?
BLUSH
SORRY, DIDN'T GIVE YA MY NAME, DID I?
IG-NORE MUCH?
ME...
I'M NANA.

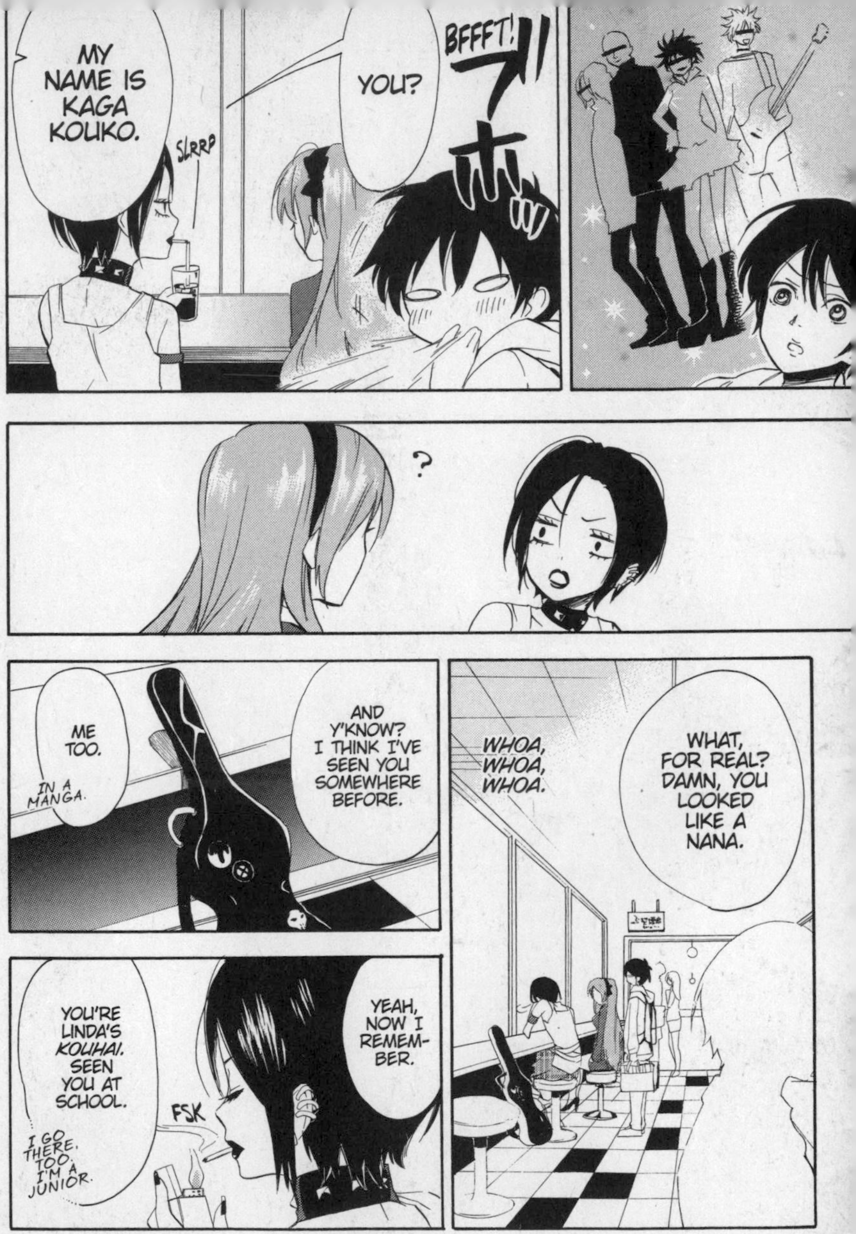
BFFFT!
YOU?
MY NAME IS KAGA KOUKO.
SLRRP
?
WHAT, FOR REAL? DAMN, YOU LOOKED LIKE A NANA.
WHOA, WHOA, WHOA.
AND Y'KNOW? I THINK I'VE SEEN YOU SOMEWHERE BEFORE.
ME TOO.
IN A MANGA.
YEAH, NOW I REMEM-BER.
YOU'RE LINDA'S KOUHAI. SEEN YOU AT SCHOOL.
FSK
I GO THERE, TOO. I'M A JUNIOR.

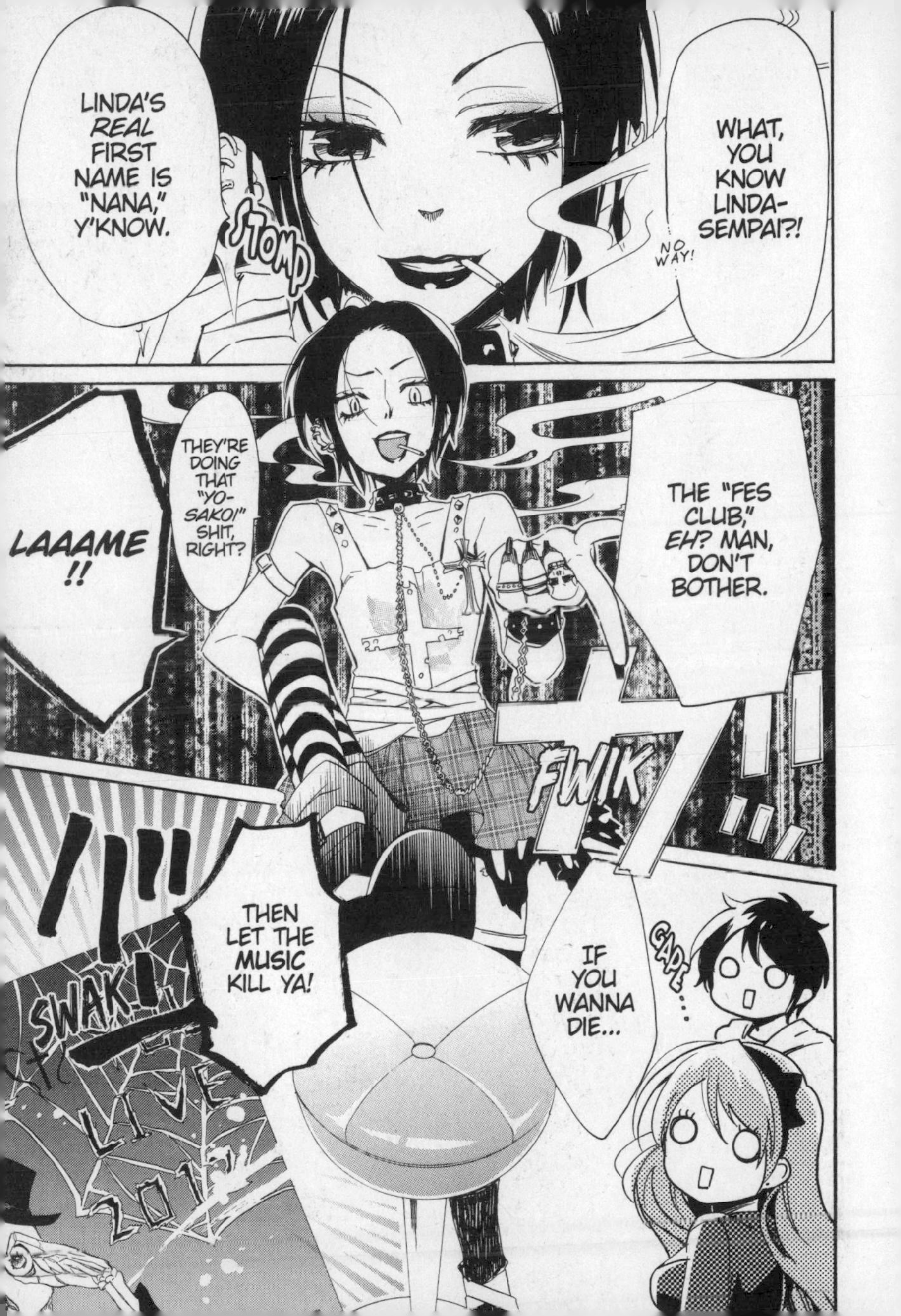
WHAT, YOU KNOW LINDA-SEMPAI?!
NO WAY!
LINDA'S *REAL* FIRST NAME IS "NANA," Y'KNOW.
STOMP
THE "FES CLUB," *EH?* MAN, DON'T BOTHER.
THEY'RE DOING THAT "YO-SAKOI" SHIT, RIGHT?
LAAAME!!
FWIK
IF YOU WANNA DIE...
GAPE...
THEN LET THE MUSIC KILL YA!
SWAK
LIVE

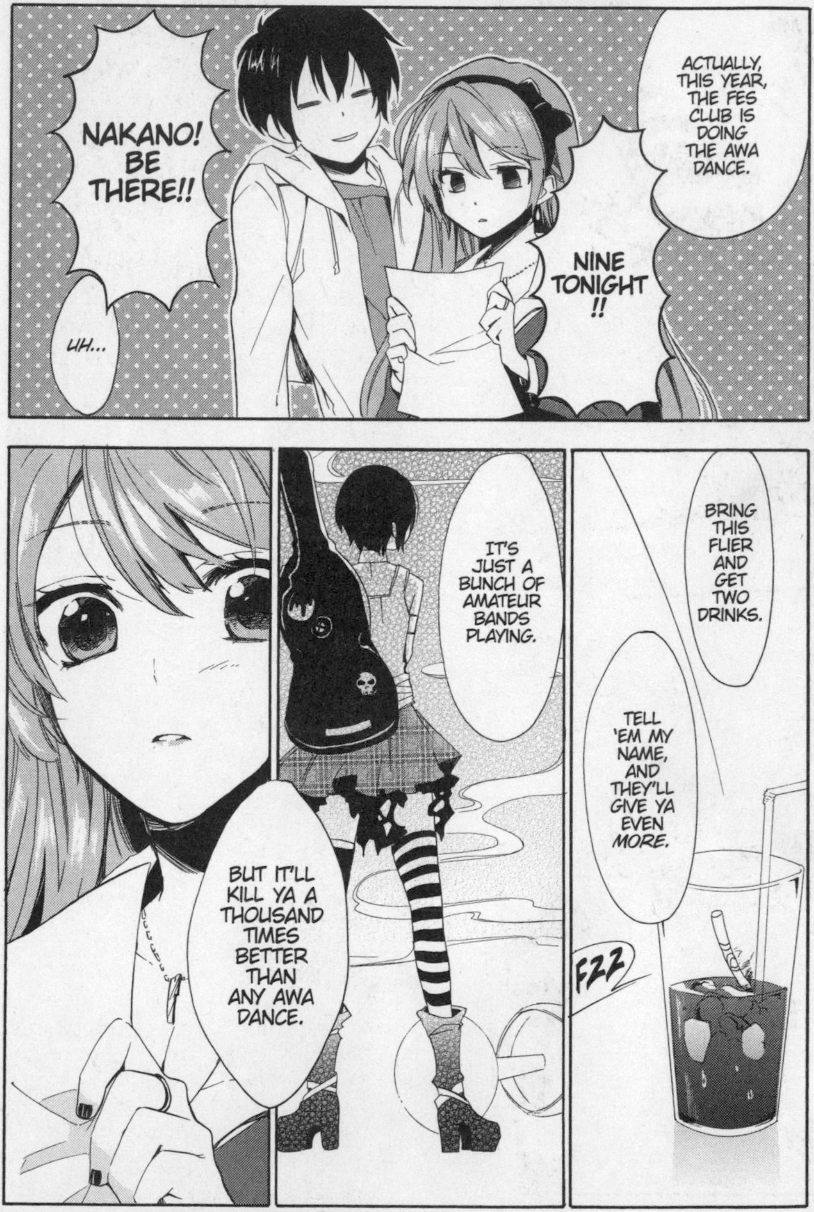
ACTUALLY, THIS YEAR, THE FES CLUB IS DOING THE AWA DANCE.
NINE TONIGHT!!
NAKANO! BE THERE!!
UH...
BRING THIS FLIER AND GET TWO DRINKS.
TELL 'EM MY NAME, AND THEY'LL GIVE YA EVEN MORE.
FZZ
IT'S JUST A BUNCH OF AMATEUR BANDS PLAYING.
BUT IT'LL KILL YA A THOUSAND TIMES BETTER THAN ANY AWA DANCE.

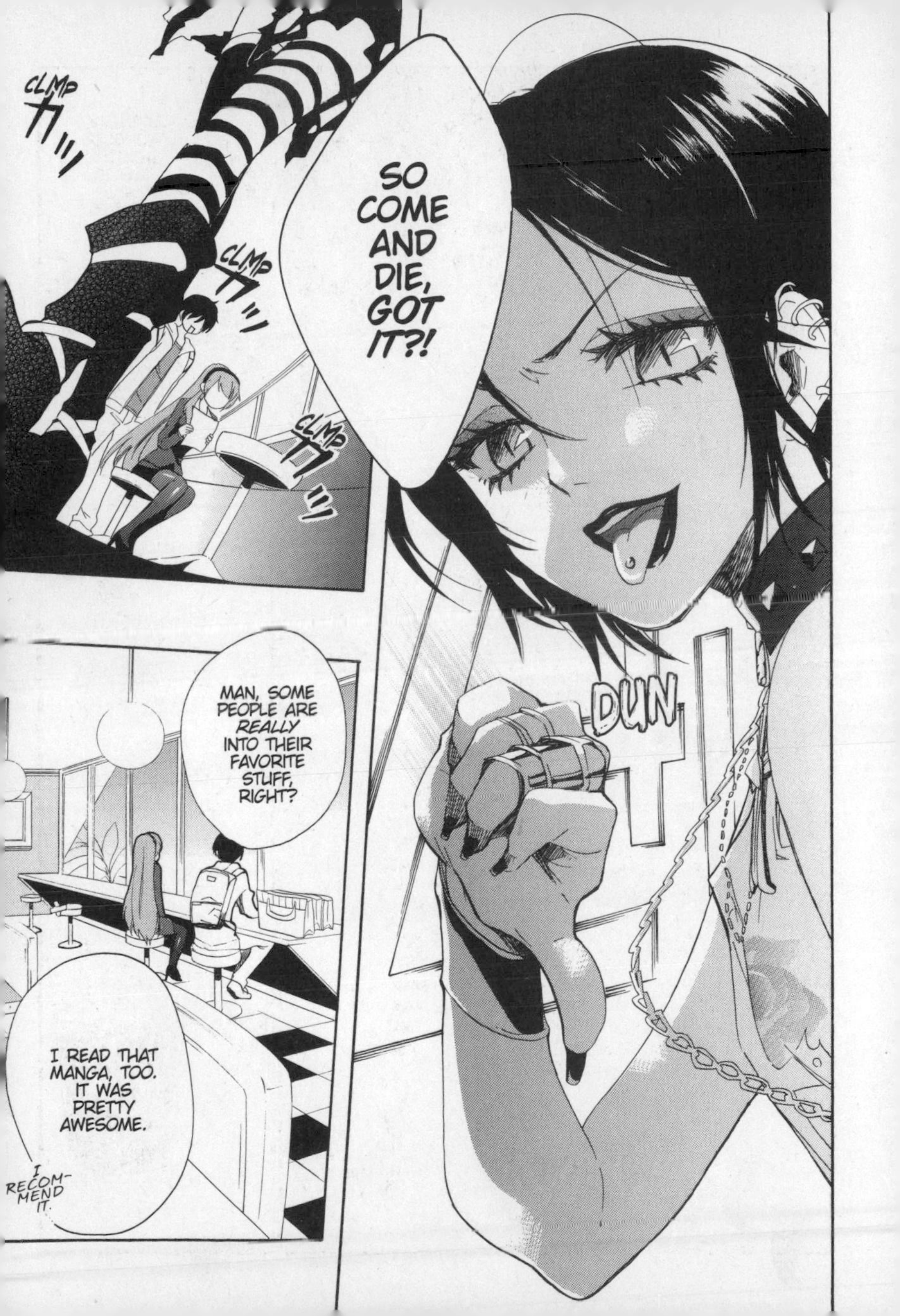
SO COME AND DIE, GOT IT?!
DUN
CLMP
CLMP
CLMP
MAN, SOME PEOPLE ARE *REALLY* INTO THEIR FAVORITE STUFF, RIGHT?
I READ THAT MANGA, TOO. IT WAS PRETTY AWESOME.
I RECOM-MEND IT.

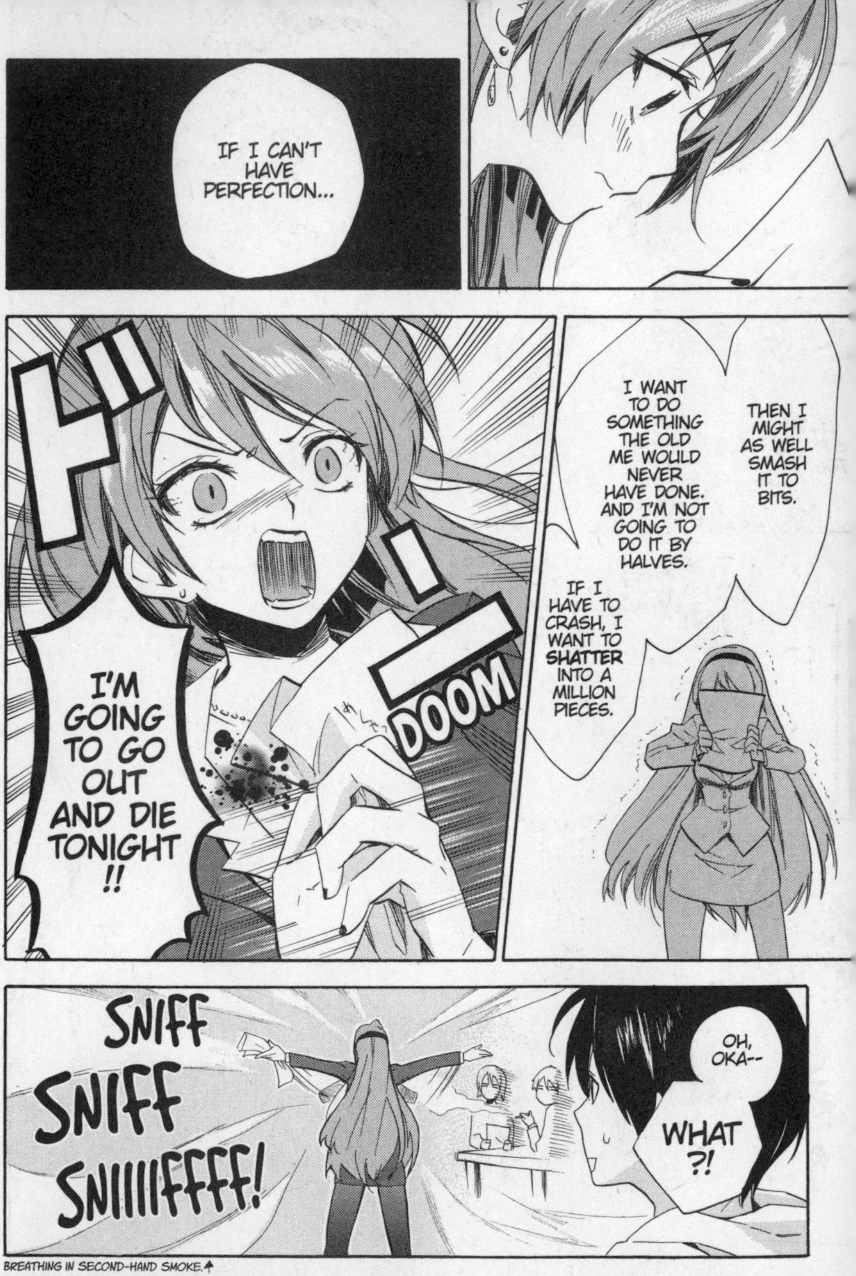
IF I CAN'T HAVE PERFECTION...
THEN I MIGHT AS WELL SMASH IT TO BITS.
I WANT TO DO SOMETHING THE OLD ME WOULD NEVER HAVE DONE. AND I'M NOT GOING TO DO IT BY HALVES.
IF I HAVE TO CRASH, I WANT TO **SHATTER** INTO A MILLION PIECES.
DOOM
I'M GOING TO GO OUT AND DIE TONIGHT!!
OH, OKA--
WHAT?!
SNIFF
SNIFF
SNIIIIFFFF!
BREATHING IN SECOND-HAND SMOKE.↑

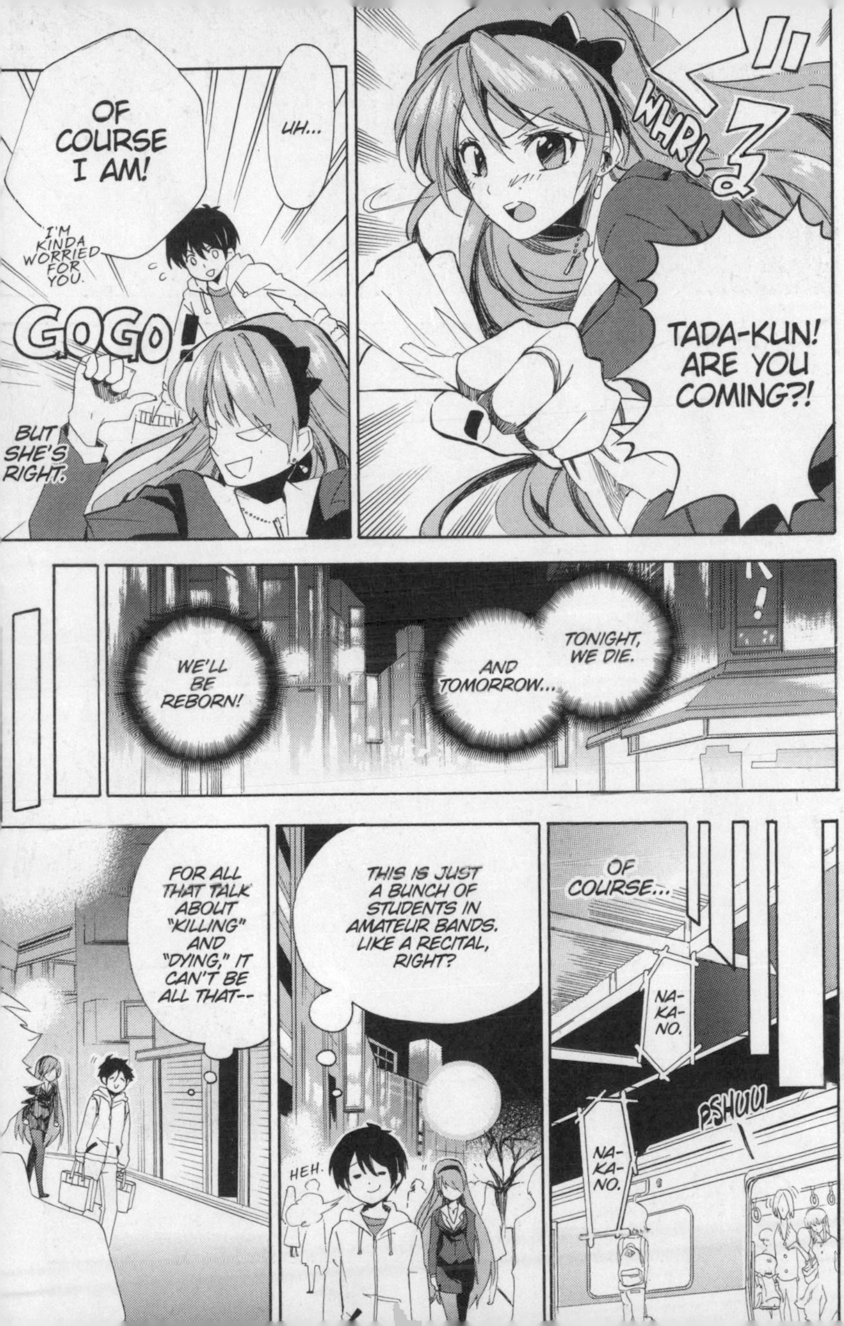
WHRL
TADA-KUN! ARE YOU COMING?!
UH...
OF COURSE I AM!
I'M KINDA WORRIED FOR YOU.
GOGO
BUT SHE'S RIGHT.
TONIGHT, WE DIE.
AND TOMORROW...
WE'LL BE REBORN!
OF COURSE...
NA-KA-NO.
PSHUU
NA-KA-NO.
THIS IS JUST A BUNCH OF STUDENTS IN AMATEUR BANDS. LIKE A RECITAL, RIGHT?
HEH.
FOR ALL THAT TALK ABOUT "KILLING" AND "DYING," IT CAN'T BE ALL THAT--

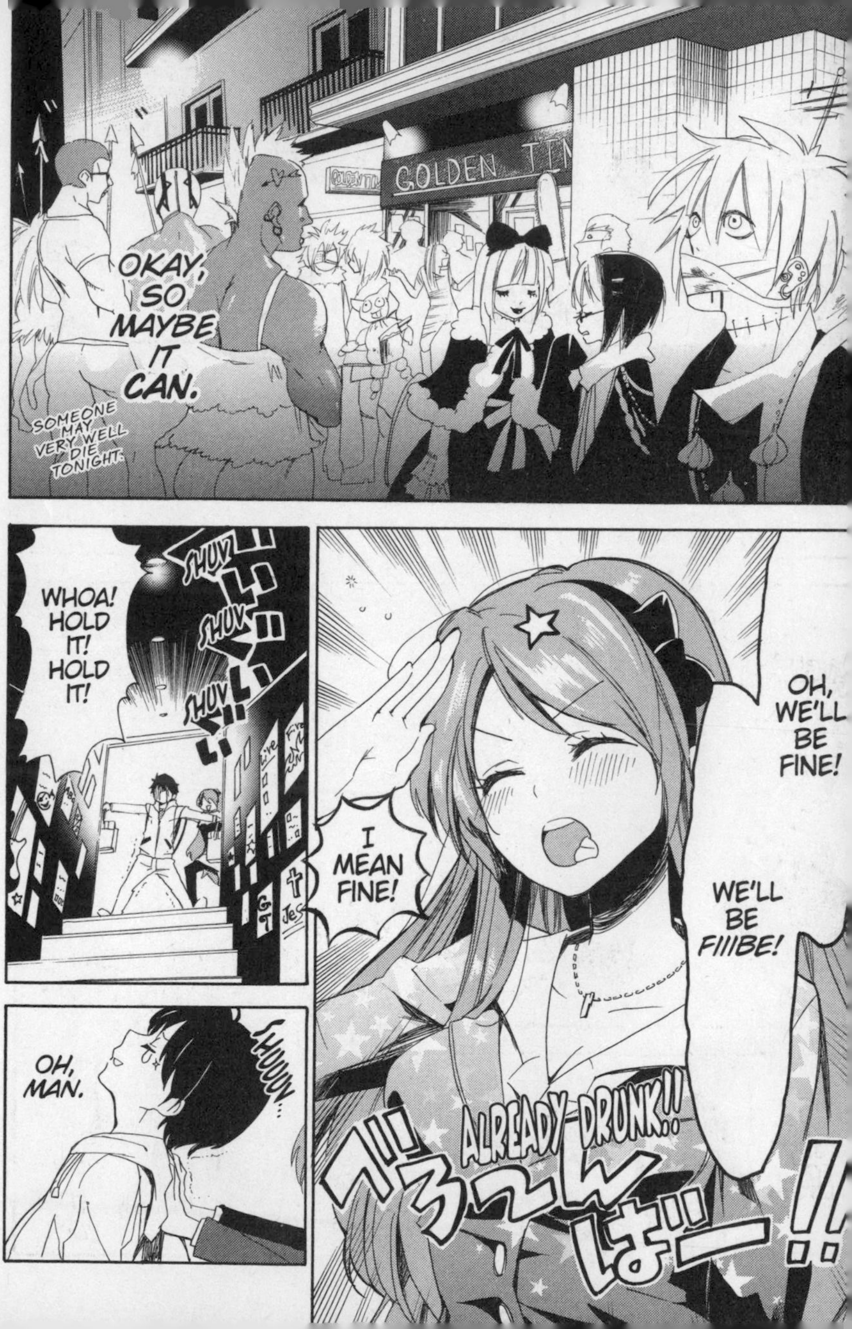
GOLDEN TIM
OKAY, SO MAYBE IT CAN.
SOMEONE MAY VERY WELL DIE TONIGHT.
OH, WE'LL BE FINE!
WE'LL BE FIIIBE!
I MEAN FINE!
ALREADY DRUNK!!
SHUV
SHUV
SHUV
WHOA! HOLD IT! HOLD IT!
OH, MAN.
SHUUUV...

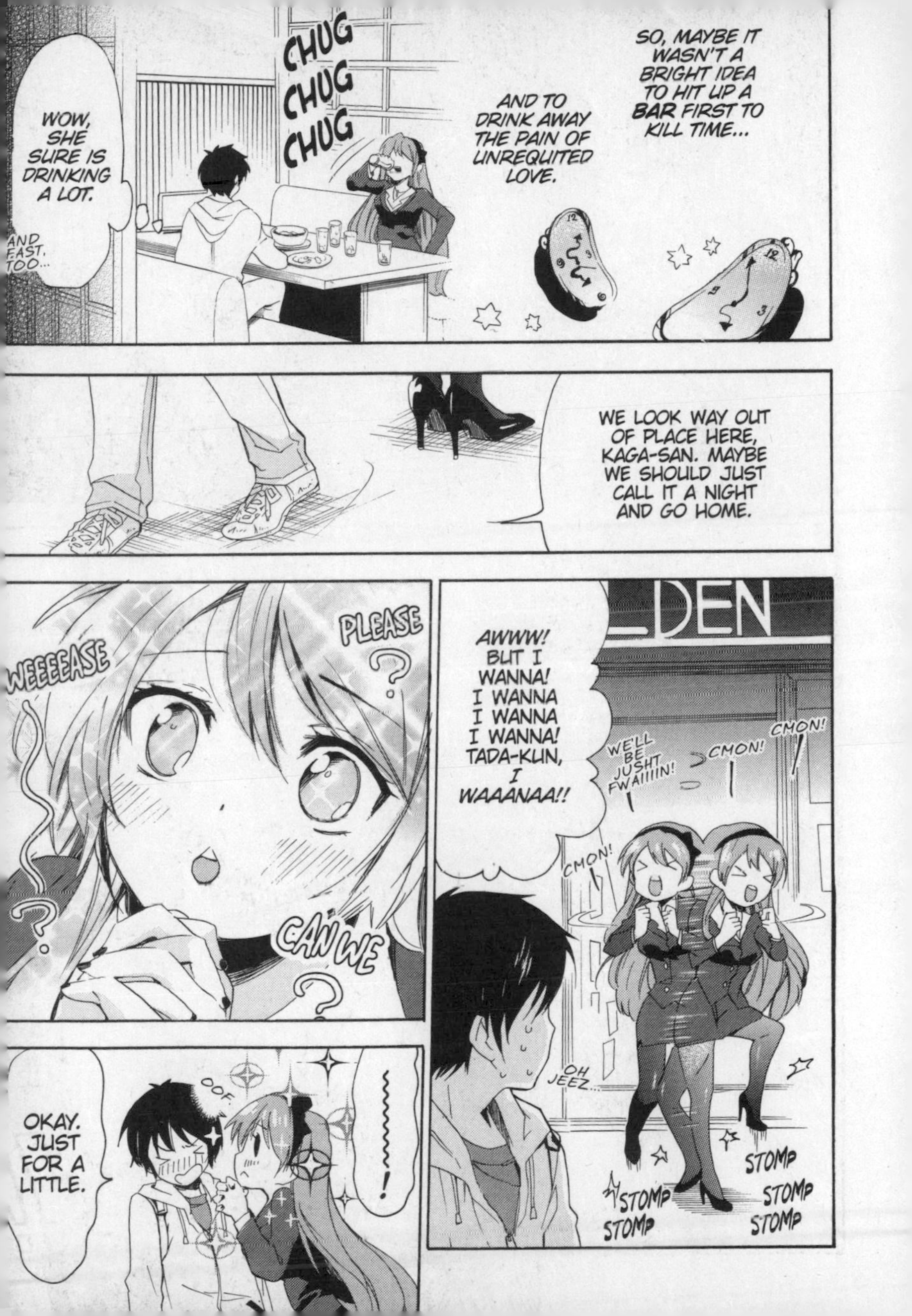
SO, MAYBE IT WASN'T A BRIGHT IDEA TO HIT UP A BAR FIRST TO KILL TIME...
AND TO DRINK AWAY THE PAIN OF UNREQUITED LOVE.
CHUG CHUG CHUG
WOW, SHE SURE IS DRINKING A LOT.
AND FAST, TOO...
WE LOOK WAY OUT OF PLACE HERE, KAGA-SAN. MAYBE WE SHOULD JUST CALL IT A NIGHT AND GO HOME.
EDEN
AWWW! BUT I WANNA! I WANNA I WANNA I WANNA! TADA-KUN, I WAAANAA!!
CMON!
CMON!
WE'LL BE JUSHT FWAIIIIN!
CMON!
OH JEEZ...
STOMP
STOMP
STOMP
STOMP
PLEASE
WEEEEASE
CAN WE
OKAY. JUST FOR A LITTLE.
OOF
~~~~!
~~~~

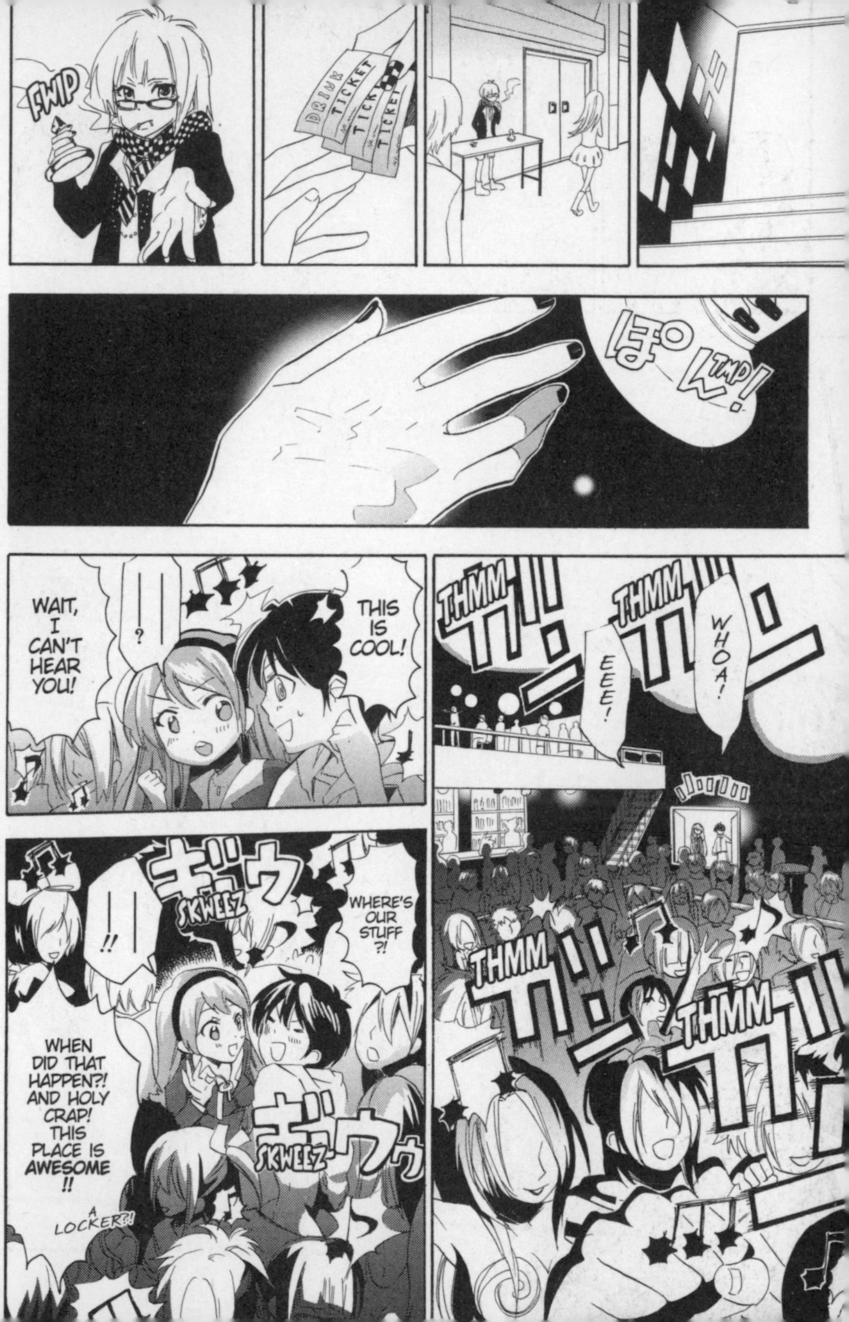
DRINK TICKET
TICKET
TICKET
FWIP
ぽん
TMP!
THMM
THMM
WHOA!
EEE!
THMM
THMM
THIS IS COOL!
?
WAIT, I CAN'T HEAR YOU!
WHERE'S OUR STUFF?!
SKWEEZ
!!
WHEN DID THAT HAPPEN?! AND HOLY CRAP! THIS PLACE IS AWESOME!!
SKWEEZ
A LOCKER?!

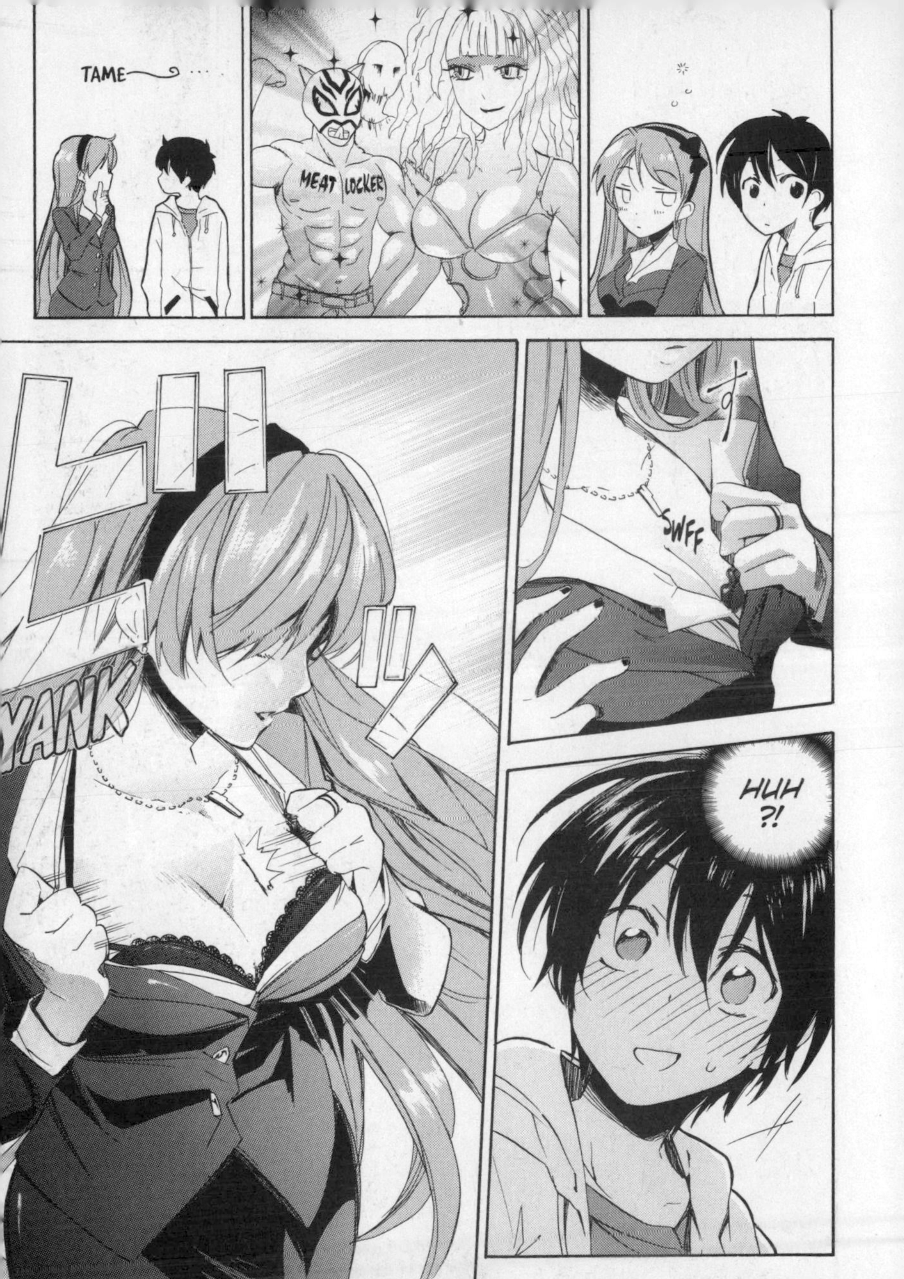
MEAT LOCKER
TAME~ ...
SWFF
HUH?!
YANK

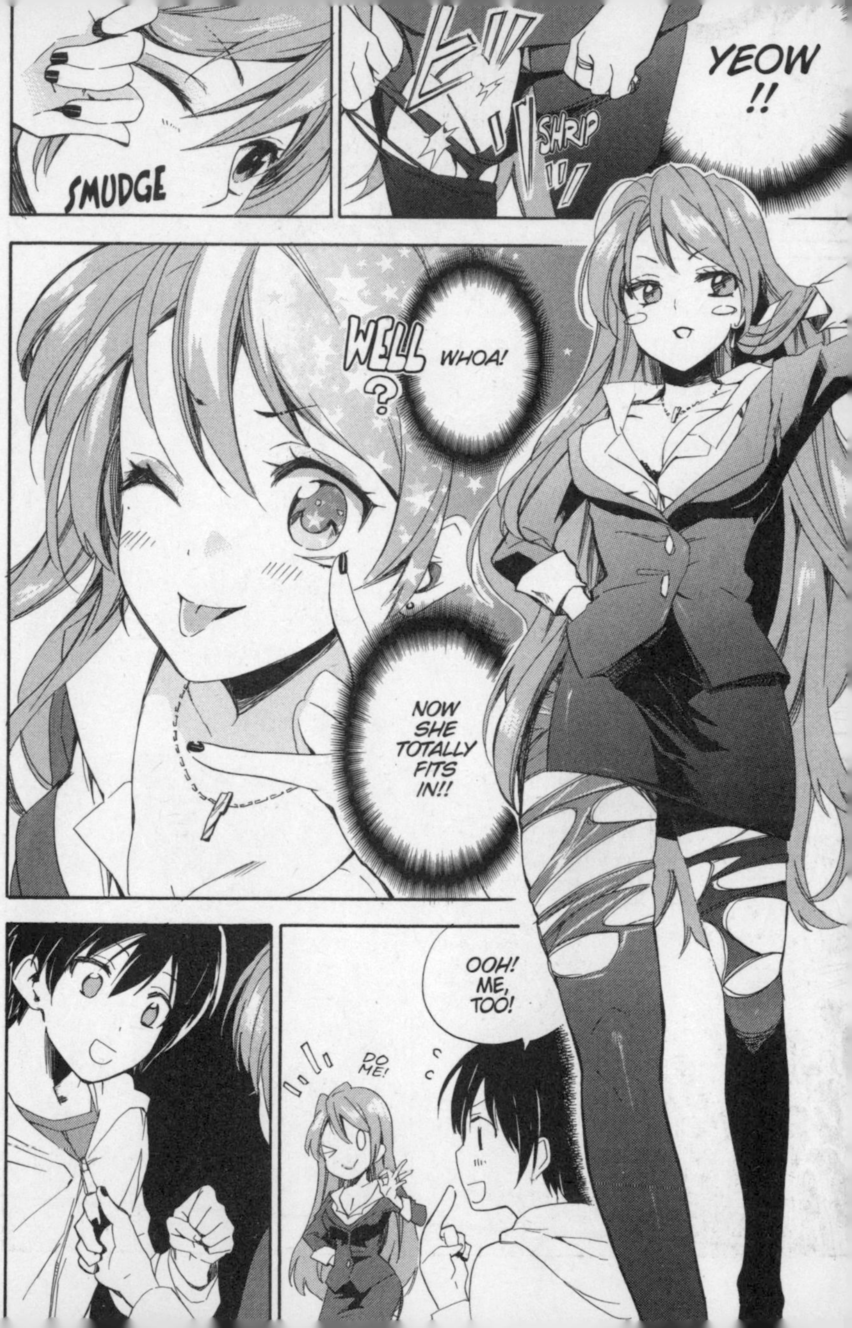
YEOW !!
SHRIP !!
SMUDGE
WELL ?
WHOA!
NOW SHE TOTALLY FITS IN!!
OOH! ME, TOO!
DO ME!

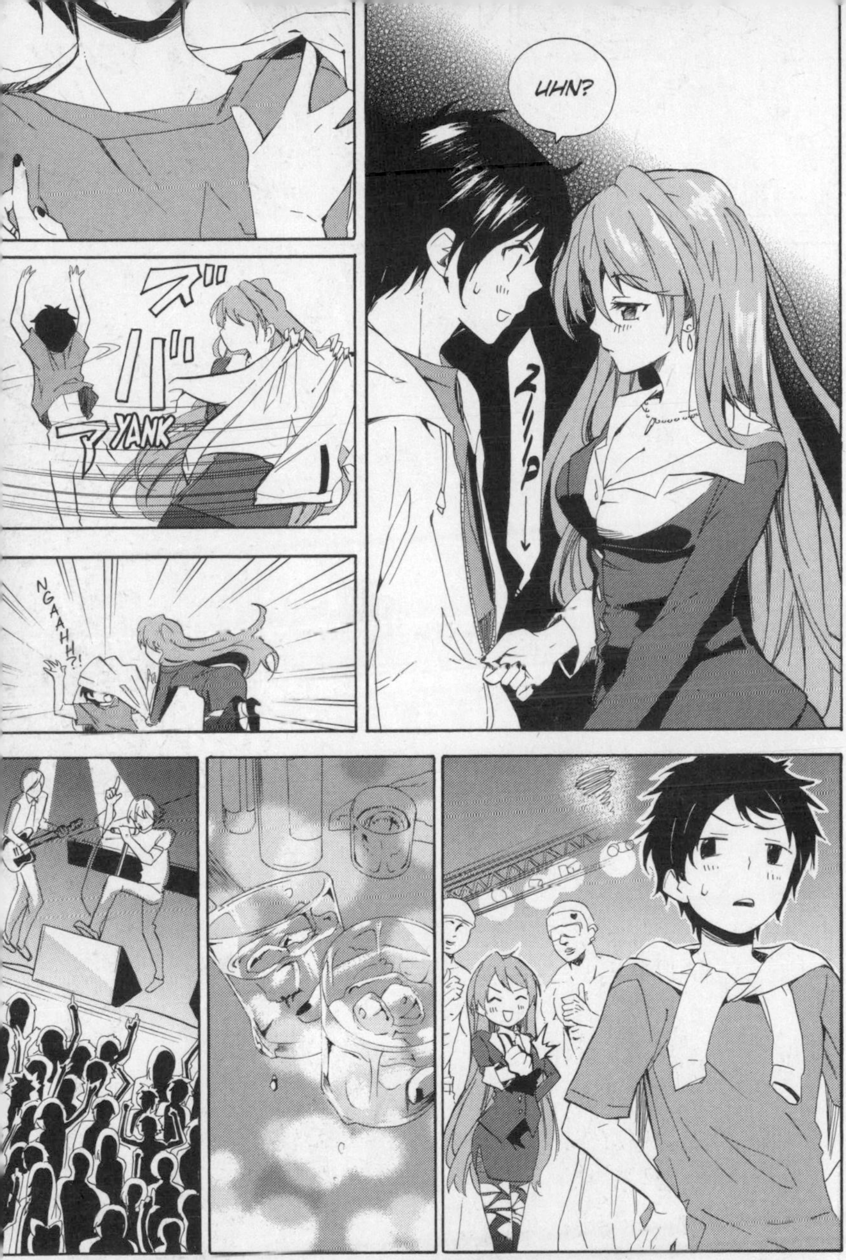
UHN?
ZIIIP
ズバア
YANK
NGAAHH?!

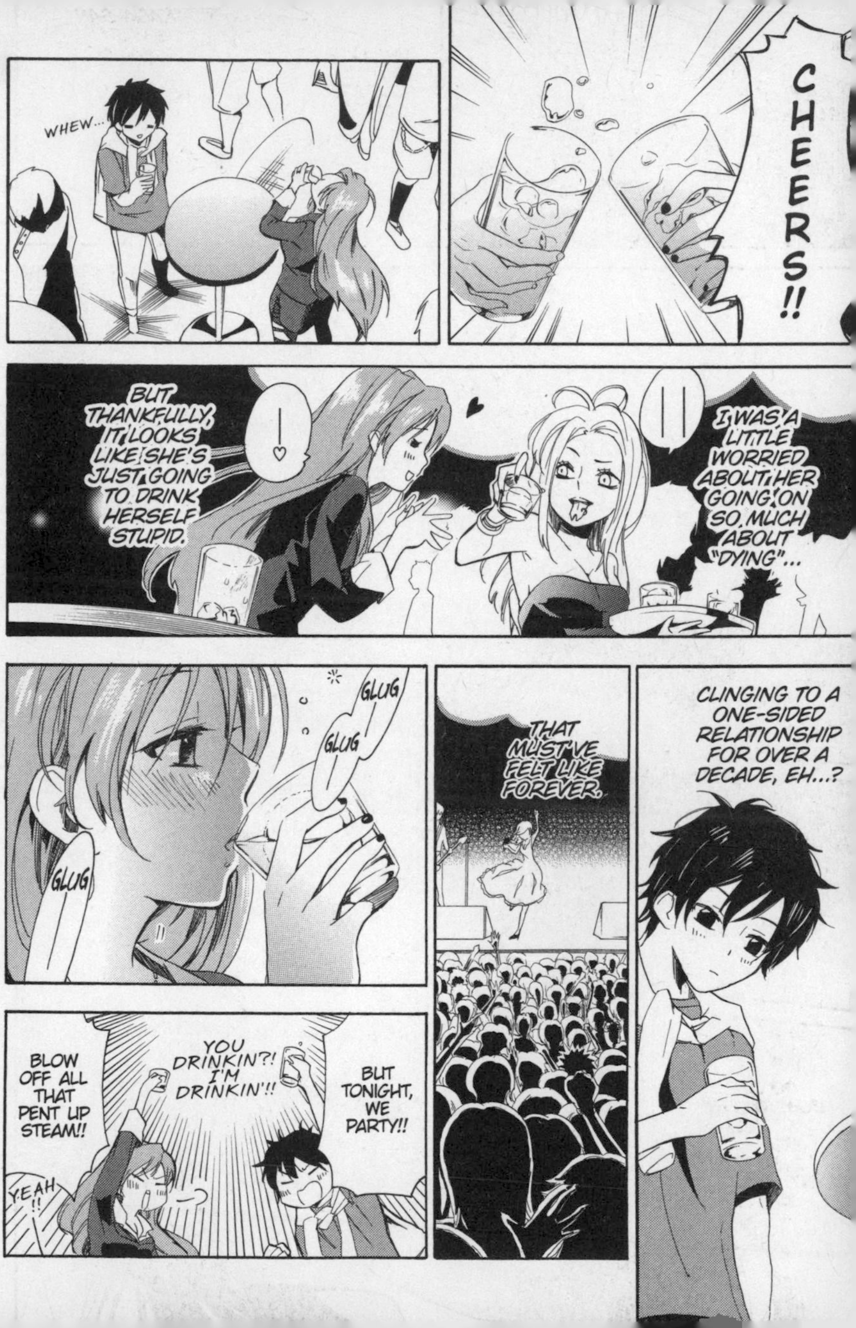

CHEERS!!
WHEW...
I WAS A LITTLE WORRIED ABOUT HER GOING ON SO MUCH ABOUT "DYING"...
!!
!♥
BUT THANKFULLY, IT LOOKS LIKE SHE'S JUST GOING TO DRINK HERSELF STUPID.
CLINGING TO A ONE-SIDED RELATIONSHIP FOR OVER A DECADE, EH...?
THAT MUST'VE FELT LIKE FOREVER.
GLUG
GLUG
GLUG
BUT TONIGHT, WE PARTY!!
YOU DRINKIN'?! I'M DRINKIN'!!
BLOW OFF ALL THAT PENT UP STEAM!!
YEAH!!

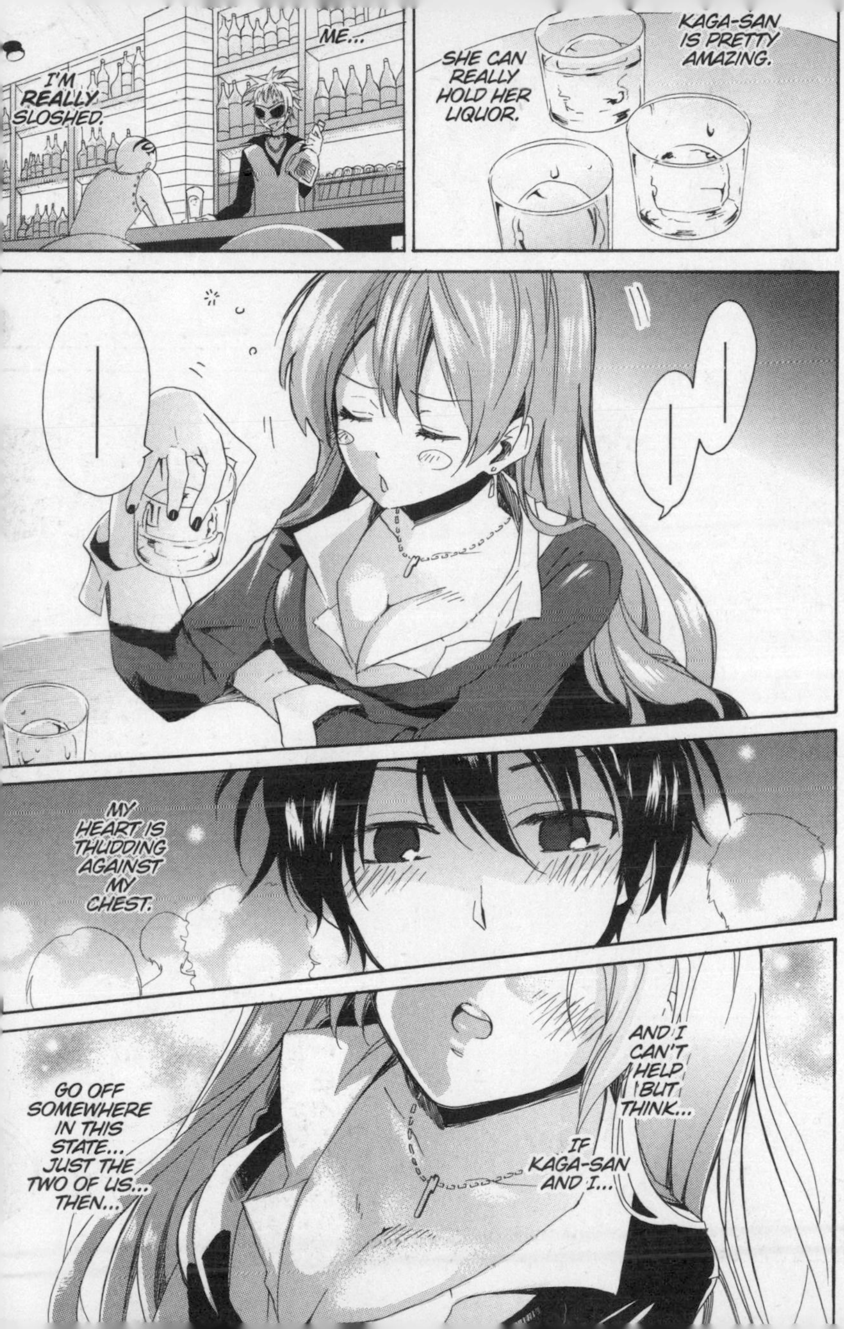
KAGA-SAN IS PRETTY AMAZING.
SHE CAN REALLY HOLD HER LIQUOR.
ME...
I'M REALLY SLOSHED.
MY HEART IS THUDDING AGAINST MY CHEST.
AND I CAN'T HELP BUT THINK...
IF KAGA-SAN AND I...
GO OFF SOMEWHERE IN THIS STATE... JUST THE TWO OF US... THEN...

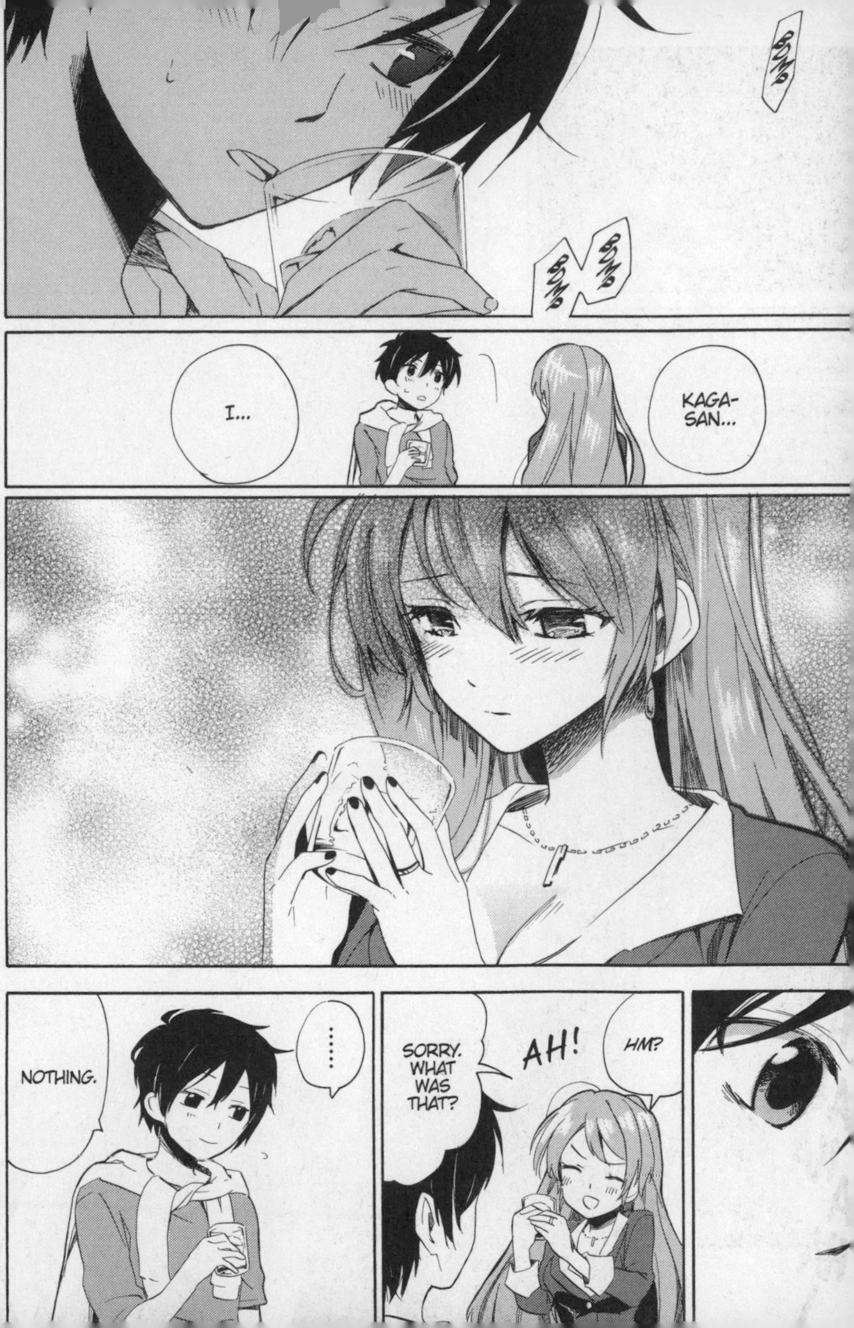
BDMP
BDMP
BDMP
KAGA-SAN...
I...
HM?
AH!
SORRY. WHAT WAS THAT?
......
NOTHING.

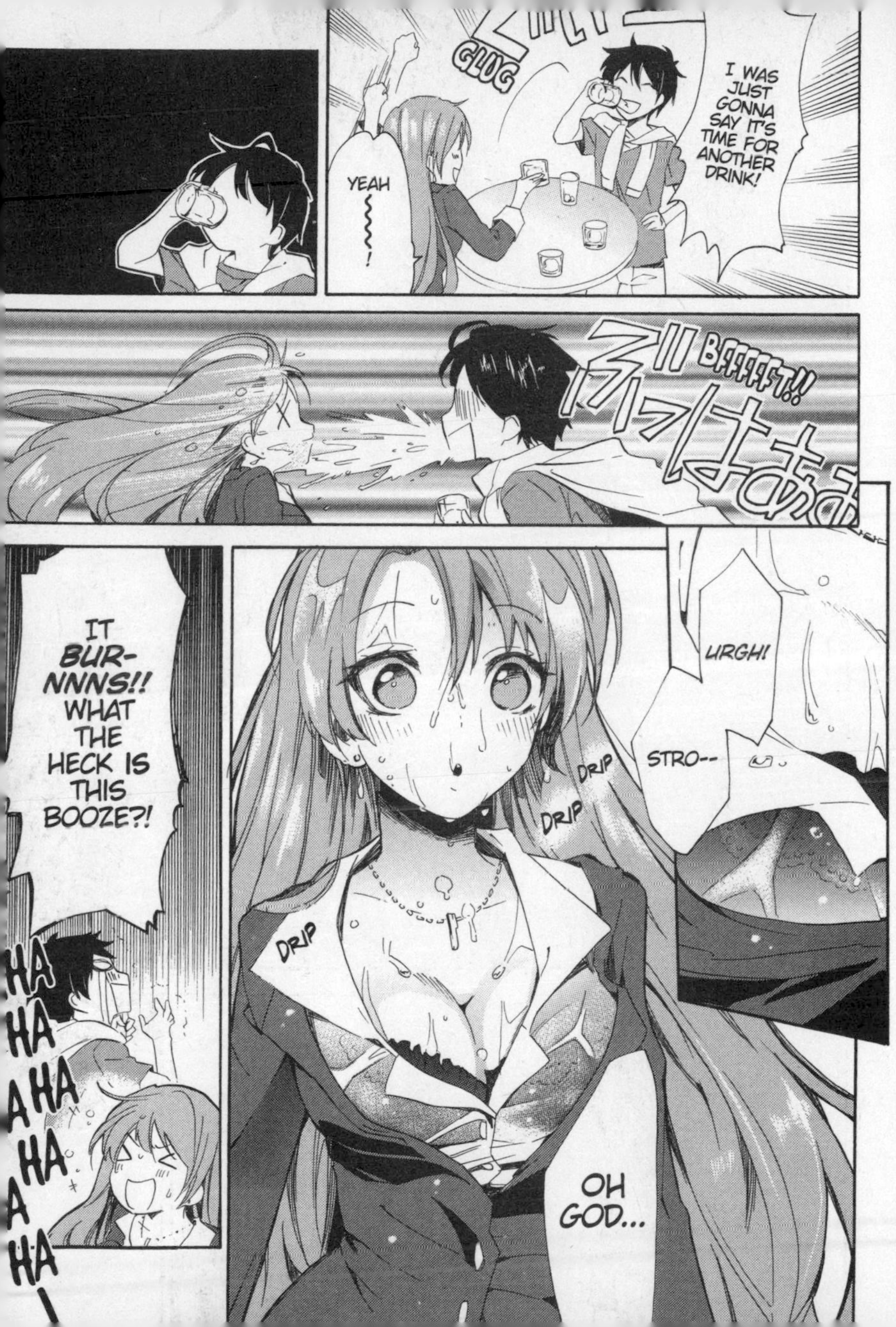
I WAS JUST GONNA SAY IT'S TIME FOR ANOTHER DRINK!
GLUG
YEAH~!
BFFFFFT!!
URGH!
STRO--
DRIP
DRIP
DRIP
OH GOD...
IT BURNNNS!! WHAT THE HECK IS THIS BOOZE?!
HA HA HA HA HA HA HA HA HA HA!

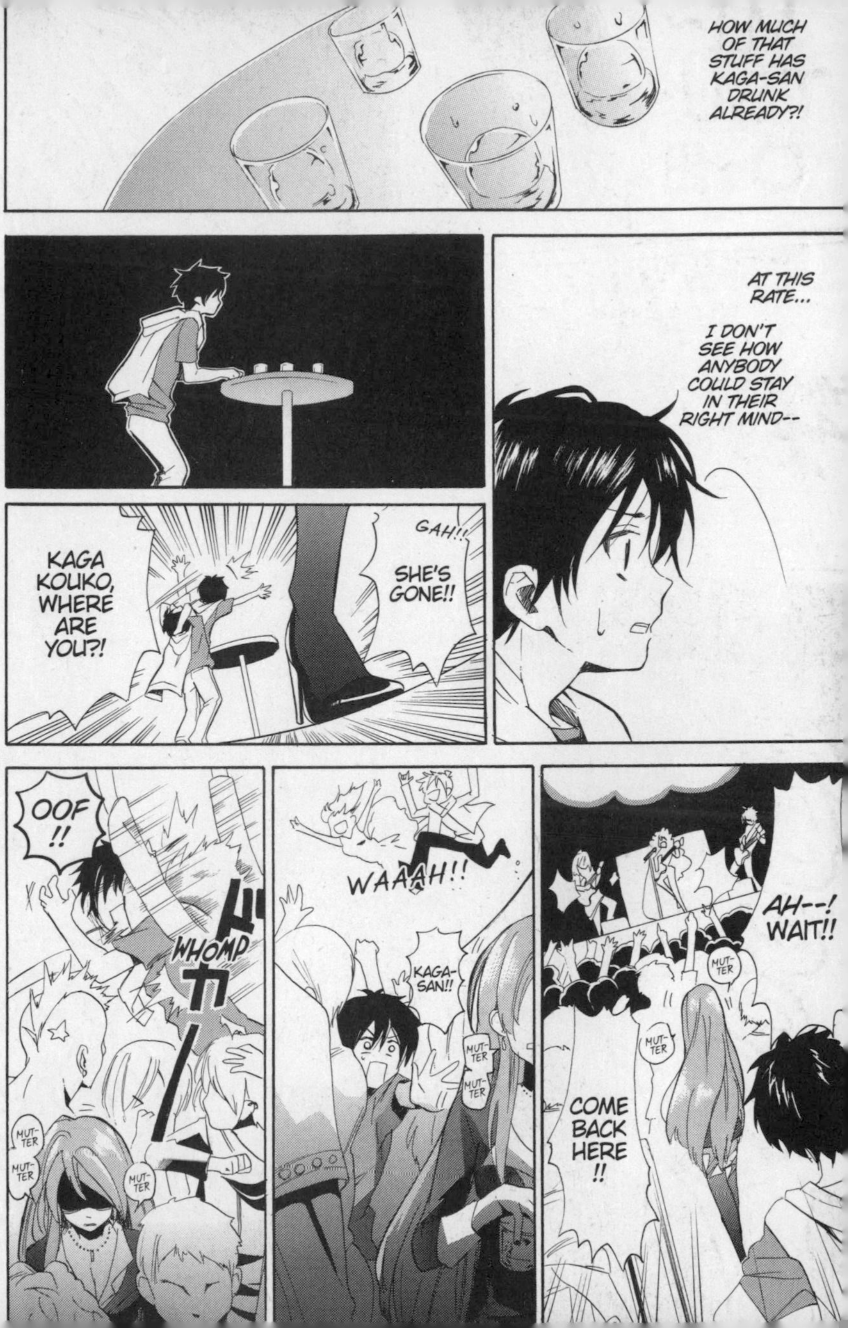
HOW MUCH OF THAT STUFF HAS KAGA-SAN DRUNK ALREADY?!
AT THIS RATE...
I DON'T SEE HOW ANYBODY COULD STAY IN THEIR RIGHT MIND--
GAH!!
SHE'S GONE!!
KAGA KOUKO, WHERE ARE YOU?!
AH--! WAIT!!
MUTTER
MUTTER
COME BACK HERE !!
WAAAH!!
KAGA-SAN!!
MUTTER
MUTTER
OOF !!
WHOMP
MUTTER
MUTTER
MUTTER

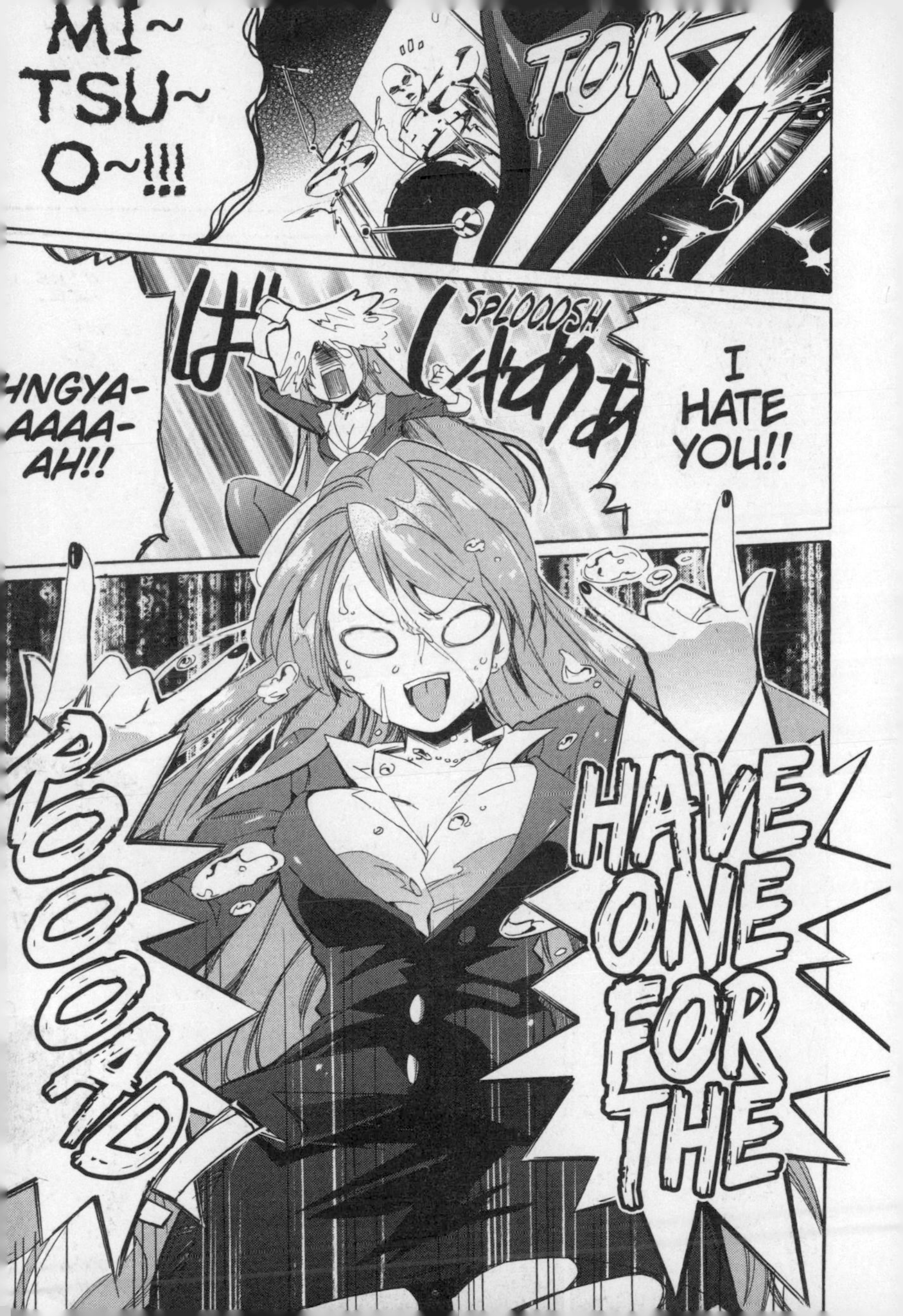
TOK
MI~TSU~O~!!!
SPLOOOSH
ばしゃあ
I HATE YOU!!
HNGYA-AAAA-AH!!
HAVE ONE FOR THE
ROOOOAD!

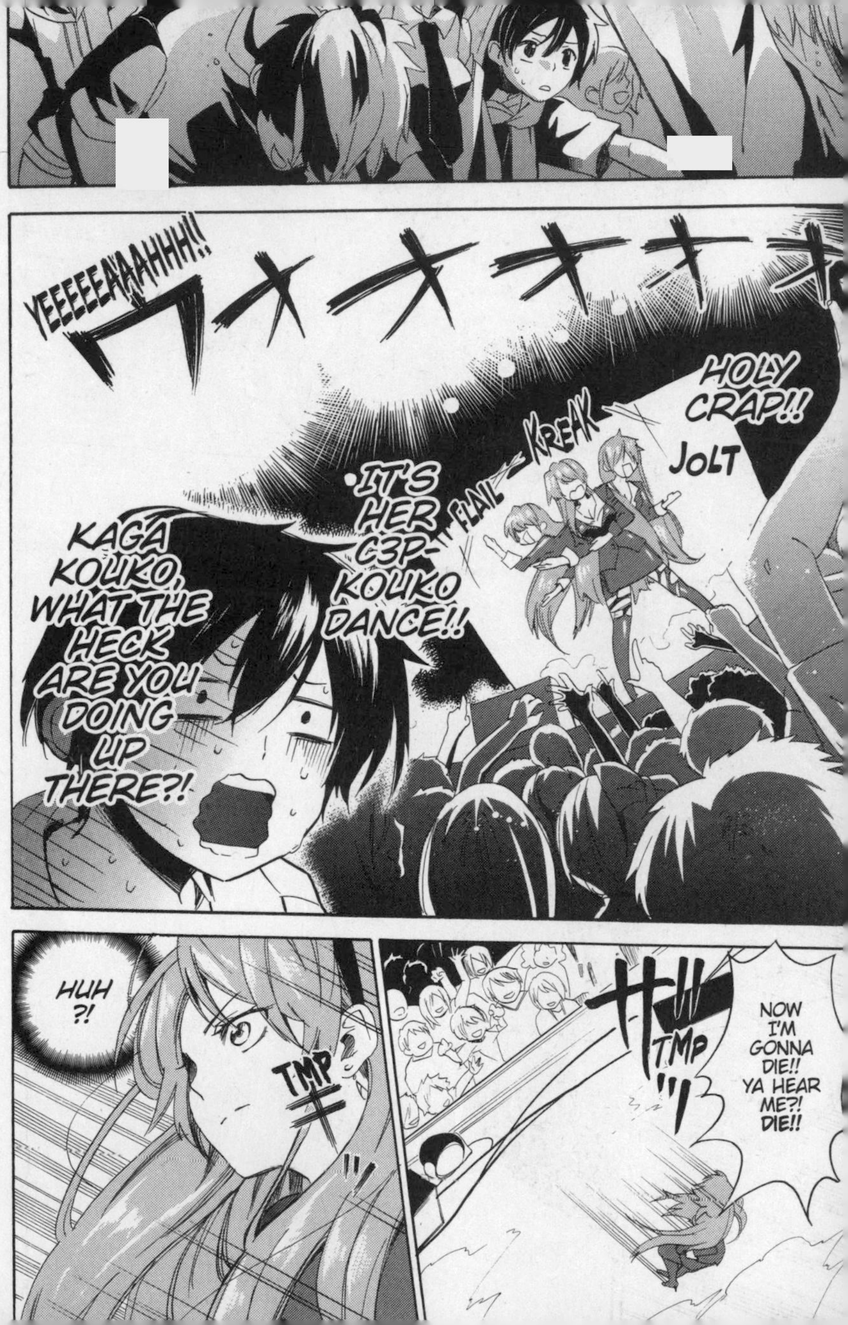
YEEEEEAAAHHH!!
HOLY CRAP!!
JOLT
KREAK
FLAIL
IT'S HER C3P-KOUKO DANCE!!
KAGA KOUKO, WHAT THE HECK ARE YOU DOING UP THERE?!
NOW I'M GONNA DIE!! YA HEAR ME?! DIE!!
TMP
TMP
HUH?!

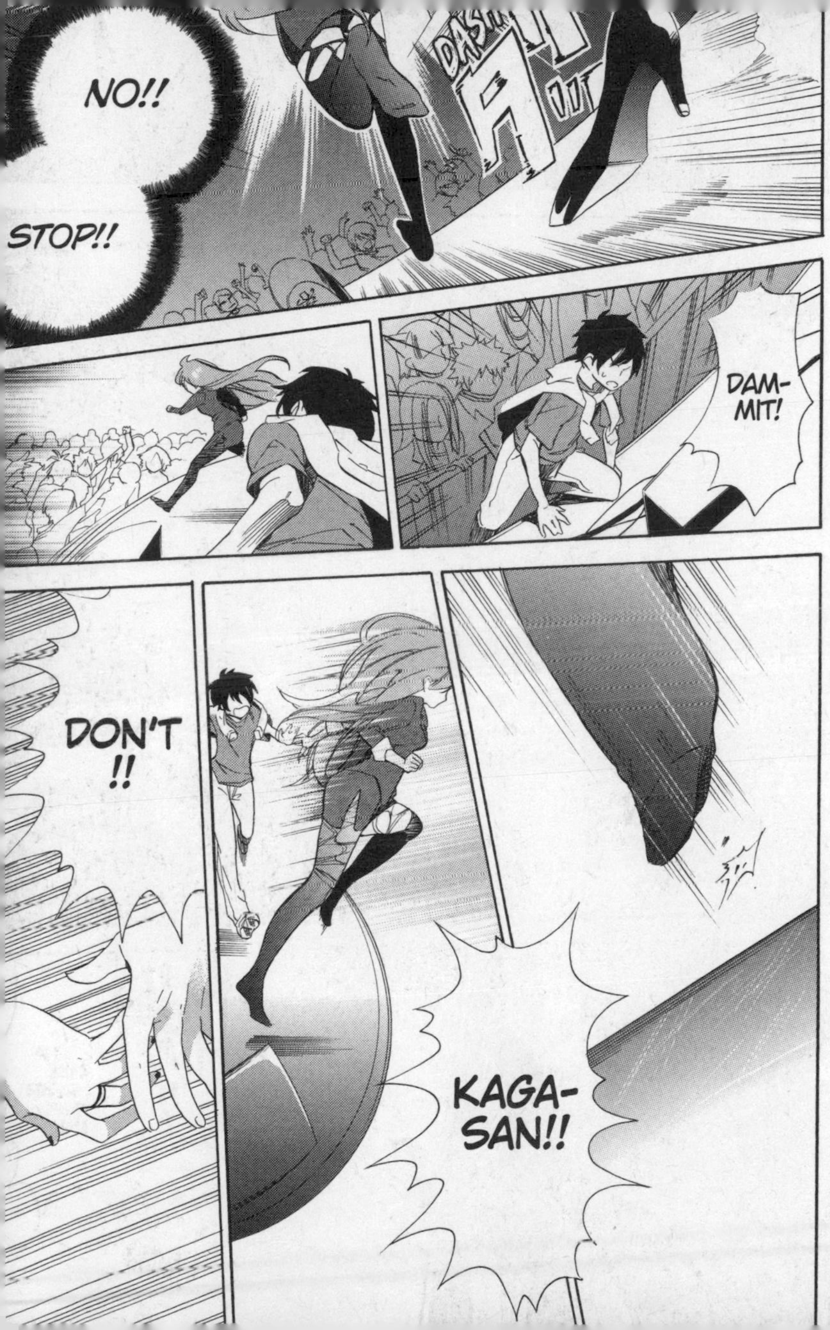
NO!!
STOP!!
DAM-
MIT!
KAGA-
SAN!!
DON'T
!!

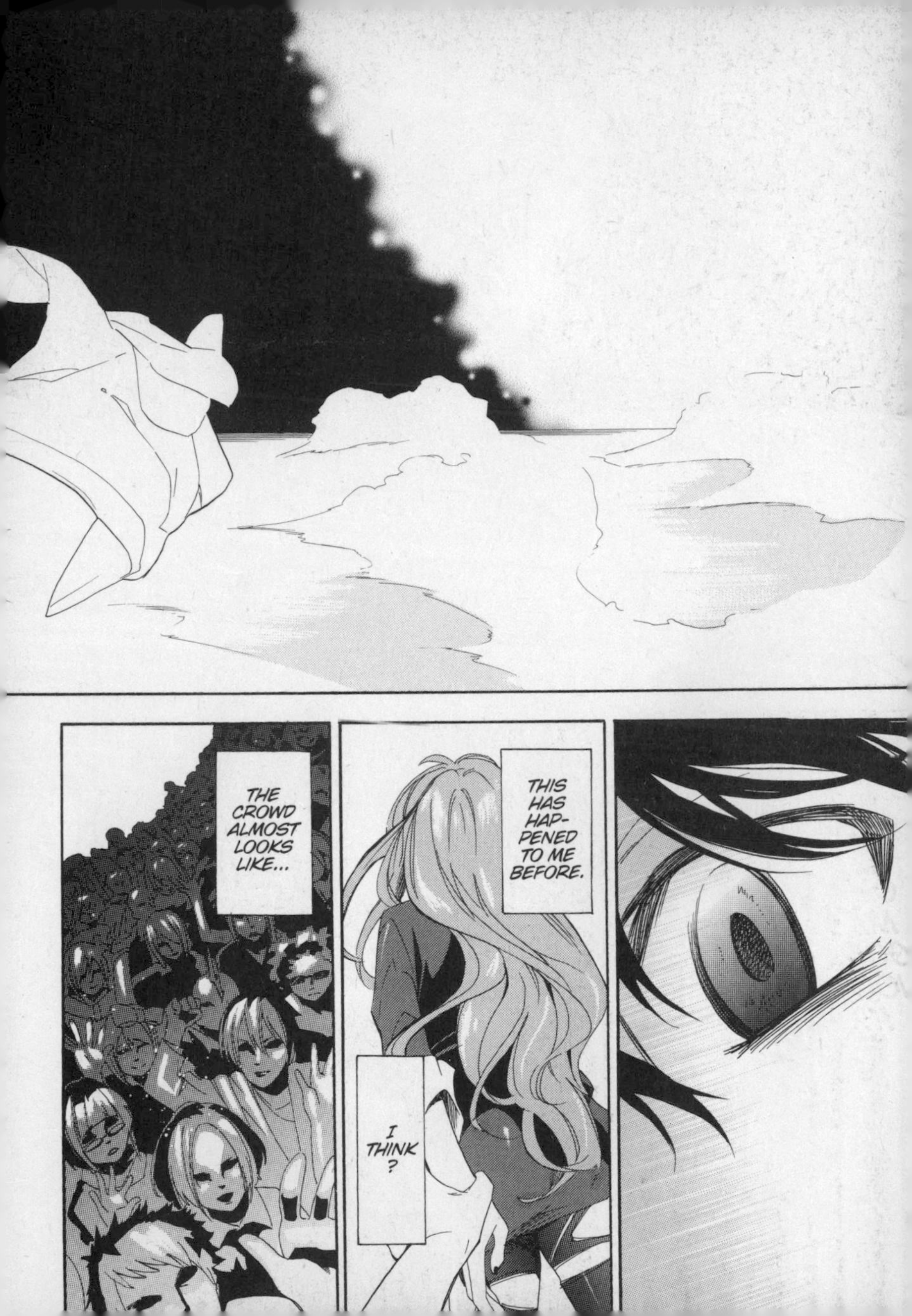
THIS HAS HAP-PENED TO ME BEFORE.
I THINK?
THE CROWD ALMOST LOOKS LIKE...

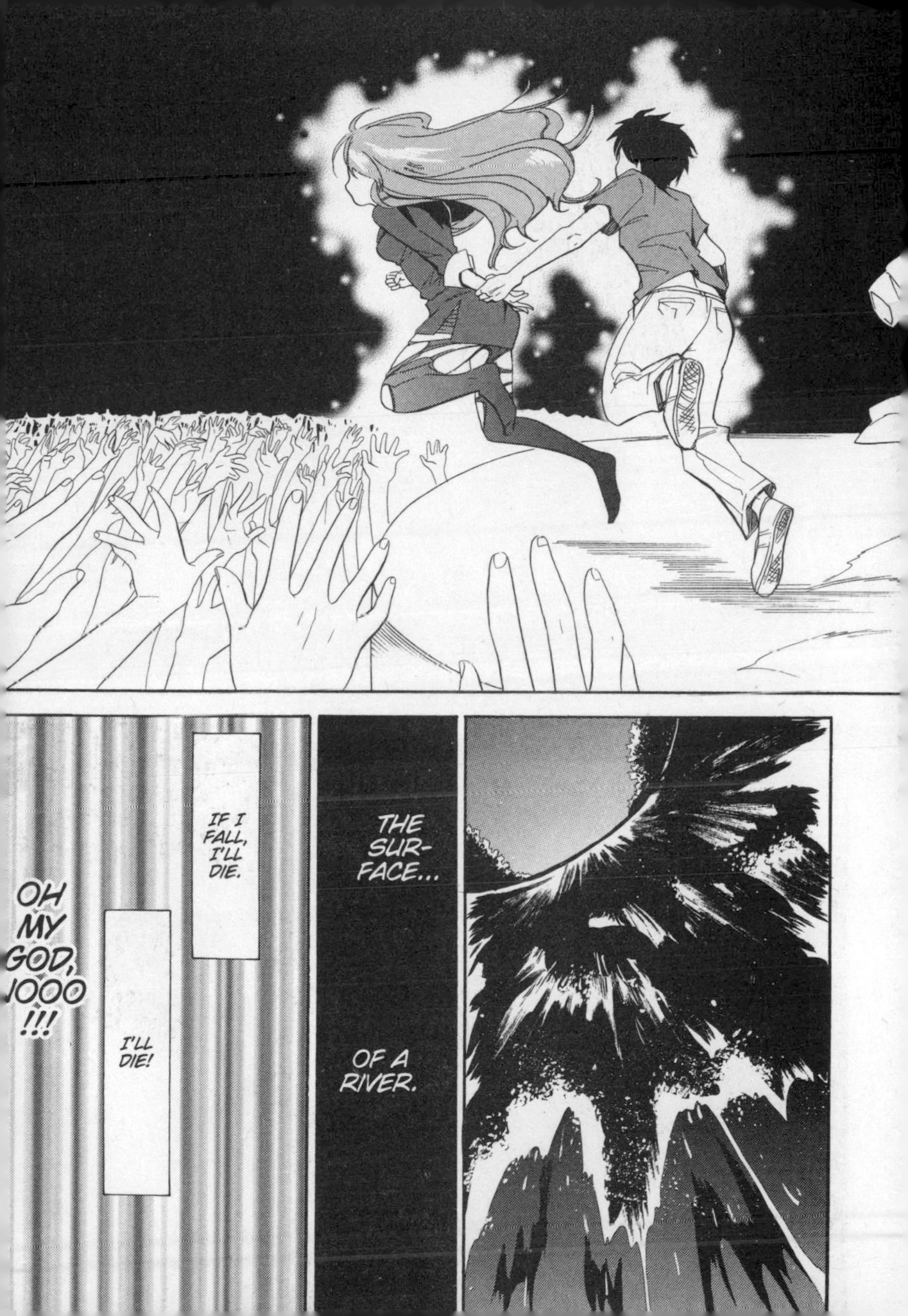
THE SUR-FACE...
OF A RIVER.
IF I FALL, I'LL DIE.
I'LL DIE!
OH MY GOD, IOOO!!!

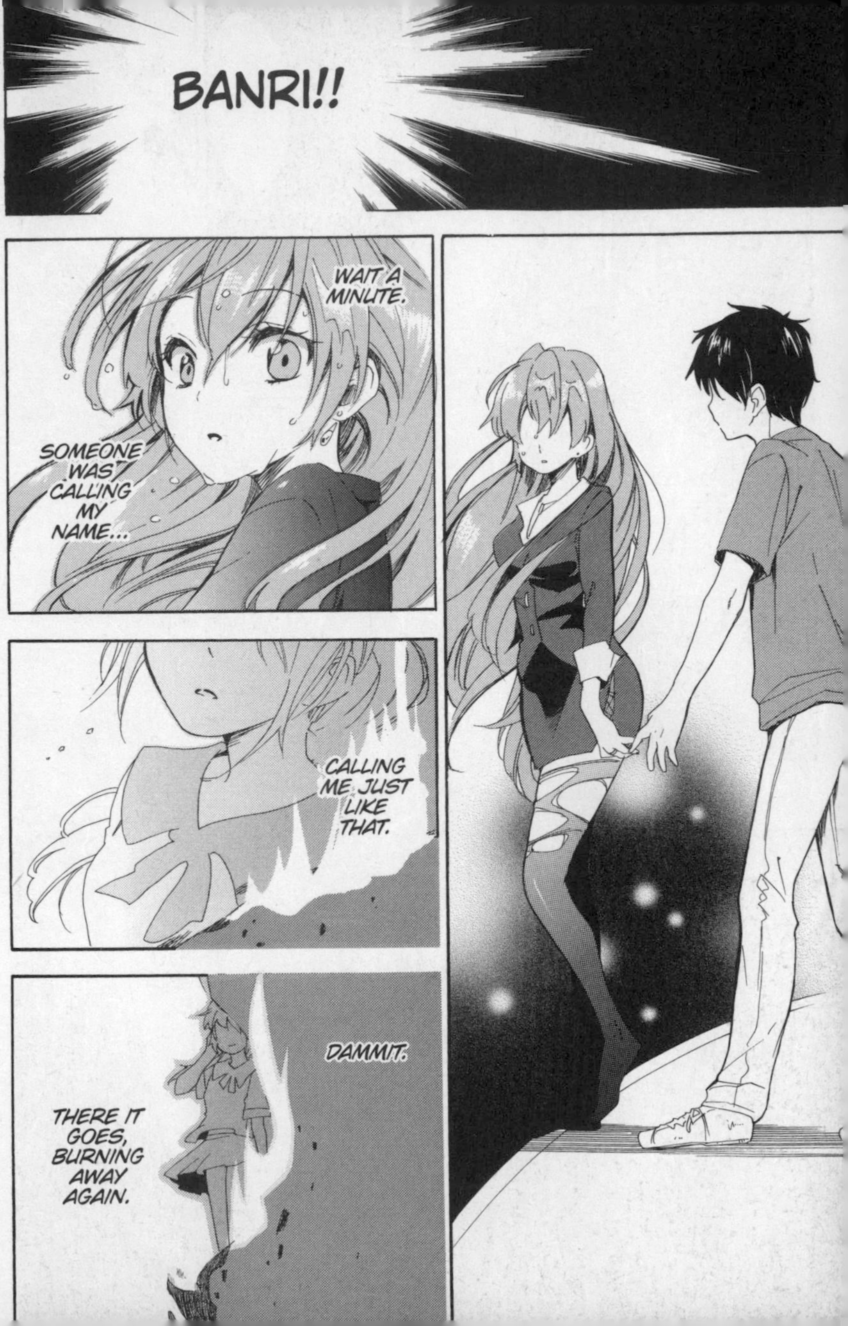
BANRI!!
WAIT A MINUTE.
SOMEONE WAS CALLING MY NAME...
CALLING ME JUST LIKE THAT.
DAMMIT.
THERE IT GOES, BURNING AWAY AGAIN.

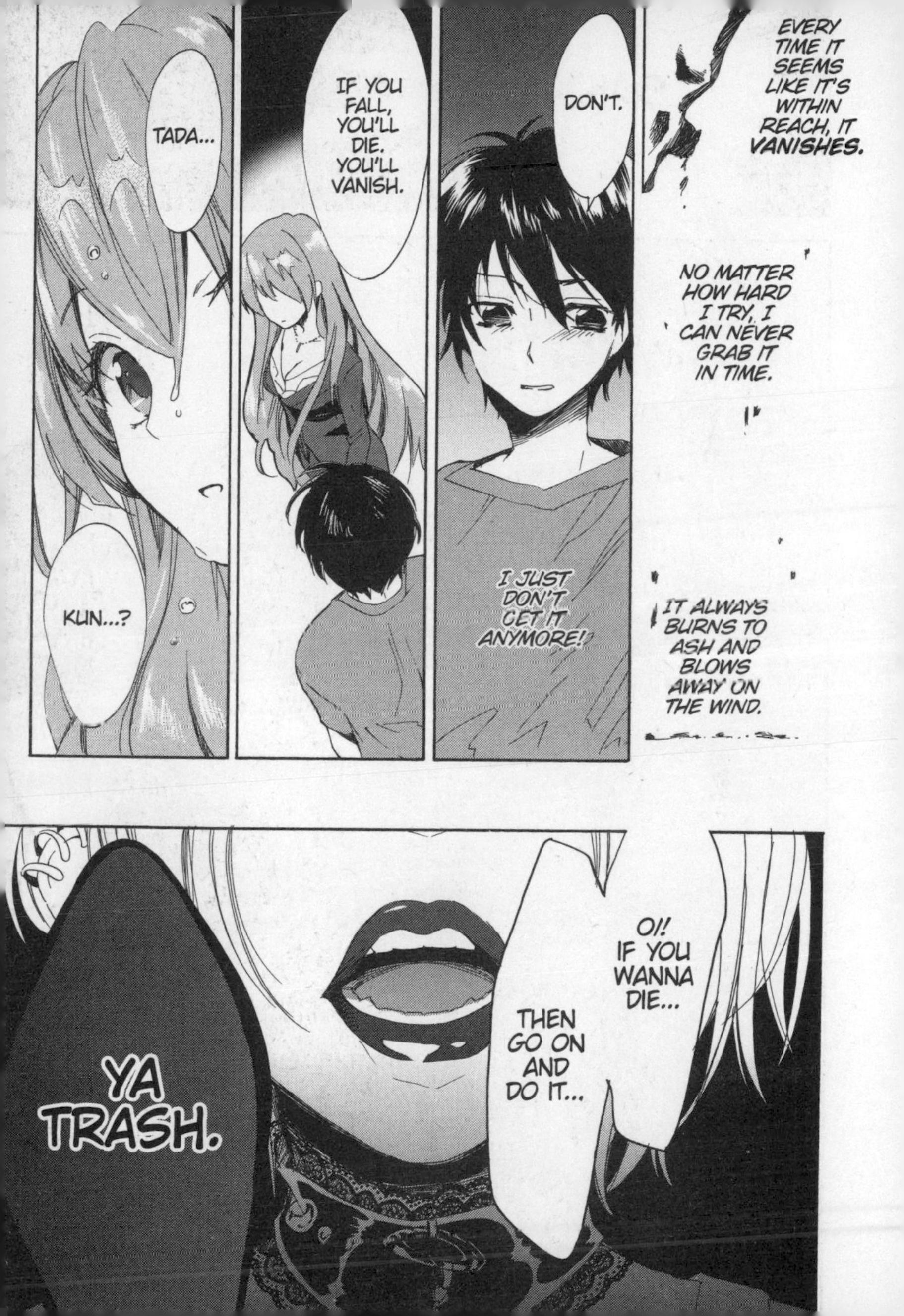
EVERY TIME IT SEEMS LIKE IT'S WITHIN REACH, IT VANISHES.
NO MATTER HOW HARD I TRY, I CAN NEVER GRAB IT IN TIME.
IT ALWAYS BURNS TO ASH AND BLOWS AWAY ON THE WIND.
DON'T.
I JUST DON'T GET IT ANYMORE!
IF YOU FALL, YOU'LL DIE. YOU'LL VANISH.
TADA...
KUN...?
OI! IF YOU WANNA DIE...
THEN GO ON AND DO IT...
YA TRASH.

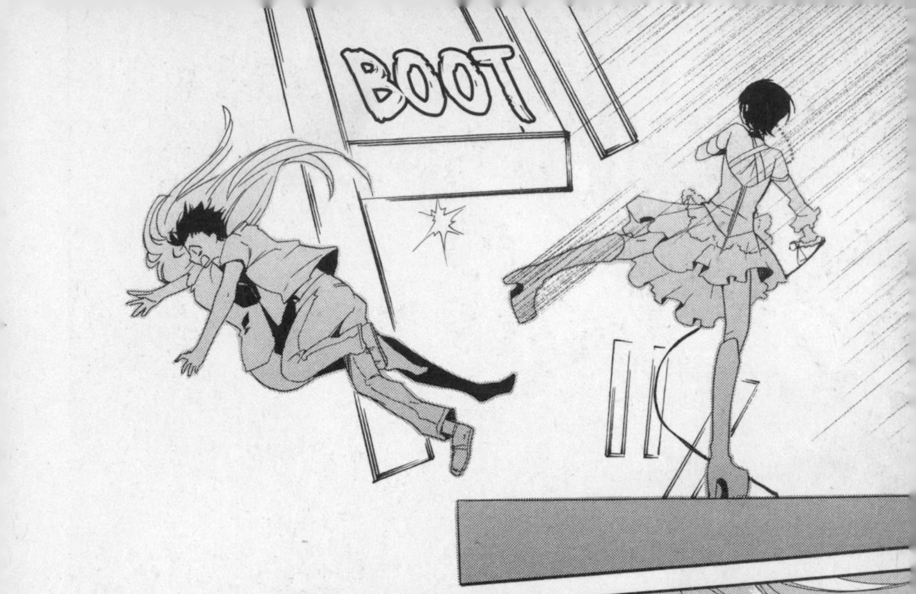
BOOT
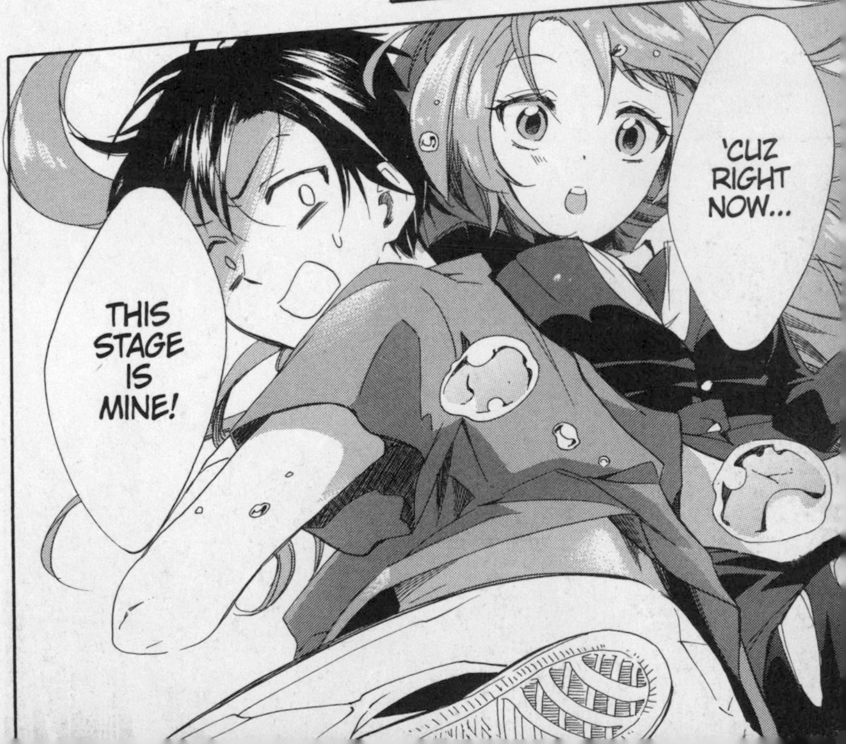
'CUZ RIGHT NOW...
THIS STAGE IS MINE!

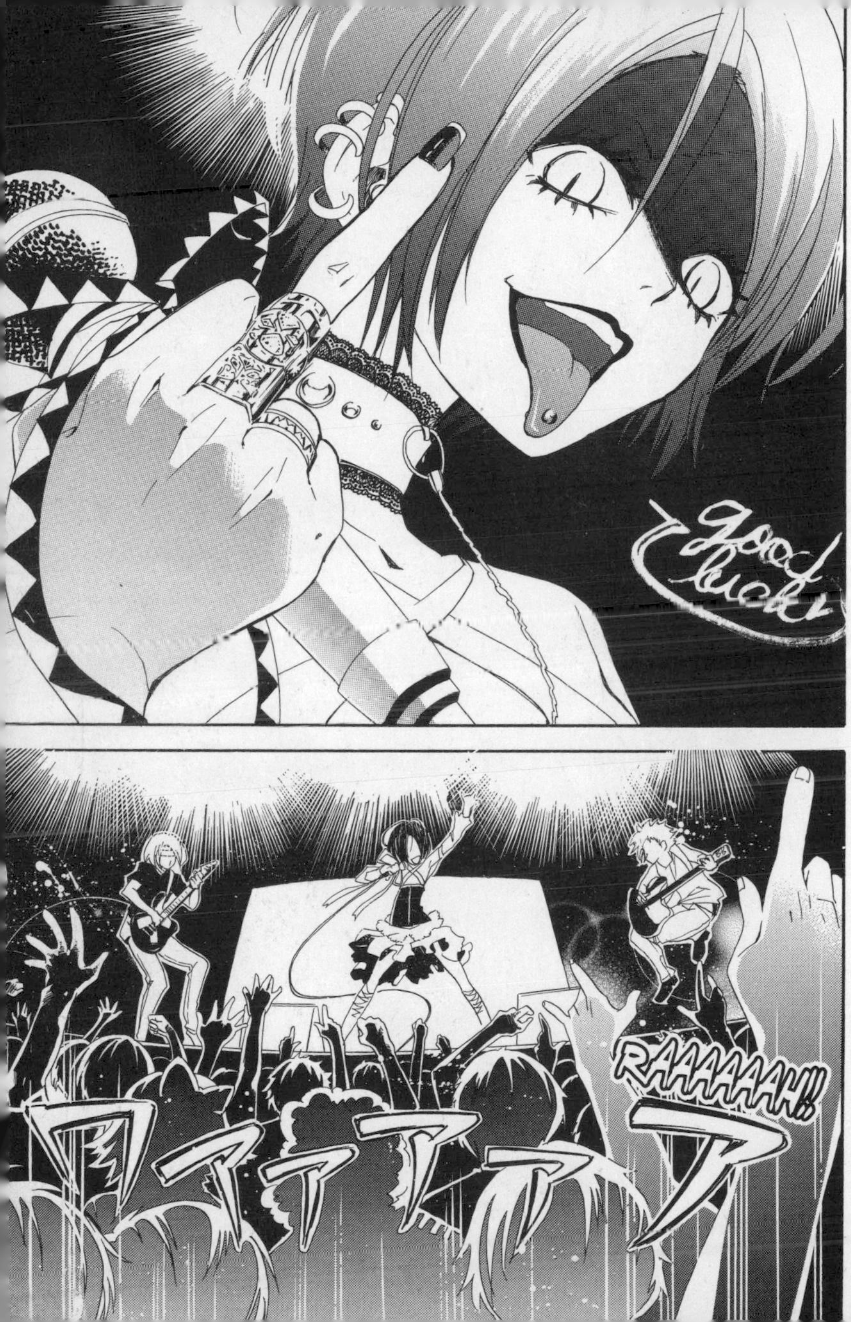
good luck
アァアーア
RAAAAAAH!!

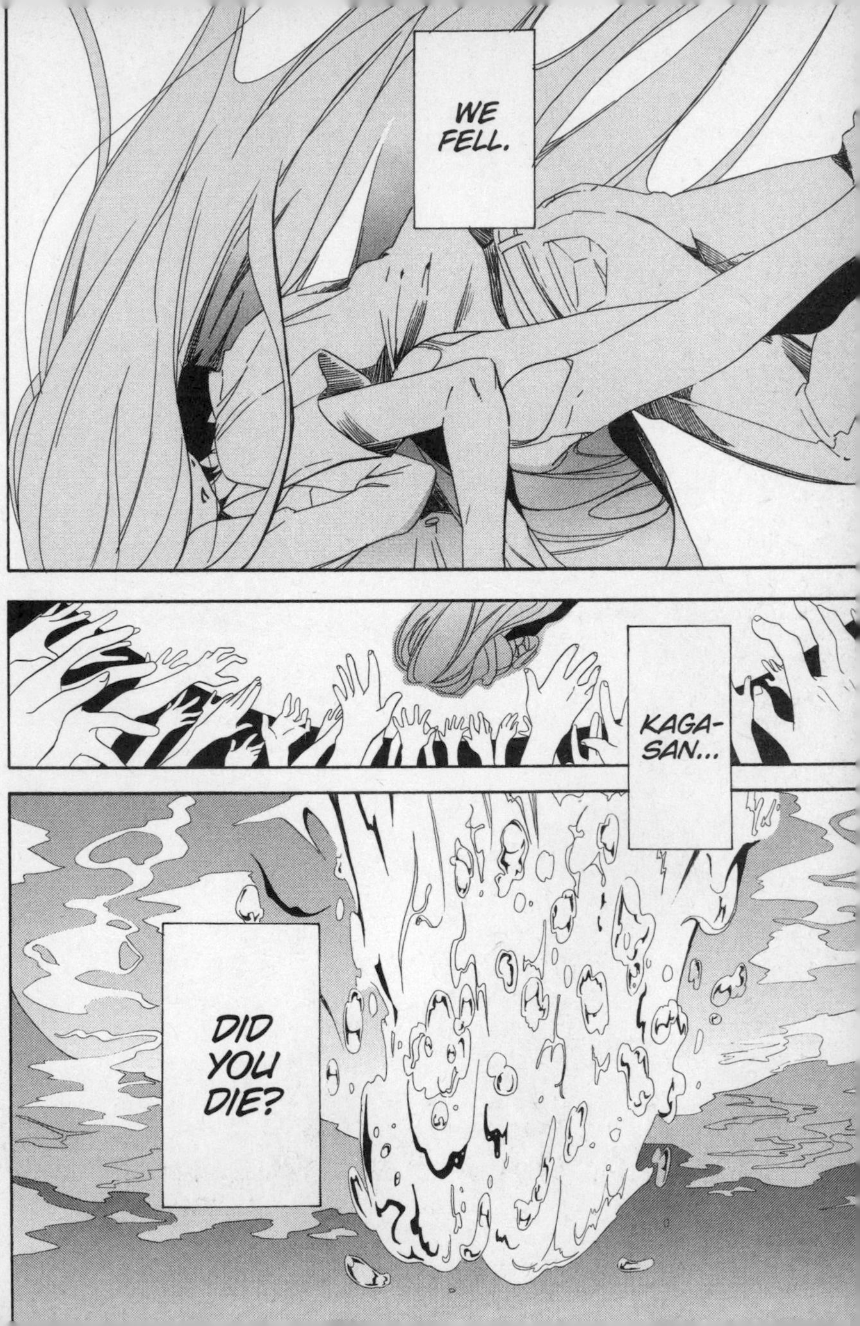
WE FELL.
KAGA-SAN...
DID YOU DIE?

GOLDEN TIME

ゴールデンタイム

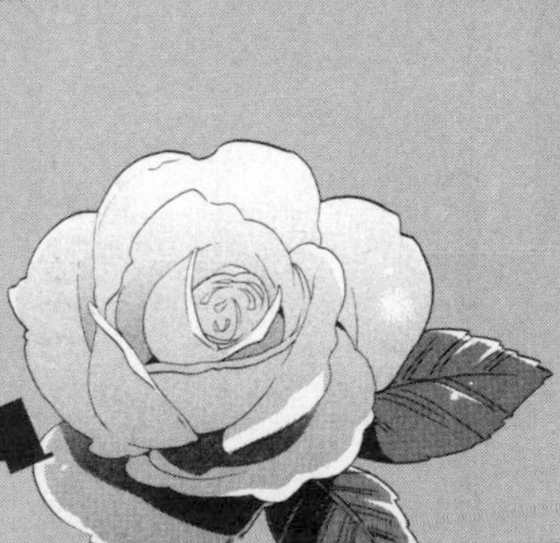

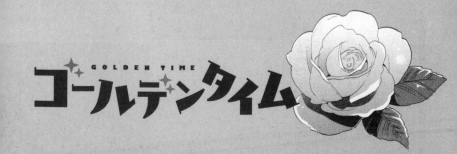

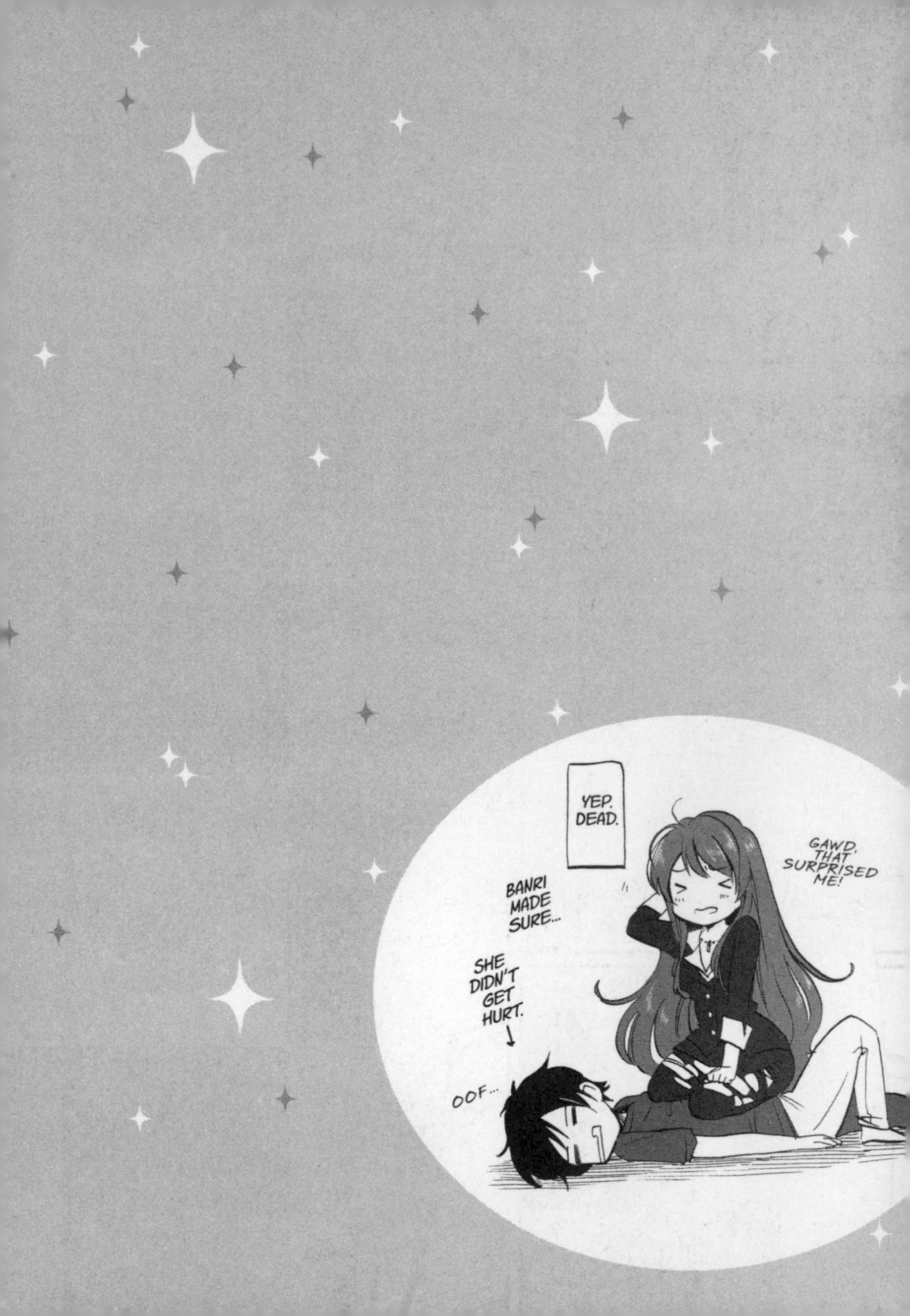
GAWD, THAT SURPRISED ME!
YEP. DEAD.
BANRI MADE SURE...
SHE DIDN'T GET HURT.
OOF...

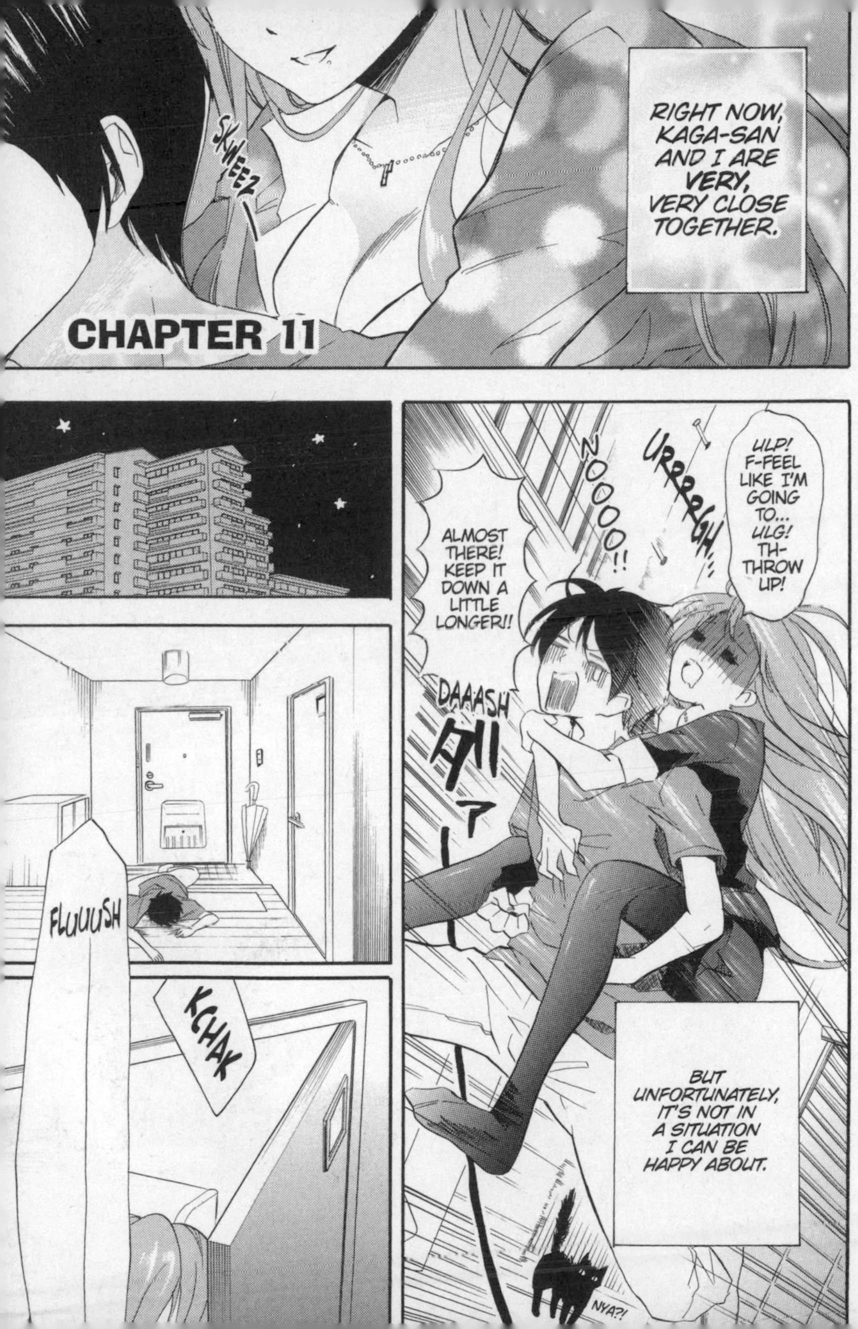
RIGHT NOW, KAGA-SAN AND I ARE VERY, VERY CLOSE TOGETHER.
SKWEEZ
CHAPTER 11
ULP! F-FEEL LIKE I'M GOING TO... ULG! TH-THROW UP!
URRRRGH!!
NOOOOO!!
ALMOST THERE! KEEP IT DOWN A LITTLE LONGER!!
DAAASH
BUT UNFORTUNATELY, IT'S NOT IN A SITUATION I CAN BE HAPPY ABOUT.
NYA?!
FLUUUSH
KCHAK

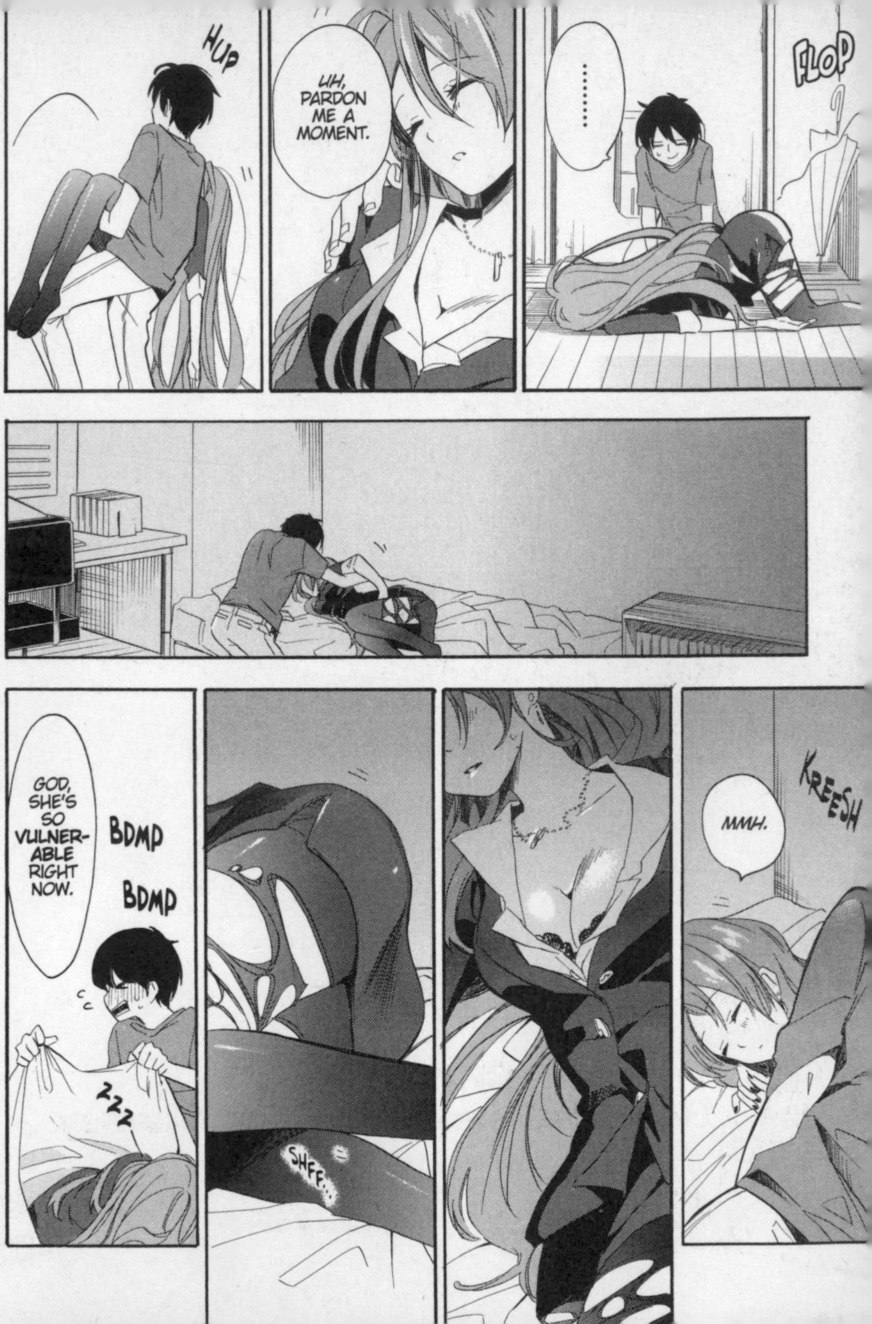

FLOP
......
UH, PARDON ME A MOMENT.
HUP
KREESH
MMH.
SHFF...
GOD, SHE'S SO VULNER-ABLE RIGHT NOW.
BDMP
BDMP
ZZZ

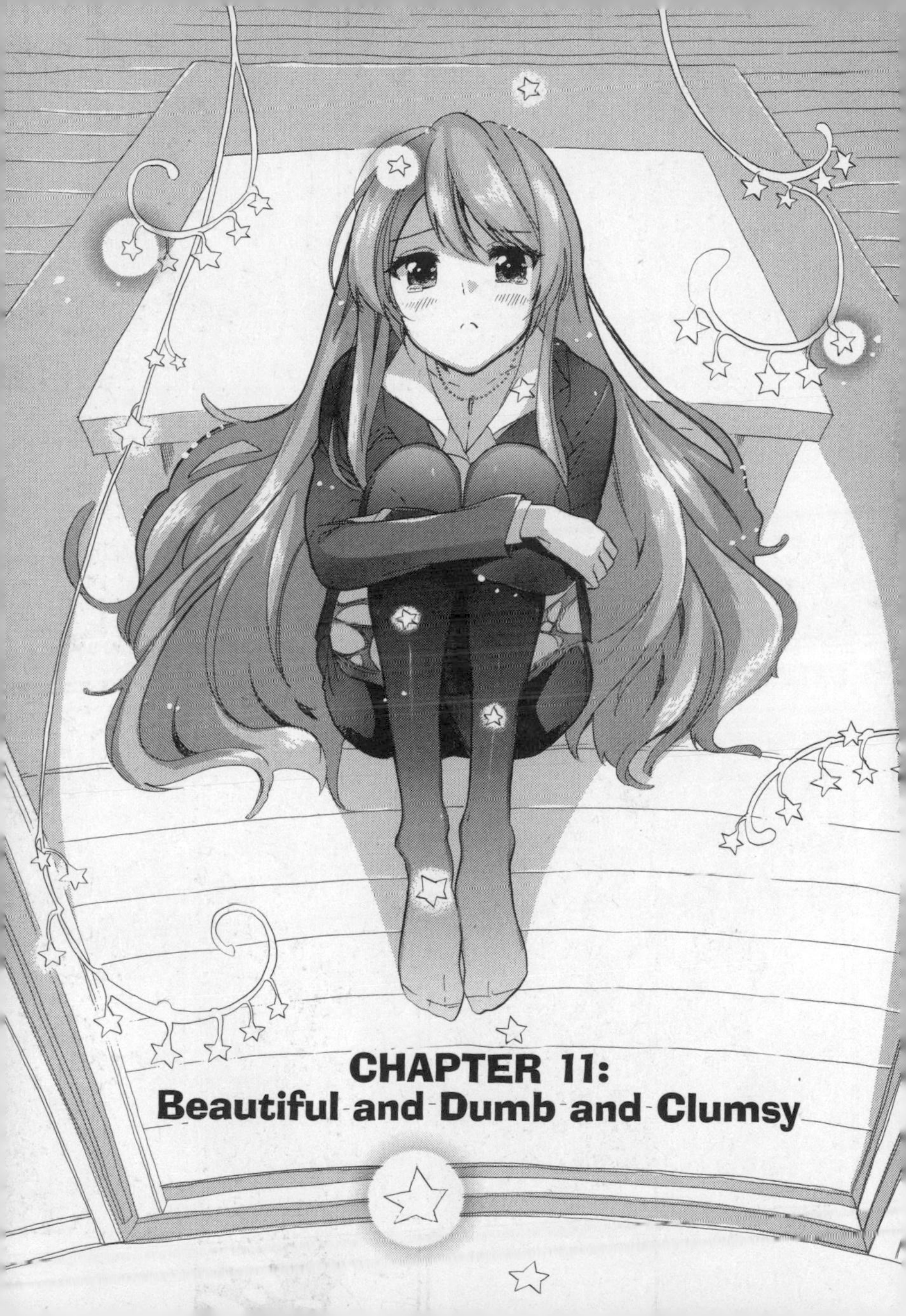

CHAPTER 11:
Beautiful and Dumb and Clumsy

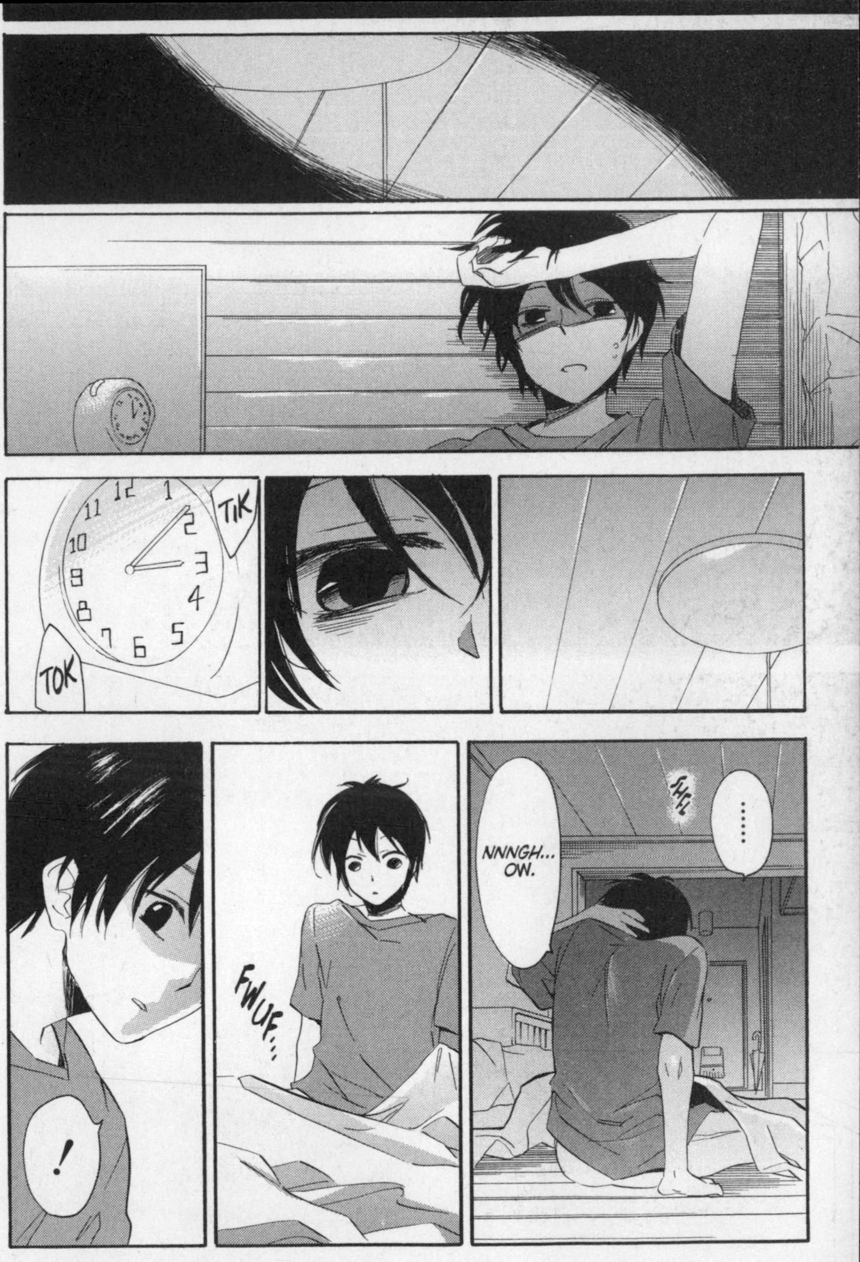
TIK
TOK
......
SHFL
NNNGH... OW.
FWUF...
!

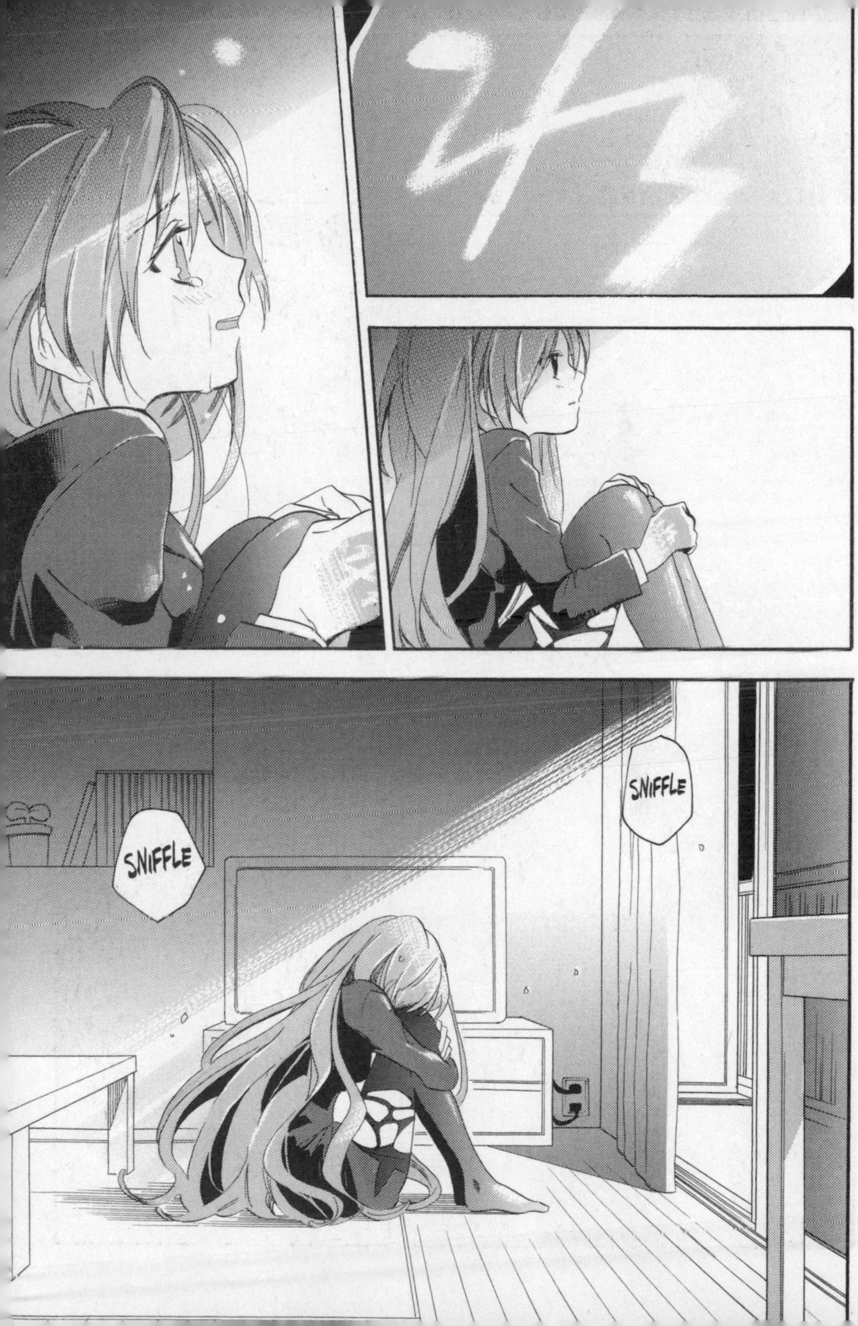
SNIFFLE
SNIFFLE

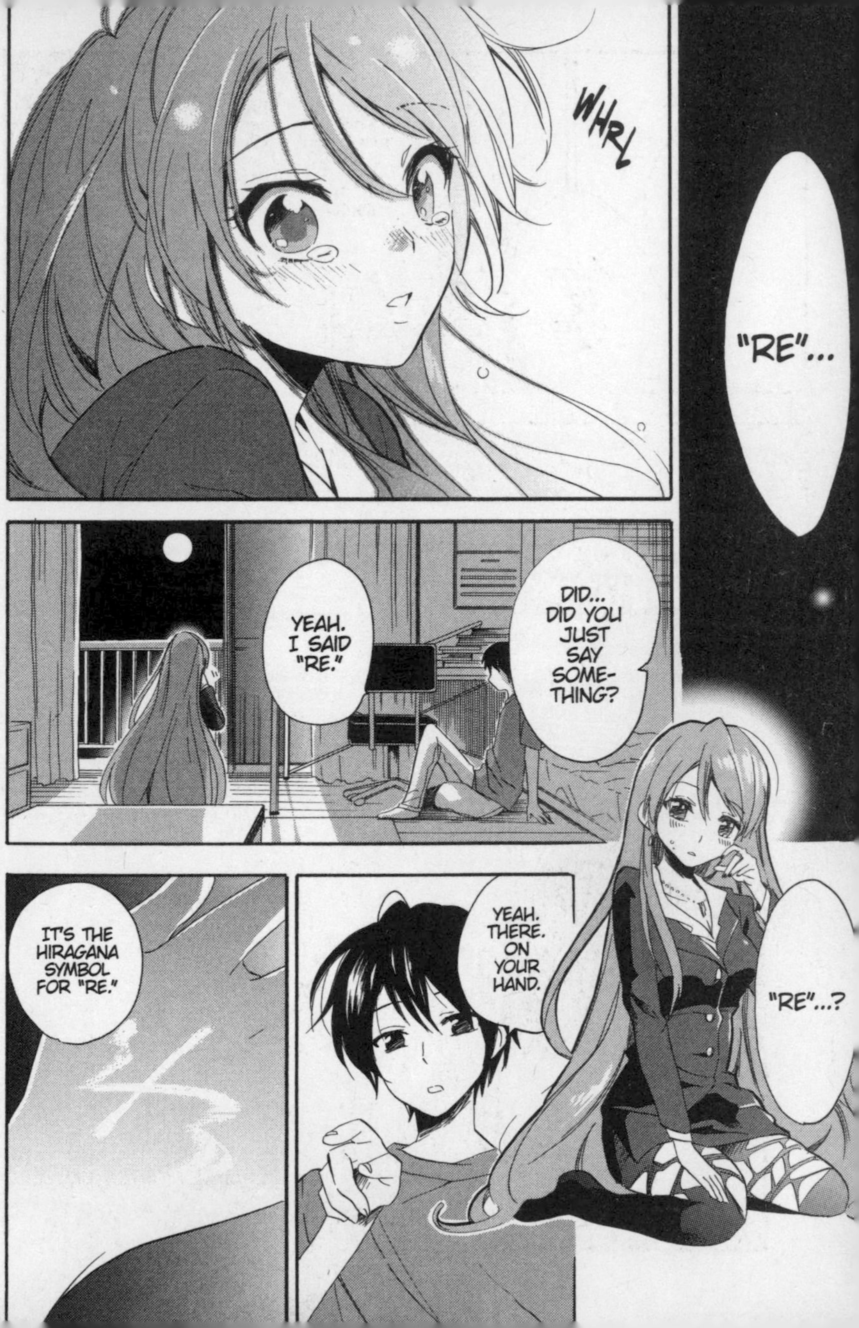
"RE"...
WHRL
DID... DID YOU JUST SAY SOMETHING?
YEAH. I SAID "RE."
"RE"...?
YEAH. THERE. ON YOUR HAND.
IT'S THE HIRAGANA SYMBOL FOR "RE."

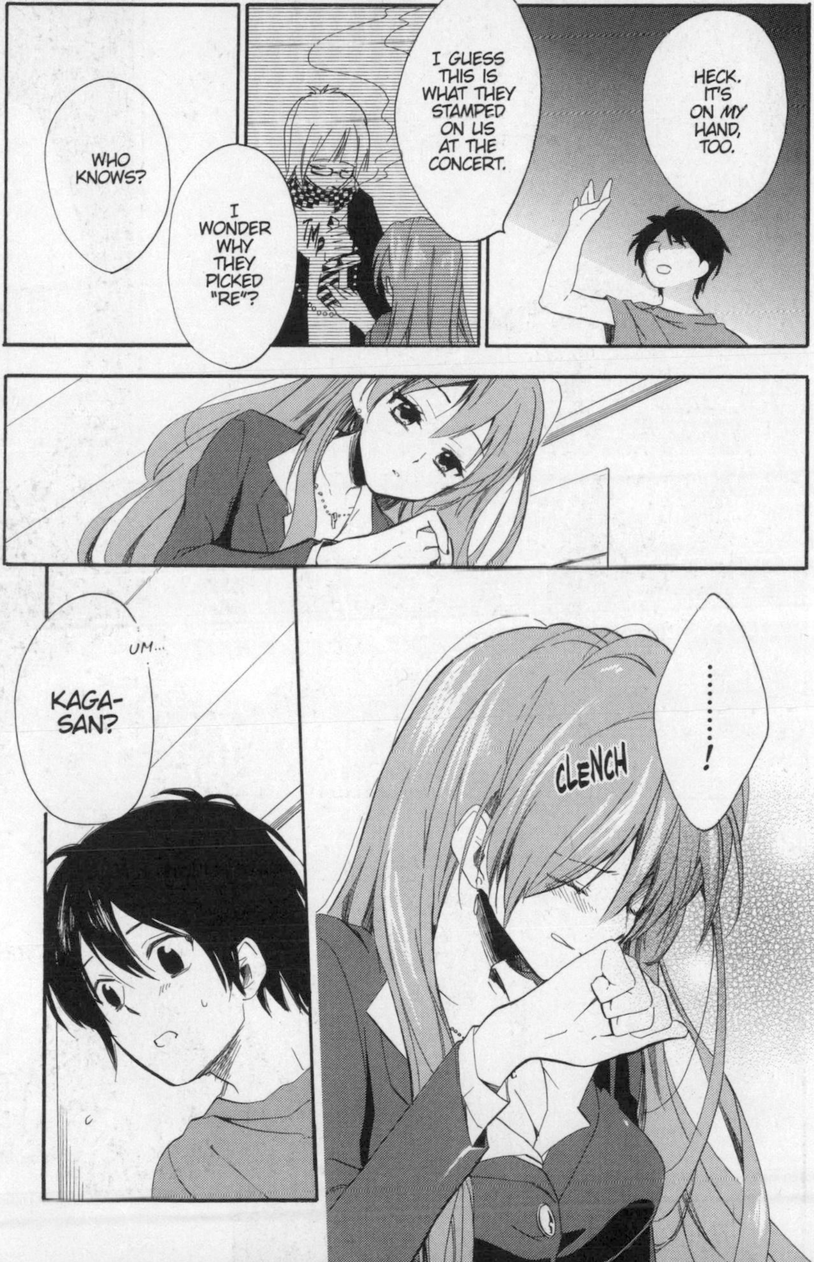
HECK. IT'S ON MY HAND, TOO.
I GUESS THIS IS WHAT THEY STAMPED ON US AT THE CONCERT.
TMP
I WONDER WHY THEY PICKED "RE"?
WHO KNOWS?
......!
CLENCH
UM...
KAGA-SAN?

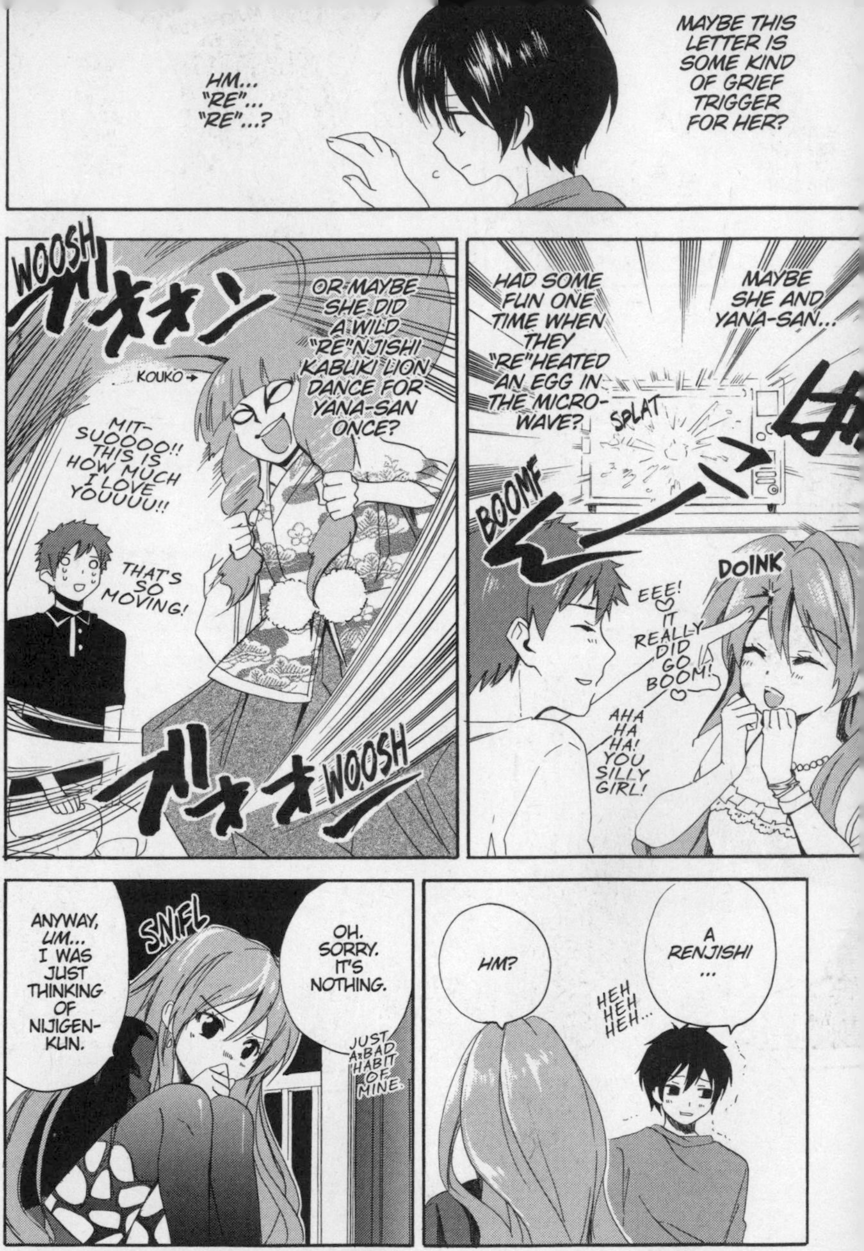
MAYBE THIS LETTER IS SOME KIND OF GRIEF TRIGGER FOR HER?
HM... "RE"... "RE"...?
MAYBE SHE AND YANA-SAN...
HAD SOME FUN ONE TIME WHEN THEY "RE"HEATED AN EGG IN THE MICRO-WAVE?
SPLAT
BOOMF
DOINK
EEE! ♡ IT REALLY DID GO BOOM! ♡
AHA HA HA! YOU SILLY GIRL!
WOOSH
OR MAYBE SHE DID A WILD "RE"NJISHI KABUKI LION DANCE FOR YANA-SAN ONCE?
KOUKO →
MIT-SUOOOO!! THIS IS HOW MUCH I LOVE YOUUUU!!
THAT'S SO MOVING!
WOOSH
A RENJISHI...
HM?
HEH HEH HEH...
OH. SORRY. IT'S NOTHING.
JUST A BAD HABIT OF MINE.
SNIFL
ANYWAY, UM... I WAS JUST THINKING OF NIJIGEN-KUN.

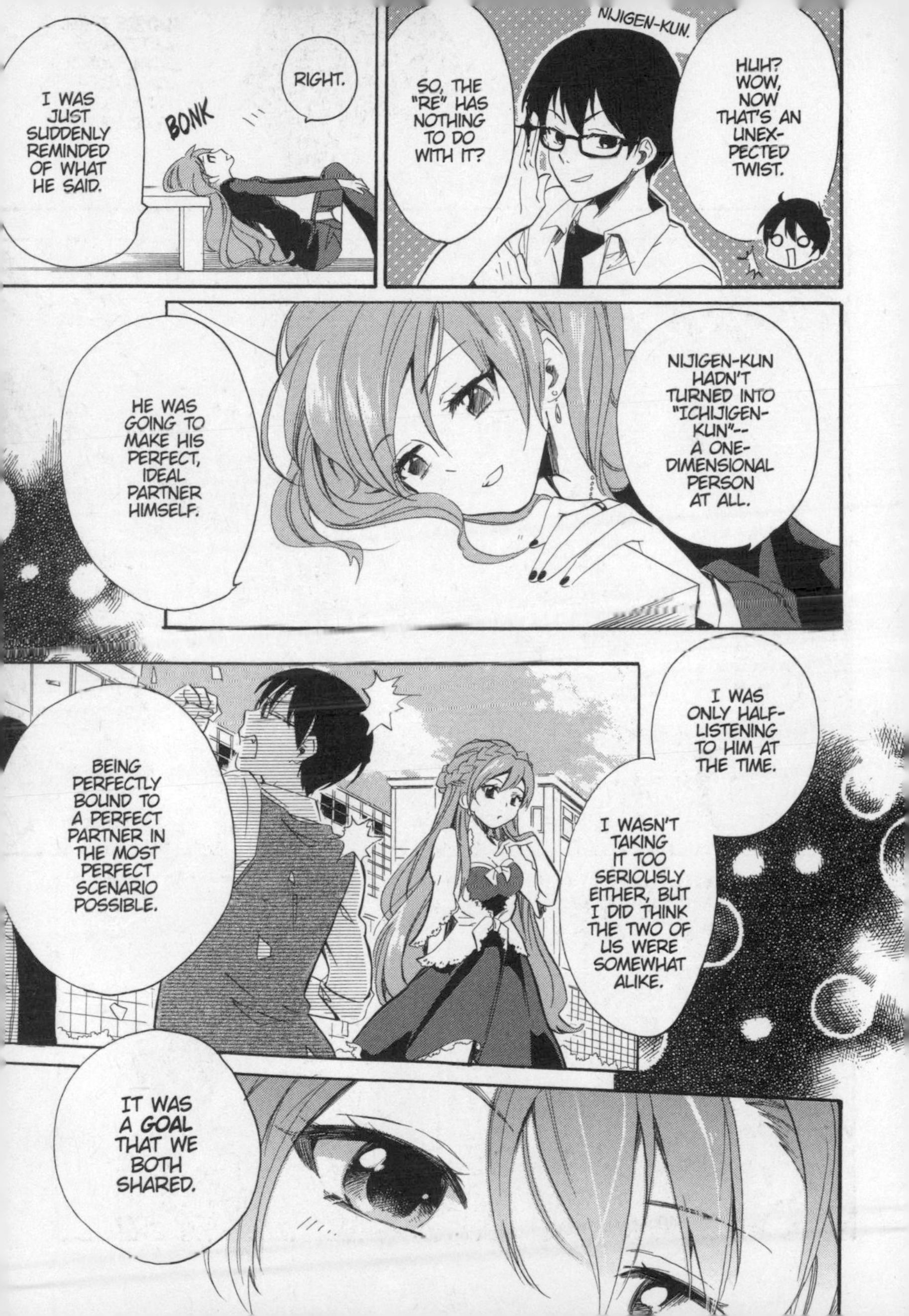
NIJIGEN-KUN.
HUH? WOW, NOW THAT'S AN UNEXPECTED TWIST.
SO, THE "RE" HAS NOTHING TO DO WITH IT?
RIGHT.
BONK
I WAS JUST SUDDENLY REMINDED OF WHAT HE SAID.
NIJIGEN-KUN HADN'T TURNED INTO "ICHIJIGEN-KUN"-- A ONE-DIMENSIONAL PERSON AT ALL.
HE WAS GOING TO MAKE HIS PERFECT, IDEAL PARTNER HIMSELF.
I WAS ONLY HALF-LISTENING TO HIM AT THE TIME.
I WASN'T TAKING IT TOO SERIOUSLY EITHER, BUT I DID THINK THE TWO OF US WERE SOMEWHAT ALIKE.
BEING PERFECTLY BOUND TO A PERFECT PARTNER IN THE MOST PERFECT SCENARIO POSSIBLE.
IT WAS A **GOAL** THAT WE BOTH SHARED.

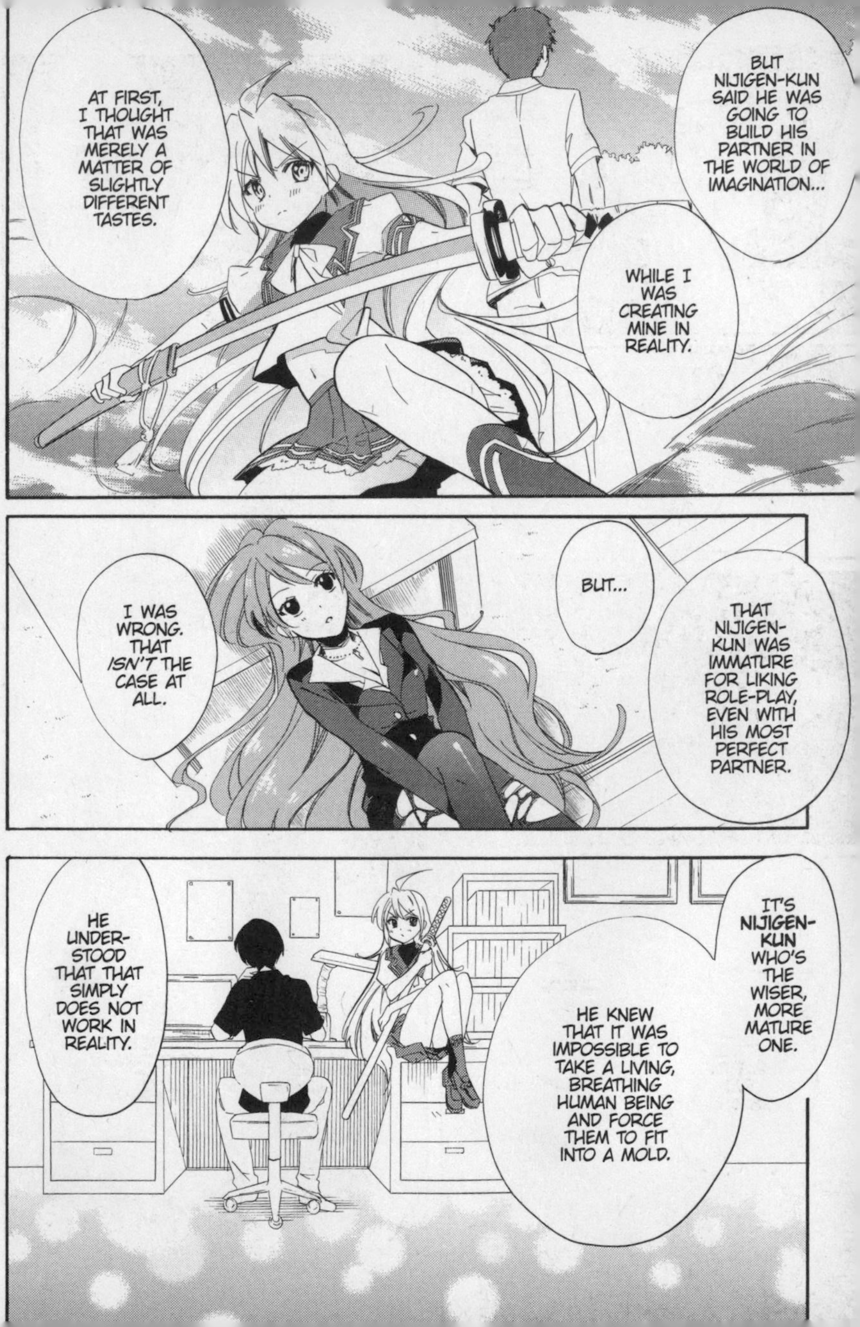
BUT NIJIGEN-KUN SAID HE WAS GOING TO BUILD HIS PARTNER IN THE WORLD OF IMAGINATION...
WHILE I WAS CREATING MINE IN REALITY.
AT FIRST, I THOUGHT THAT WAS MERELY A MATTER OF SLIGHTLY DIFFERENT TASTES.
BUT...
THAT NIJIGEN-KUN WAS IMMATURE FOR LIKING ROLE-PLAY, EVEN WITH HIS MOST PERFECT PARTNER.
I WAS WRONG. THAT *ISN'T* THE CASE AT ALL.
IT'S NIJIGEN-KUN WHO'S THE WISER, MORE MATURE ONE.
HE KNEW THAT IT WAS IMPOSSIBLE TO TAKE A LIVING, BREATHING HUMAN BEING AND FORCE THEM TO FIT INTO A MOLD.
HE UNDER-STOOD THAT THAT SIMPLY DOES NOT WORK IN REALITY.

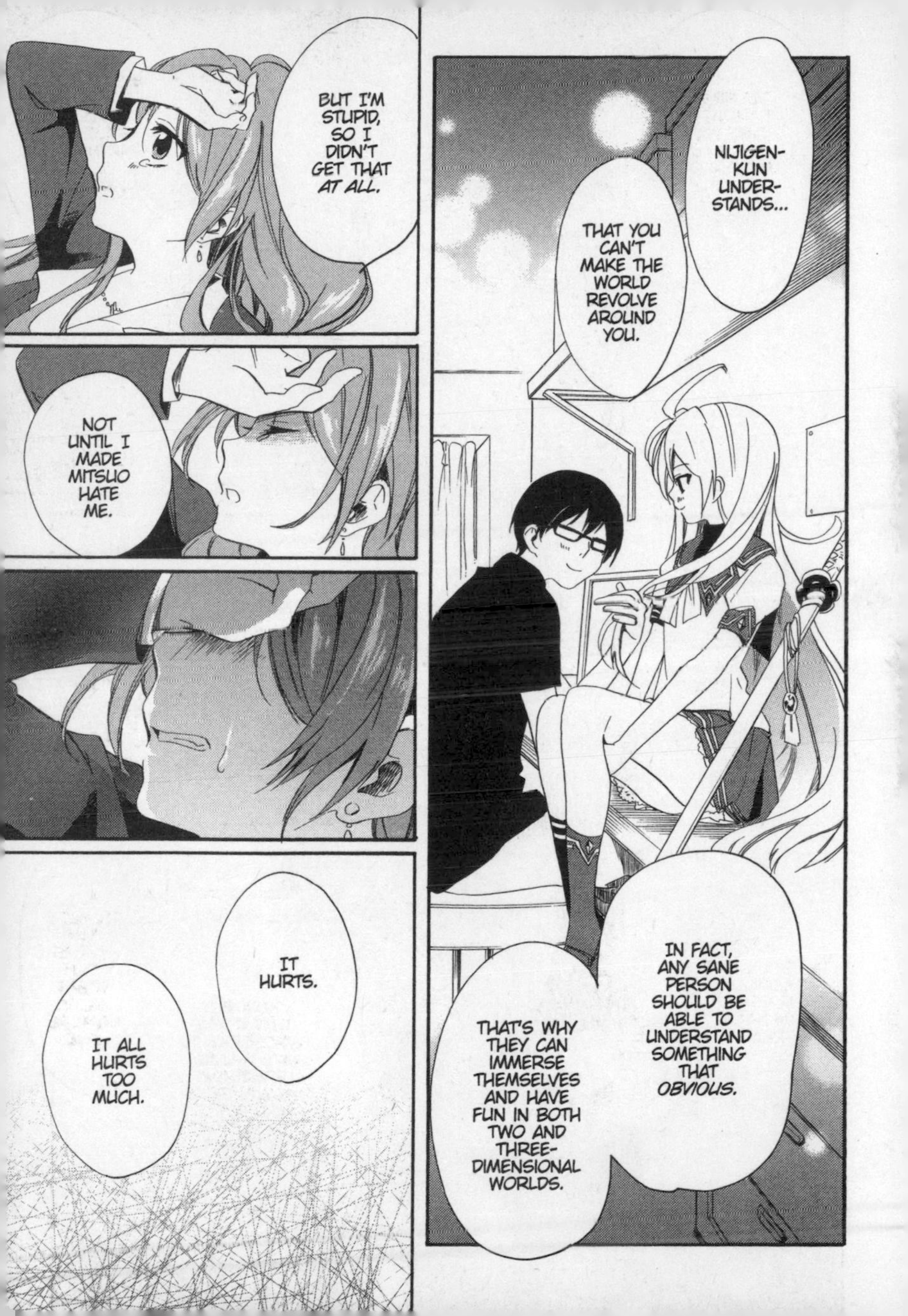
NIJIGEN-KUN UNDERSTANDS...
THAT YOU CAN'T MAKE THE WORLD REVOLVE AROUND YOU.
IN FACT, ANY SANE PERSON SHOULD BE ABLE TO UNDERSTAND SOMETHING THAT *OBVIOUS.*
THAT'S WHY THEY CAN IMMERSE THEMSELVES AND HAVE FUN IN BOTH TWO AND THREE-DIMENSIONAL WORLDS.
BUT I'M STUPID, SO I DIDN'T GET THAT *AT ALL.*
NOT UNTIL I MADE MITSUO HATE ME.
IT HURTS.
IT ALL HURTS TOO MUCH.

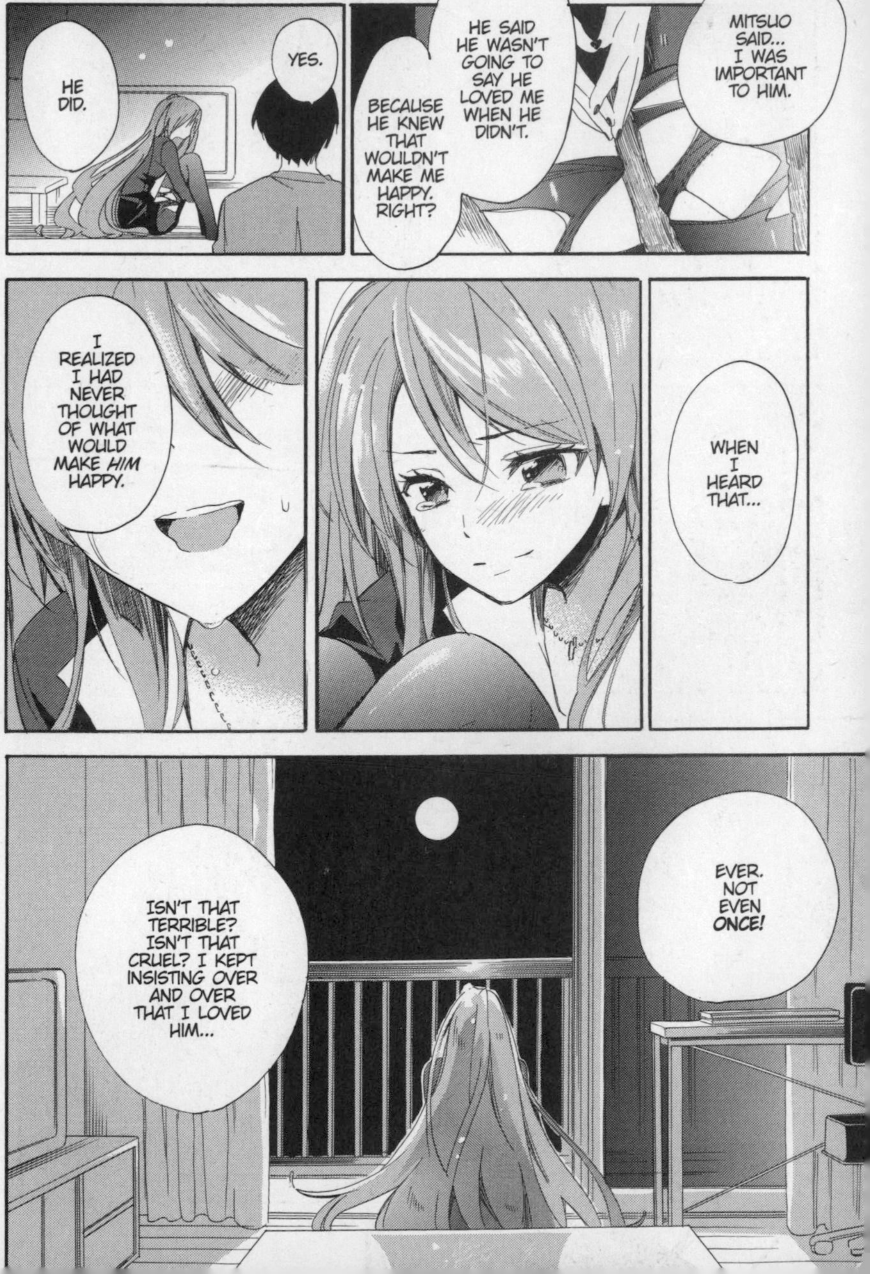
MITSUO SAID... I WAS IMPORTANT TO HIM.
HE SAID HE WASN'T GOING TO SAY HE LOVED ME WHEN HE DIDN'T.
BECAUSE HE KNEW THAT WOULDN'T MAKE ME HAPPY. RIGHT?
YES.
HE DID.
WHEN I HEARD THAT...
I REALIZED I HAD NEVER THOUGHT OF WHAT WOULD MAKE *HIM* HAPPY.
EVER. NOT EVEN ONCE!
ISN'T THAT TERRIBLE? ISN'T THAT CRUEL? I KEPT INSISTING OVER AND OVER THAT I LOVED HIM...

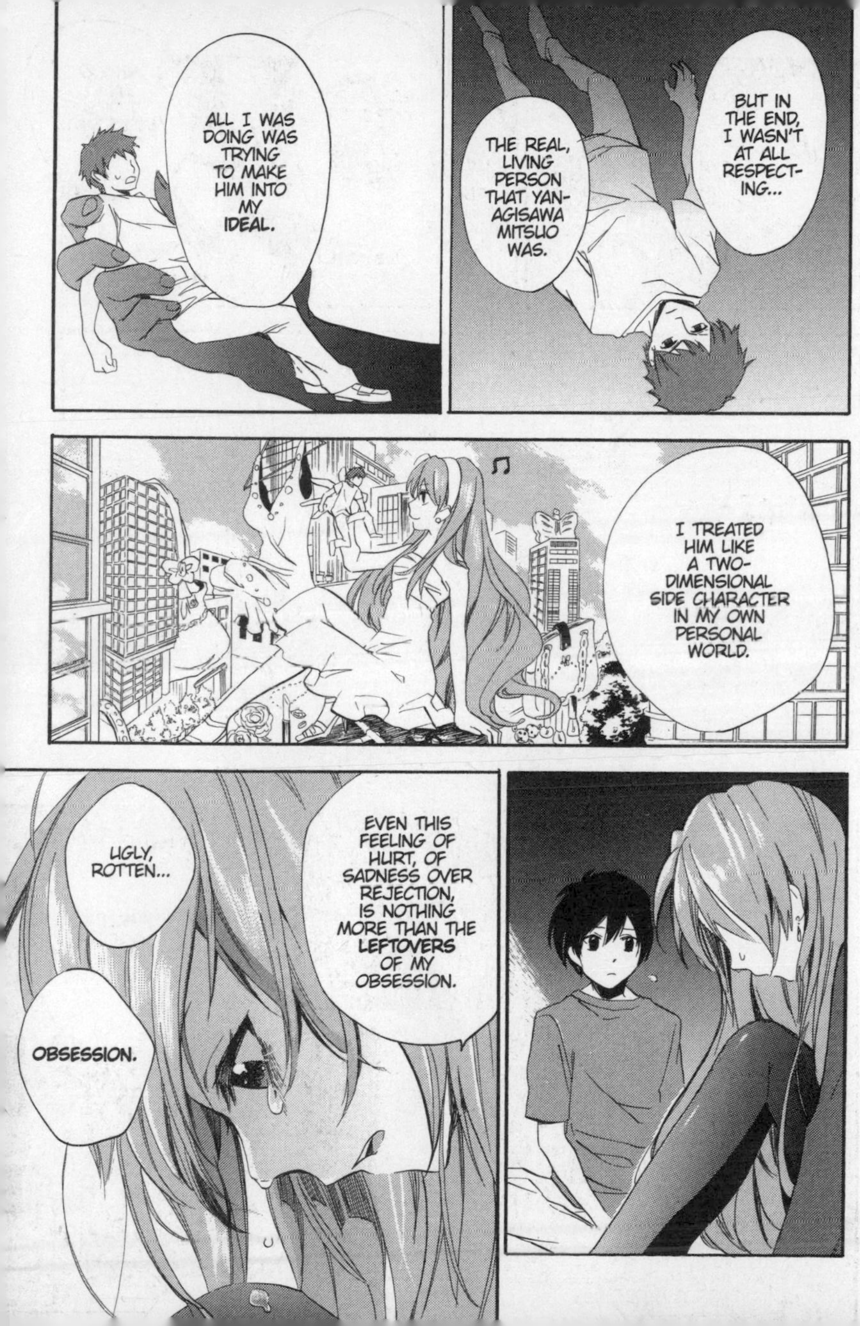
BUT IN THE END, I WASN'T AT ALL RESPECTING...
THE REAL, LIVING PERSON THAT YANAGISAWA MITSUO WAS.
ALL I WAS DOING WAS TRYING TO MAKE HIM INTO MY IDEAL.
I TREATED HIM LIKE A TWO-DIMENSIONAL SIDE CHARACTER IN MY OWN PERSONAL WORLD.
EVEN THIS FEELING OF HURT, OF SADNESS OVER REJECTION, IS NOTHING MORE THAN THE LEFTOVERS OF MY OBSESSION.
UGLY, ROTTEN...
OBSESSION.

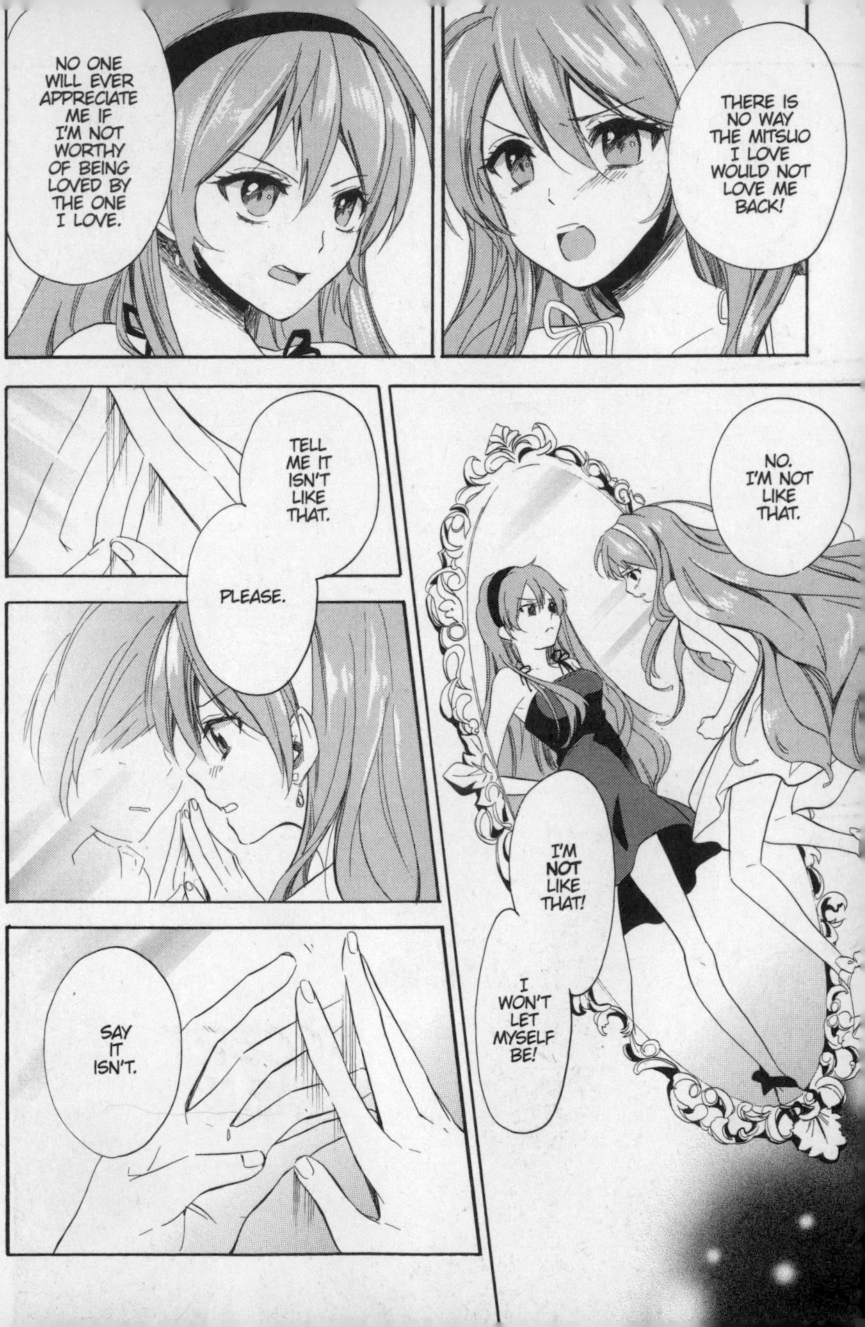
THERE IS NO WAY THE MITSUO I LOVE WOULD NOT LOVE ME BACK!
NO ONE WILL EVER APPRECIATE ME IF I'M NOT WORTHY OF BEING LOVED BY THE ONE I LOVE.
NO. I'M NOT LIKE THAT.
I'M NOT LIKE THAT!
I WON'T LET MYSELF BE!
TELL ME IT ISN'T LIKE THAT.
PLEASE.
SAY IT ISN'T.

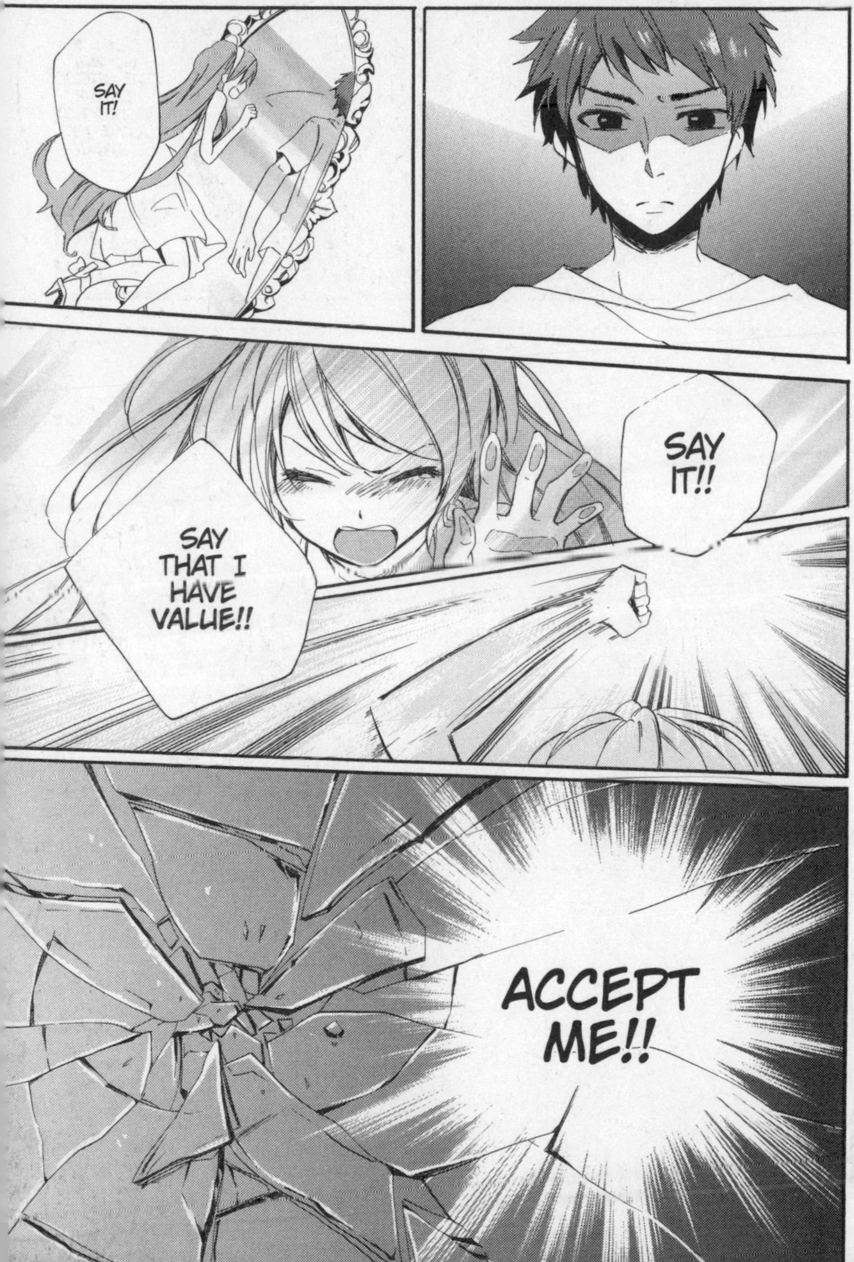
SAY IT!
SAY IT!!
SAY THAT I HAVE VALUE!!
ACCEPT ME!!

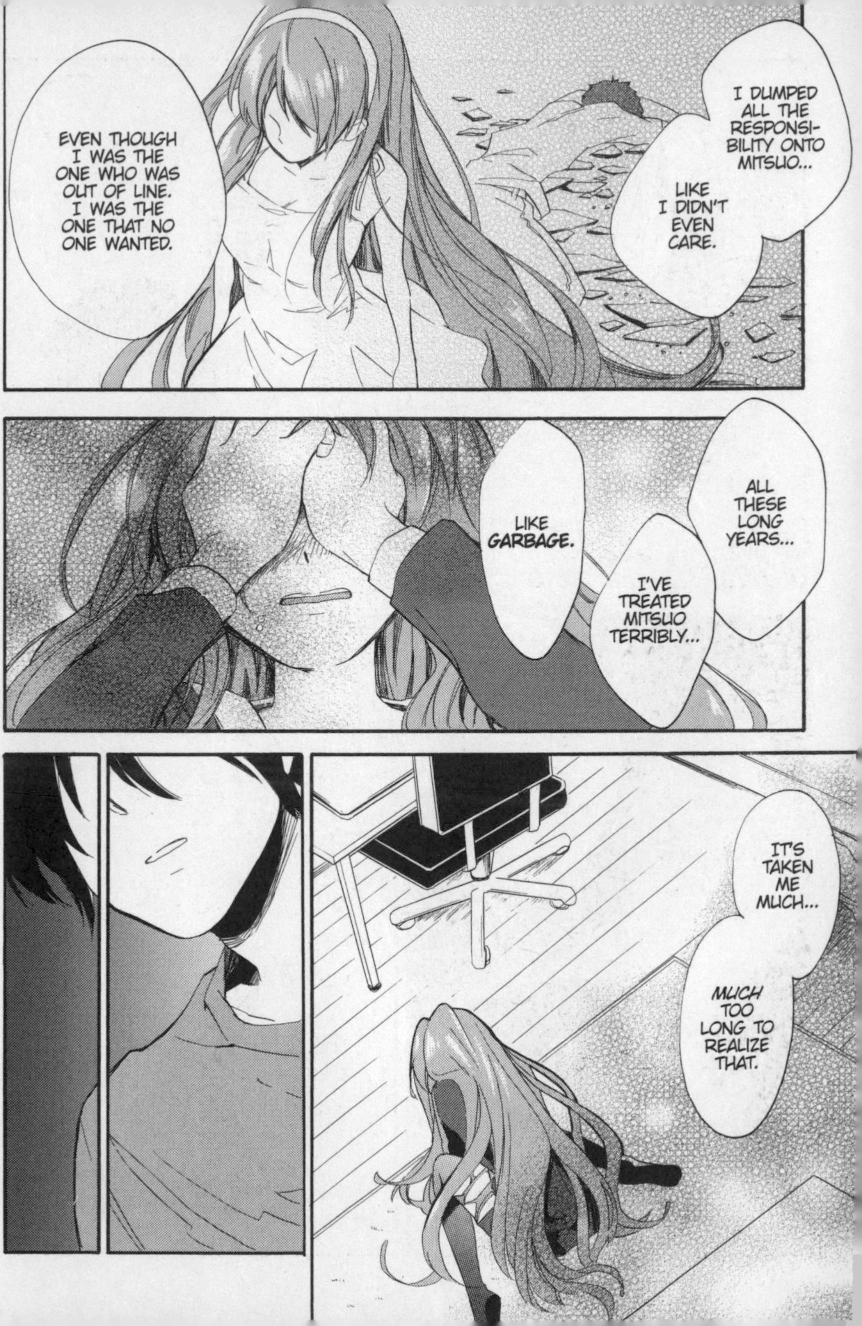
I DUMPED ALL THE RESPONSIBILITY ONTO MITSUO...
LIKE I DIDN'T EVEN CARE.
EVEN THOUGH I WAS THE ONE WHO WAS OUT OF LINE. I WAS THE ONE THAT NO ONE WANTED.
ALL THESE LONG YEARS...
I'VE TREATED MITSUO TERRIBLY...
LIKE GARBAGE.
IT'S TAKEN ME MUCH...
MUCH TOO LONG TO REALIZE THAT.

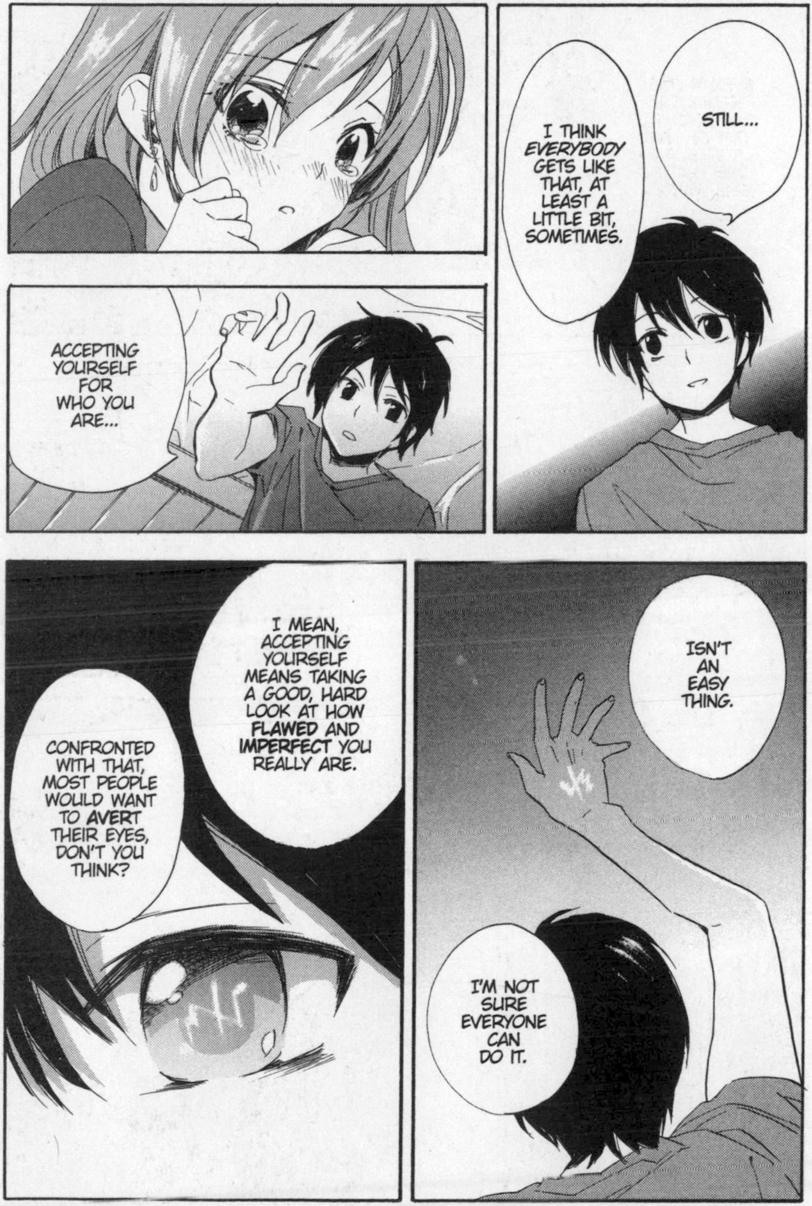
STILL...
I THINK EVERYBODY GETS LIKE THAT, AT LEAST A LITTLE BIT, SOMETIMES.
ACCEPTING YOURSELF FOR WHO YOU ARE...
ISN'T AN EASY THING.
I'M NOT SURE EVERYONE CAN DO IT.
I MEAN, ACCEPTING YOURSELF MEANS TAKING A GOOD, HARD LOOK AT HOW FLAWED AND IMPERFECT YOU REALLY ARE.
CONFRONTED WITH THAT, MOST PEOPLE WOULD WANT TO AVERT THEIR EYES, DON'T YOU THINK?

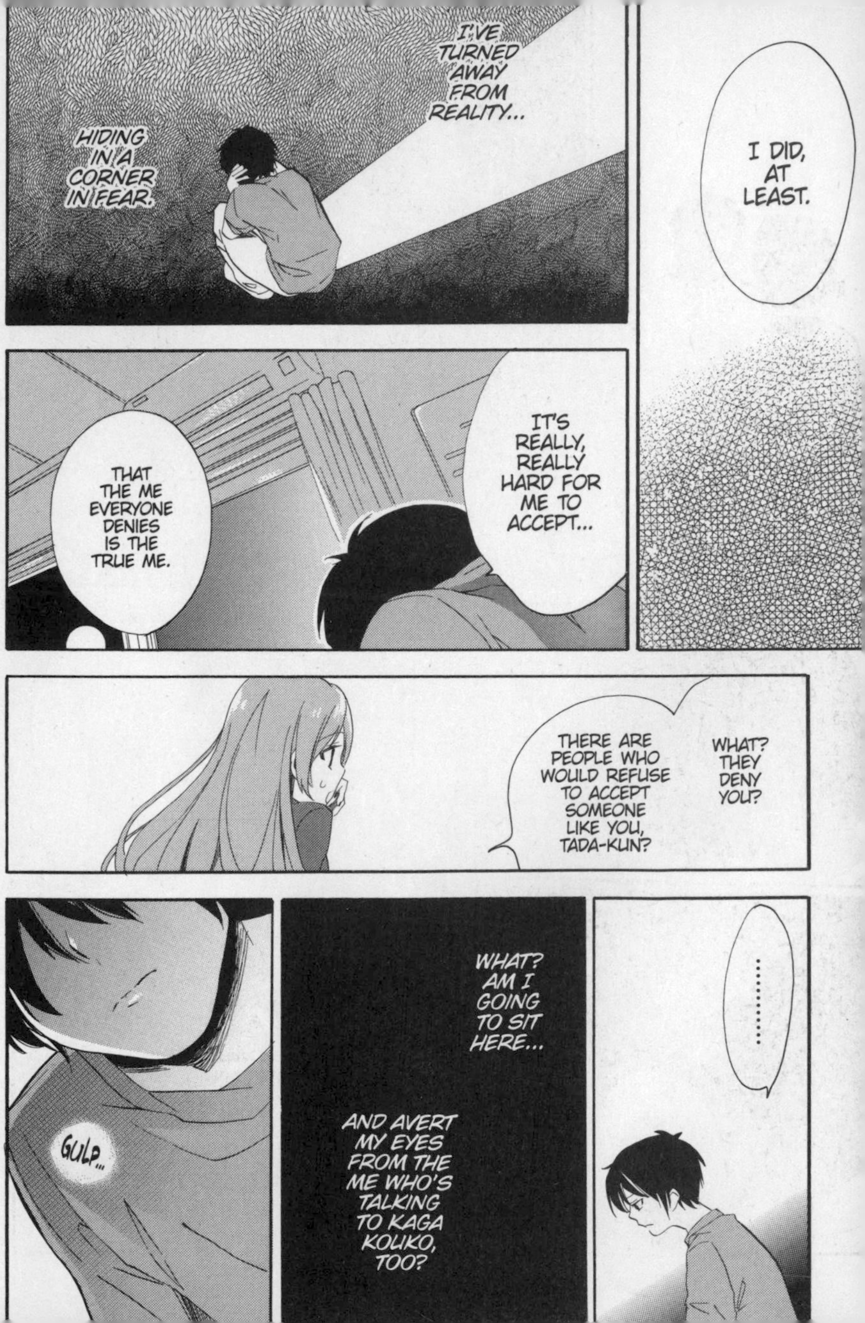
I DID, AT LEAST.
I'VE TURNED AWAY FROM REALITY...
HIDING IN A CORNER IN FEAR.
IT'S REALLY, REALLY HARD FOR ME TO ACCEPT...
THAT THE ME EVERYONE DENIES IS THE TRUE ME.
WHAT? THEY DENY YOU?
THERE ARE PEOPLE WHO WOULD REFUSE TO ACCEPT SOMEONE LIKE YOU, TADA-KUN?
......
WHAT? AM I GOING TO SIT HERE...
AND AVERT MY EYES FROM THE ME WHO'S TALKING TO KAGA KOUKO, TOO?
GULP...

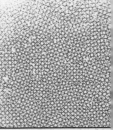

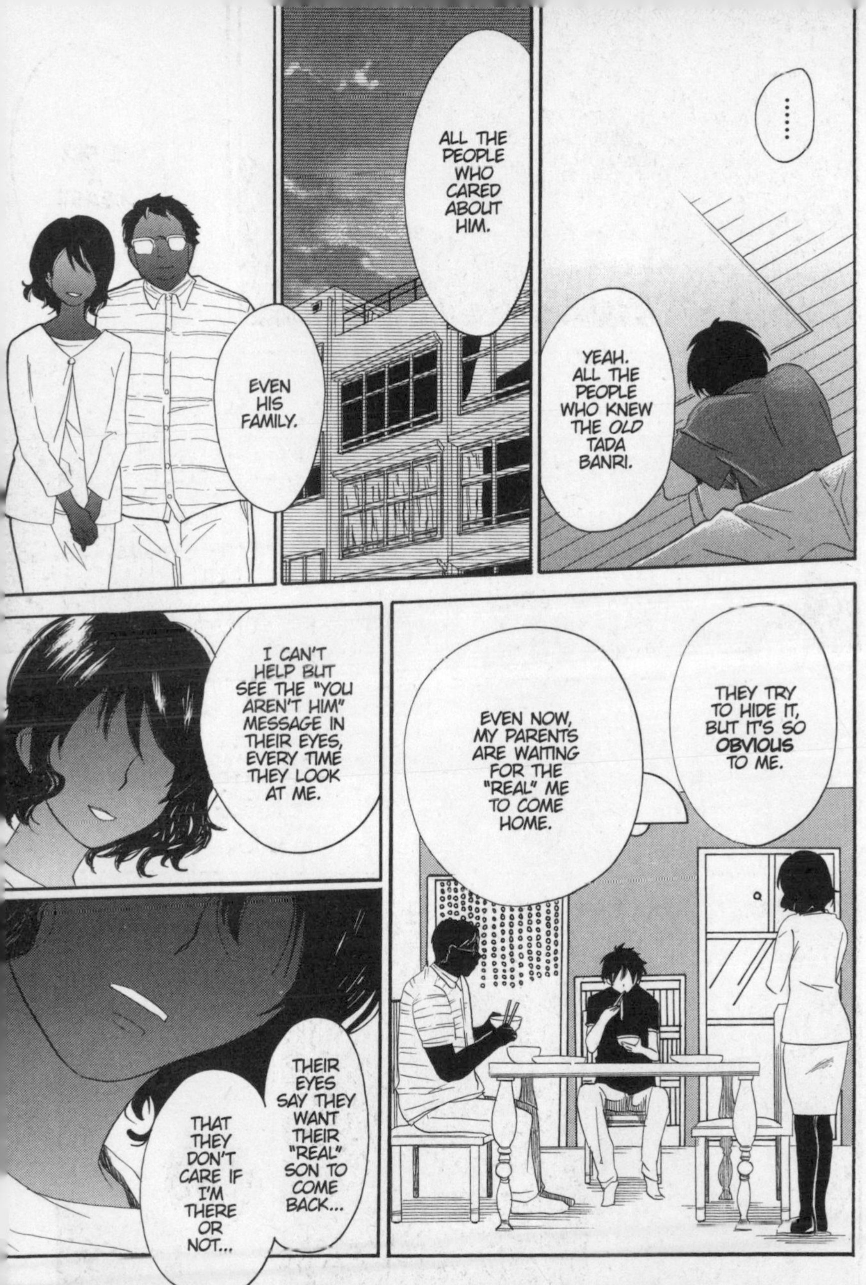
......
YEAH. ALL THE PEOPLE WHO KNEW THE *OLD* TADA BANRI.
ALL THE PEOPLE WHO CARED ABOUT HIM.
EVEN HIS FAMILY.
THEY TRY TO HIDE IT, BUT IT'S SO **OBVIOUS** TO ME.
EVEN NOW, MY PARENTS ARE WAITING FOR THE "REAL" ME TO COME HOME.
I CAN'T HELP BUT SEE THE "YOU AREN'T HIM" MESSAGE IN THEIR EYES, EVERY TIME THEY LOOK AT ME.
THEIR EYES SAY THEY WANT THEIR "REAL" SON TO COME BACK...
THAT THEY DON'T CARE IF I'M THERE OR NOT...

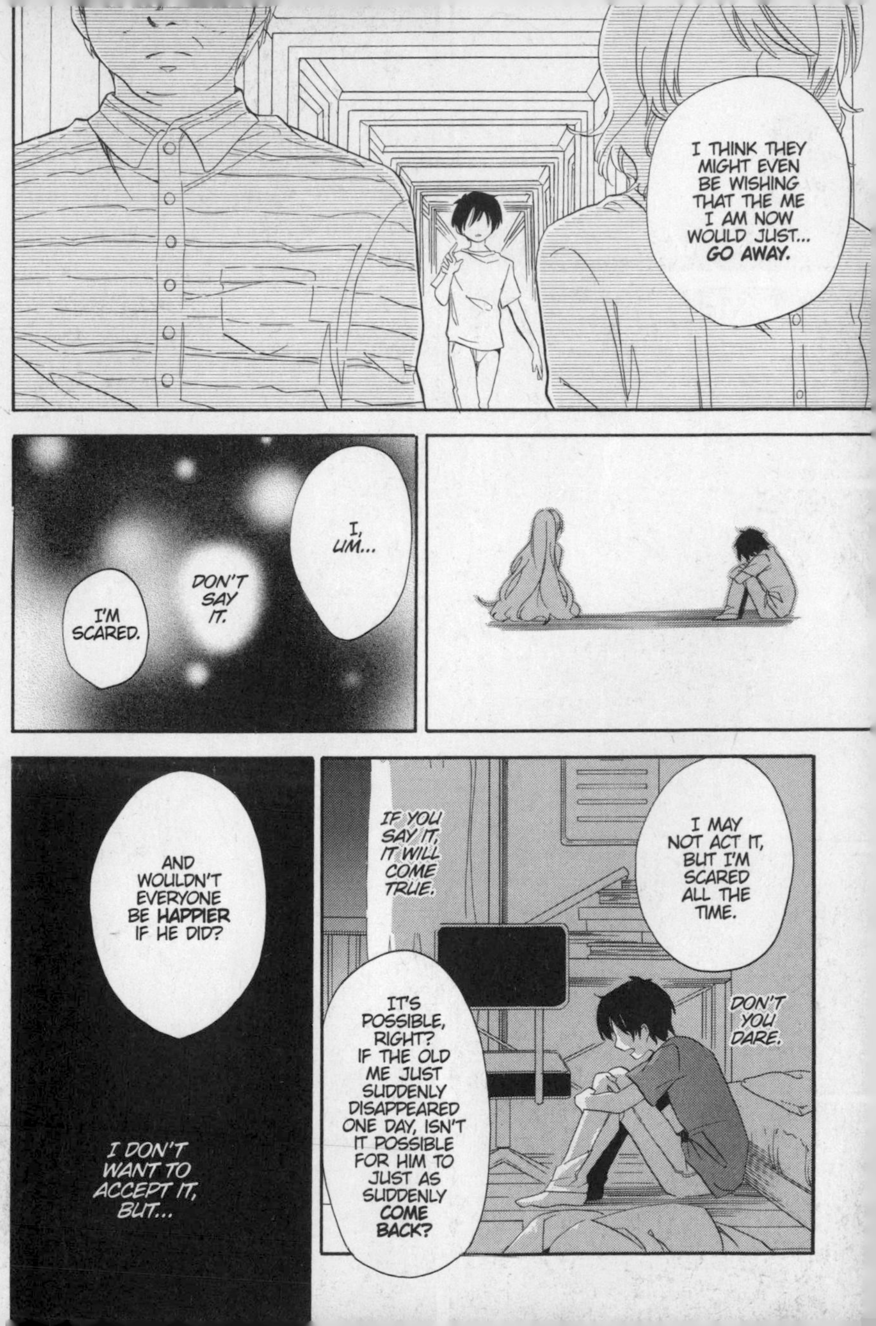
I THINK THEY MIGHT EVEN BE WISHING THAT THE ME I AM NOW WOULD JUST... **GO AWAY.**
I, UM...
DON'T SAY IT.
I'M SCARED.
I MAY NOT ACT IT, BUT I'M SCARED ALL THE TIME.
IF YOU SAY IT, IT WILL COME TRUE.
DON'T YOU DARE.
IT'S POSSIBLE, RIGHT? IF THE OLD ME JUST SUDDENLY DISAPPEARED ONE DAY, ISN'T IT POSSIBLE FOR HIM TO JUST AS SUDDENLY **COME BACK?**
AND WOULDN'T EVERYONE BE **HAPPIER** IF HE DID?
I DON'T WANT TO ACCEPT IT, BUT...

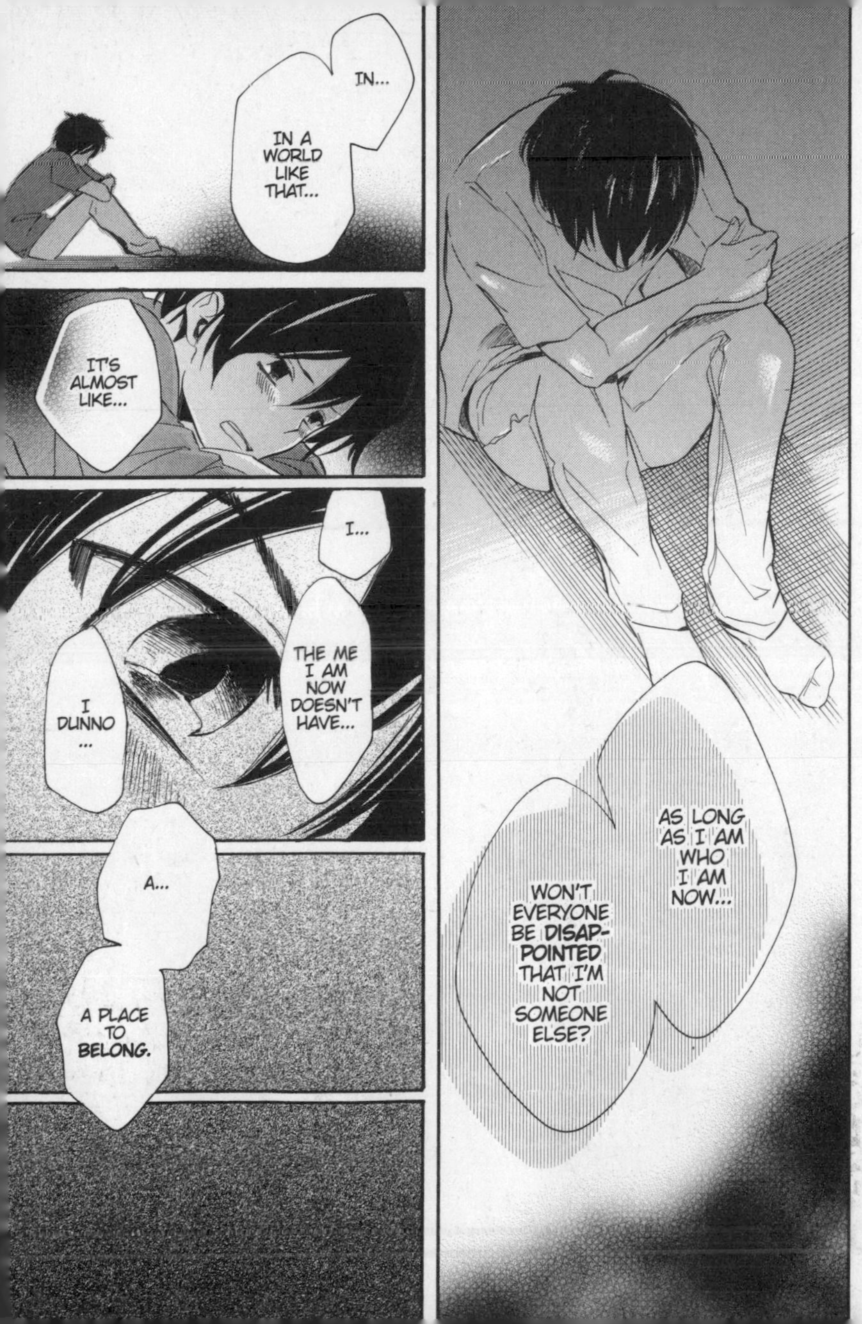
AS LONG AS I AM WHO I AM NOW...
WON'T EVERYONE BE DISAPPOINTED THAT I'M NOT SOMEONE ELSE?
IN...
IN A WORLD LIKE THAT...
IT'S ALMOST LIKE...
I...
THE ME I AM NOW DOESN'T HAVE...
I DUNNO...
A...
A PLACE TO BELONG.

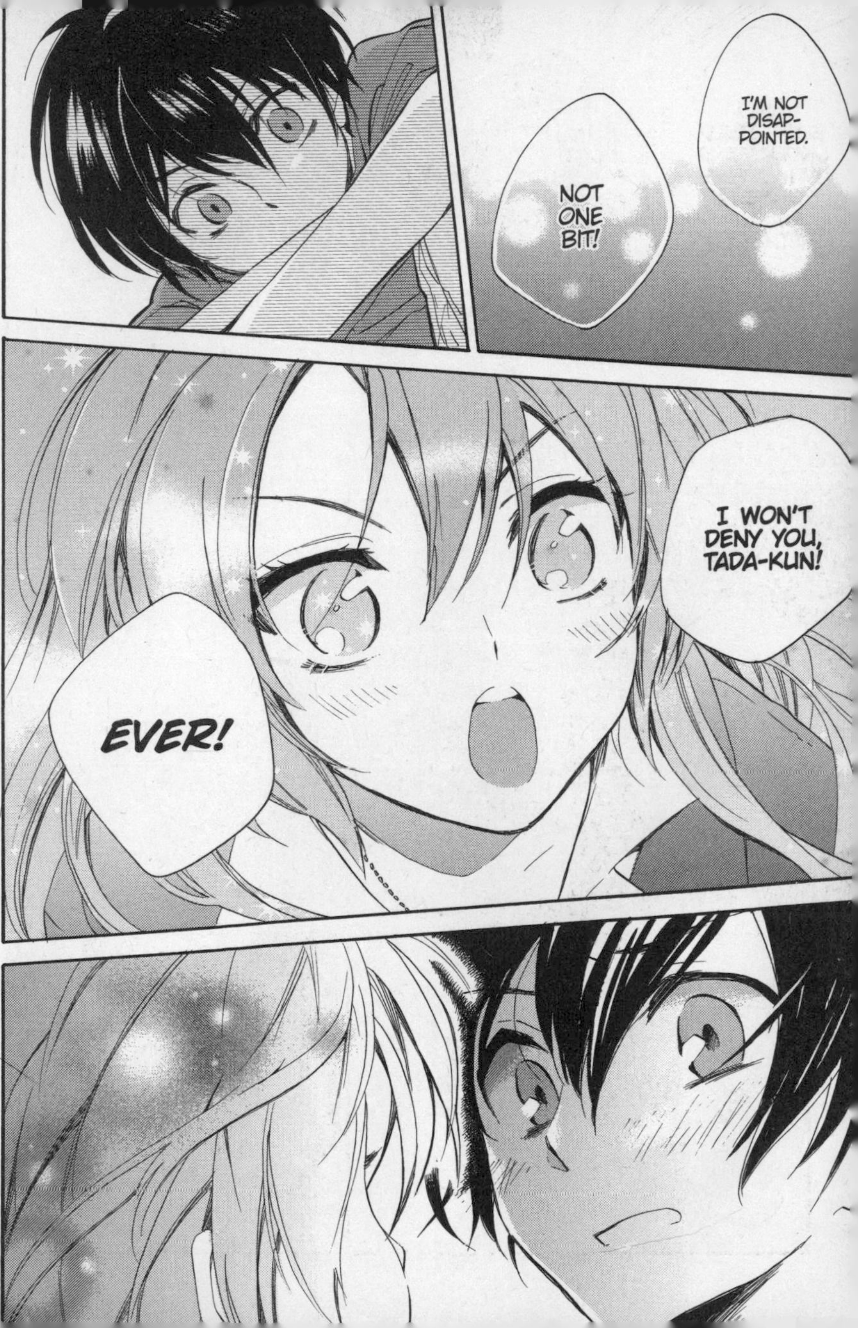
I'M NOT DISAP-POINTED.
NOT ONE BIT!
I WON'T DENY YOU, TADA-KUN!
EVER!

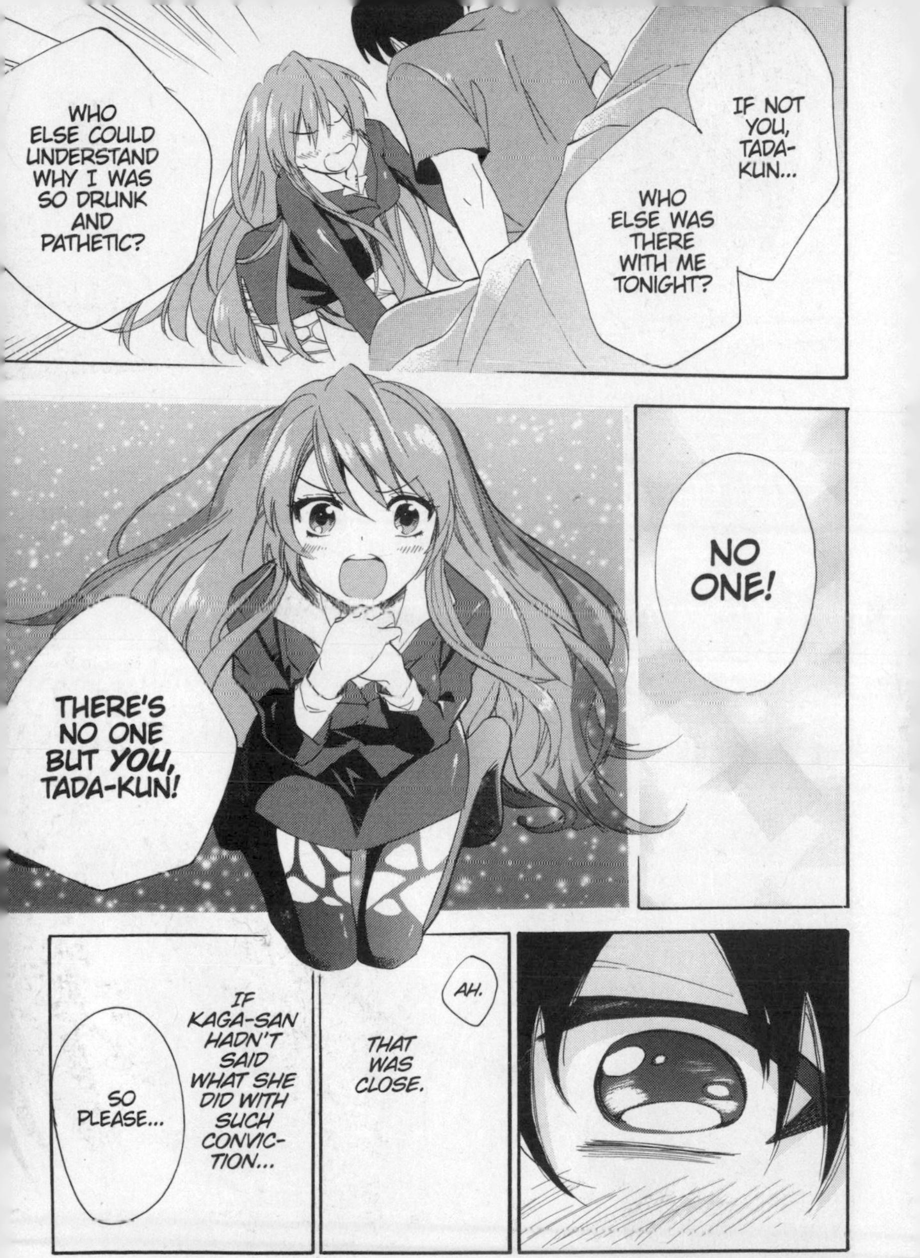
IF NOT YOU, TADA-KUN...
WHO ELSE WAS THERE WITH ME TONIGHT?
WHO ELSE COULD UNDERSTAND WHY I WAS SO DRUNK AND PATHETIC?
NO ONE!
THERE'S NO ONE BUT YOU, TADA-KUN!
AH.
THAT WAS CLOSE.
IF KAGA-SAN HADN'T SAID WHAT SHE DID WITH SUCH CONVICTION...
SO PLEASE...

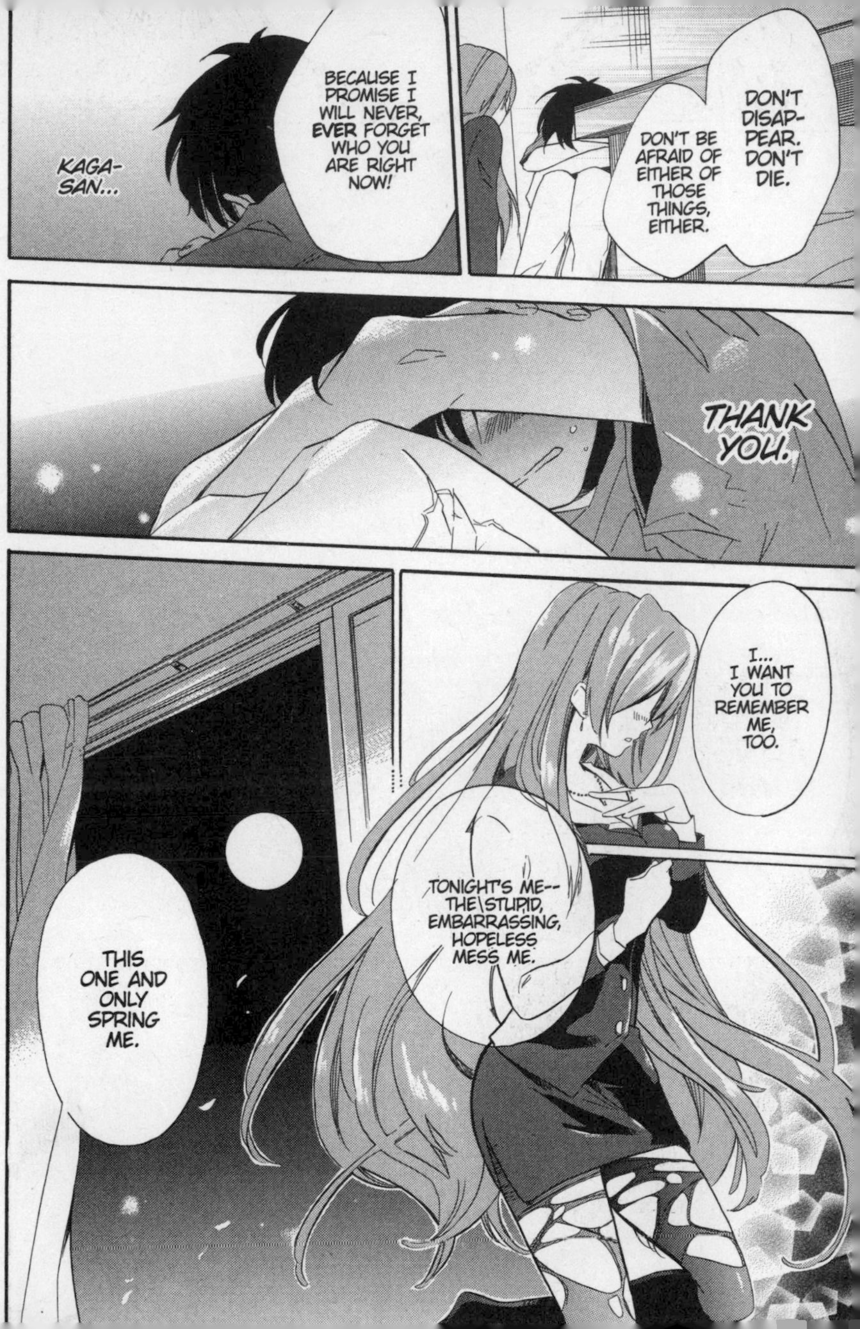
DON'T DISAPPEAR. DON'T DIE.
DON'T BE AFRAID OF EITHER OF THOSE THINGS, EITHER.
BECAUSE I PROMISE I WILL NEVER, EVER FORGET WHO YOU ARE RIGHT NOW!
KAGA-SAN...
THANK YOU.
I... I WANT YOU TO REMEMBER ME, TOO.
TONIGHT'S ME-- THE STUPID, EMBARRASSING, HOPELESS MESS ME.
THIS ONE AND ONLY SPRING ME.

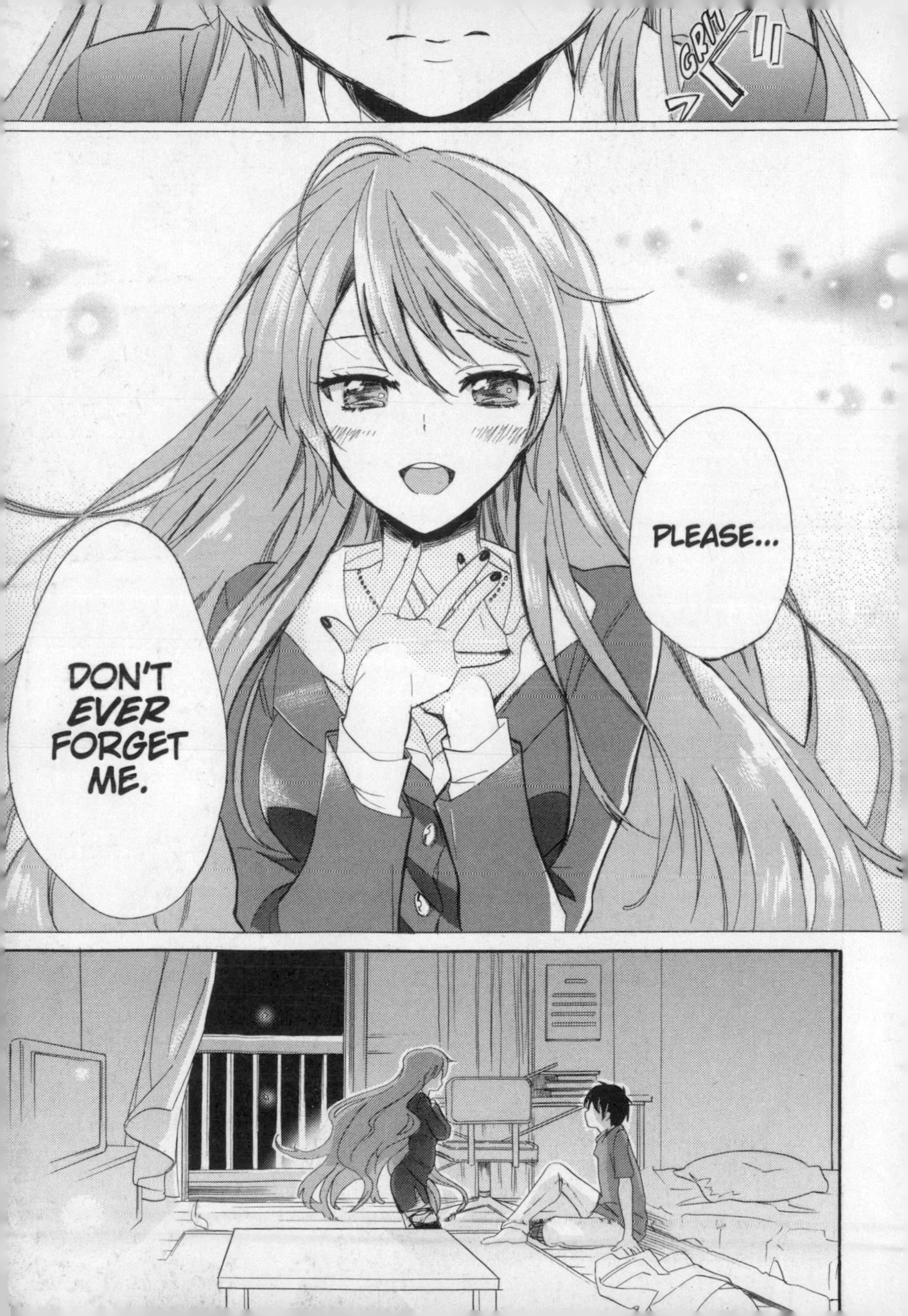
GRIT
PLEASE...
DON'T EVER FORGET ME.

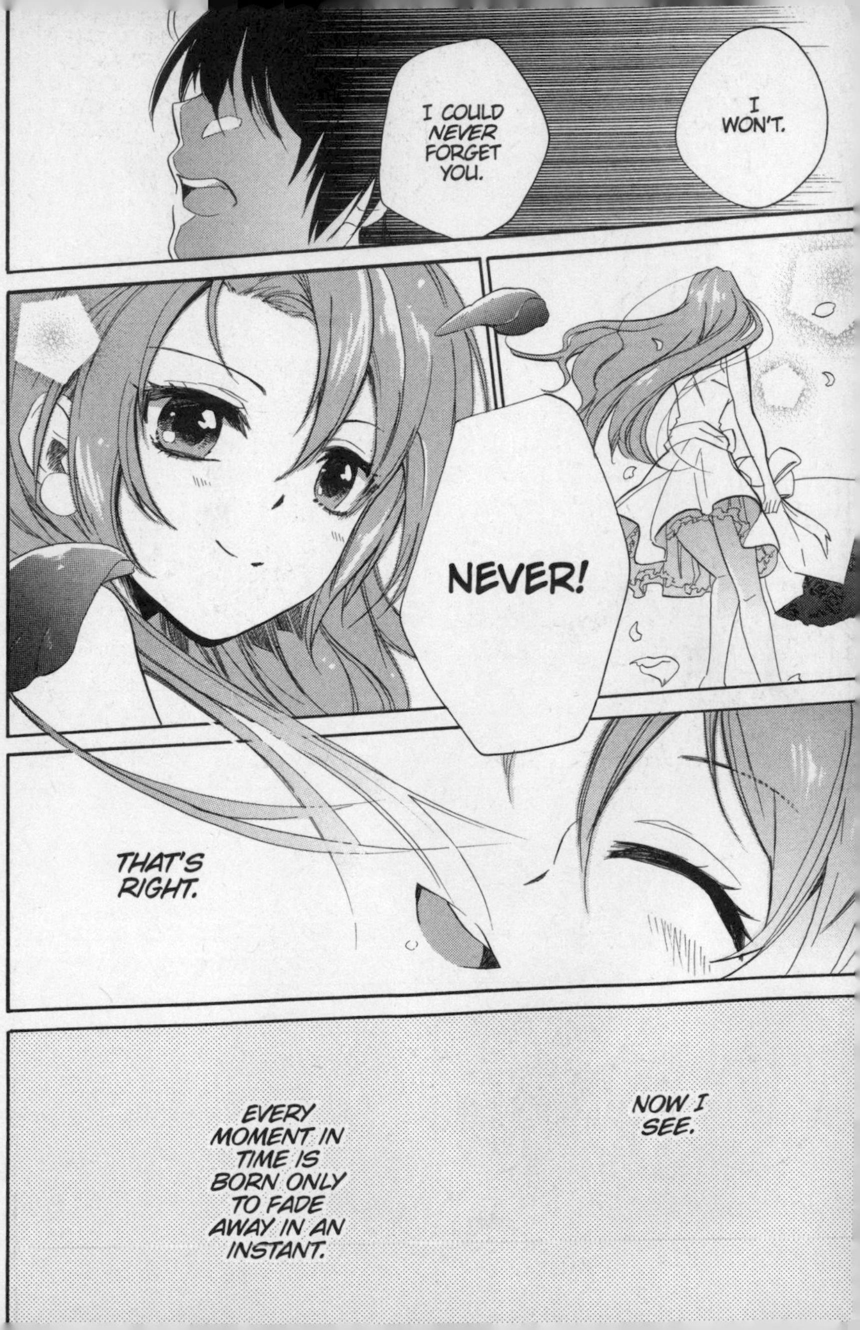
I WON'T.
I COULD NEVER FORGET YOU.
NEVER!
THAT'S RIGHT.
NOW I SEE.
EVERY MOMENT IN TIME IS BORN ONLY TO FADE AWAY IN AN INSTANT.

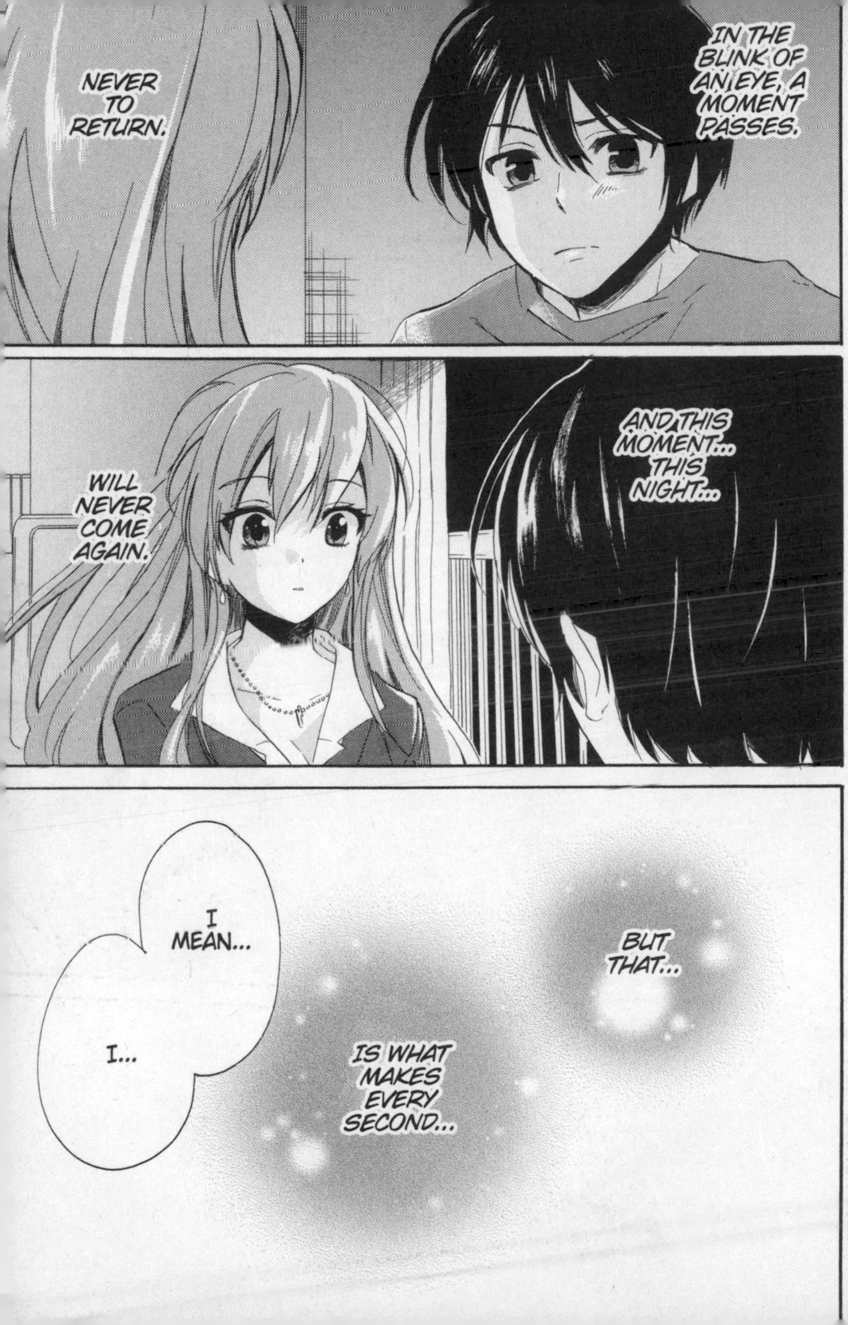
IN THE BLINK OF AN EYE, A MOMENT PASSES.
NEVER TO RETURN.
AND THIS MOMENT... THIS NIGHT...
WILL NEVER COME AGAIN.
BUT THAT...
IS WHAT MAKES EVERY SECOND...
I MEAN...
I...

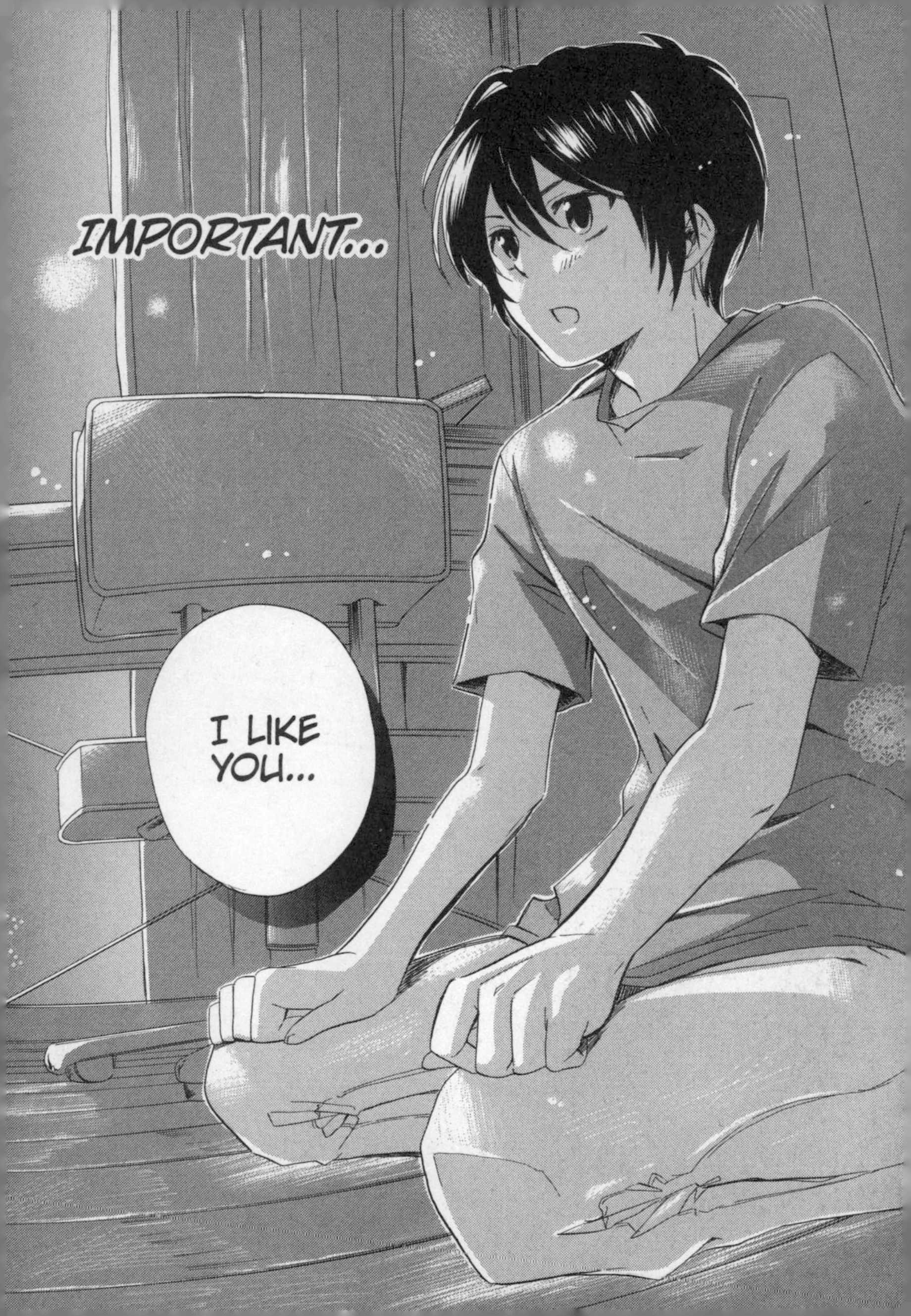
IMPORTANT...
I LIKE YOU...

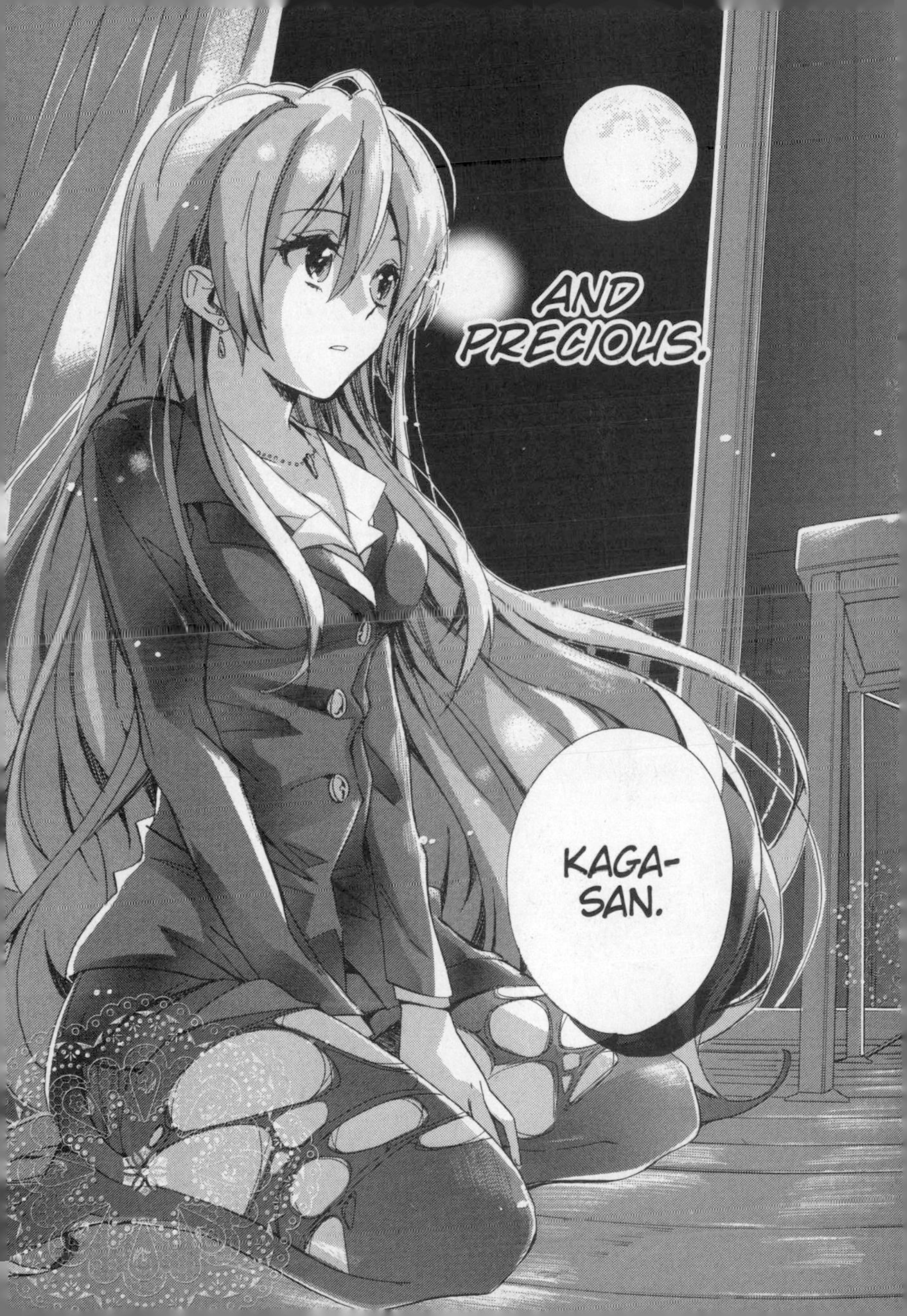
AND PRECIOUS.
KAGA-SAN.

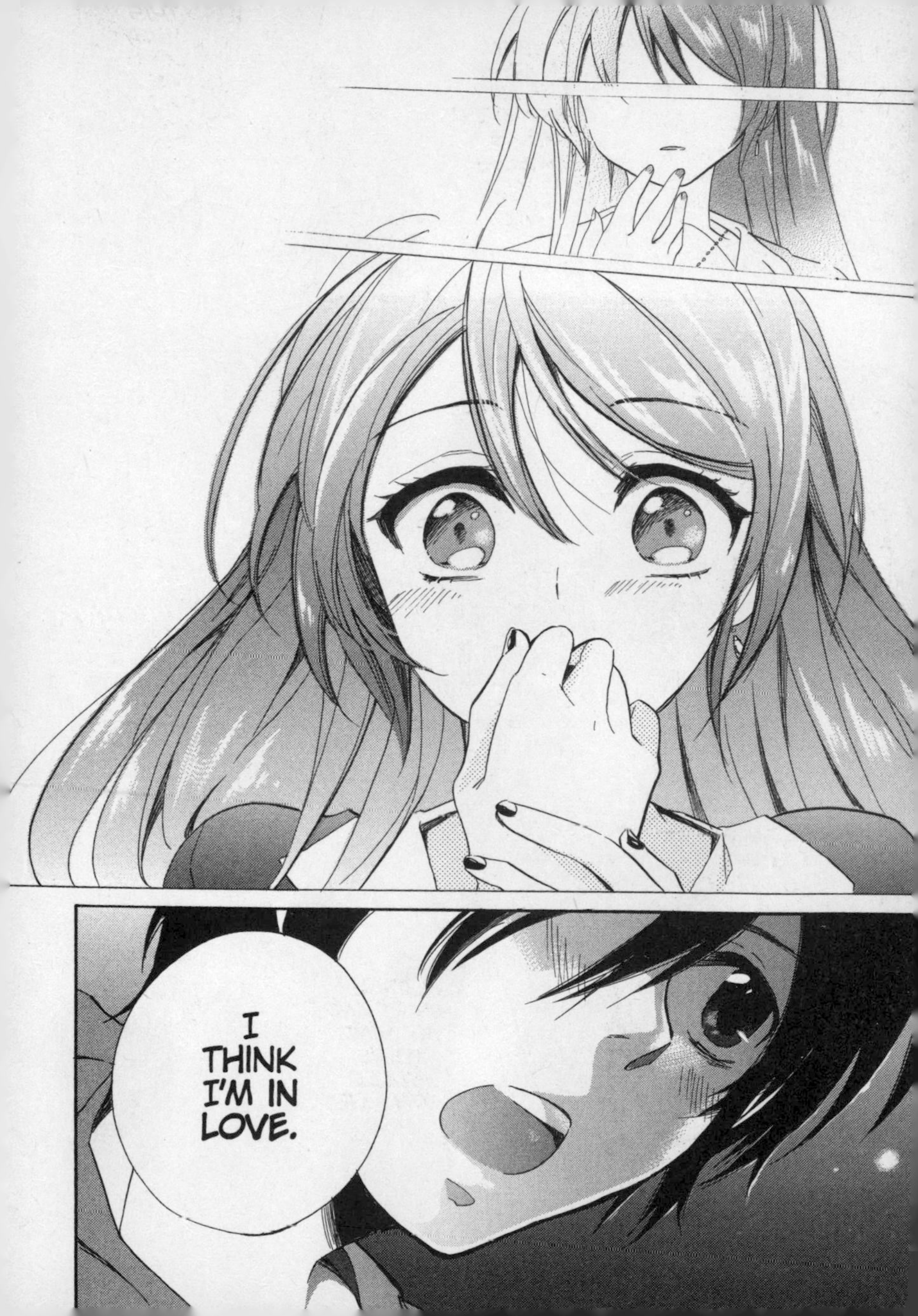
I THINK I'M IN LOVE.

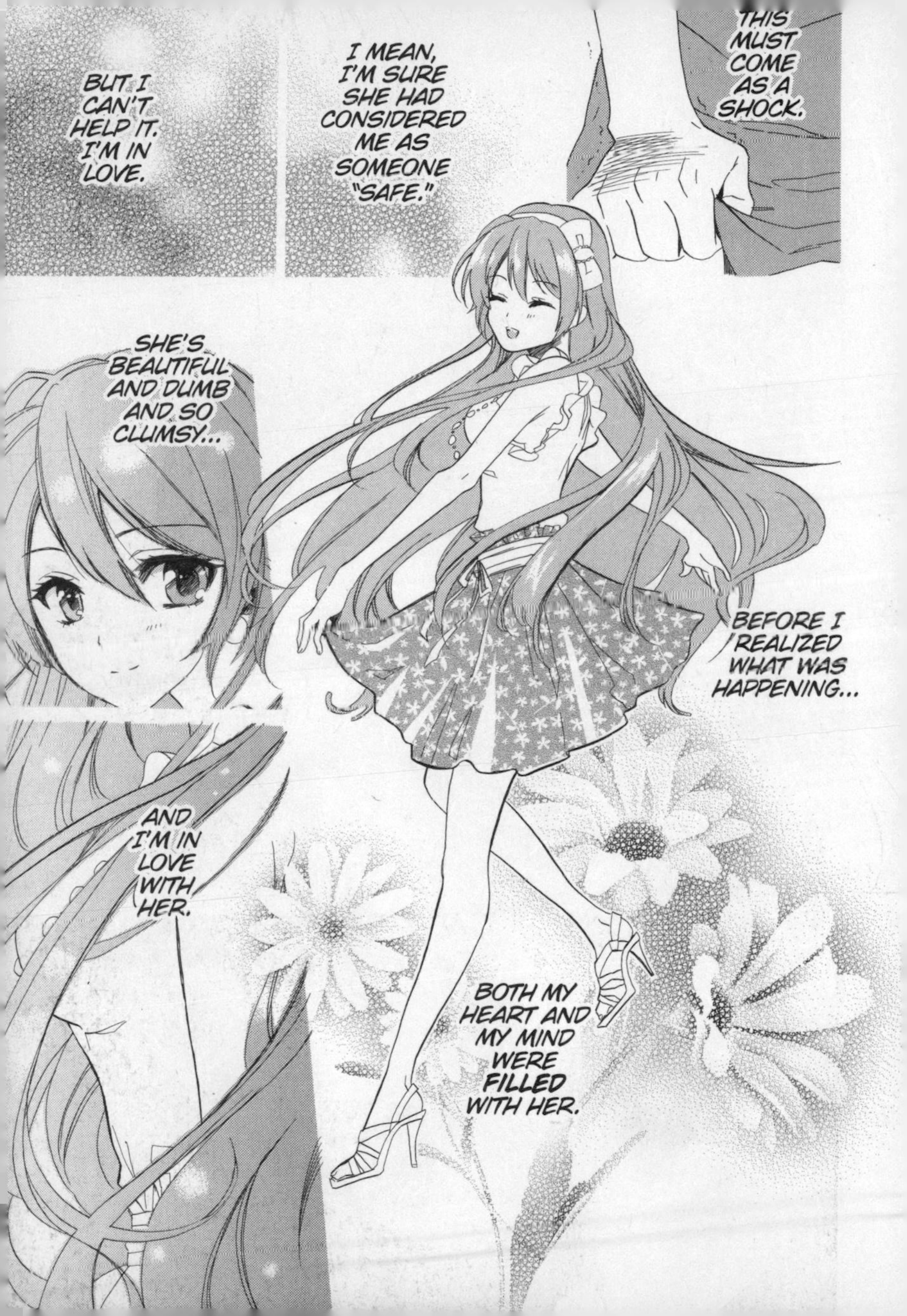
THIS MUST COME AS A SHOCK.
I MEAN, I'M SURE SHE HAD CONSIDERED ME AS SOMEONE "SAFE."
BUT I CAN'T HELP IT. I'M IN LOVE.
BEFORE I REALIZED WHAT WAS HAPPENING...
BOTH MY HEART AND MY MIND WERE FILLED WITH HER.
SHE'S BEAUTIFUL AND DUMB AND SO CLUMSY...
AND I'M IN LOVE WITH HER.

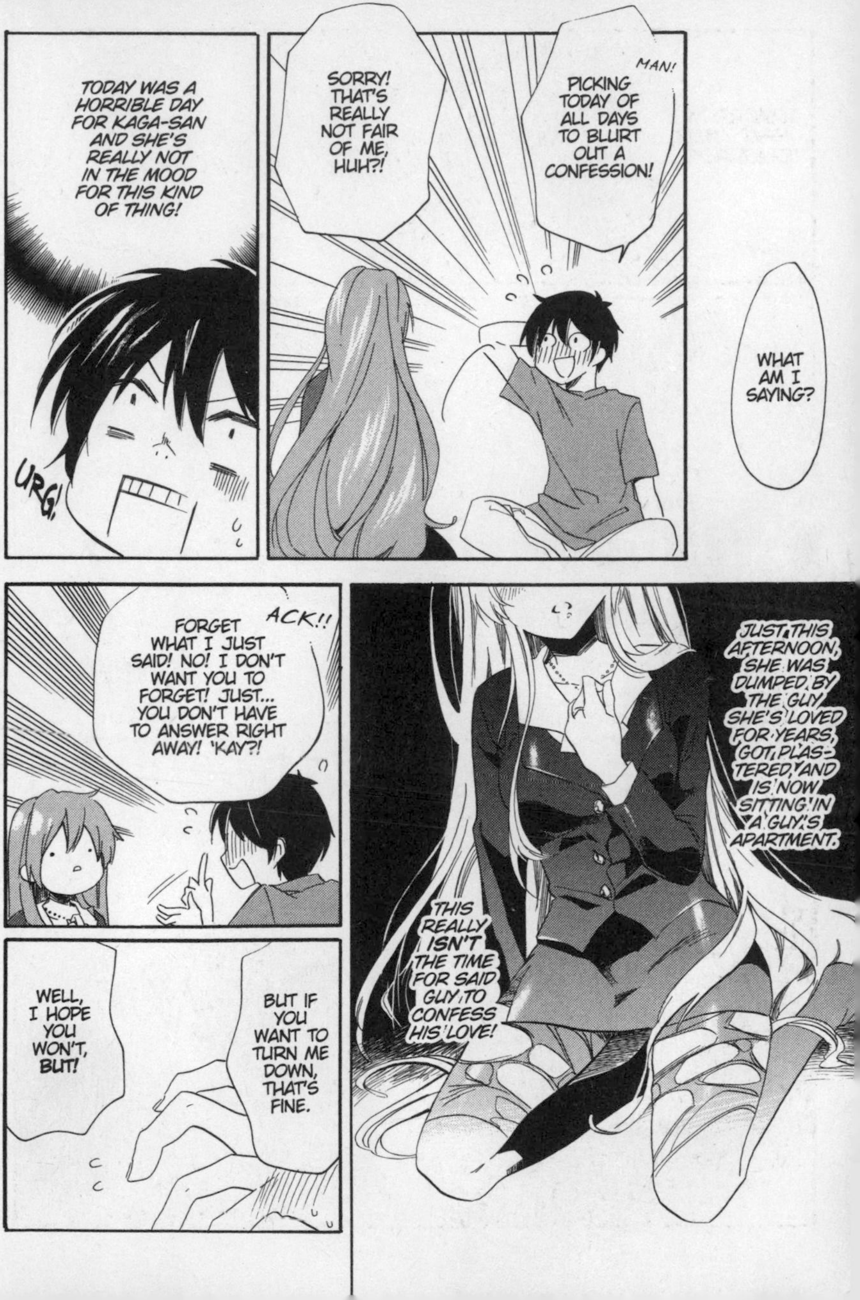
MAN!
PICKING TODAY OF ALL DAYS TO BLURT OUT A CONFESSION!
SORRY! THAT'S REALLY NOT FAIR OF ME, HUH?!
WHAT AM I SAYING?
TODAY WAS A HORRIBLE DAY FOR KAGA-SAN AND SHE'S REALLY NOT IN THE MOOD FOR THIS KIND OF THING!
URG!
JUST THIS AFTERNOON, SHE WAS DUMPED BY THE GUY SHE'S LOVED FOR YEARS, GOT PLASTERED, AND IS NOW SITTING IN A GUY'S APARTMENT.
THIS REALLY ISN'T THE TIME FOR SAID GUY TO CONFESS HIS LOVE!
ACK!!
FORGET WHAT I JUST SAID! NO! I DON'T WANT YOU TO FORGET! JUST... YOU DON'T HAVE TO ANSWER RIGHT AWAY! 'KAY?!
BUT IF YOU WANT TO TURN ME DOWN, THAT'S FINE.
WELL, I HOPE YOU WON'T, BUT!

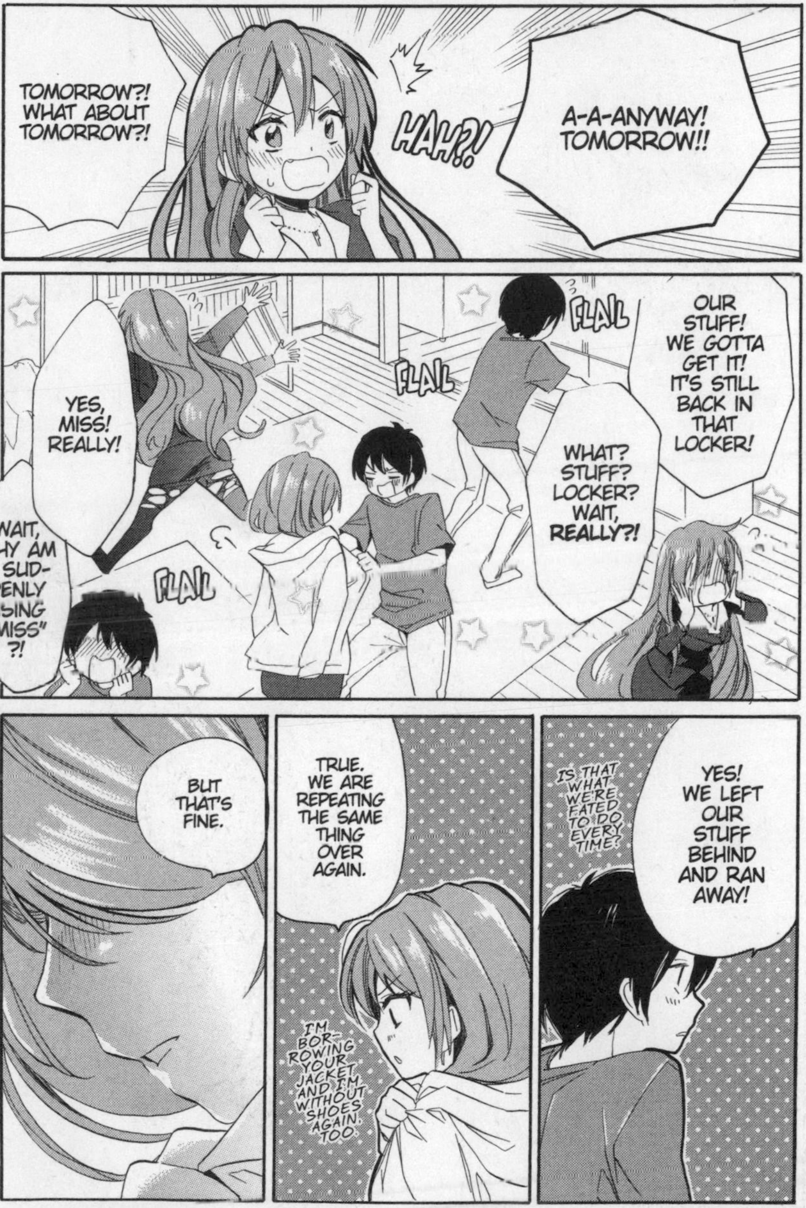
A-A-ANYWAY! TOMORROW!!
HAH?!
TOMORROW?! WHAT ABOUT TOMORROW?!
OUR STUFF! WE GOTTA GET IT! IT'S STILL BACK IN THAT LOCKER!
FLAIL
WHAT? STUFF? LOCKER? WAIT, REALLY?!
FLAIL
YES, MISS! REALLY!
FLAIL
WAIT, WHY AM I SUD-DENLY USING "MISS"?!
YES! WE LEFT OUR STUFF BEHIND AND RAN AWAY!
IS THAT WHAT WE'RE FATED TO DO EVERY TIME?
TRUE. WE ARE REPEATING THE SAME THING OVER AGAIN.
I'M BOR-ROWING YOUR JACKET AND I'M WITHOUT SHOES AGAIN, TOO.
BUT THAT'S FINE.

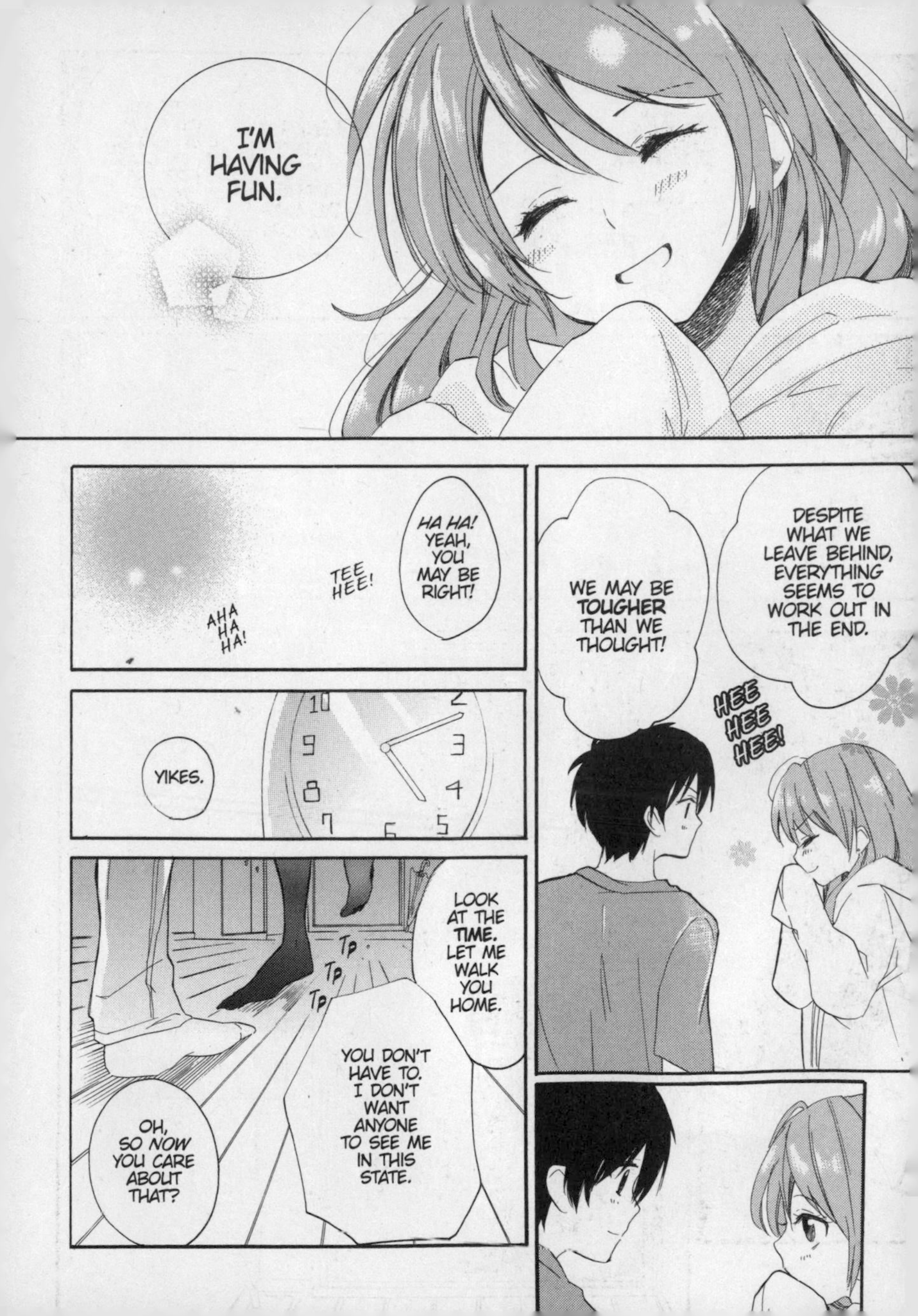
I'M HAVING FUN.
DESPITE WHAT WE LEAVE BEHIND, EVERYTHING SEEMS TO WORK OUT IN THE END.
WE MAY BE TOUGHER THAN WE THOUGHT!
HEE HEE HEE!
HA HA! YEAH, YOU MAY BE RIGHT!
TEE HEE!
AHA HA HA!
YIKES.
LOOK AT THE TIME. LET ME WALK YOU HOME.
Tp Tp Tp
YOU DON'T HAVE TO. I DON'T WANT ANYONE TO SEE ME IN THIS STATE.
OH, SO NOW YOU CARE ABOUT THAT?

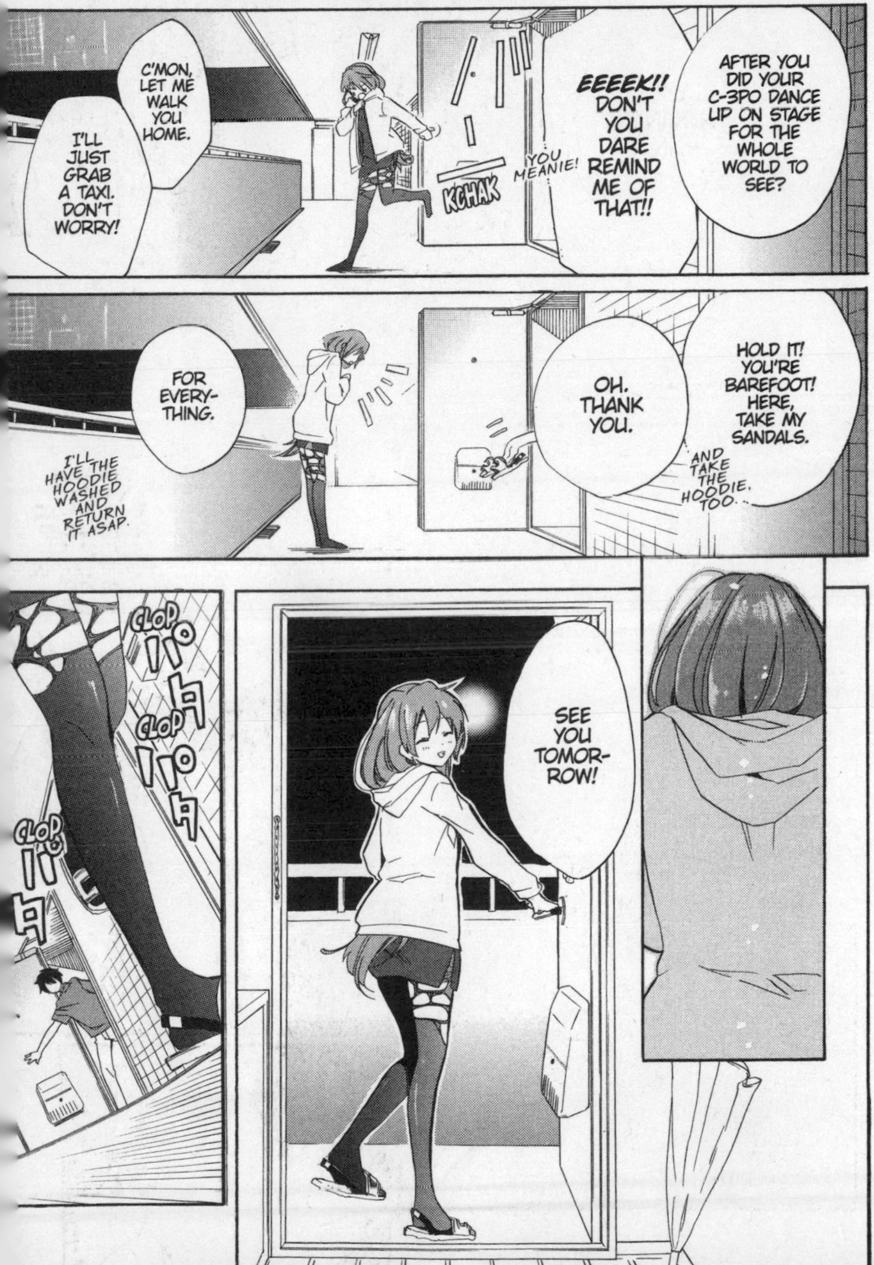

AFTER YOU DID YOUR C-3PO DANCE UP ON STAGE FOR THE WHOLE WORLD TO SEE?
EEEEK!! DON'T YOU DARE REMIND ME OF THAT!!
YOU MEANIE!
KCHAK
C'MON, LET ME WALK YOU HOME.
I'LL JUST GRAB A TAXI. DON'T WORRY!
HOLD IT! YOU'RE BAREFOOT! HERE, TAKE MY SANDALS.
AND TAKE THE HOODIE, TOO...
OH. THANK YOU.
FOR EVERY-THING.
I'LL HAVE THE HOODIE WASHED AND RETURN IT ASAP.
SEE YOU TOMOR-ROW!
CLOP
CLOP
CLOP

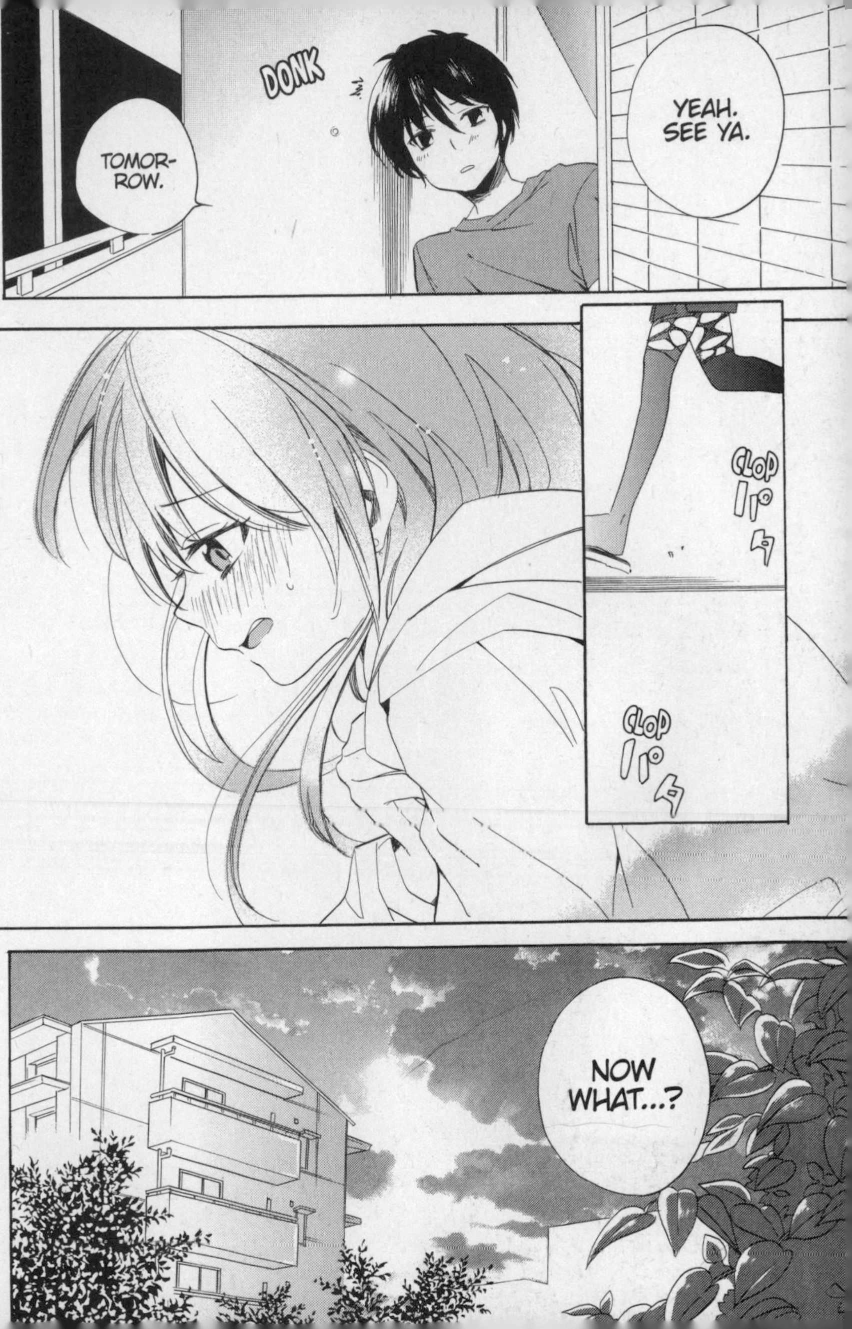
YEAH. SEE YA.
DONK
TOMOR-ROW.
CLOP パタ
CLOP パタ
NOW WHAT...?

GOLDEN TIME

ゴールデンタイム

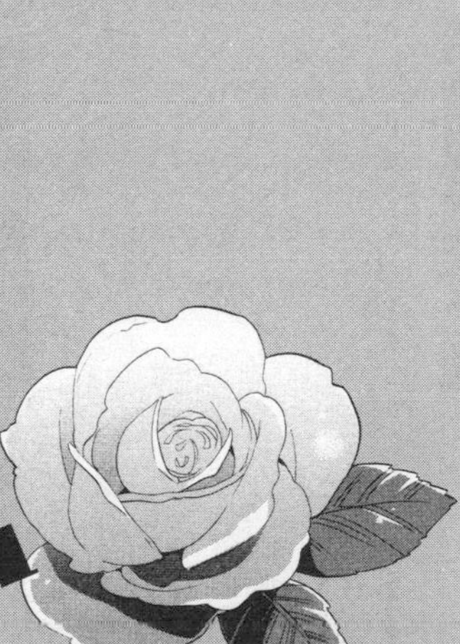

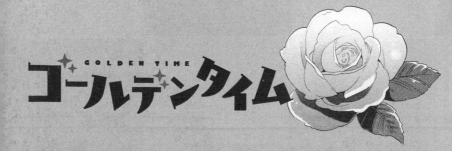

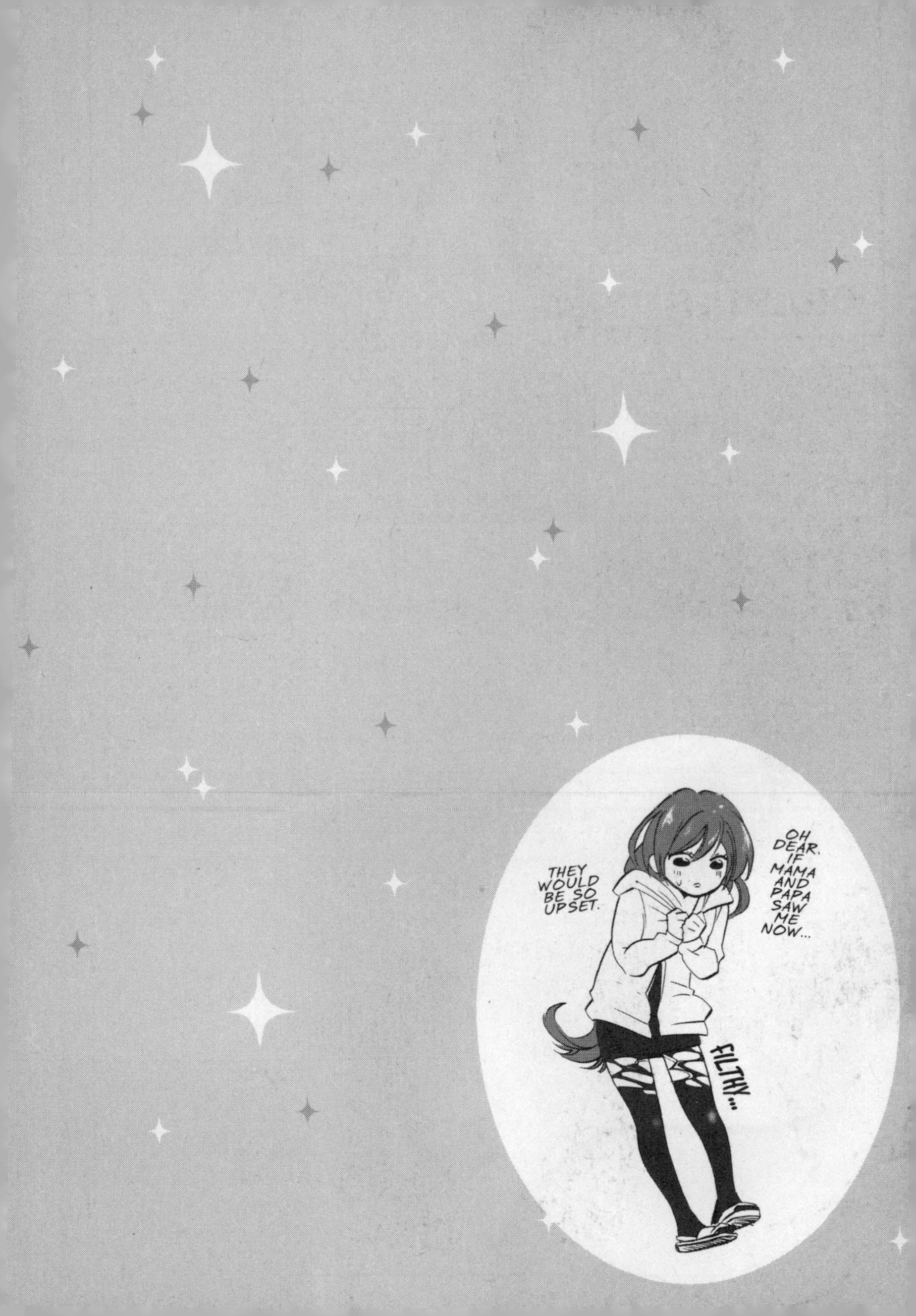
OH DEAR. IF MAMA AND PAPA SAW ME NOW...
THEY WOULD BE SO UPSET.
FILTHY...

CHAPTER 12

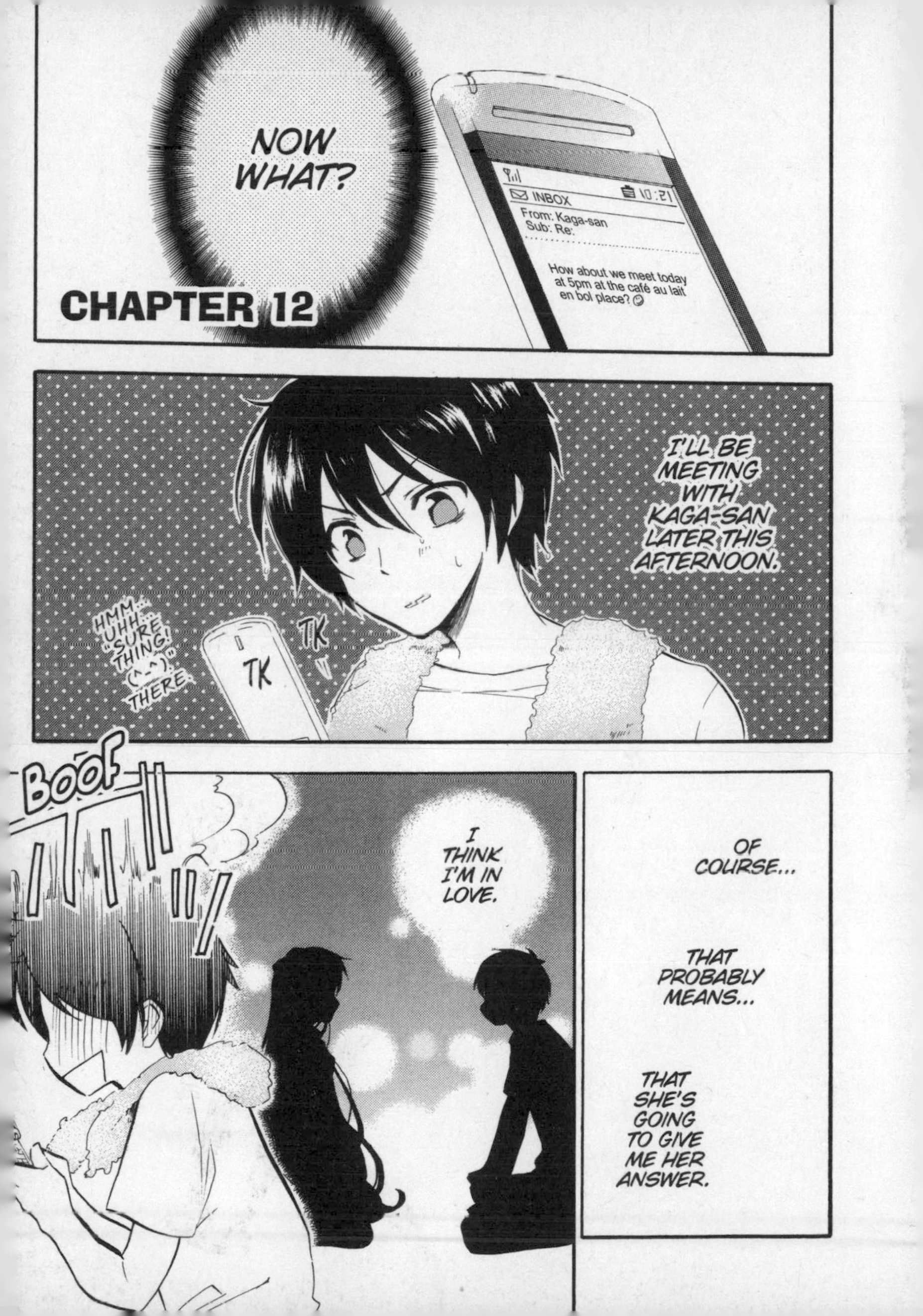
INBOX 10:21
From: Kaga-san
Sub: Re:
How about we meet today at 5pm at the café au lait en bol place? ☺
NOW WHAT?
I'LL BE MEETING WITH KAGA-SAN LATER THIS AFTERNOON.
TK
TK
HMM... UHH... "SURE THING! (^_^)" THERE.
OF COURSE...
THAT PROBABLY MEANS...
THAT SHE'S GOING TO GIVE ME HER ANSWER.
I THINK I'M IN LOVE.
BOOF

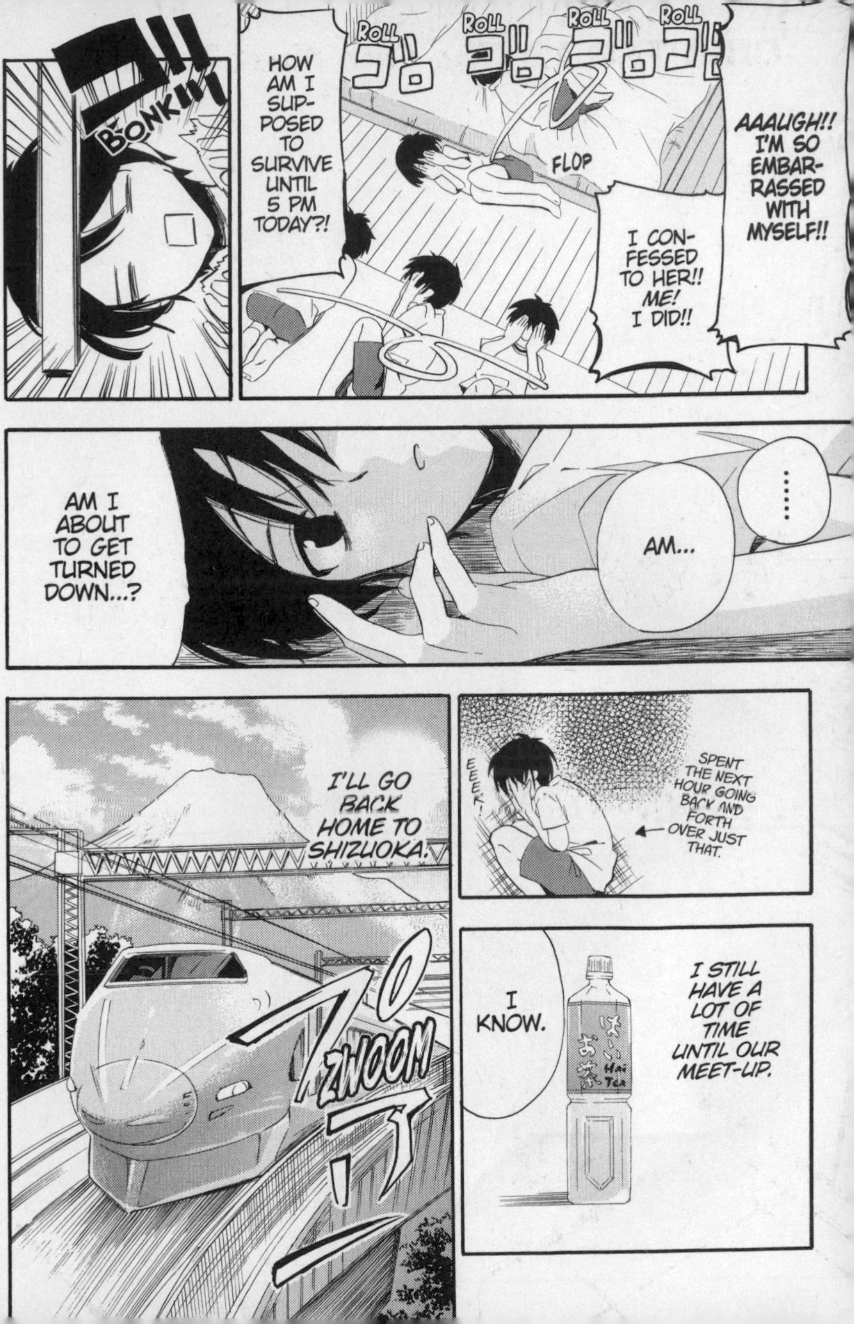
ROLL ゴロ ROLL ゴロ ROLL ゴロ ROLL ゴロ
AAAUGH!! I'M SO EMBARRASSED WITH MYSELF!!
I CONFESSED TO HER!! ME! I DID!!
FLOP
HOW AM I SUPPOSED TO SURVIVE UNTIL 5 PM TODAY?!
BONK!!!
......
AM...
AM I ABOUT TO GET TURNED DOWN...?
SPENT THE NEXT HOUR GOING BACK AND FORTH OVER JUST THAT.
EEEK!
I STILL HAVE A LOT OF TIME UNTIL OUR MEET-UP.
I KNOW.
はいお茶
Hai Tea
I'LL GO BACK HOME TO SHIZUOKA.
ZWOOM

CHAPTER 12: The One Next To Me

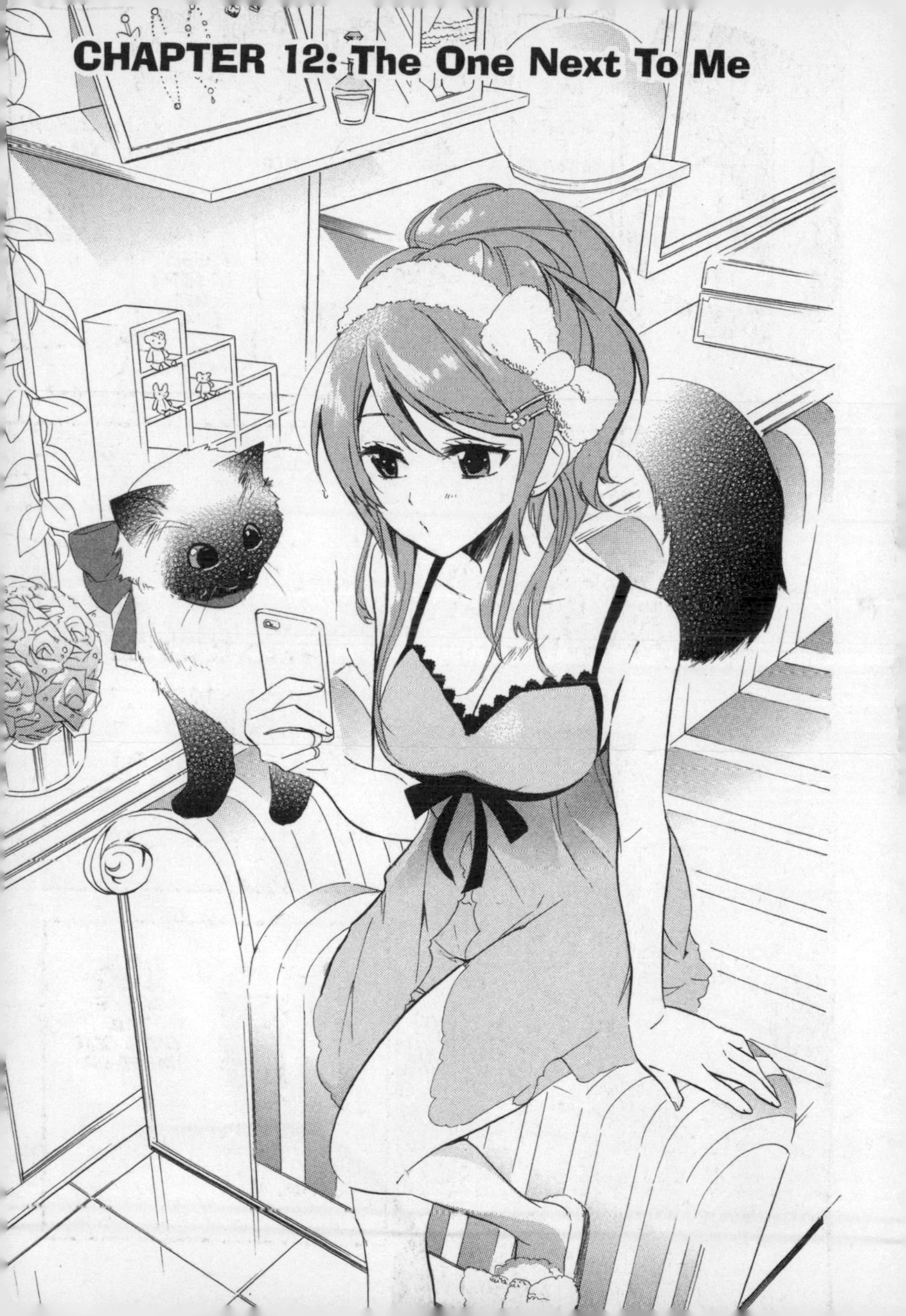

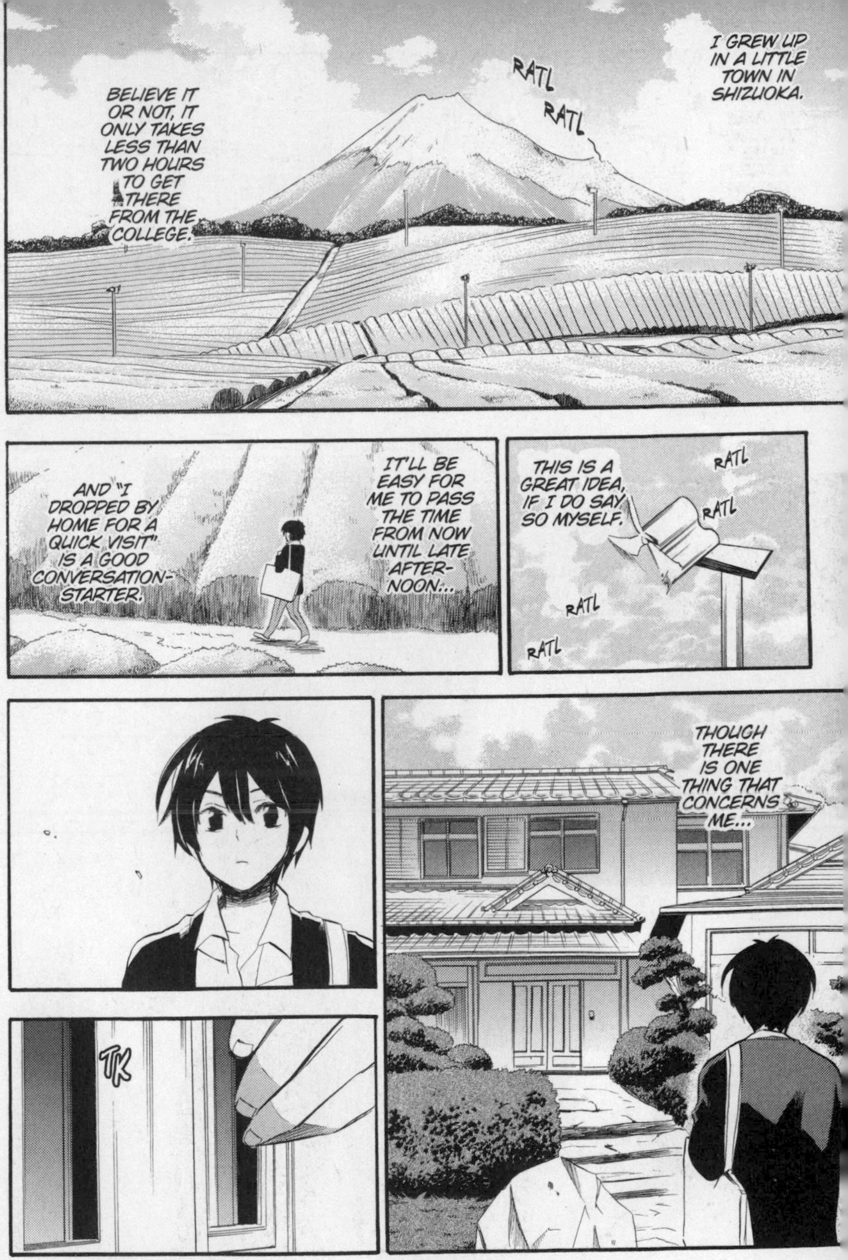
I GREW UP IN A LITTLE TOWN IN SHIZUOKA.
RATL
RATL
BELIEVE IT OR NOT, IT ONLY TAKES LESS THAN TWO HOURS TO GET THERE FROM THE COLLEGE.
RATL
THIS IS A GREAT IDEA, IF I DO SAY SO MYSELF.
RATL
RATL
RATL
IT'LL BE EASY FOR ME TO PASS THE TIME FROM NOW UNTIL LATE AFTER-NOON...
AND "I DROPPED BY HOME FOR A QUICK VISIT" IS A GOOD CONVERSATION-STARTER.
THOUGH THERE IS ONE THING THAT CONCERNS ME...
TK

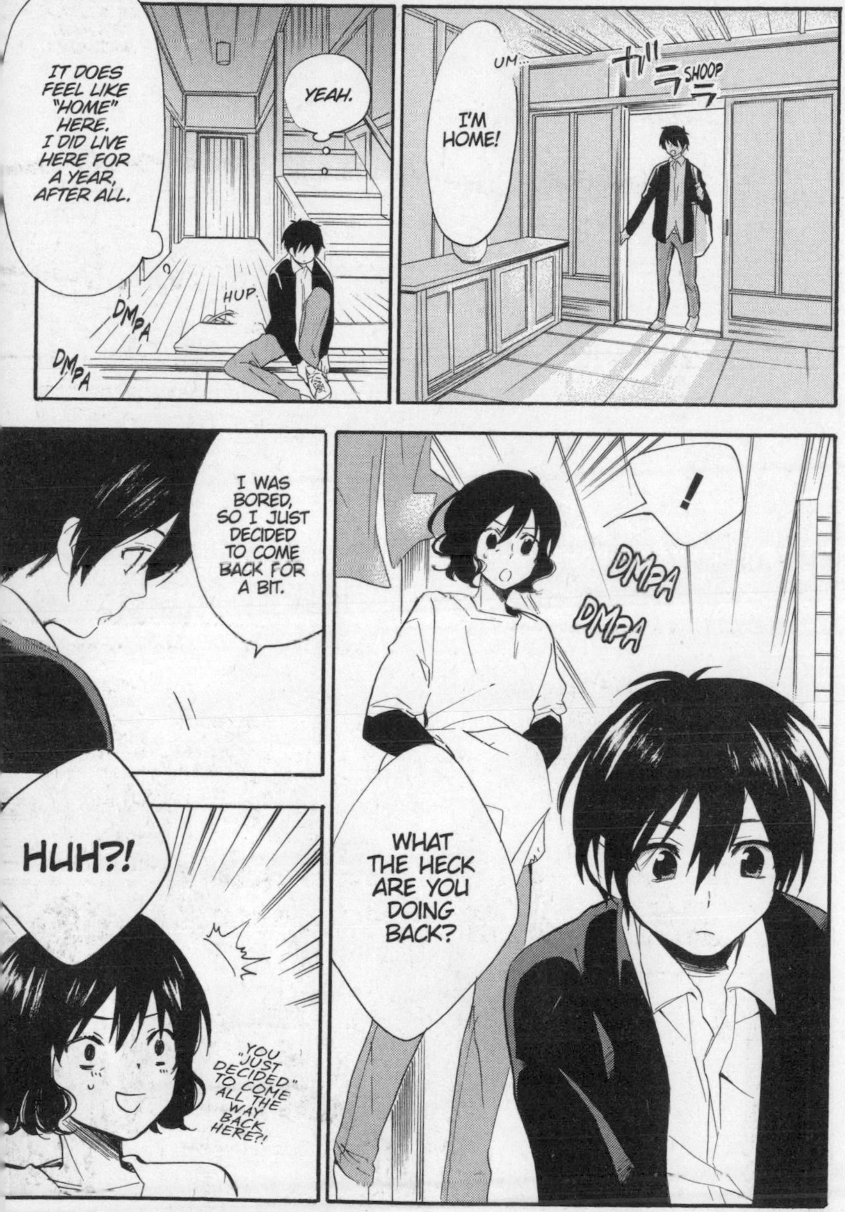
SHOOP
UM...
I'M HOME!
YEAH.
IT DOES FEEL LIKE "HOME" HERE. I DID LIVE HERE FOR A YEAR, AFTER ALL.
HUP.
DMPA
DMPA
!
DMPA
DMPA
WHAT THE HECK ARE YOU DOING BACK?
I WAS BORED, SO I JUST DECIDED TO COME BACK FOR A BIT.
HUH?!
"YOU "JUST DECIDED" TO COME ALL THE WAY BACK HERE?!

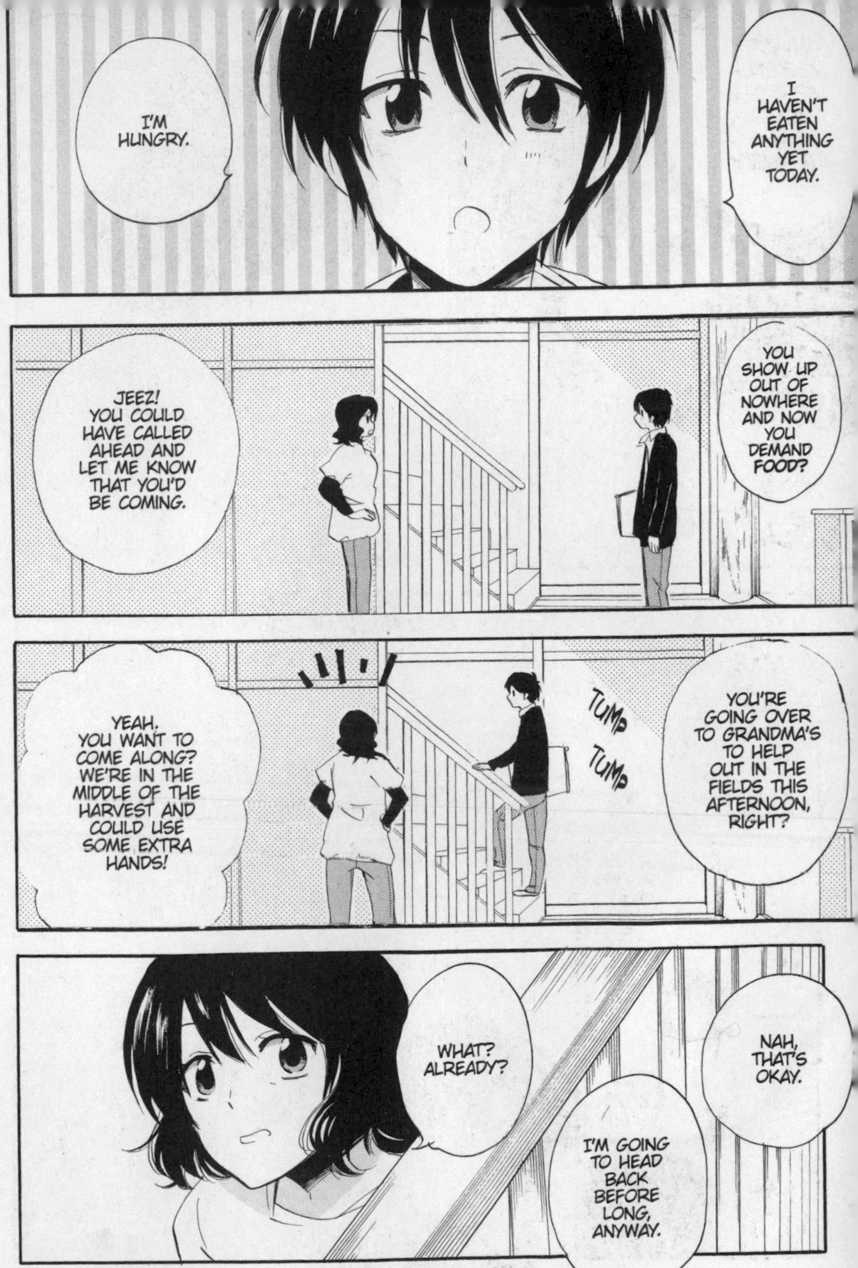
I HAVEN'T EATEN ANYTHING YET TODAY.
I'M HUNGRY.
YOU SHOW UP OUT OF NOWHERE AND NOW YOU DEMAND FOOD?
JEEZ! YOU COULD HAVE CALLED AHEAD AND LET ME KNOW THAT YOU'D BE COMING.
YOU'RE GOING OVER TO GRANDMA'S TO HELP OUT IN THE FIELDS THIS AFTERNOON, RIGHT?
TUMP
TUMP
YEAH. YOU WANT TO COME ALONG? WE'RE IN THE MIDDLE OF THE HARVEST AND COULD USE SOME EXTRA HANDS!
NAH, THAT'S OKAY.
I'M GOING TO HEAD BACK BEFORE LONG, ANYWAY.
WHAT? ALREADY?

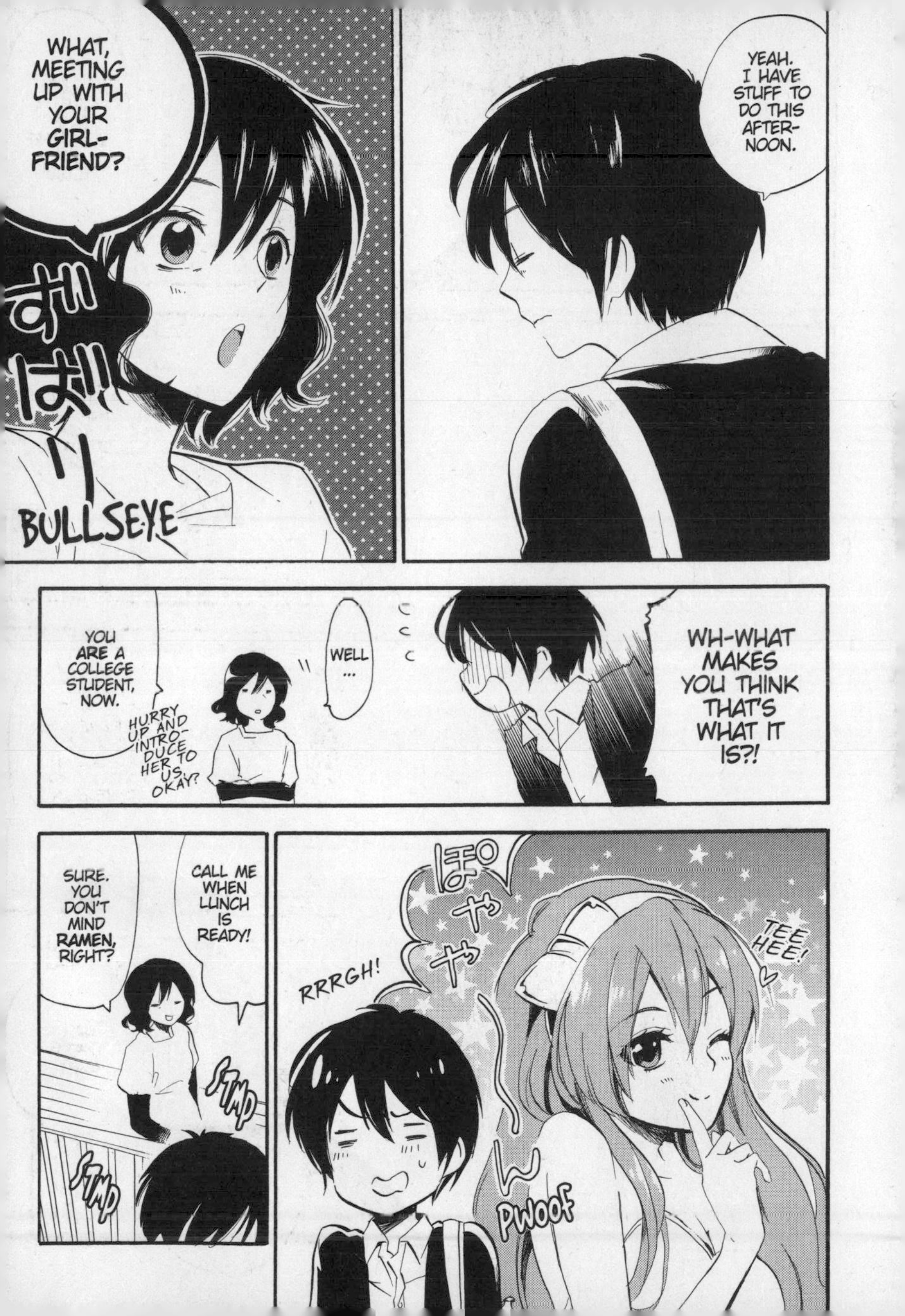
YEAH. I HAVE STUFF TO DO THIS AFTER-NOON.
WHAT, MEETING UP WITH YOUR GIRL-FRIEND?
ずばり
BULLSEYE
WH-WHAT MAKES YOU THINK THAT'S WHAT IT IS?!
WELL ...
YOU ARE A COLLEGE STUDENT, NOW.
HURRY UP AND INTRO-DUCE HER TO US, OKAY?
ぽやや～ん
PWOOF
TEE HEE!
RRRGH!
CALL ME WHEN LUNCH IS READY!
SURE. YOU DON'T MIND RAMEN, RIGHT?
STMP
STMP

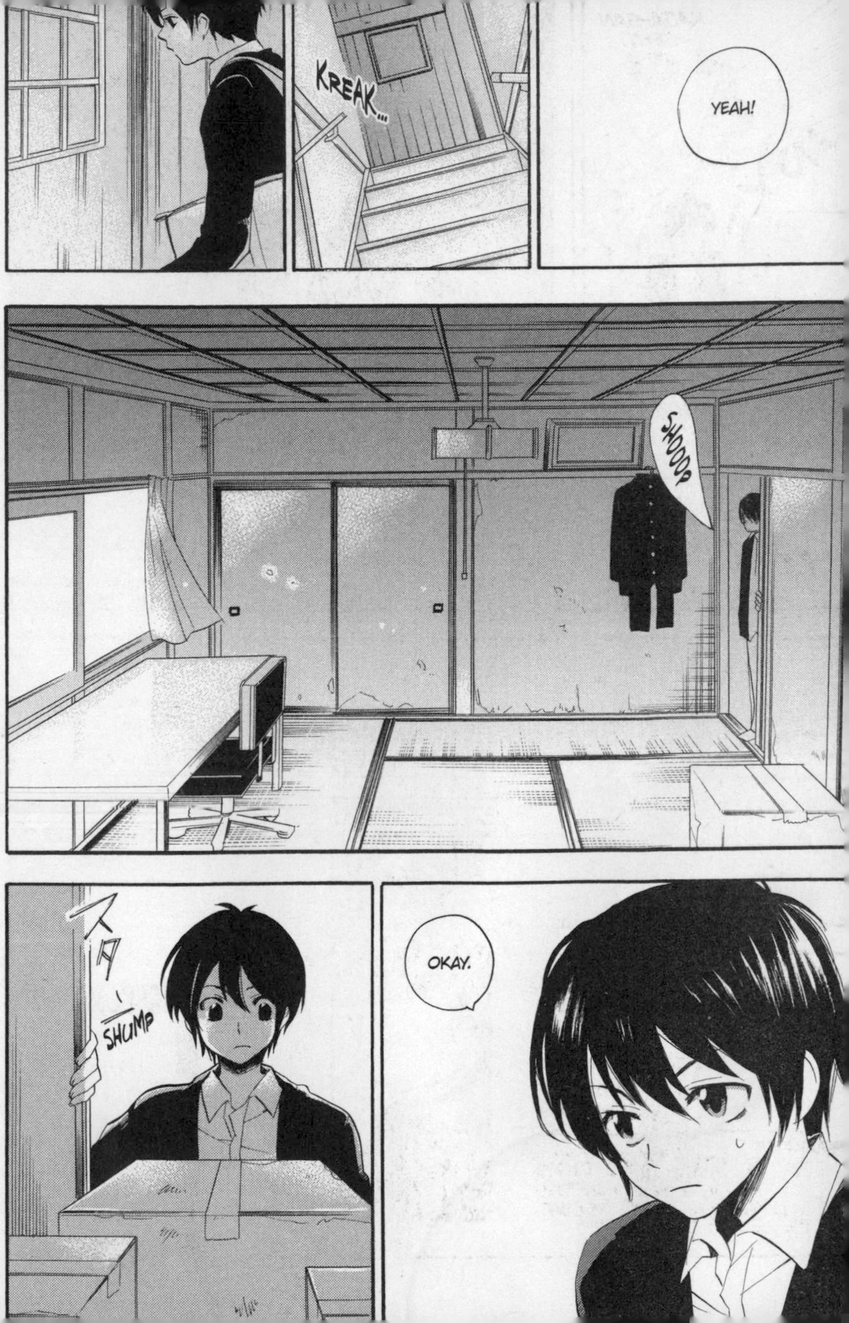
YEAH!
KREAK...
SHOOP
OKAY.
スタ
SHUMP

SWFF
ずる
A FEW HOURS AGO...
KAGA-SAN SENT ME A TEXT.
VRRRT
VRRRT
TWITCH
びくっ
IT... IT'S FROM KAGA-SAN!
BDMP
BDMP
"MAYBE IT FEELS LIKE YOU ARE BEING DENIED BY THE ONES YOU LOVE...
"...BECAUSE THEY FEEL LIKE YOU ARE DENYING THEM."
SHE HAD A POINT.
RIIIP
FMP
I MAY HAVE BEEN SHUTTING OUT THE PEOPLE WHO KNEW AND LOVED THE OLD BANRI AS MUCH AS I WAS SHUTTING HIM OUT.

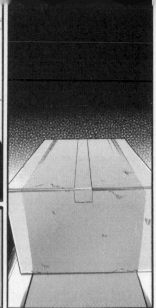

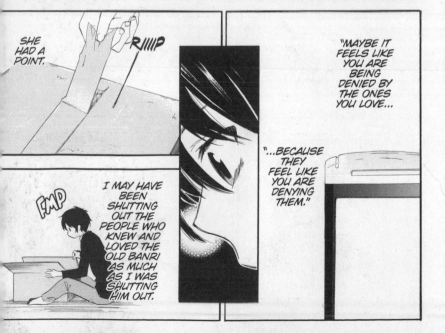

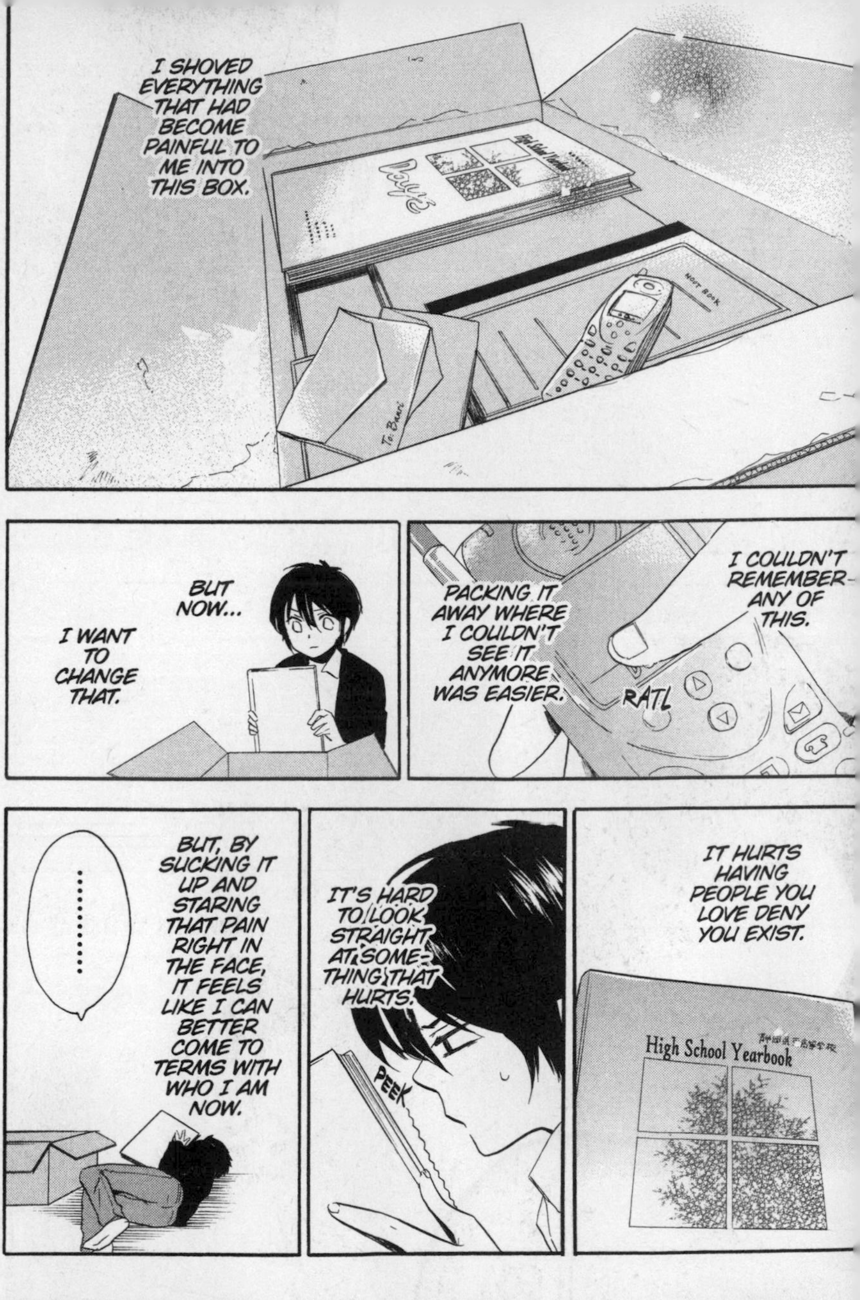
I SHOVED EVERYTHING THAT HAD BECOME PAINFUL TO ME INTO THIS BOX.
I COULDN'T REMEMBER ANY OF THIS.
PACKING IT AWAY WHERE I COULDN'T SEE IT ANYMORE WAS EASIER.
RATL
BUT NOW...
I WANT TO CHANGE THAT.
IT HURTS HAVING PEOPLE YOU LOVE DENY YOU EXIST.
High School Yearbook
IT'S HARD TO LOOK STRAIGHT AT SOME-THING THAT HURTS.
PEEK
BUT, BY SUCKING IT UP AND STARING THAT PAIN RIGHT IN THE FACE, IT FEELS LIKE I CAN BETTER COME TO TERMS WITH WHO I AM NOW.
....

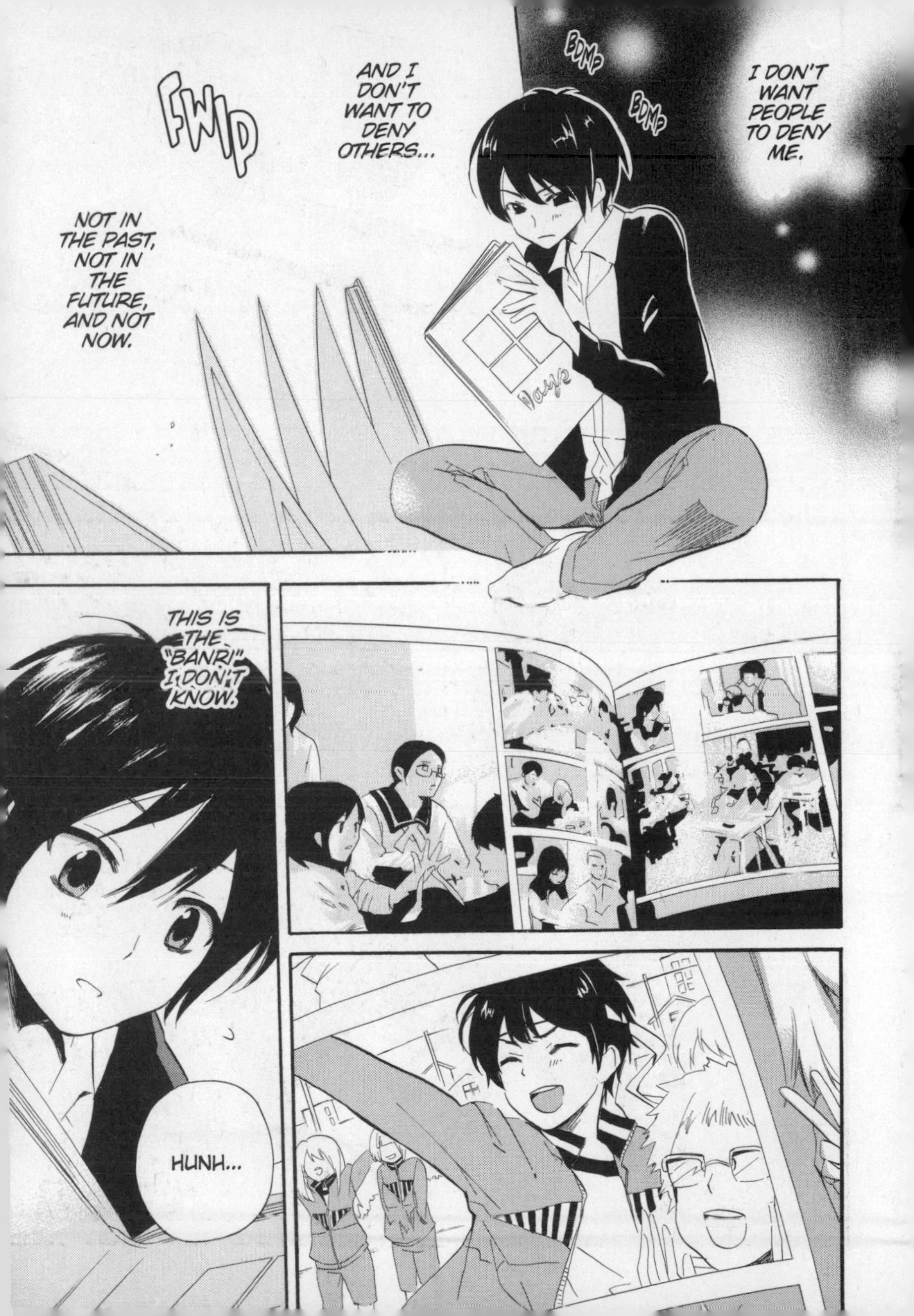
I DON'T WANT PEOPLE TO DENY ME.
BDMP
BDMP
AND I DON'T WANT TO DENY OTHERS...
FWIP
NOT IN THE PAST, NOT IN THE FUTURE, AND NOT NOW.
THIS IS THE "BANRI" I DON'T KNOW.
HUNH...

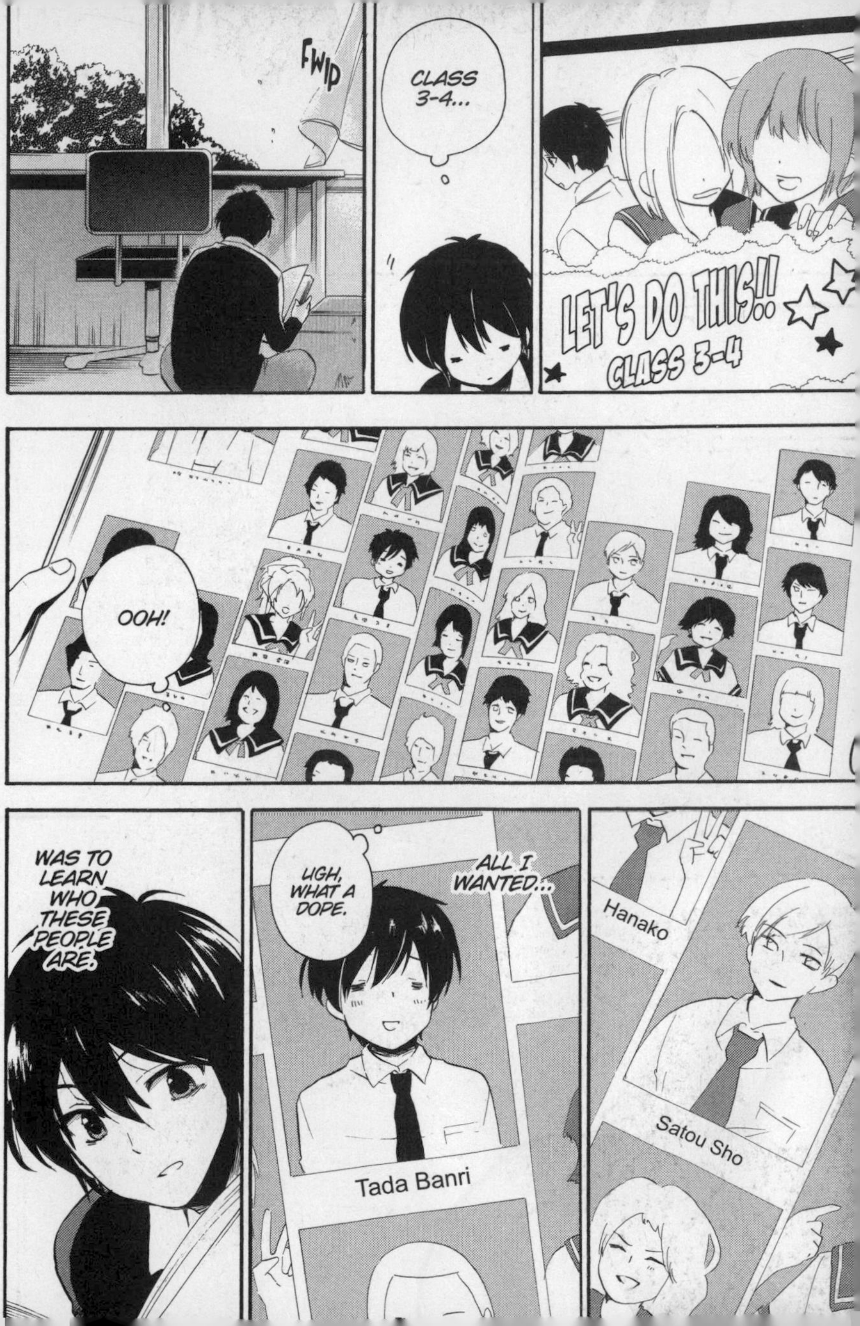
LET'S DO THIS!!
CLASS 3-4
CLASS 3-4...
FWIP
OOH!
Hanako
Satou Sho
ALL I WANTED...
UGH, WHAT A DOPE.
Tada Banri
WAS TO LEARN WHO THESE PEOPLE ARE.

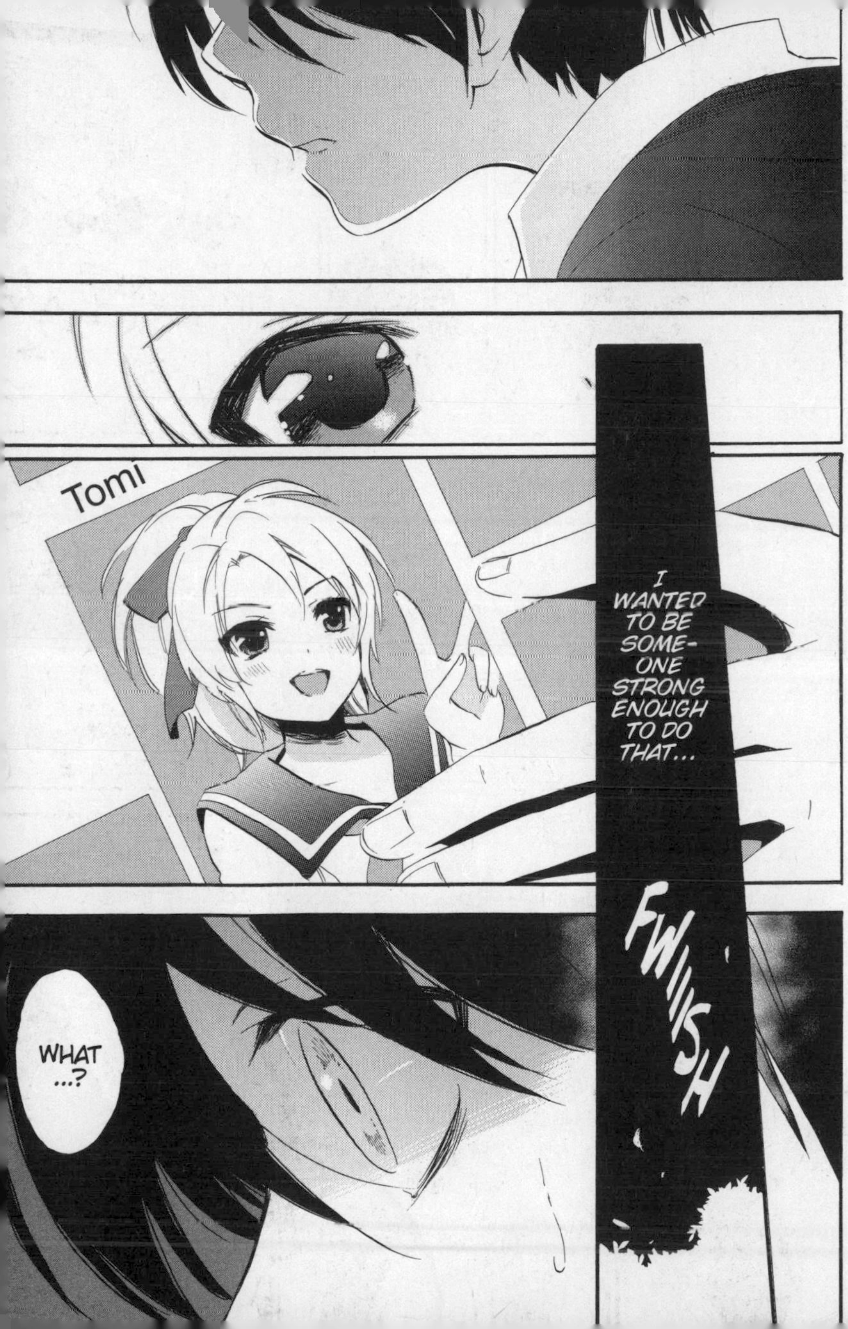
I WANTED TO BE SOME-ONE STRONG ENOUGH TO DO THAT...
Tomi
FWIIISH
WHAT ...?

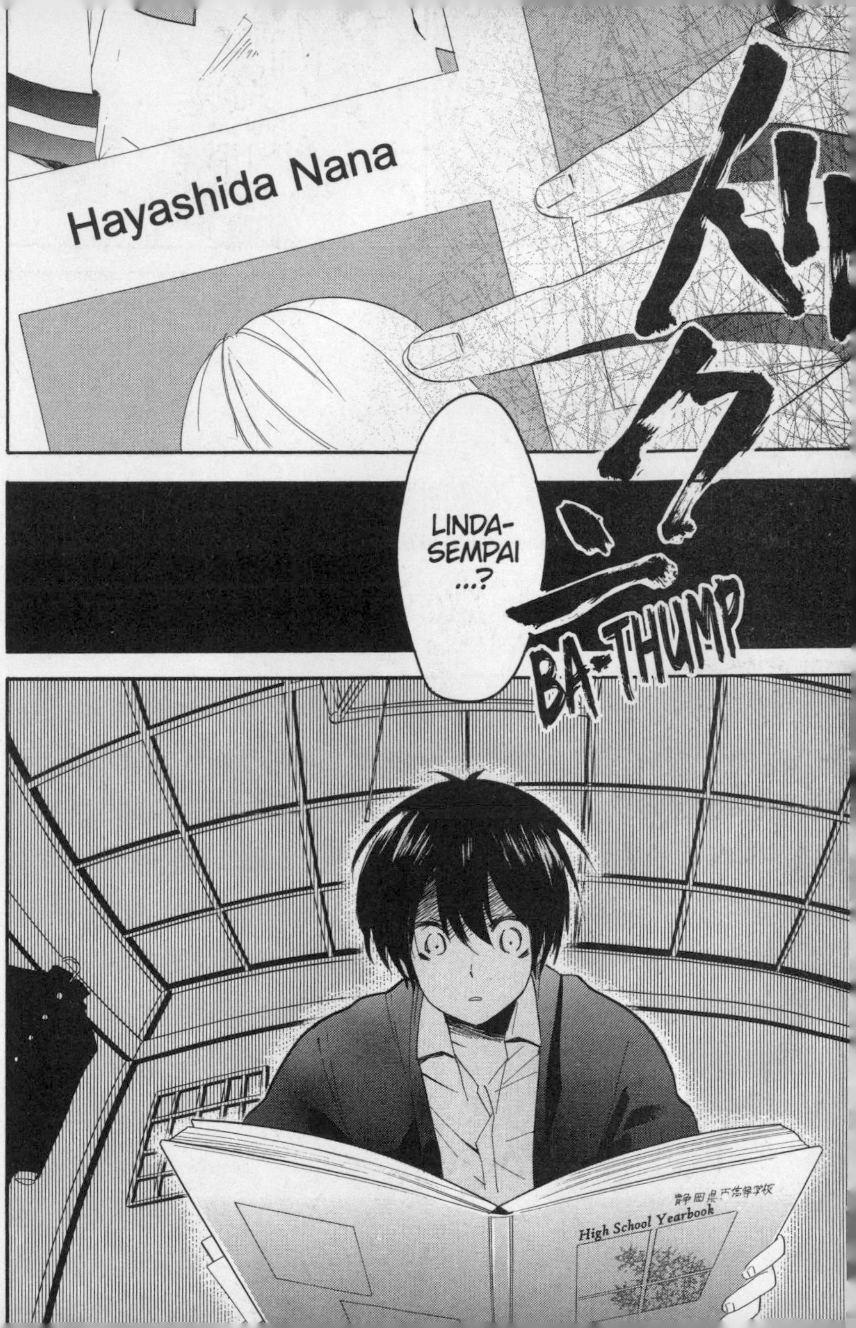
Hayashida Nana
LINDA-SEMPAI ...?
BA-THUMP
High School Yearbook

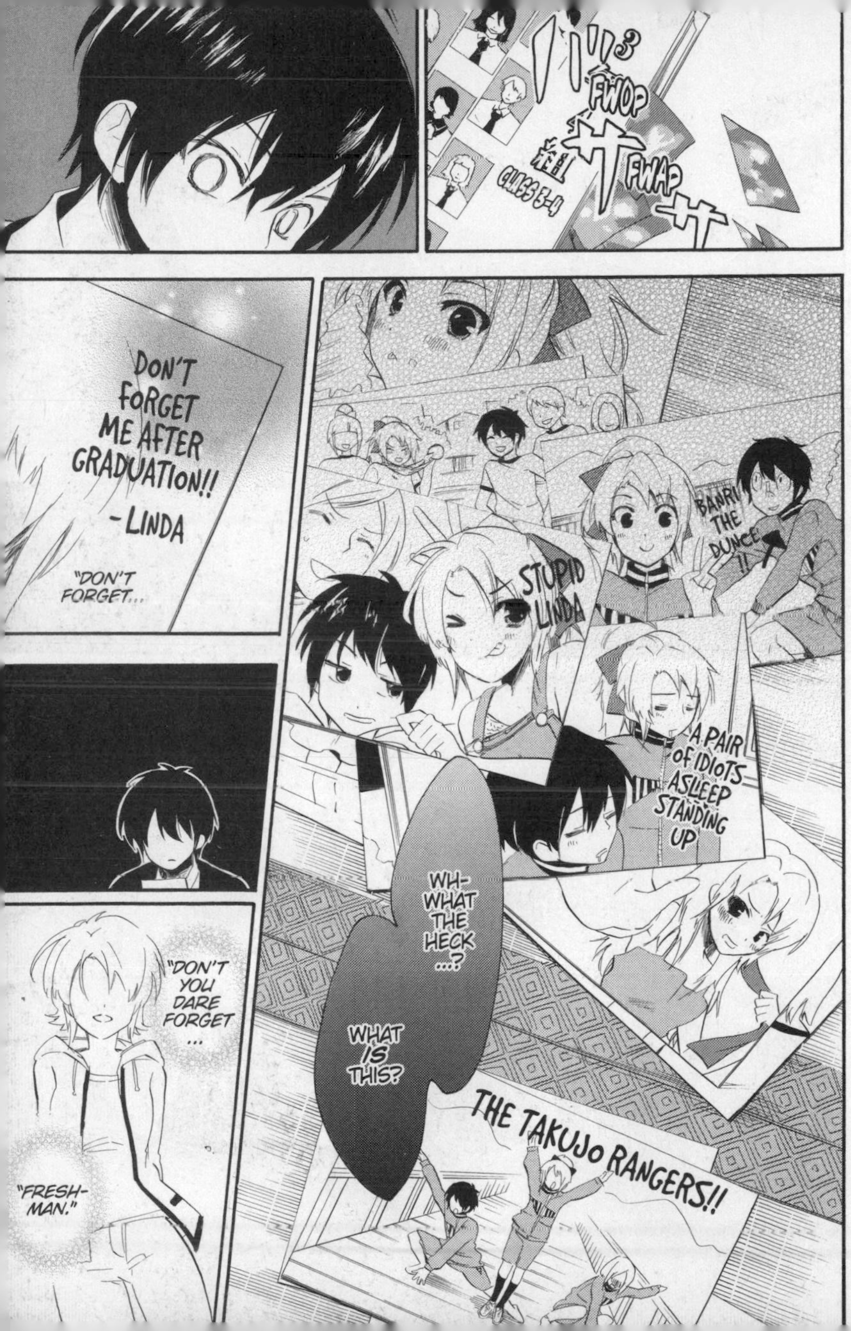
FWOP
FWAP
CLASS 3-4
BANRI THE DUNCE!!
STUPID LINDA
A PAIR OF IDIOTS ASLEEP STANDING UP
WH-WHAT THE HECK...?
WHAT IS THIS?
THE TAKUJO RANGERS!!
DON'T FORGET ME AFTER GRADUATION!! -LINDA
"DON'T FORGET...
"DON'T YOU DARE FORGET...
"FRESHMAN."

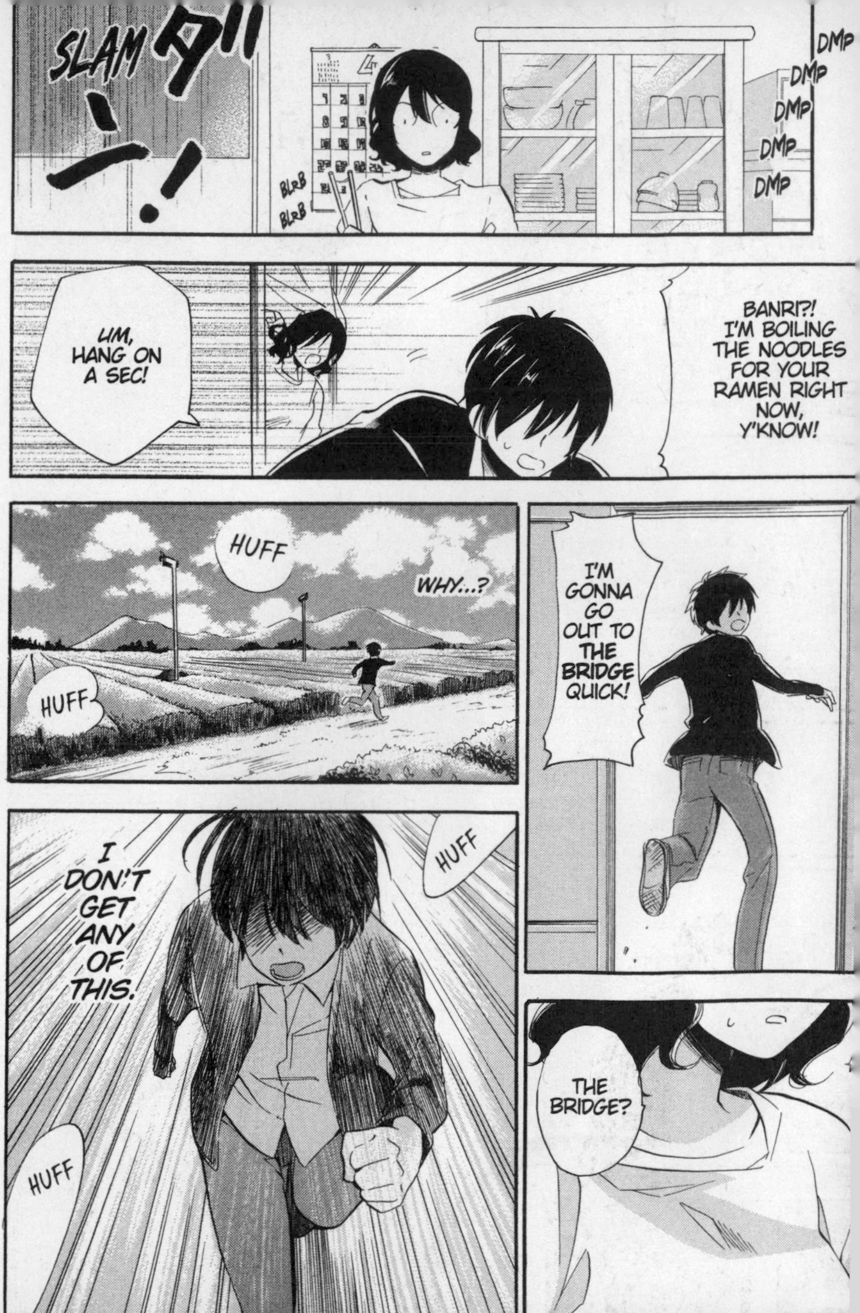
DMP
DMP
DMP
DMP
DMP
BLRB
BLRB
SLAM
タッ
ン!
BANRI?! I'M BOILING THE NOODLES FOR YOUR RAMEN RIGHT NOW, Y'KNOW!
UM, HANG ON A SEC!
I'M GONNA GO OUT TO THE BRIDGE QUICK!
THE BRIDGE?
HUFF
WHY...?
HUFF
HUFF
I DON'T GET ANY OF THIS.
HUFF

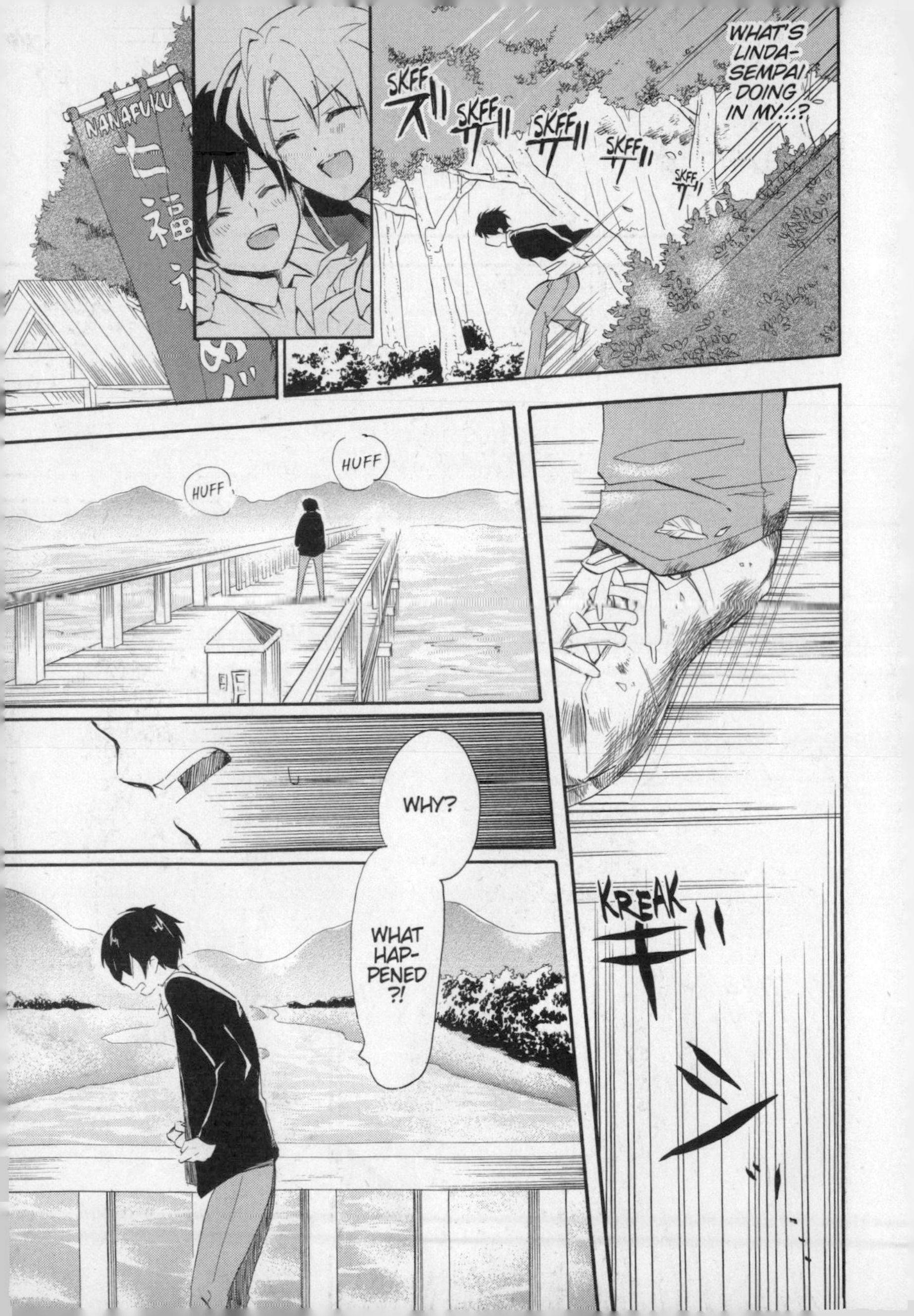

WHAT'S LINDA-SEMPAI DOING IN MY...?
SKFF
SKFF
SKFF
SKFF
SKFF
NANAFUKU
KREAK
HUFF
HUFF
WHY?
WHAT HAP-PENED?!

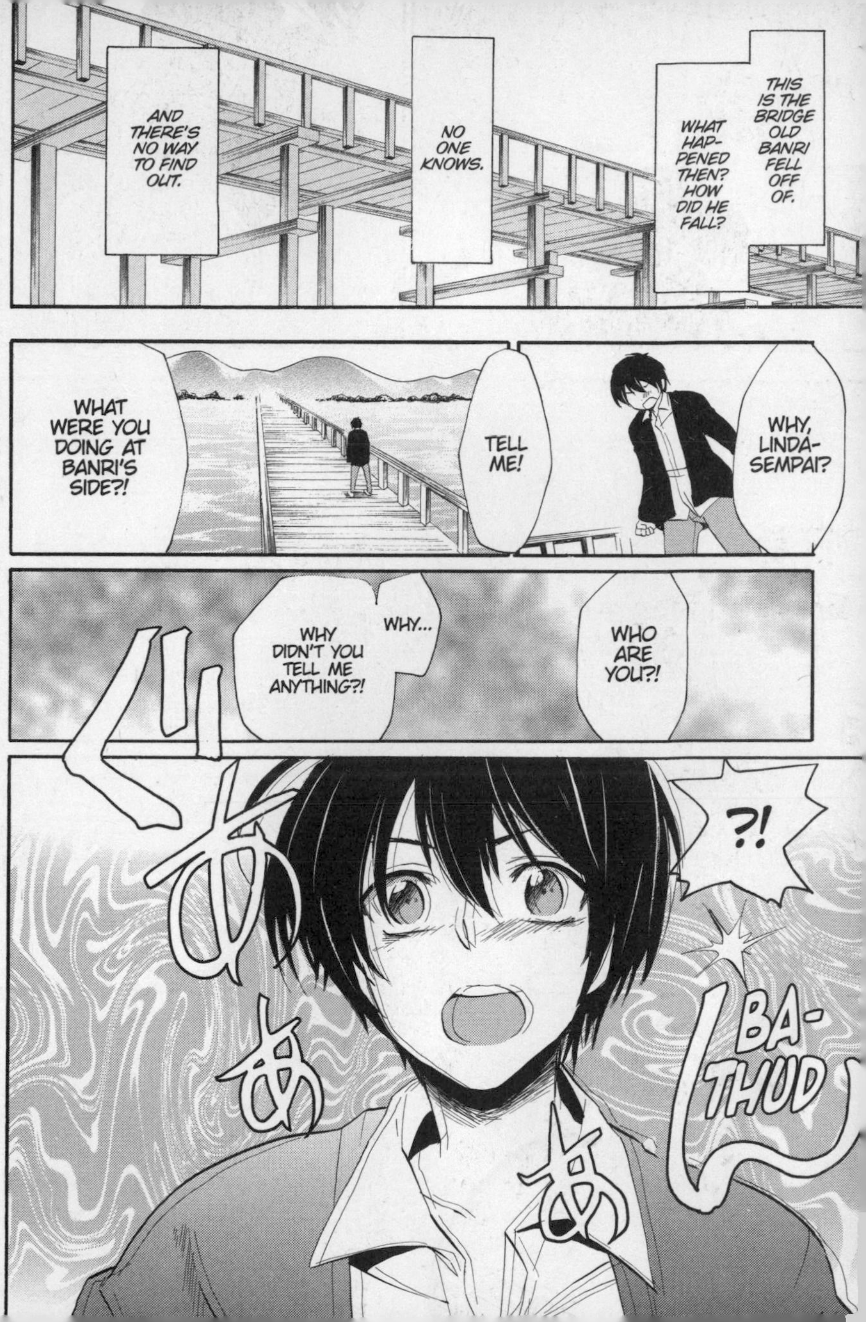
THIS IS THE BRIDGE OLD BANRI FELL OFF OF.
WHAT HAPPENED THEN? HOW DID HE FALL?
NO ONE KNOWS.
AND THERE'S NO WAY TO FIND OUT.
WHY, LINDA-SEMPAI?
TELL ME!
WHAT WERE YOU DOING AT BANRI'S SIDE?!
WHO ARE YOU?!
WHY...
WHY DIDN'T YOU TELL ME ANYTHING?!
?!
BA-THUD

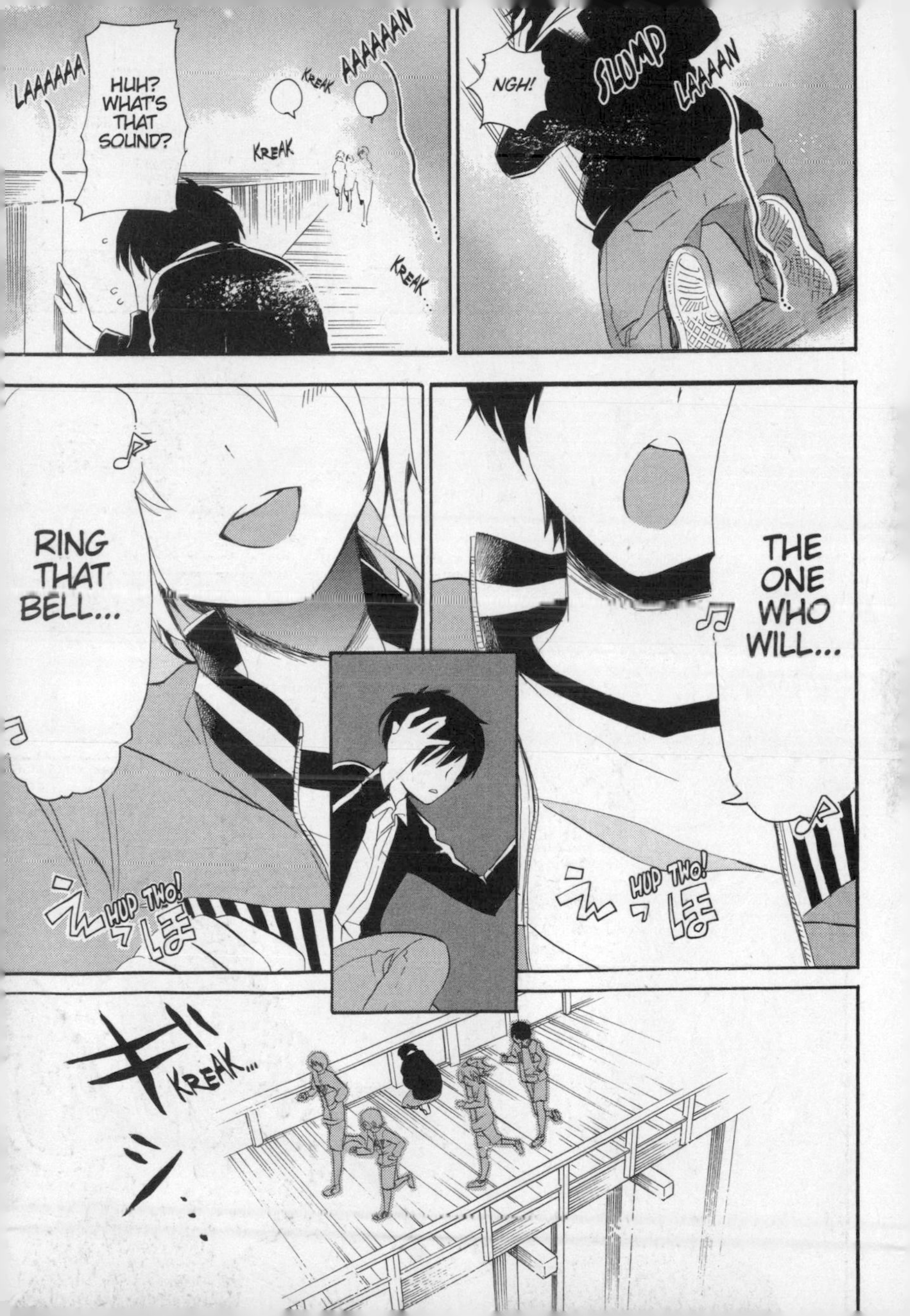
NGH!
SLUMP
LAAAAN
AAAAAAN
KREAK
LAAAAAA
HUH? WHAT'S THAT SOUND?
KREAK
KREAK...
THE ONE WHO WILL...
HUP TWO!
えっほ
RING THAT BELL...
HUP TWO!
えっほ
KREAK...

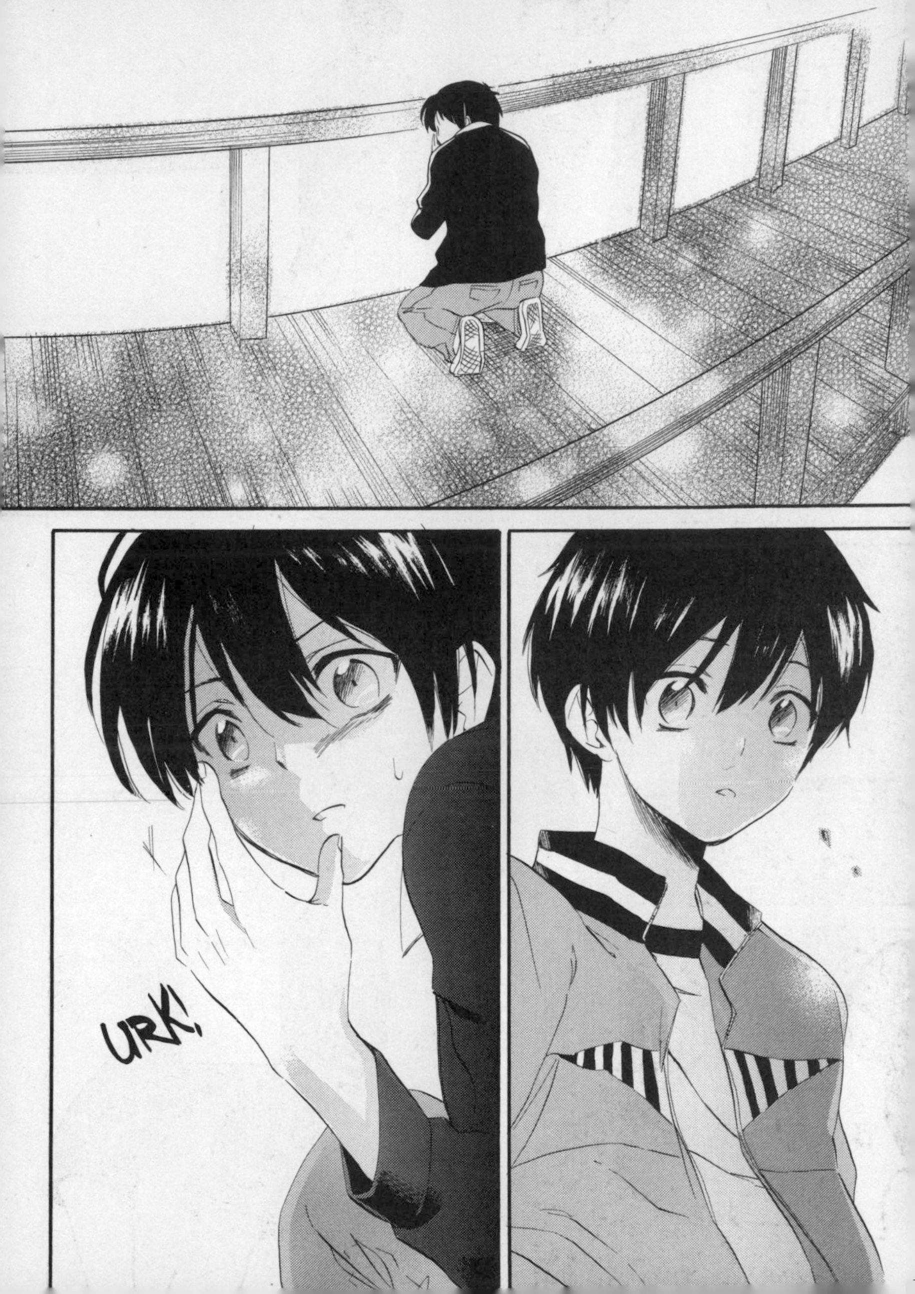
URK!

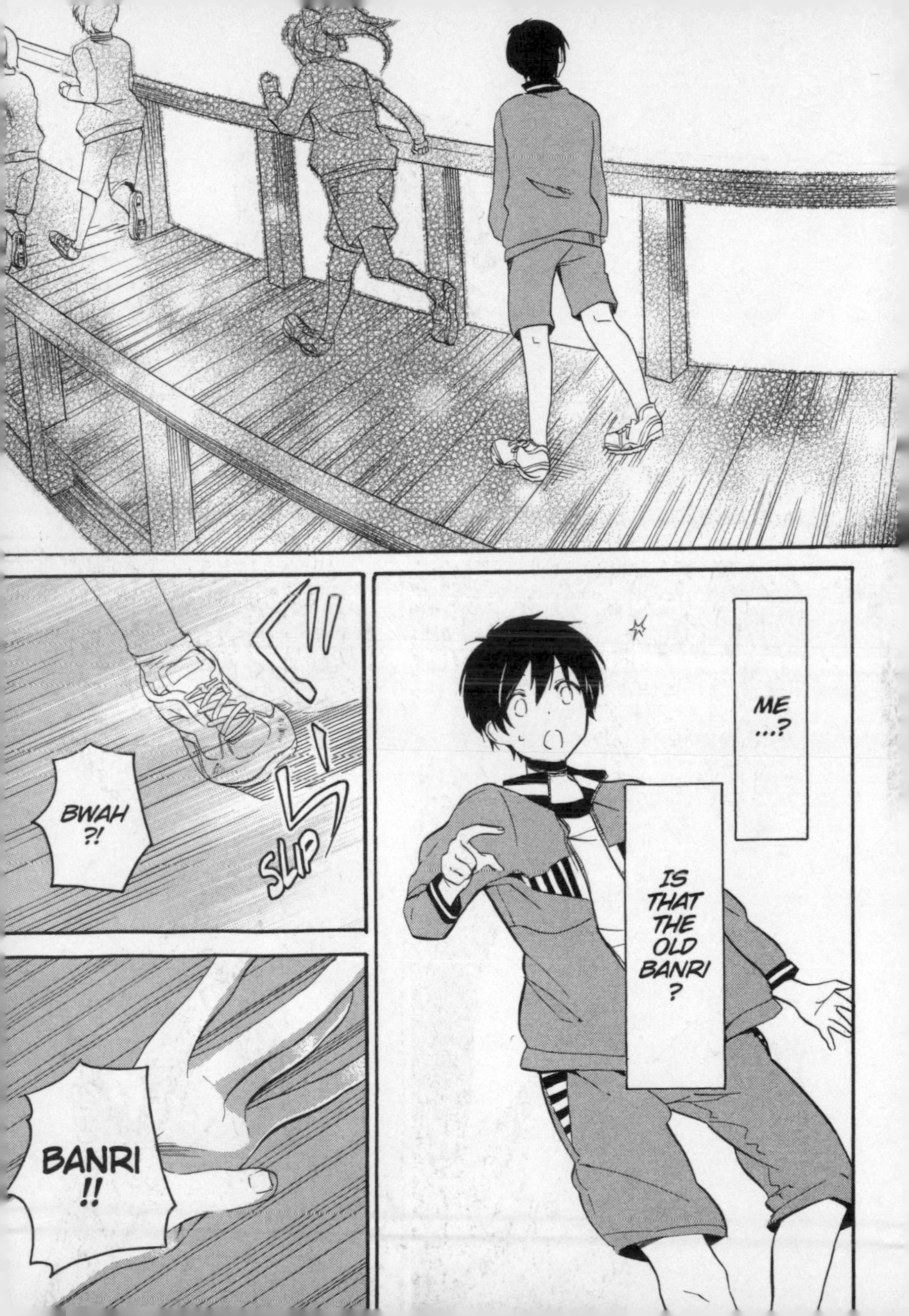
ME ...?
IS THAT THE OLD BANRI ?
SLIP
BWAH ?!
BANRI !!

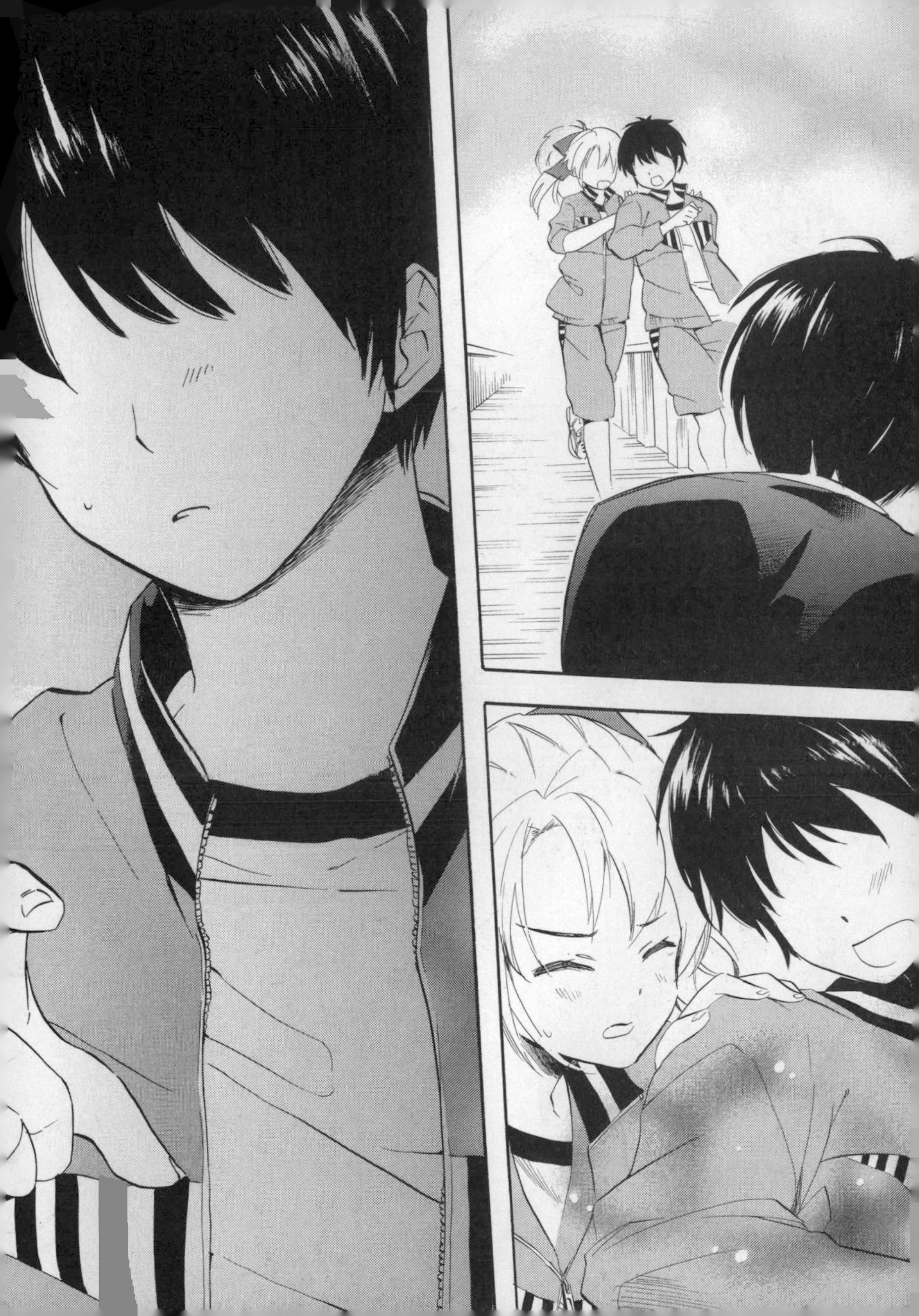

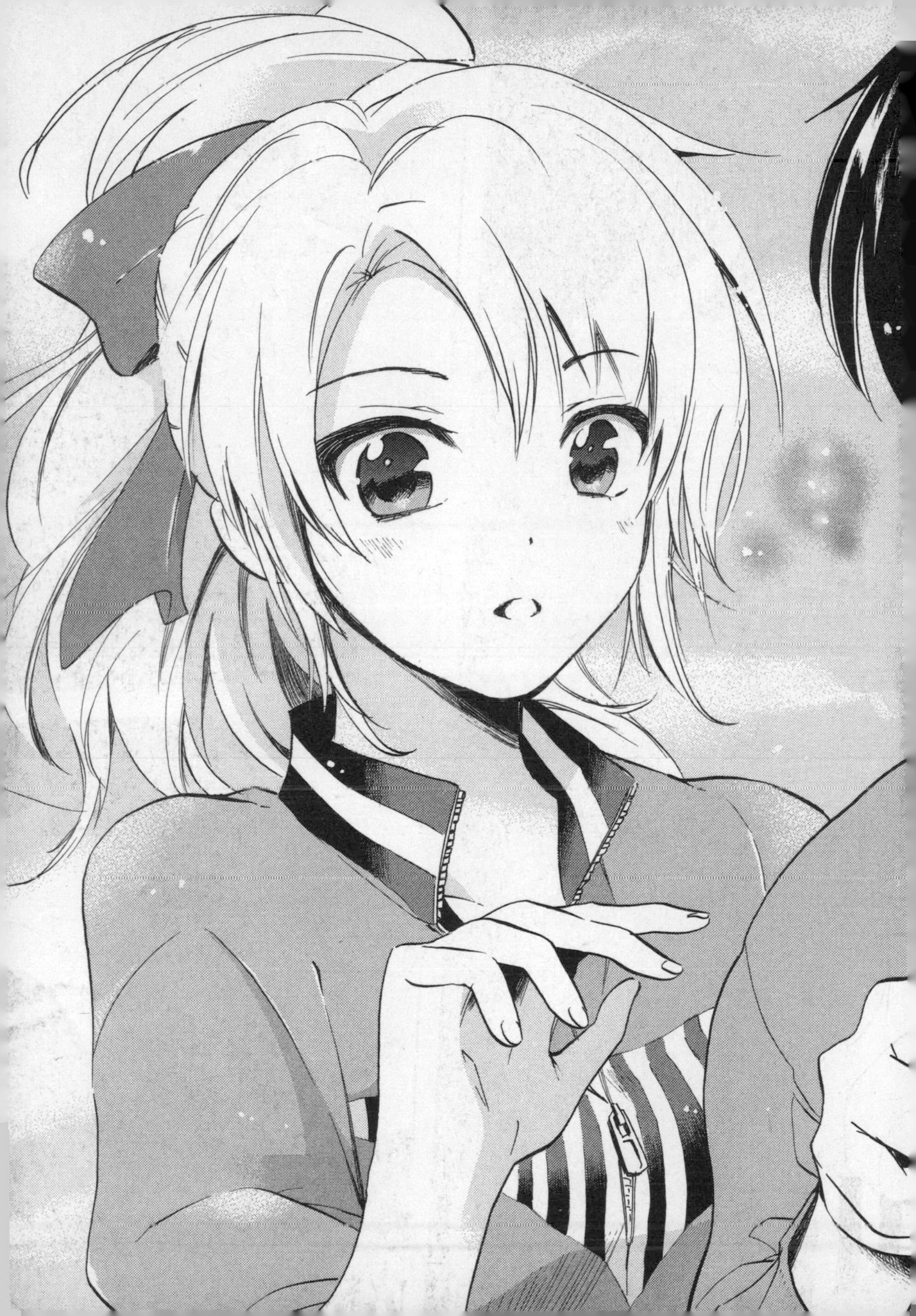

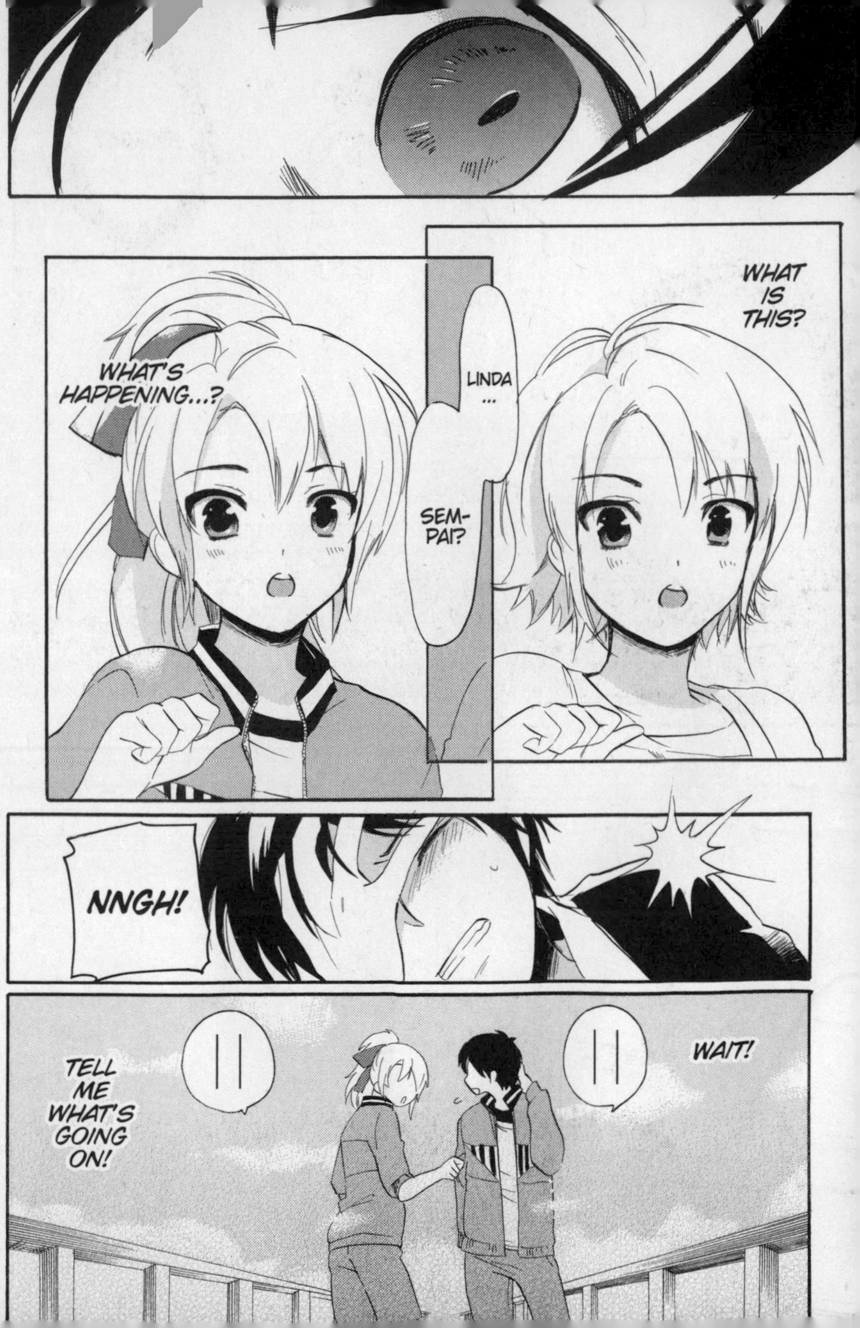
WHAT IS THIS?
LINDA ...
SEM-PAI?
WHAT'S HAPPENING...?
NNGH!
WAIT!
TELL ME WHAT'S GOING ON!

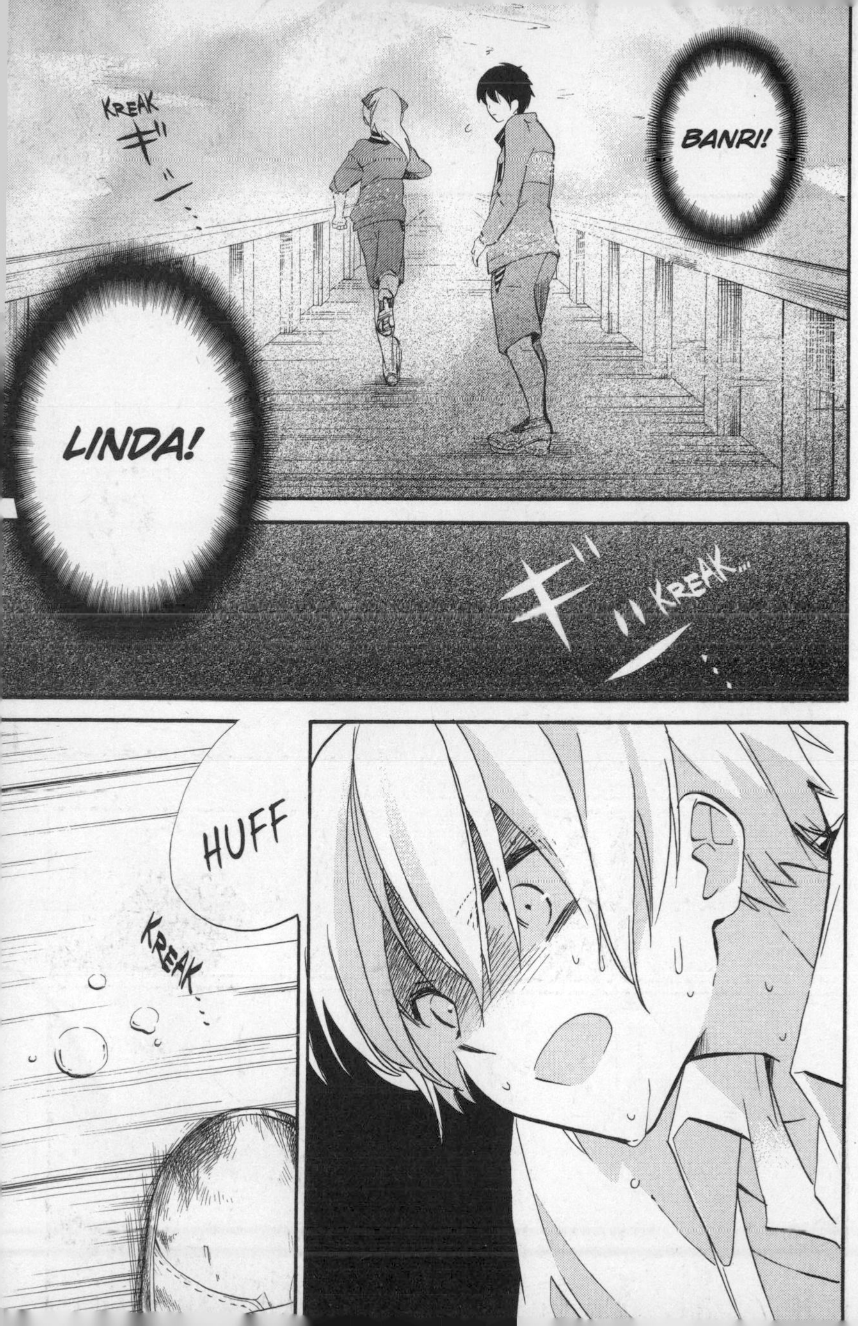
BANRI!
KREAK
LINDA!
KREAK...
HUFF
KREAK...

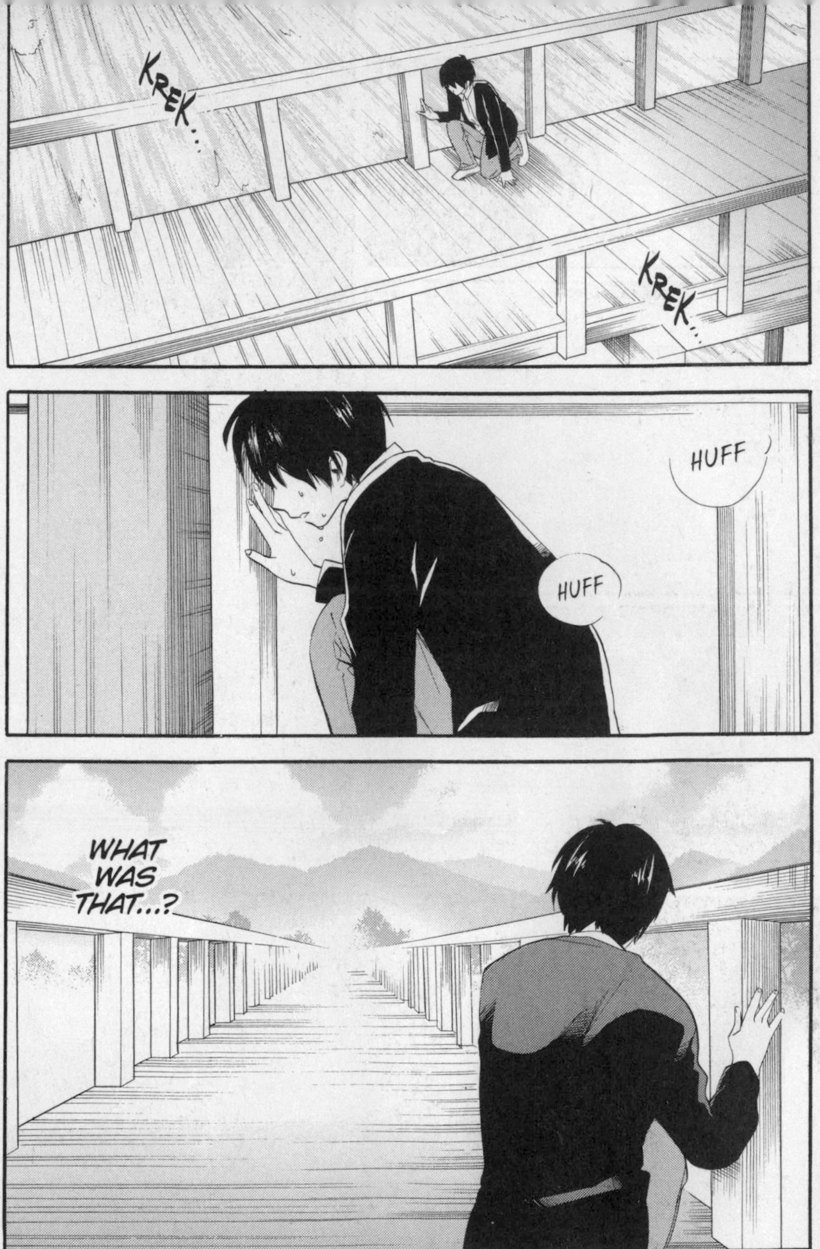
KREK...
KREK...
HUFF
HUFF
WHAT WAS THAT...?

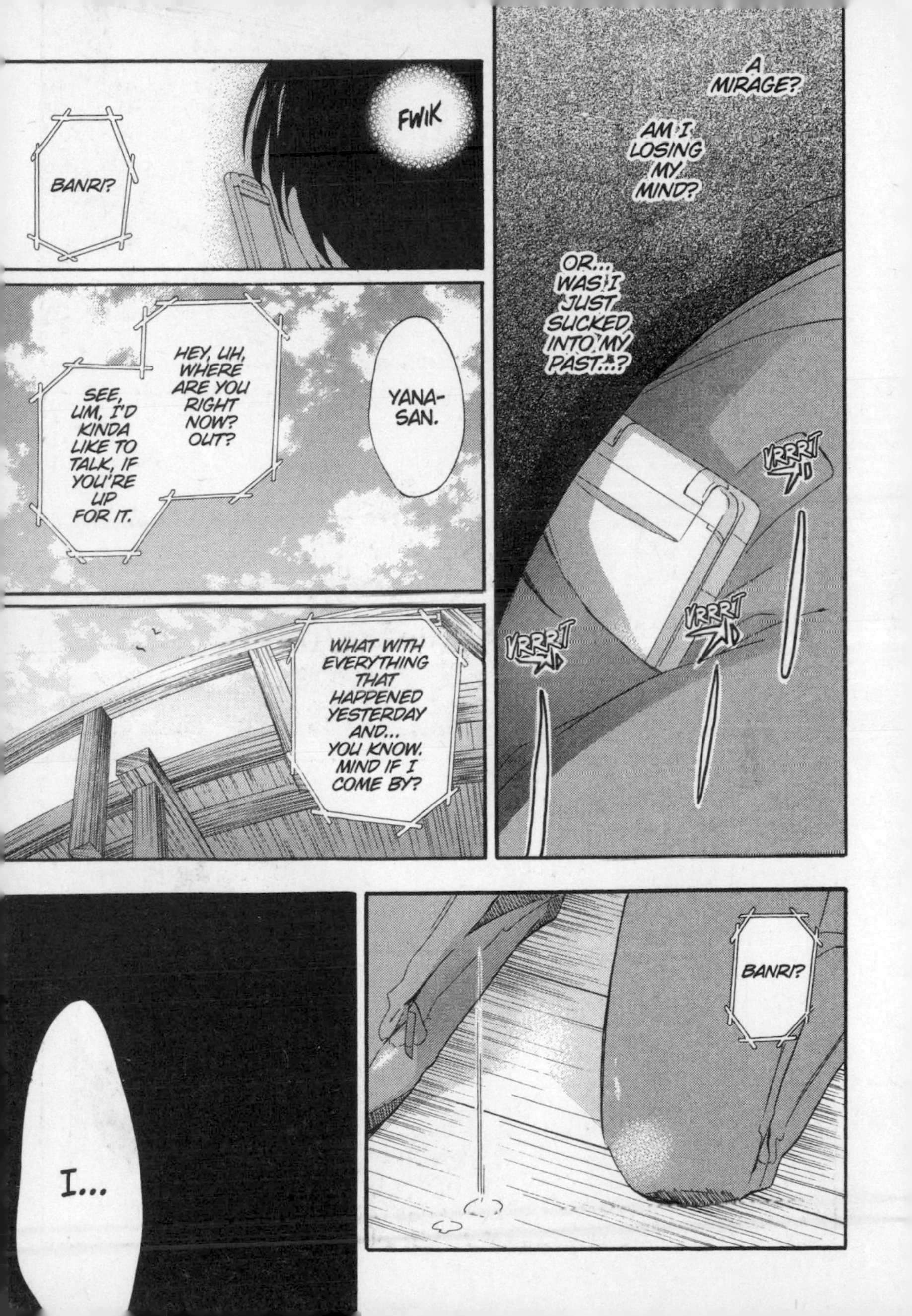
A MIRAGE?
AM I LOSING MY MIND?
OR... WAS I JUST SUCKED INTO MY PAST...?
VRRRT
VRRRT
VRRRT
FWIK
BANRI?
YANA-SAN.
HEY, UH, WHERE ARE YOU RIGHT NOW? OUT?
SEE, UM, I'D KINDA LIKE TO TALK, IF YOU'RE UP FOR IT.
WHAT WITH EVERYTHING THAT HAPPENED YESTERDAY AND... YOU KNOW. MIND IF I COME BY?
BANRI?
I...

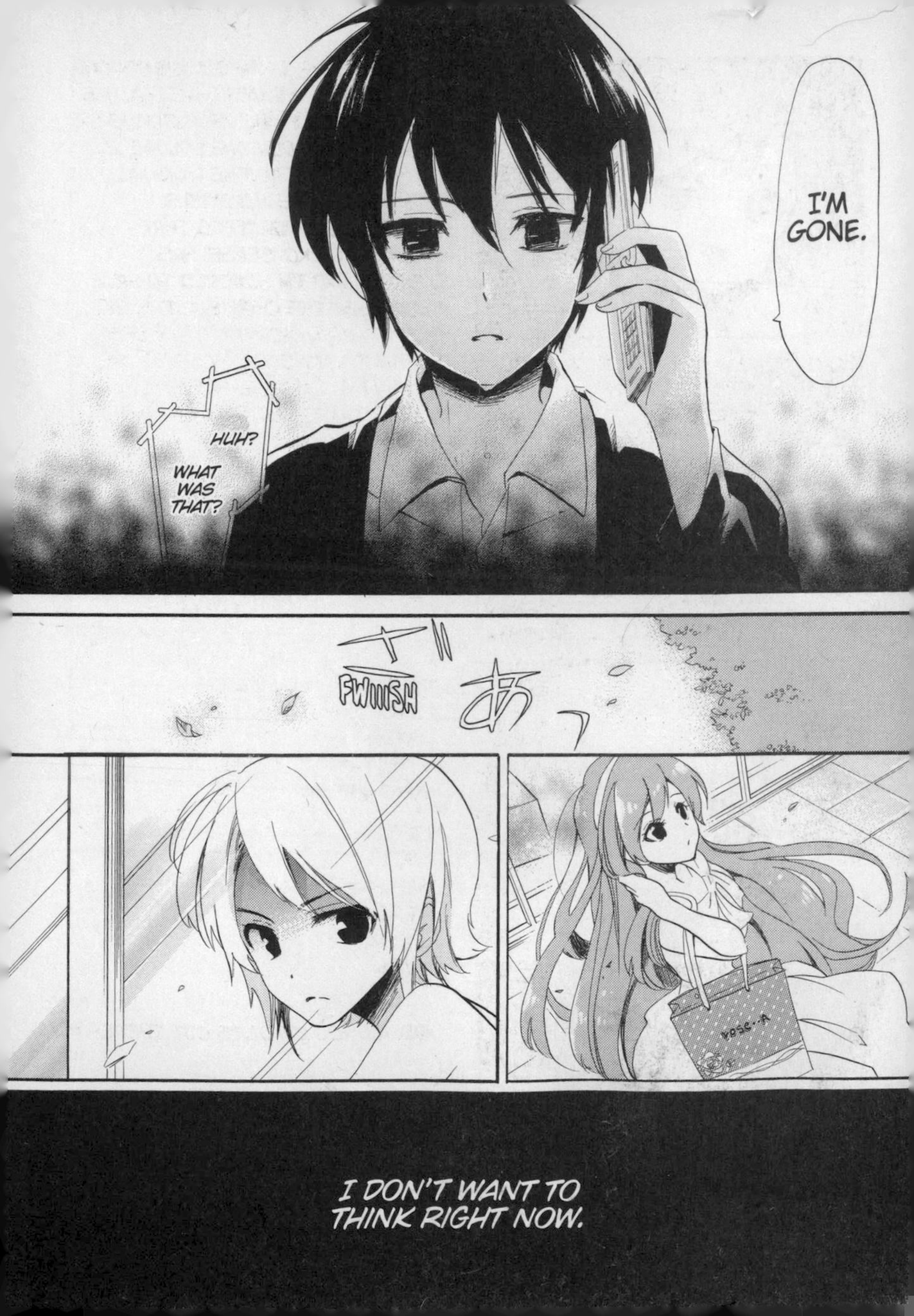
I'M GONE.
HUH?
WHAT WAS THAT?
あっ
FWIIISH
I DON'T WANT TO THINK RIGHT NOW.